ROUTLEDGE LIBRARY EDITIONS: THE ECONOMY OF THE MIDDLE EAST

Volume 22

NORTH AFRICA

NORTH AFRICA
Contemporary Politics and Economic Development

Edited by
RICHARD LAWLESS AND ALLAN FINDLAY

LONDON AND NEW YORK

First published in 1984

This edition first published in 2015
by Routledge
2 Park Square, Milton Park, Abingdon, Oxon, OX14 4RN

and by Routledge
711 Third Avenue, New York, NY 10017

Routledge is an imprint of the Taylor & Francis Group, an informa business

© 1984 R.I. Lawless and A.M. Findlay

All rights reserved. No part of this book may be reprinted or reproduced or utilised in any form or by any electronic, mechanical, or other means, now known or hereafter invented, including photocopying and recording, or in any information storage or retrieval system, without permission in writing from the publishers.

Trademark notice: Product or corporate names may be trademarks or registered trademarks, and are used only for identification and explanation without intent to infringe.

British Library Cataloguing in Publication Data
A catalogue record for this book is available from the British Library

ISBN: 978-1-138-78710-0 (Set)
eISBN: 978-1-315-74408-7 (Set)
ISBN: 978-1-138-81014-3 (Volume 22)
eISBN: 978-1-315-74472-8 (Volume 22)
Pb ISBN: 978-1-138-82025-8 (Volume 22)

Publisher's Note
The publisher has gone to great lengths to ensure the quality of this reprint but points out that some imperfections in the original copies may be apparent.

Disclaimer
The publisher has made every effort to trace copyright holders and would welcome correspondence from those they have been unable to trace.

North Africa

CONTEMPORARY POLITICS

AND

ECONOMIC DEVELOPMENT

**Edited by Richard Lawless
and Allan Findlay**

CROOM HELM
London & Canberra
ST. MARTIN'S PRESS
New York

©1984 R.I. Lawless and A.M. Findlay
Croom Helm Ltd, Provident House, Burrell Row,
Beckenham, Kent BR3 1AT

Croom Helm Australia Pty Ltd, 28 Kembla St.,
Fyshwick, ACT 2609, Australia

British Library Cataloguing in Publication Data

North Africa: contemporary politics and economic
  development.
  1. Africa, North — Social aspects
  2. Africa, North — Political aspects
  I. Lawless, Richard I.   II. Findlay, Allan M.
  961'.04   HDT177

ISBN 0-7099-1609-4

All rights reserved. For information, write:
St. Martin's Press, Inc., 175 Fifth Avenue, New York, NY 10010
First published in the United States of America in 1984

Library of Congress Cataloging in Publication Data
Main entry under title:

North Africa, contemporary politics and economic
development.

  Includes index.
   1. Africa, North — Politics and government. 2. Africa,
North — Economic conditions. I. Lawless, Richard I.
DT204.N67   1984   320.961   83-43001
ISBN 0-312-57812-1

Printed and bound in Great Britain

CONTENTS

List of Tables	vii
List of Figures	ix
Preface	xi
Currency Exchange Rates	xiii

PART ONE

Introduction		1
1	The Politics of Algerian Socialism *Hugh Roberts*	5
2	Modern Morocco: Political Immobilism, Economic Dependence *Peter Sluglett and Marion Farouk-Sluglett*	50
3	Tunisia: Contemporary Politics *Werner Ruf*	101
4	State and Labour in Libya *Pandeli Glavanis*	120

PART TWO

Introduction		150
5	Algeria: The Contradictions of Rapid Industrialisation *Richard Lawless*	153
6	The Moroccan Economy in the 1970s *Anne Findlay*	191
7	Tunisia: The Vicissitudes of Economic Development *Allan Findlay*	217
8	Libya: Problems of a *Rentier* State *Stace Birks* and *Clive Sinclair*	241

Index	277

TABLES AND FIGURES

Tables

5.1	Sectoral Composition of GDP 1963/1978	158
5.2	Oil Production and Revenues	162
5.3	Rate of Growth of GDP by Sector 1967-78	165
5.4	Planned and Actual Investment 1967-1977	165
5.5	Level of Utilisation of Industrial Capacity in 1978	169
5.6	Crop Production and Cultivated Area by Sector-Season 1977-1978	174
5.7	Evolution of Agricultural Production 1970-77 (1967-1970=100)	178
5.8	Planned Investment 1980-84 (In 000 million AD)	178
5.9	Structure of Planned Investments 1967-1984	178
6.1	The Sectoral Allocation of Investment of the Moroccan National Plans (% of Total Investment)	194
6.2	Growth and Structure GDP	196
6.3	Agricultural Production	196
6.4	Irrigation Schemes in Morocco	200
6.5	Phosphate Exports, 1970-1980	204
6.6	Growth in Manufacturing Production 1970-1980 (Volume Index 1969=100)	204
6.7	Moroccanisation of Enterprises 1973-1977	207
6.8	Labourforce by Occupational Category (%)	207
6.9	Income from Remittances (millions MD)	211
6.10	Investment Projects Agreed 1979 by Major Centres	211
7.1	Tunisian Phosphate and Oil Production	220
7.2	Tunisian Population Growth and Other Demographic Characteristics, 1936-1980	220
7.3	Volume and Value of Tunisian Petroleum and Petroleum Product Exports	225
7.4	Projects and Jobs Created as a Result of Laws 72-38 and 74-74 from Contracts Signed 1973-1978	225
7.5	Indices of Tunisian Industrial Production (100= base year : 1970)	231

7.6	Percentage Distribution of Public and Private Investment by Manufacturing Sector	231
7.7	Production of Selected Crops (1000 tons)	233
7.8	Percentage Distribution of Tunisian Exports by Sector	233
7.9	Percentage Distribution of Tunisian Imports by Sector	235
7.10	Tunisian Investment for the Sixth Plan	235
8.1	Population and GNP Per Capita of North Africa 1978	242
8.2	Gross National Product Per Capita (US dollars) 1978	242
8.3	Oil Production Reserves, Revenues and Duration of Oil Reserves in 1978 for Selected Arab States	243
8.4	Libya: Plan Allocations, 1973-1975, 1976-1980 Million LD	243
8.5	Libya: Oil Production, Revenue, Take per Barrel and Gross National Product, 1962-1981	249
8.6	Libya National Expenditure (Income) Accounts 1975-1980	250
8.7	Libya: Distribution of Gross Domestic Product by Economic Sector, 1970 and 1978 (at current prices)	251
8.8	Libya: Gross Fixed Capital Formation in 1975 and 1980 (Constant 1975 Prices) and Cumulative Gross Fixed Capital Formation 1981-1985 (1979 Prices)	251
8.9	Libya: Distribution of Non-Oil Gross Domestic Product by Economic Sector, 1975, 1980 & 1985 (1979 Prices)	253
8.10	Libya: Balance of Payments 1970-1980 (US dollars million)	254
8.11	Libya: Terms of Trade, 1974-1980	255
8.12	Libya: Land Use in 1979	255
8.13	Libya: Selected Agricultural Indices, 1958, 1962, 1967 and Various Recent Years (LD million)	257
8.14	Libya: Index of Output of Selected Agricultural Items, 1970 to 1977	259
8.15	Libya: Growth of Selected Agricultural Indices 1976-1980	260
8.16	Libya: Expansion of Enrolment in Primary Schools 1950/51 to 1976/77	260
8.17	Libya: Enrolment of Libyans in Schools, Colleges, Universities, 1976/77	260
8.18	Libya: Distribution of Nationals' Employment by Economic Sector, 1973, 1975 and 1980	266
8.19	Libya: Growth of Migrant Workers in Libya, Official and Estimated Figures	268
8.20	Libya: Distribution of Migrant Workers by Economic Sectors, 1975 and 1980	269

8.21	Libya: Migrant Workers in 1975 and 1980	271

Figures

	A General Map of NorthWest Africa	xv
5.1	Location Map of Algeria	154
6.1	Morocco: Trends in Wheat Production & Demand	198
6.2	Distribution of Mineral Resources in Morocco	202
7.1	Location Map of Tunisia	218
8.1	Location Map of Libya	248

PREFACE

This volume aims to be a reader on the politics and economies of the four countries of NorthWest Africa - Algeria, Morocco, Tunisia and Libya - for the decade of the 1970s. The colonial history of the Maghreb states linked them traditionally to the politics and economy of Europe, but contemporary political and economic changes both within NorthWest Africa and in the world economy has led to these countries becoming increasingly marginalised by the European nations. Although the political courses pursued by Algeria, Morocco, Tunisia and Libya have been strikingly different, one from another, during the 1970s, they have all been strongly influenced by international economic forces such as the international division of labour, the dependence on technology provided by the major international corporations, and in the case of Tunisia and Morocco by international aid programmes. By the late 1970s all the NorthWest African nations were increasingly being drawn into a complex political and economic involvement with the Mashreq or Arab East, acting both as mediators in the conflicts of the Arab world and as major recipients of finance from the oil-rich states of the Middle East. All these forces have had the effect of introducing common constraints on the independent economic and political courses being sought by the different nations of NorthWest Africa.

This reader devotes one chapter to the politics of each nation followed in the second half of the book by a chapter which concentrates on the economic aspects of change in each state. The boundary between political and economic aspects of development is a hard one to define, and for this reason some minor overlap between chapters has been permitted so that chapters on the contemporary politics of each nation can be read independently from those on the economy. Likewise the authors of each chapter have been given considerable academic freedom in their approach, resulting in light being thrown on the important issues from a number of different perspectives.

The editors gratefully acknowledge their thanks to Nancy Smart (Centre for Middle Eastern & Islamic Studies, University of Durham) for undertaking preparation of the camera-ready copy of the book with great patience and care. Without her considerable efforts the publication of this book would not have been possible. Acknowledgements are also due to Dennis Ewbank (Centre for Middle Eastern & Islamic Studies, University of Durham) for his help in preparing the tables for final publication; to Margaret Cape, who drew most of the maps; and to Leslie Hill (Photographic Unit of the Department of Geography, University of Glasgow) for his help. In addition we are most grateful to Marion Farouk-Sluglett, Anne Findlay and Peter Sluglett who completed some translation work on our behalf.

                                    Richard Lawless   Allan Findlay
                                          Durham   Glasgow

CURRENCY EXCHANGE RATES

Year	£= ALGERIA Dinar (AD)	MOROCCO Dirham (MD)	TUNISIA Dinar (TD)	LIBYA Dinar (LD)
1970	11.82	12.06	1.25	0.857
1971	11.67	11.97	1.24	0.857
1972	11.85	12.06	1.24	0.853
1973	10.40	10.90	1.13	0.853
1974	9.07	9.45	0.943	0.687
1975	9.20	9.65	0.930	0.695
1976	7.95	8.34	0.840	0.600
1977	7.05	7.40	0.690	0.500
1978	7.93	8.15	0.772	0.567
1979	7.81	8.05	0.827	0.604
1980	8.77	8.55	0.831	0.652

Year	$= ALGERIA Dinar (AD)	MOROCCO Dirham (MD)	TUNISIA Dinar (TD)	LIBYA Dinar (LD)
1970	4.96	5.1	0.53	0.36
1971	4.96	5.1	0.53	0.36
1972	4.75	4.6	0.483	0.329
1973	4.33	4.54	0.471	0.355
1974	3.91	4.07	0.406	0.296
1975	3.90	4.10	0.395	0.295
1976	3.95	4.17	0.425	0.295
1977	4.13	4.49	0.430	0.295
1978	4.14	4.33	0.413	0.295
1979	3.82	3.94	0.405	0.296
1980	3.98	3.88	0.377	0.296

Source: Middle East Economic Digest (the figures refer to January of each year).

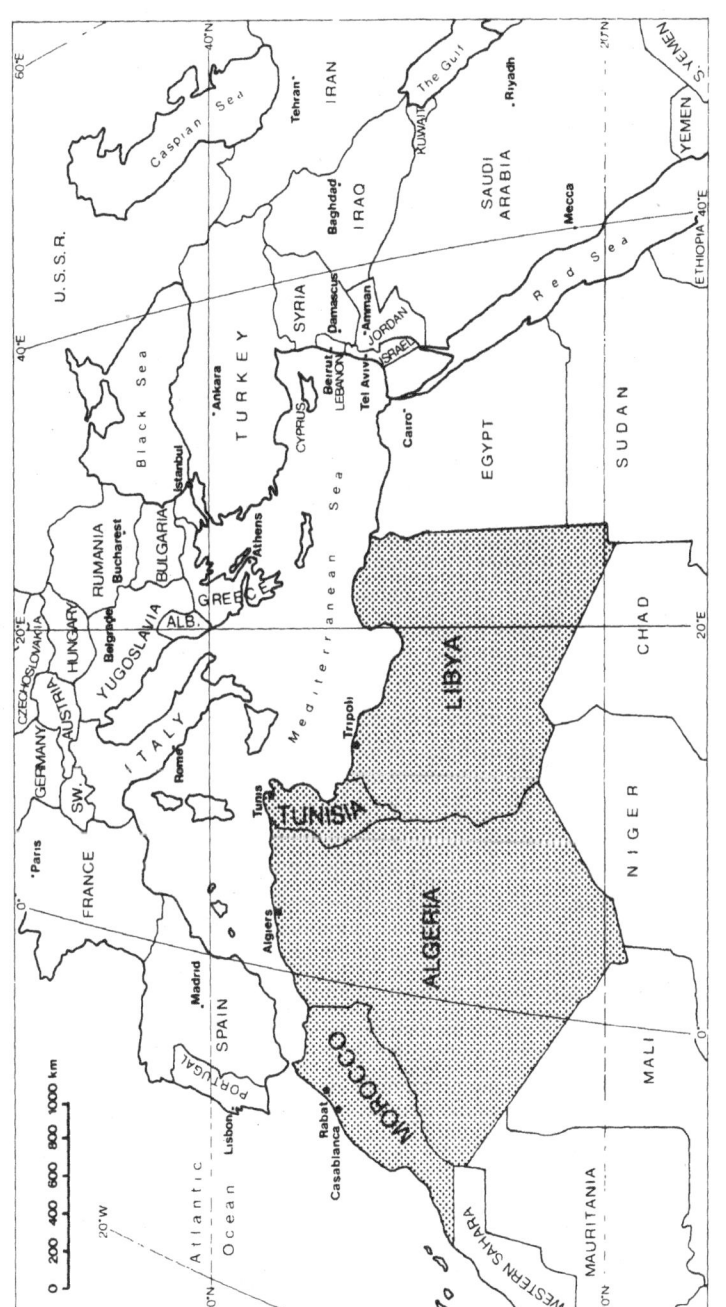

A GENERAL MAP OF NORTHWEST AFRICA

PART ONE

CONTEMPORARY POLITICS OF NORTHWEST AFRICA : INTRODUCTION

Werner Ruf

How can one justify another book on North Africa, especially when it is almost impossible to find one's way through the existing literature? The authors of this book have tried to tackle this very problem, and have attempted to produce a wide ranging review of the state of political and economic development in the Maghreb countries at the beginning of the 1980s.

Such an attempt to draw up a balance sheet is important for a number of reasons. In the first place, the gradual concentration of economic relations, transport networks and communications systems has meant that the world has become smaller, and in this context North Africa lies at the southern door of Europe. Secondly, the Mediterranean basin is becoming increasingly important in the general context of the rising tensions in international relations; such tensions include the so-called crisis in Afghanistan, which broke out, perhaps not entirely fortuitously, shortly after the fall of the Shah, the Americans' most 'reliable' ally, and the war between Iran and Iraq, which may well lead to a dangerous destabilisation of both regimes and which has already been responsible for a substantial check to Soviet influence in the area. An important consequence of the Iran/Iraq war has been the collapse of OPEC, but its impact has not been confined to the price of oil and the revenues of the oil producing states in the region. In the medium term it may well have serious implications for the international financial system, particularly if the Gulf states are no longer able to fund their ambitious development plans with current revenues from oil and are forced to withdraw their enormous deposits from Western banks.

Again, there is the continuous and escalating crisis in the Palestine conflict, which has already dealt a staggering blow to the Lebanese political system and now threatens the further destabilisation of Jordan, Syria and possibly Egypt. Political developments thus become harder to evaluate and more difficult for the super-powers to control, although in fact, outside Syria, Libya and possibly Algeria, given the strength of the Western presence, it is probably more accurate to think in terms of a single super-power, the United States, and its ally the European Community, bound together by a complex network of competitive relationships.

The growing instability of almost all the regimes in the region is a reflection of the acute social contradictions in the various countries. Food riots, (in Egypt in 1979 and Morocco in June 1981), uncontrolled urbanisation, the massive increase in illegal migration (1), the harsh repression of any opposition and the tacit condoning of such repression on the part of the outside world (Turkey, Iraq, Morocco, Tunisia, Saudi Arabia), the growth of fundamentalist Islamic movements – all these are the result of a combination of policies of exploitation and the increasing political and ideological isolation of the elites and the ruling classes from the mass of the population in these countries over the past 20 years.

The accession of Greece, Spain and Portugal to the EEC may be seen partly as strengthening the European Community's influence in the Mediterranean, and to a certain extent as competing with the American presence there. On the other hand, Spain's desire to become a member of NATO means an expansion of NATO interests and presence in the area, especially as the Mediterranean basin and the oil-producing states of the Middle East have been declared a NATO security zone, according to recent defence plans (2). It is certain that the accession of these three newcomers to the EEC will affect the trade relations of most of the Mediterranean EEC associate states, particularly Morocco and Tunisia, because Western Europe is the traditional market for their agricultural exports.

Another clear indication of the extent to which the Mediterranean is incorporated into US (and NATO) global strategy is the agreement between the US and Morocco to allow the US military to use bases in Morocco, as well as persistent rumours about the reopening of the old naval base at Bizerta on the straits between Sicily and Tunisia for the use of the Sixth Fleet. It is difficult to decide whether US pressure on the pro-Western governments of Tunisia and Morocco will simply increase the American presence in the Mediterranean, or whether the proposed bases will provide logistical and strategic springboards for the Rapid Deployment Force, or whether a direct American presence in these countries is intended to have a stabilising effect on their increasingly shaky regimes (see the chapters on Morocco and Tunisia). Such developments certainly have their counterproductive aspects: in particular, they are highly unpopular among the citizens of these countries, and are also especially likely to encourage the growth of Islamic fundamentalist movements.

Of course, North Africa itself is not free of internal conflicts: the war between Polisario and Morocco, which has continued for some eight years, threatens to take on an international dimension as a result of massive US support for the Moroccan government. There are constant attempts to undermine the regime in Libya, and latent border conflicts between Morocco and Algeria as well as the apparently unbridgeable ideological gap between the more conservative and more self-proclaimed progressive systems within the Maghrib, which have their roots in the various historical, economic, social and cultural experiences of the four countries which can all be manipulated to order.

Any analysis of the political system of North Africa and of their profoundly differing development policies (or economic strategies) must therefore be based upon an historical study of their social structures, a study of the existing class formation and particularly of the ruling classes and their aspirations as reflected in their political and socio-economic orientations, and the specific contradictions which result. Here we must bear in mind that pre-colonial North Africa exhibited a number of common socio-economic, cultural and political structures. Although their numbers varied from place to place, the nomads were always a significant element in the population. While generally posing a latent threat to the various dynasties, they also made an important contribution to both east-west and north-south trade, in their capacity as protectors of the caravans. Hence as well as being a danger to the very existence of the coastal trading cities and to the hinterlands which the rulers of these cities controlled, the nomads were of vital importance in ensuring the continuity of trade. Another important feature of pre-colonial North Africa was the opposition between the city and the countryside, between the rulers of the coastal towns and the sedentary peasants behind, who had to pay 'taxes' to them.

Although Morocco was not part of the Ottoman Empire, it followed the same path of development as the other states; commercial capitalist penetration in the late eighteenth and early nineteenth centuries was succeeded by finance capitalism, which culminated in the establishment of the protectorates in Tunisia and Morrocco. Here the lines begin to diverge; leaving Libya aside because of its very different colonial history. French influence is generally taken to be the decisive common factor in the later development of the other three countries. Although this is certainly important, particularly on the cultural level, it must be emphasised that the colonisation of Algeria actually caused its *deculturation*, while in Tunisia and Morocco a dual Arab/French culture developed, each with its own particular features.

In general, our particular concern is with the socio-economic transformation undergone by each of these countries. The savage and almost total agrarian colonisation of Algeria made the emergence of a national landowning bourgeoisie almost impossible, and this may well have facilitated the introduction of a tentative land reform some years after independence. In contrast, the Tunisian and Moroccan bourgeoisie developed quite differently, as a result of the particular colonial and finance capitalist penetration to which their societies were subjected. Here Libya is particularly difficult to analyse because of its virtual 'non-development' (rather than under-development).

This collection of essays is not intended purely as an academic analysis of the history and political systems of each Maghreb state, and it does not attempt any detailed prognosis of future political and economic development. It tries to show the divergent and often antagonistic interests of the various strata and classes within each society. Thus it is impossible to understand the development of each class, stratum or group without reference to the whole spectrum of social and political interactions both inside and outside each country, and to the general historical framework. For example, the particular features of the struggle and successes of the organised working class movement in all four countries must be taken into account.

Despite sharing the same geographical space, a common Islamic-cultural identity, and a similar colonial past, the North African countries today present a widely differentiated spectrum of social classes and interests (3), which results in considerable variation both in domestic policies and external alliances. One of the principal purposes of this book is to examine and unravel the political determinants of each nation state. The variety and complexity of these determinants make it difficult to apply a common analytical approach in each case, and the various authors have followed their own academic and theoretical interests in the different case studies. Hence the wide variety of political and social developments surveyed in this volume is to some extent paralleled by a degree of plurality in the methodological approach adopted by the contributors. This feature of the book has both advantages and disadvantages. On the one hand, the editors did not intend to provide a comparative analysis which could only have been achieved by adopting a common methodological framework. On the other hand, the variety of approaches adopted enables the reader to ask what other answers might have been forthcoming if a different form of analysis had been utilised in some of the contributions.

The book will have fulfilled its purpose if it is able to provide the interested reader with the basic information, insight and bibliographical background to help him deepen his knowledge of the history and politics of contemporary North Africa. We believe that the venture is of particular importance because it is appearing at a time when North Africa is playing a new and crucial role in vital international political developments.

NOTES AND REFERENCES

1. See the papers from the seminar on Labour Movements in the Mediterranean, (Inter-University Centre, Dubrovnik, 21 March - 1 April, 1983), to be published by the Friedrich-Ebert Foundation, Bonn.

2. This problem is dealt with by Heinz-Jürgen Axt in 'Konkurrenz und "Arbeitsteilung" : Griechenlands EG-Beitritt und die amerikanisch-westeuropeäische Mittelmeer-, Nahost- und Mittelostpolitik', Blätter für deutsche und internationale Politik, no.5, 1981, pp.542-560.

3. See Werner Ruf, 'Struktur- und Entwicklungs probleme des Maghreb', in Nohlen and Nuscheler (eds), Handbuch der Dritten Welt, vol.6 (revised and extended edition), Hoffman und Campe, 1983, pp.12-36

Chapter 1.

THE POLITICS OF ALGERIAN SOCIALISM

Hugh Roberts

Algeria is a socialist one-party state without a clear socialist doctrine or a ruling party worthy of the name. It is a republic in which Islam is the state religion but it is far from being an Islamic Republic in the sense in which this is understood in Iran, with whose revolutionary government Algeria nevertheless enjoys excellent relations. It is ruled in the name of the people by a self-conscious and self-confident elite whose particular interests and internal divisions are masked by a populist and nationalist rhetoric which expresses respect for, and mistrust of, those it governs in about equal proportions, a complex of sentiments which are generally reciprocated by the latter. In the last 20 years it has undergone exceptionally rapid economic and social change, the benefits of which have been unusually widely distributed, by comparison with other oil-rich states of the Third World. It is a country characterized, *inter alia*, by a high level of social tension, but which has nevertheless displayed a rare degree of continuity in its political orientations and arrangements since its accession to Independence in 1962. The nature of these orientations and arrangements and the manner in which they have evolved over the last two decades are matters of controversy, as keenly debated by academic observers as they are by the Algerians themselves.

FACTIONALISM AND THE EMPIRICAL MODE OF DEVELOPMENT

Brendan Clifford has recently written

> two lines of socialist development have been occurring throughout the century. Russia has been the prime example of the one, Britain of the other. In the one case there has been comprehensive theoretical coherence and the political determination of developments. In the other case development has been economically determined amidst theoretical confusion (1).

The uniqueness of the Algerian case lies in the fact that, while differing in crucial respects from both of these extremes, it is, in fact, a peculiar hybrid of the two, resembling the Soviet experience in certain formal respects, but not all, and the British case in a cardinal matter of substance, but in no other. The form of government has been dictatorial, as in Russia, and there has been a measure of both theoretical coherence and political determination of development but the first has been far less explicit and the second less effective than in the Russian case, for circumstances have not permitted the *Front de Libération Nationale* (FLN) to perform the same functions as the CPSU. The corollary of this is that there has also been a substantial degree of economic determination of development, reflected in the severely empirical approach of the political leadership to the formulation of policy and its almost British aversion to doctrinal debate (2).

Within the regime which came to power in 1965, the principal architects of policy have possessed a realistic vision and a coherent strategy for achieving rapid social and economic development and for consolidating their own rule. On the other hand, the regime has not possessed a strong enough social base in one section of the population to enable it to impose radical changes on the rest in the way the Bolsheviks did, by deliberately precipitating social conflicts and employing a combination of mass mobilisation and coercion to achieve the desired outcome. Instead, the government has been obliged to temporise with a wide range of social forces and interests and propose changes rather than impose them. At the same time, objective circumstances, chief among them Algeria's oil and gas resources and a comparatively favourable international environment, have made it possible for the government to pursue its ambitious development policies while eschewing radical methods.

Part of the reason for this, of course, is that, unlike the Bolsheviks, the victors of the power struggle within the wartime FLN did not come to power as the political leadership of a class, committed to reconstructing society in the interest of this class and able to mobilise its support. On the contrary, they came to power as the leadership of a national revolution, a leadership which was itself a coalition of various factions and which represented, although rather obliquely, all classes in Algeria, for all had, in varying degrees, participated in the anti-colonial struggle. The resulting ideological heterogeneity and rhetorical syncretism have not implied theoretical incoherence, however. A good deal of coherence can be inferred from, because it is presupposed by, the strategy which the regime has pursued in matters of economic development and especially in its handling of social change in the countryside. On the other hand, the diversity of social interests represented within the regime and the potential for division which this contains have both limited the extent to which theoretical coherence has been possible - for it has been far from comprehensive - and, in particular, inhibited the explicit formulation or explanation (as opposed to rationalisation) of government strategy, outside non-contentious matters. Indeed, a Byzantine secrecy has shrouded government thinking for most of the time, with public suspicion the natural counterpart of the leaders' lack of confidence in the led. The same social and ideological heterogeneity of the regime and its origin in an anti-colonial, not anticapitalist or even anti-feudal, revolution have precluded the recourse to the massive political mobilisation of the population on class lines which has been fundamental to the Soviet and Chinese experiences.

There is a more profound reason for this absence, however, for if we cannot speak of a revolution from above, still less a reign of terror, in post-colonial Algeria, this is in large measure because both of these occurred prior to the conquest of state power by the FLN in 1962, during the war itself which, as Pierre Bourdieu has insisted, was indeed a social as well as a national revolution (3). The FLN used ruthless coercion and intimidation in the course of eliminating collaborators and informers and asserting its claim, against those of rival organisations, to be the unique political representative of the Algerian nation. At the same time, the total mobilisation of the Muslim population during the war brought about a fundamental and many-sided transformation of the attitudes of individual Algerians. As Bourdieu observed at the time:

> everywhere the same consciousness of their rights is now in evidence: the right to work, the right to decent housing, the right to the different social benefits (social security, family allowances, etc). For the attitude of the beggar who comes humbly to solicit a charitable gift there has been substituted a demanding and revolutionary state of mind which is inducing the Algerians to insist on their rights to social benefits and services (4).

This radicalisation of the popular consciousness during the war is the source of the immense pressure which the government of the independent state has been under to provide rapid but also egalitarian access to the material benefits of a modern industrial economy. For, in Jean Leca's words, 'the Algerian citizen is above all an aggressive consumer who expects from the State all that the colonial State refused him' (5). In the short term, however, the political repercussions of this mobilisation created obstacles to the fulfilment of popular aspirations. Precisely because of its popular character, the war did not mobilise the population on unambiguously national lines. The nationwide structure of the FLN, divided for operational purposes into six *wilayat* (commands) (6) and, within each *wilaya*, into 'zones', 'regions' and 'sectors', reflected but also made explicit the long-standing cultural and also political differences resulting from the low level of national integration and the regionally differentiated impact of French colonialism on Algerian society. Because of the relative isolation of the wilayat from one another and from the overall leadership, the more truly popular the FLN became, the more its operational commanders became the captives of the specific local or regional interests which they had mobilised. Thus the political differences between regions were accentuated in the course of the war and, although contained for its duration by the imperative of national unity against the French, inevitably surfaced in the form of intense factionalism once independence was achieved.

As a result, any subsequent recourse to the Jacobin methods of the wartime FLN was out of the question, for such legitimacy as these methods had acquired in virtue of the dramatic exigencies of the national liberation struggle disappeared with the advent of independence and, simultaneously, the wartime FLN itself disintegrated. In consequence, the factions which triumphed in the struggle for power were initially confronted with a plethora of only narrowly defeated - and by no means discredited - rivals ever ready to mobilise popular resistance to the arbitrary use of state power. Thus the same imperative of national unity which made Jacobin methods necessary during the war ruled them out thereafter, with the result that the government of the independent state has lacked the means as well as the will to engage in coercive social engineering.

A corollary of this state of affairs is that the capacity of the government to adopt coherent and effective policies for economic and social development such as could meet popular expectations has been seriously limited by the need, which has arisen every time a major choice has had to be made, to establish anew a consensus between the various factions of which the regime has been composed. Since the ideological assumptions common to all - nationalism, anti-imperialism, respect for Islam, (more or less sincere) adherence to (one or another conception of) socialism - have not, in general, furnished clear guidance for the practical business of formulating particular policies, pragmatic arguments have been decisive in achieving consensus at each stage, while a kind of gentlemen's agreement to differ on ideological matters has been in operation.

Part of the reason for this is that, for the first decade of independence at least, the factions within the regime were not primarily ideological in character. With the exception of the Marxist Left led by Mohamed Harbi and the Liberal Right led by Ferhat Abbas, neither of which tendencies had a substantial following in the national liberation movement (7), alliances were based on personal loyalties rather than doctrinal agreements, so that there was no simple or direct correspondence between political rivalries and ideological divisions. If all regimes and political parties contain factions, it is nevertheless of considerable importance for the conduct of government whether ideology or mere self-interest is the basis of the main political conflicts. In the Soviet Communist Party in the 1920s, as in the British Labour Party since 1951, the competition between clienteles has been subsidiary to doctrinal differences. In Algeria, it has been the other way round: factions have represented clienteles rather than tendencies, at any rate for most of the time.

FROM BEN BELLA TO BOUMEDIENE: DEMOBILISATION AND THE CONSTRUCTION OF THE STATE 1962-1971

The contradictory political legacy of the Revolution confronted the President of the newly independent state, Ahmed Ben Bella, with a major dilemma. The disintegration of the wartime FLN into a plethora of factions representing clienteles rather than tendencies meant that as many of these as possible had to be accommodated in order to forestall opposition which the regime was initially too weak to suppress. In addition, because, in the incessant manoeuvring of the 1962-1965 period, all factions, though essentially clientelist in nature, nonetheless resorted, when convenient, to ideological arguments in support of their claims to positions of influence, the regime had to be extremely catholic or chameleon-like in its ideological complexion. In order to achieve coherence in policy, on the other hand, it was necessary either to reduce the number of factions within the regime or to contain their interplay within tolerable limits by submitting it to binding arbitration.

Ben Bella primarily attempted the first tactic in dealing respectively with the challenges from the trade union leadership (8), the party head Mohamed Khider (9), the Ferhat Abbas-Ahmed Francis group (10), the Kabyle opposition (11) and the 'Oujda clan' (12). The fundamental weakness of this approach was that it was one thing to eliminate a political rival but quite another to neutralise or absorb the constituency for which he spoke. Thus the challenge was, in most cases, not defeated but merely deflected temporarily. The result was a perpetual juggling act, in which Ben Bella sought to play the various factions off against one another, but therefore actually needed to refrain from decisively alienating any one group in order to be able to call on its support at a later stage, if need be. For example, in sharp contrast to the events of January 1963, when independently-minded trade union leaders had been voted out of office by the first UGTA Congress, packed with Party militants on Khider's orders, the second Congress of the UGTA, in March 1965, was remarkable for the freedom and vigour of the debates, the rejection of four of the six reports presented by the tame leadership installed two years previously and the election of one of the chief critics of this leadership, Mouloud Oumeziane, as General Secretary (13) - striking evidence of Ben Bella's willingness to make concessions to the UGTA in the hope of securing its support in the context of the approaching showdown with Boumediène and the 'Oujda clan'. Similarly, having crushed the revolt of the Kabyle *Front des Forces Socialistes* (FFS) in 1963-1964 and secured the arrest of its leader, Hocine Ait Ahmed, Ben Bella not only commuted the death sentence passed on the latter to one of imprisonment but negotiated a secret agreement with Ait Ahmed and his supporters whereby all FFS prisoners, including Ait Ahmed, would be released and allowed to rejoin the FLN (14). It was widely believed subsequently that he had even offered Ait Ahmed the post of Foreign Minister (15), then held by Boumediène's close ally, Abdelaziz Bouteflika. That these moves were designed to win Kabyle support in the duel with Boumediène and the 'Oujda clan' is suggested by, among other things, the fact that these negotiations were conducted without the knowledge of the rest of the government, who learned of the agreement when *Le Peuple* published a communique from the FFS on 15 June 1965 (16). The *coup d'état* followed four days later.

The resort to the first tactic proper, that of definitively reducing the number of factions in play, could not in the circumstances be successful in the short run. The process of neutralising the social bases of the various political clienteles would inevitably take time. Ben Bella's problem was that he was equally unable to employ with success the second tactic, that of submitting the factional interplay to binding arbitration. To do so required him to accord a pre-eminent position within his regime to the sole disciplined and organised force which was national in character, namely the regular *Armée Nationale Populaire* (ANP) (17) under Boumediène's command as Minister of Defence. But the legitimacy of the ANP was vigorously contested by a wide range of groups at the time, from the Marxist Left to the Liberal Right and, above all, by many of the surviving and still highly influential former guerrilla commanders. Unable, therefore, and probably unwilling to acknowledge the army's claim to the role of arbiter of the factional conflicts within the regime, Ben Bella treated those who principally represented it, Boumediène and his allies of the 'Oujda clan', as simply another faction to be played off against the others in the same way, in the short run, until the army could be induced to retire to its barracks for good (18). Thus, in September 1963, on the eve of the showdown with Ait Ahmed's FFS, Ben Bella had brought two more of Boumediène's Oujda clan allies, Kaid Ahmed and Cherif Belkacem, into his government, as Minister of Tourism and Minister of Education and National Orientation respectively, to join Ahmed Medeghri and Bouteflika, both of whom were confirmed in their posts. As soon as the FFS revolt and that of Colonel Mohamed Chaabani in the south (19) had been quelled, however, Ben Bella felt less dependent upon Boumediène's army and set about purging the Oujda clan from the government. Thus he forced Medeghri, Minister of the Interior since 1962, to resign on 9 July 1964 and Kaid to do so three weeks later and secured the demotion of Cherif to Minister of Education *tout court* the following December (20).

It was this incessant factional manoeuvring and the concomitant lack of continuity in government personnel which was responsible for the general confusion and incoherence of government policy during the first three years of independence and, if it was the attempted eviction of Bouteflika (whether or not in favour of Ait Ahmed) which precipitated the coup d'état of 19 June 1965, it was the question of the political role of the army - of fundamental importance for the form of government of the independent state - which was at stake in the final confrontation between Ben Bella and Boumediène.

The Boumediène regime was also, initially, composed of a wide range of factions, equally clientelist in nature. The level of infighting and instability was sharply diminished, however, for instead of trying to reduce the number of factions directly by eliminating their leading figures, Boumediène was able to act effectively as the arbiter of their interplay, since through him and his allies the political weight of the army was institutionalised. Without making a frontal assault upon them, Boumediène nevertheless managed gradually to eliminate certain factions definitively, especially those linked to ex-guerrilla commanders, usually by coaxing their leading members into substantial responsibilities outside the government (for example, Lakhdar Ben Tobbal (21), Ali Kafi (22) and

Omar Ouseddik (23)) or into purely token positions within it (notably Salah Boubenider (24), Mohand ou el Hadj (25), Mohammedi Said (26) and Khatib Youcef (27)), in which they were badly placed to maintain an organised following of political significance. The only serious difficulty he encountered in this delicate process was the attempted coup in December 1967 by Colonel Tahar Zbiri, Chief of Staff of the ANP and formerly commander of the guerrilla forces in wilaya I (Aurès), and this was because of the exceptionally labyrinthine character of the faction in question (28) and the fact that it held key positions within the army itself (29).

By the end of 1967, then, the internal profile of the regime had been effectively rationalised, the factions reduced to a manageable number and, with the consequent stability, it was possible for coherent policy-making at last to be undertaken. The next four years saw the consolidation of the state apparatus at regional as well as national level, the beginnings of central economic planning, the comprehensive nationalisation of foreign capital and the rapid development of the state sector of the economy. The architects of this were the central core of the regime, Boumediène and the Oujda clan, with as junior partners in the enterprise a number of essentially apolitical ministers who were in no practical sense the spokesmen for particular constituencies but possessed high educational qualifications and technical expertise. During this period, the government appeared suspended in space, distant from a population denied effective participation in the political process at the national level following the eviction of its erstwhile representatives, not only the former guerrilla commanders but also the more combative trade union leaders, notably Mouloud Oumeziane (30), and the liberal spokesmen for the urban middle class With the major exception of education, in which a massive effort was undertaken, the government's concern to lay the foundations of a modern industrial economy precluded the immediate fulfilment of popular aspirations for material advancement and the political weakness of the regime in relation to the society ruled out any direct attempt to transform social relations. In particular, private agriculture was neglected and the 'self-managed' sector was allowed to stagnate. Policy was thus essentially elitist in concept and method and the mass of the population was reduced to the role of onlooker, with 'a disquieting degree of depoliticization, notably among youth' the inevitable result (31).

POLITICAL REMOBILISATION: THE IMPLICATIONS AND RATIONALE OF THE 'AGRARIAN REVOLUTION'

By late 1971, the process of laying the economic and administrative foundations of a modern state had been largely completed and the political alliance which had constituted the solid core of the regime and the basis of its coherence began to break up as alternative lines of development emerged. The more conservative line involved moving directly, if cautiously, towards political liberalisation and abstaining from any development of public property at the expense of domestic private property. The immediate positive proposal in this perspective was to complete the process of creating representative institutions begun at the local level in 1967 with the 'communal popular assemblies' (APC) and the regional level in 1969 with the 'wilaya popular assemblies' (APW) by reconvening the National Assembly, prorogued in June 1965. This would have provided the urban middle class with a national forum through which to participate in the political process; it would have thus widened the social basis of the regime while accentuating its bourgeois character and, crucially, providing a potential check on the executive's capacity for arbitrary action. As Hubert Michel has noted 'certain indications suggested that 1971 would be the year of the national institutions' (32). Not the least significant of the events of 1971 was the confounding of these expectations by the government's decision not to move in this direction.

Instead, it decided to embark upon the long promised and repeatedly postponed task of transforming the private sector of agriculture. As ever, the argument which proved decisive in the internal debates was undoubtedly a pragmatic one (33) – the critical state of private agriculture, reflected in the growing national deficit in foodstuffs and the accelerating rural exodus, which latter was creating massive social problems in the coastal cities built by Europeans for Europeans and which were now having to accommodate twice their populations of the colonial period. But the change in the regime's policy was none the less radical, as subsequent developments were to confirm, for having been rooted in the pragmatic consideration of earthy realities (34).

The aims of the Agrarian Revolution were several. Given Algeria's ability to pay for food imports with her revenues from oil and gas, it is unlikely that the poor performance of private agriculture was, in itself, the main reason for the reform. More convincing is the view that the growing state-owned industries required an expanding internal market for their products. This too is probably only part of the explanation, although certain authors have accorded it primary importance (35), for there was almost certainly a directly political rationale as well, the concern to incorporate the somewhat refractory population of the countryside into the national political community by responding to its material aspirations – thereby reinforcing the legitimacy of the regime – and bringing it more firmly within the purview of the state apparatus in several ways at once: in production, distribution, education, health, religious and cultural life, and so on. Finally, there was the undoubted need to halt or at least slow down the exodus from the countryside.

In theory, all these objectives neatly dovetailed. For example, the last objective could be attained only by substantially raising rural living standards and therefore, as a prerequisite, rural incomes. The latter could be achieved in a non-inflationary way only if total agricultural output rose but for this to happen productivity had to be substantially increased. This required a major injection of capital which, in turn, presupposed the transformation of production relations and the form of property and the constitution of 'production cooperatives' (*Coopératives Agricoles de Production de la Révolution*

Agraire: CAPRA). The latter, being in reality collective farms dependent in a variety of ways upon the state apparatus, contributed to the attainment of the political objective referred to above. They were complemented in this by the new socialist agricultural villages, 1000 of which were planned, in which many members of the CAPRA were accommodated, and which were elaborately equipped with modern amenities (electricity, gas, running water, a café) but also institutions diffusing the modernist ideology of the state power and permitting the reinforcement of its political control (school, clinic, mosque, cinema, party and union offices). At the same time, the villages and the CAPRA, through the intermediary of new multi-purpose service cooperatives *(Coopératives Agricoles Polyvalentes Communales de Service CAPCS)*, were to constitute a new source of domestic demand for the products of the state industries.

Ten years later it appears that the reform was, on balance, unsuccessful in attaining these objectives. Numerous observers have pointed out shortcomings of both implementation and conception (36). In the short run, however, its political repercussions were far more important than its impact upon the rural sector of the economy and it is in these repercussions, I believe, that we may discern the real political rationale for Boumediène's conspicuous personal commitment to the reform, for, while it is highly likely that the factions within the regime had different motives for approving the reform and that the need to halt the influx of rural migrants into the crowded cities was the common denominator, the decision to embark upon it clearly had a number of radical political implications.

To begin with, it involved the first effective attack on domestic private property and therefore made necessary the continuing political disenfranchisement, at the national level, of the developing bourgeoisie. Second, it required the mobilisation of popular support, in the countryside in particular, and thus the revitalisation of the various mass organisations, above all the party itself. Third, it led to the development of a temporary parallel administrative structure designed to outflank the influence of vested interests. The nature of the routine administrative apparatus made it particularly unsuitable for the implementation of controversial measures; accordingly, Boumediène by-passed it as much as possible by creating new, *ad hoc*, bodies or modifying existing ones. At the national level, it was not the Ministry of Agriculture and Agrarian Reform which supervised the reform, despite its nominal competence in this area, but the National Commission of the Agrarian Revolution (CNRA), on which the representatives of the ministry were heavily outnumbered by those of the presidency, the army, the party, the trade union and ten other ministries (37). At the level of the wilaya responsibility for the implementation of the reform was entrusted, not to the existing wilaya Director of Agriculture, but to a specially appointed Commissioner for the Agrarian Révolution. Finally, at the local level, the Communal Popular Assemblies (APC), charged with the task of expropriation and redistribution of land, were specially enlarged for the duration of this function by the inclusion of local representatives of the party, the War Veterans Association, the trade union, the National Union of

Algerian Women and the party youth organisation, in addition to a minimum of six members of the newly constituted National Union of Algerian Peasants and a number of technical advisers, while former APC members who owned land liable to be affected by the nationalisation measures were excluded (38).

Fourth, an early, if unexpected, development following the promulgation of the reform was the constitution, in the summer of 1972, of a student voluntary service (*Volontariat*) for the Agrarian Revolution, with committees being formed in each university, plus some high schools in Algeria but also in France, where numerous Algerians were studying. For several years running, between 3,000 and 5,000 students carried out propaganda and educational as well as manual work in the countryside during their vacations and reported directly to the presidency on abuses and deficiencies at the local level. The Volontariat has been regarded by some observers as a manoeuvre by the regime to 'incorporate' ('*recuperer*') the intellectual Left. However, it is important to note that it was the student activists who proposed the scheme to the regime rather than vice-versa. Its establishment occurred after the clandestine Algerian Communist Party (*le Parti de l'Avant-Garde Socialiste:* PAGS) had announced its support for the regime (39) and PAGS militants were undoubtedly active in student political circles. As one of them put it to me, '*le Volontariat était un acquis des étudiants*'; (40) indeed, the students deliberately chose not to approach the party or the Ministry of Agriculture, whose hostility or at least lack of enthusiasm was taken for granted in advance, but instead obtained the support of the left-wing Minister of Higher Education, Mohamed Benyahia, and through him that of Boumediène himself, who fully endorsed the idea and thereafter gave it every encouragement. Public (and televised) meetings between Boumediène and the student volunteers were held at the end of each vacation's volontariat, at which detailed and most interesting – because comparatively candid and well-researched – reports were presented by the spokesmen of the *comités de volontariat* of the three universities, Algiers, Constantine and Oran. These reports were also published *in extenso* (41).

Fifth, it led to the increased and more explicit participation of the army in the application of government policy and thus the general process of economic and social transformation. Following 19 June 1965, the army had stayed in the background of the political process. The ANP had been built on the fusion of the old 'army of the frontiers' and those elements of the interior *maquis* susceptible to incorporation into a regular army. The artisans of this conversion, under Boumediène's general direction, were a group of regular officers who had originally served in the French army. Highly proficient technically, they lacked substantial political followings having played at most a marginal role during the war. The favouring of such officers by Boumediène was badly received by many an ex-guerrilla chief and probably lay behind both Chaabani's revolt in July 1964 and that of Zbiri in December 1967. The repressive role of the ANP in the 1962-1967 period did little for its popularity and its conversion into a modern fighting force absorbed the energies of its officer corps.

and, when these two functions had been accomplished, the introduction of National Service in 1968 continued to keep it preoccupied with its own affairs. This permitted the regime to slough off its military image to some extent, neither Boumediène nor any of the other ex-army officers in the government ever appearing in uniform, for example. The army had, however, been engaged throughout in productive work, possessing its own network of agricultural and industrial enterprises coordinated since 1963 by the *Direction Nationale des Coopératives de de l'Armée Nationale Populaire* (DNC-ANP), and had undertaken a number of major engineering and construction projects, notably those of the Trans-Saharan highway and the University of Constantine. With the advent of the agrarian reform, this role was extended and acquired political ramifications. It was the army which undertook the construction of many of the new socialist agricultural villages (42) and that of the *barrage vert*, the ambitious reafforestation project along the northern edge of the Sahara, and the army also participated in the application of the reform at the national level through its two representatives on the CNRA as well as, more discreetly, through the *Sécurité Militaire*, the Algerian equivalent of MI5, which was responsible for monitoring actual or potential opposition to the reform measures. These developments were echoed in the increasingly radical, indeed *marxisant*, tone of *El Djeich*, the monthly review published by the army's Political Commissariat, markedly to the left of the party weekly, *Révolution Africaine*, in its analysis and editorial content. It was in *El Djeich*, not *Révolution Africaine*, that the first elaborate theoretical statement of Boumediène's perspective on the Agrarian Revolution was published in the summer of 1972, in a two-part article by one of his advisers, Mustapha Lacheraf (43), entitled *De la Révolution agraire à la Revolution sociale* (44).

The application of the agrarian reform had a number of other repercussions. In particular, the expropriation of the large landowners was followed in late 1974 by the elimination of the private wholesalers of agricultural produce with the state take-over of marketing via the CAPCS at the communal level and the COFEL (*Coopérative des Fruits et Legumes*) at the wilaya level. This measure, intended to assist government attempts at price control and prevent hoarding and speculation and at the same time to guarantee a fair return to the new CAPRA, aroused a good deal of resentment and appears to have been far from successful in strictly economic terms in the short run, as a substantial black market developed. In political terms, however, we can see that the attack on private capital was widening and state intervention increasing by 1974 and it is in this context that we can understand the significance of the other measures introduced at this time, all of which appear to have been intended to evoke greater popular support for the regime in the face of growing bourgeois opposition to its agrarian policy. Thus the minimum wage was raised by 20 per cent (by 25 per cent in agriculture) on 3 January 1974 at the same time as the free medicine system (*la gratuité des soins*) came into nationwide operation, unwelcomed, it need hardly be added, by the private practitioners. Perhaps the most important of these measures was the reform of industrial relations in the state sector through the introduction of institutionalised workers' participation of a consultative kind. The Charter of 'Socialist Management' (*la Gestion Socialiste des Entreprises*: GSE) provided for the election of a Workers' Assembly in each *société nationale* (SN) at the national level (*l'Assemblée des Travailleurs de l'Entreprise*: ATE) as well as in each unit of production of which the SN in question was composed (*l'Assemblée des Travailleurs de l'Unité*: ATU); ultimately, the system was to be extended to the enterprises of the private sector as well (45). Although the Charter had been published on 16 November 1971 (that is, eight days after the Charter of the Agrarian Revolution), it began to be applied only in early 1974 with the election of the workers' assemblies in an initial sample of eleven SNs. The delay appears to have been caused, at least in part, by the resistance of senior management to the introduction of the reform; it is notable that the most important SN, SONATRACH (the state oil and gas corporation) was not affected by the new measures until four years later (the autumn of 1978), although the second most important state enterprise, the *Société Nationale de Sidérurgie* (SNS), conspicuously figured among the first eleven. Finally, 1974 saw another major measure of substantial interest to the mass of the population, the redrawing of the national administrative map with the increase in the number of wilayat from 15 to 31, (46) thereby effectively halving, *grosso modo*, the time wasted, distance travelled and expense incurred by the vast numbers of ordinary people requiring access, in order to obtain anything from a pension to an exit visa, to the administration at the regional level.

Thus the promulgation of the agrarian reform in 1971 inaugurated a range of developments in government policy broadly beneficial to those sectors of the population which, as John Dunn has put it, in Yeats's graphic phrase, had been 'breaking stone' (47) during the first six years of the Boumediène regime, developments which were clearly inimical to many of those interests which had prospered during this period. This change in direction was reflected in the audible hardening of Boumediène's rhetoric, in increasingly marked contrast to the blander pronouncements of the other members of the government. For example, in the early days of the reform in 1972, he had warned that 'either the Agrarian Revolution will succeed in bringing justice, or it will fail and we shall come up against a new Algerian bourgeoisie which will, perhaps, be harder and more vile than its colonial predecessor.' (48) He followed this up in April 1973 with the attack on the private sector to which we have already referred and, above all, with a major series of speeches in the summer of 1974, at Constantine, Tlemcen and Tizi Ouzou, in which he denounced corruption and opportunism in high places and stressed the need for an authentic vanguard party composed of committed socialists. Indeed, 1974 was the year in which matters came to a head. As *Le Monde's* correspondent, Paul Balta, observed in December of that year:

> since the beginning of the year, President Boumediène's government has been engaged in a trial of strength with the three principal sectors of the bourgeoisie: the large landowners, the

big private merchants and industrialists and, lastly, certain elements of the technocrats. The development of the conflict has been muffled and masked, as is often the case in Algeria, and this for two reasons: the different strata of the bourgeoisie are too ill-assorted to do battle in the open and the state power is strong enough to control the conflicts and prevent them from degenerating into open crises. From time to time, a split occurs, revealing the underlying tensions (49).

These tensions were reflected within the regime itself with increasing clarity from 1972 onwards and were ultimately resolved only with the destruction of the group of politicians hitherto fundamental to its stability, the famous 'Oujda clan'.

BOUMEDIENE AND THE END OF THE OUJDA CLAN

The Oujda clan consisted of five men with five things in common. First, they were from or connected with the urban middle class of western Algeria: Kaid Ahmed from Tiaret, Ahmed Medeghri from Saida, Cherif Belkacem and Abdelaziz Bouteflika both born in Morocco but possessing links with Tlemcen and Mohamed Tayebi from Sfisef near Sidi Bel Abbes (50). Second, none of them played roles during the war such as had enabled them to construct popular followings: they had all served as staff officers at the Moroccan HQ of wilaya V (Oranie) and subsequently of the 'army of the frontiers' at Oujda (51) (whence their collective sobriquet) and Tayebi's earlier stint in the maquis of wilaya V had been prejudicial, rather than beneficial, to his political prospects (52). Third, and in consequence, they were all heavily reliant upon Boumediène for their political advancement: their control of the Oujda HQ made their support vital to Boumediène in the last years of the war but they owed their army posts to him and forfeited them on obtaining government office after independence. Fourth, they were all notably unenthusiastic and unconvincing in their espousal of socialist ideals, having at most merely flirted with Fanonist notions during the war. Fifth, they all possessed considerable abilities which Boumediène needed to enlist: Medeghri was undoubtedly an extremely able administrator who deserves much of the credit for the construction of the state apparatus; Bouteflika, flamboyant but also eloquent and highly astute, proved an excellent foreign minister; Kaid was more than equal to the task of asserting the regime's authority over recalcitrant elements in the party, the trade union and the student union, which was essentially all that was asked of him in the late 1960's; Cherif and Tayebi were also undoubtedly competent in their respective ministerial posts, the former, as Minister of State without portfolio, acting as a kind of trouble-shooter and the latter presiding over the Ministry of Agriculture.

As such, then, they were especially useful to Boumediène during the first phase of his regime, from 1965 to 1971, as they had been in his earlier rise to power in the wartime army and in the power struggle with Ben Bella. By the early 1970's, however, they had largely rendered such services as they were capable of and had become an obstacle to the policies upon which Boumediène now seemed decided. Precisely in what way this was so is open to argument: the intricate dialectic of changes in policy and changes in personnel is a complex enough matter for analysis at the best of times and one can never be sure of one's interpretation of political developments conducted behind closed doors. It would seem, however, that the change in the direction of government policy inaugurated by the agrarian reform, in particular the growing emphasis on popular mobilisation and participation, required, if it was to carry conviction, the elimination of those figures specifically associated with the more elitist and, in certain respects, repressive content of policy in the earlier phase of the regime. New measures required new men, for whom room had to be made at the top. At the same time, the Oujda clan had already ceased to exist *qua* 'clan', for its triumph over the other clientelist factions in the mid-1960's had removed the external condition of its own cohesion, and the attempts of its individual members to bolster their personal power bases gave rise to divisions which could be exploited by Boumediène. On the other hand, while one can see that, in the context of the left-ward change in policy from 1971 onwards, the elimination of the Oujda clan made political sense from Boumediène's point of view, it would appear that considerations of political stability, as well as subjective factors – the long-standing personal ties between Boumediène and the five – ruled out any recourse to a wholesale purge or 'night of the long knives', but rather enjoined a piecemeal approach, so that specific motives and circumstances had an important part to play in each individual case. Just as the adoption of major policy measures required the emergence of a consensus as to their necessity, so the elimination of important figures was equally conditional upon the existence of collective agreement within the regime and, as such, the product of a wide range of only temporarily congruent calculations.

The fall of Kaid Ahmed in 1972 is an interesting case in point, as is that of Ahmed Medeghri two years later. Kaid's role as party head had been essentially repressive: it was he who had supervised the purging of all, but primarily left-wing, opposition to the regime within the party itself, the UGTA and the students' union (*Union Nationale des Etudiants Algériens:* UNEA, dissolved 15 January 1971). As such, he was eminently unsuitable for the task of revitalising the party in so far as this required the remobilisation of radical elements. At the same time, having domesticated the party and, in effect, reduced it to his personal instrument, he was, by 1972, seeking to expand its formal prerogatives, like Khider nine years earlier, by demanding that the party should be responsible for key administrative appointments, notably those of ambassadors and *walis*, (53) thereby increasing his own power at the expense of Bouteflika and Medeghri respectively. There was thus a clear basis for agreement, between Boumediène on the one hand and his two most senior ministers on the other, that Kaid should go. At the same time, opposition in the countryside to the expropriatory aspects of the agrarian reform was reflected in the appreciable inactivity of the party at the local level and in Kaid's own lack of enthusiasm for a measure which, as a large landowner himself, he was badly placed to advocate with conviction. Matters came to a head with a well-timed scandal. In the wake of revelations (published in the Oran daily *La République* (54), but for which the student volunteers deserve the credit) concerning the failure of local party and administrative officials to carry out the reform in Kaid's native region of Tiaret in the summer of 1972, Boumediène addressed a 'message to the nation' on 31 October in which he proclaimed the necessity of a 'radical transformation of the FLN', both in its modes of leadership and its 'methods of action' (55). Six weeks later, on 20 December, Kaid resigned for 'imperious reasons of health'(56).

The elimination of Medeghri in December 1974 is a much more complicated affair. Following the departure of Kaid, it appeared to be Bouteflika who was losing out in the power game, as the leftward turn of internal policy was accompanied by a more vigorous assertion of the anti-imperialist content of Algeria's foreign policy. Prior to 1973, Bouteflika had enjoyed a free hand in the running of Algerian diplomacy while Boumediène concerned himself exclusively with internal affairs. From 1973 onwards, however, his personal authority over this domain was increasingly overshadowed by Boumediène's own intervention in the conduct of foreign relations, notably at the Conference of the Non-Aligned Countries at Algiers in September 1973, his dramatic flight to Moscow at the height of the October war, his tour of Arab capitals (Cairo, Riyadh and Damascus) a few weeks later, his controversial speech to the Islamic Summit at Lahore the following spring (57) on his way to visit Peking, Pyongyang and Hanoi and, above all, his remarkable address to the Extraordinary Session of the United Nations General Assembly on Primary Commodities (convened at his request) on 10 April 1974. Increasingly it appeared that Bouteflika had full control only over Algeria's relations with the West while Boumediène, who visited the USA only on the above-mentioned occasion and never once, after independence, set foot in Europe, personally handled relations with the Third World as well as the Communist bloc, either by direct contact between heads of state or through his personal representatives, in particular such long-standing confidants as Colonel Mohamed Benahmed Abdelghani, Commander of the 5th Military Region (Constantine), entrusted with numerous missions to the Middle East, and Mustapha Lacheraf, whom he notably dispatched to Argentina on Perón's return to power there.

The impression of a conflict between Boumediène and Bouteflika was reinforced by the speech given by Boumediène at Constantine on 6 June 1974. The tone of this was unprecedently frank and hard, it was given maximum coverage in the official media and created a considerable stir in the country. Its political kernel is contained in the following extract:

> I draw today a red line between us and those intruders who have wormed their way into the body of the Revolution...As for those whose sole concern is to make money, they must know once and for all that there is no place for them in the State, the Party

and the Army...In order for the militant of the vanguard to be the example, he must answer to himself before all others. He must also be aware of the bourgeois tendencies which are beginning to infiltrate our society...The Revolution has need of a Party, the ranks of which are composed of the elite of the militants and socialists...(58).

This was in sharp contrast to the complacency which characterised the responses made by Bouteflika during a five-hour teach-in with the students in Algiers on 28 May; Bouteflika's performance, in the face of a somewhat hostile audience, was much criticised; as Etienne has put it, *'cela ne plut pas à tous'* (59), above all on the Left, and it received an extraordinary ambiguous review in the Party journal, *Révolution Africaine* (60). Since Bouteflika had explicitly claimed to be speaking in Boumediène's name on that occasion (61), Boumediène's own speech nine days later appeared to be, amongst other things, an attempt to disassociate himself from his own Foreign Minister, regarded by left-wing Algerians as the personification *par excellence* of *'les tendances bourgeoises'*.

The Constantine speech was followed, as promised, by another in the same vein, at Tlemcen on 11 July. This radicalisation of Boumediène's rhetoric, with its menacing implications for many in the upper as well as the lower reaches of the regime, occurred at a time of growing middle class discontent with policies for which he was, by now, regarded as personally responsible. In particular, the fall in agricultural output occasioned by the initially disruptive change in production relations had led to hoarding and speculation by private wholesalers and the resulting shortages and inflation in the approach to Ramadan, the month of fasting in which consolation for diurnal self-denial is traditionally sought in nocturnal self-indulgence, gave rise to considerable unrest, in Algiers at least. It was in these circumstances and amidst wild rumours, that an abortive attempt to dislodge Boumediène appears to have been made by his more conservative colleagues in August 1974. The state take-over of agricultural wholesaling followed shortly afterwards, in October. But it was not Bouteflika who fell in the wake of this crisis, for the man behind the attempted coup, if such it was, was Ahmed Medeghri and it was he who paid the price for having gambled and lost. *Cui bono?*.

Shortly beforehand, in July 1974, Boumediène had demanded that each regional governor *(wali)* should report directly to him on the progress of the agrarian reform instead of, as before, to Medeghri at the Ministry of the Interior. That this demand precipitated a bitter dispute between the two men and so led to the crisis in August is clear. That the control of the walis was the substance of the dispute is doubtful, however, although this is notably Etienne's account of the matter (62). The problem with this interpretation is that it fails to explain why Boumediène should have risked alienating a loyal and able colleague over such a minor matter. That the demand in itself was of substantial importance to Boumediène is most improbable. There was, at this stage, no reason to doubt Medeghri's loyalty to the

President, going back to the war years, so that Boumediène could easily have obtained the information he required of the walis via Medeghri if he so desired. In any case, Boumediène had other sources of information at his disposal, for example Military Intelligence (*Sécurité Militaire*), which was under his control as Minister of Defence and undoubtedly as competent to assess developments on the ground as any wali. That the demand was an intolerable affront to Medeghri, on the other hand, is certain. It explicitly challenged his authority over the prefectoral corps and thus undermined his personal clientele at the very moment that he was about to expand this by doubling the number of wilayat and so too the number of walis in his charge. Above all, however, the demand must have come as a profoundly shocking insult and humiliation, for it was in precisely this way that Ben Bella had forced Medeghri to resign exactly ten years earlier. It is inconceivable that Boumediène was unaware of the effect his demand would have. Indeed, it was open to only one interpretation, as Boumediène's brutally unequivocal, if also characteristically laconic and oblique, way of indicating to Medeghri that his services were no longer required and that his distinguished political career was over. It is understandable, therefore, that Medeghri should have resorted to the desperate gamble of an attempted coup, for by this stage he had little left to lose (63). Boumediène's motives, on the other hand, appear to have been far more devious.

In Medeghri's case, unlike that of Kaid Ahmed, the problem for Boumediène does not appear to have resided in the former's undoubtedly conservative and elitist outlook, for the man who replaced him as Minister of the Interior, Colonel Abdelghani, was very much in the same mould, a crisp, efficient administrator, middle class in origin and, while personally loyal to the President, certainly no leftist. Rather, Medeghri, simply by continuing to occupy a key ministry, constituted a major bottleneck in the complex game of chess upon which Boumediène was engaged by mid-1974.

The basis of Boumediène's power, like that of any political leader, had throughout consisted, in part, of his ability to appoint, sack and transfer ambitious men. This ability was limited by that of his ministerial colleagues, to whom substantial, although not total, autonomy in their respective departments was necessarily conceded. In the army, however, over which he had nominal control, Boumediène's ability to move powerful subordinates around was constrained by the limited number of posts to play with. Whereas there were some 20 ministries in the government, their principal equivalent in the army, the military regions, were only five in number, three in northern Algeria, Blida, Constantine and Oran and two in the Sahara (Bechar in the west and Ouargla in the east), to which may be added, as a post of comparable stature, the command of the *Gendarmérie nationale*. Their commanders accordingly enjoyed considerable power and privileges and could not easily be moved, except sideways; of the three northern regions, Oran had been commanded by Colonel Chadli Bendjedid without interruption since June 1964, Blida by Colonel Abdallah Belhouchet since December 1967 and Constantine since the same date by Colonel Abdelghani, while the Gendarmérie national had been commanded by

Colonel Ahmed Bencherif since September 1962. By mid-1974, the leftward turn in government policy had been accompanied, as we have seen, by the increased participation of the army in the political process and explicitly articulated, more clearly than elsewhere, in the columns of *El Djeich*. *El Djeich* cannot be said to have reflected the views of the army as a whole, however. Rather, it reflected the outlook of the younger generation of officers, many of whom had been trained in the Soviet Union or other Communist countries after having passed through the Combined Services Military Academy at Cherchell, of which the Director, since 1969, was Colonel Mohamed Salah Yahiaoui. These officers were in marked contrast to the older men who commanded the military regions, ex-maquisards with no left-wing leanings – indeed, reputedly conservative in outlook and apparently out of sympathy with the trend of government policy. By 1974 Boumediène clearly felt that he needed to place at least one left-wing officer in command of a military region, whether simply to appease the ambitions of a potential source of radical agitation in the army or to counterbalance the potential opposition of the conservative colonels or, as is most likely, for a combination of these reasons. The man he chose to replace Abdelghani at Constantine was Lt. Colonel El Hachemi Hadjerès, Director of the army's Political Commissariat (64), in which capacity he had been responsible for the editorial content of *El Djeich* (65) and had served as one of two representatives of the Ministry of Defence on the CNRA. That it should have been Abdelghani rather than Chadli or Belhouchet who was replaced in this way is easily under-stood given, first, the fact that he was the most highly educated of the three and so most likely to meet the requirements of ministerial office and, second, the fact that he was a westerner, from Maghnia on the Moroccan border (66), unlike Chadli or Belhouchet, both of whom come from the Annaba region of eastern Algeria. As such, in so far as the maintenance of a regional balance in the complexion of the government was a consideration, only Abdelghani could replace Medeghri. At the same time, it is unlikely that Abdelghani would have been willing to relinquish his post at Constantine for anything less than Medeghri's ministry.

Thus the decision to deprive Medeghri of his control over the walis can be explained as a deliberate provocation intended to force his resignation in order to permit a major series of new appointments and transfers, for, with Medeghri out of the way, it was possible to ensure that a large number of the new walis came from the army, since Abdelghani had an interest in bringing some of his personal clients with him, thus permitting the promotion of other young officers, in addition to Lt. Colonel Hadjerès, to new responsibilities. The crisis it precipitated was short-lived and appears to have been confined to the inner circle of the government; in particular, there is no evidence of any active military support for Medeghri. Thus, while it was certainly the most serious conflict within the regime since the Zbiri affair, it was decidedly less serious than the latter. Boumediène's position in 1974 was far stronger than it had been in 1967 and, although he appeared to have sustained physical injury in the course of the crisis, he soon reappeared in public, notably at

Tizi Ouzou on 16 September where, visibly sporting a wig, he delivered a sequel to his speeches at Constantine and Tlemcen. As for Medeghri, he died at his home on 12 December. The sacking, in the summer of 1975, of Cherif Belkacem, who had been the subject of some of the more unsavoury rumours of the previous August, was probably motivated, at least in part, by his association with the discredited and the dead and may be seen as the coda to a battle which had already been decided.

THE FRUITS OF VICTORY : POLITICAL CHANGE 1975-1977

Although it was by no means self-evident at the time, 1971 can be seen in retrospect to have witnessed a turning point in the evolution of the regime established by the 'revolutionary re-adjustment' of 19 June 1965 and the process of change continued unabated during the last seven years of Boumediène's presidency. Five features of this process remain to be considered: the changed character of factional conflict within the regime, the reconvening of the National Assembly, the consolidation of Boumediène's personal power, the abolition of the Council of the Revolution and the attempted transformation of the party.

With the elimination of Kaid, Medeghri and Cherif the last major clientelist faction from the war years had been destroyed. Only two members of the former Oujda clan remained in office, Bouteflika and Tayebi, both of whom had suffered a decline in their influence: the former had been incresingly overshadowed by Boumediène in the conduct of foreign relations and the latter, as we have seen, had been by-passed to a substantial extent in the conception and execution of the agrarian reform. Shorn of old allies in addition, neither was able to proffer serious objections to Boumediène's policies. With the break-up of the Oujda clan, factional politics within the regime were changed in nature: clienteles had, at least temporarily, given way to tendencies as the basis of factional division and political rivalries had come to correspond more directly to ideological disagreements as popular mobilisation and participation in the political process gradually developed not only to a degree unprecedented since the first year of independence but also on new lines, those of support for, or opposition to, the increasingly socialist policies of Boumediène rather than, as in the Ben Bella period, support for particular factions engaged in a largely non-ideological struggle for position.

Following the defeat of the conservative tendency within the regime, Boumediène announced his decision to reconvene the National Assembly in a speech on 19 June 1975 marking the tenth anniversary of the 'revolutionary readjustment' which had brought him to power (67). He also announced, in the same speech, that a National Charter setting out the balance sheet and, more important, the future perspectives of the government would be submitted to the public for discussion and amendment. The draft, explicitly socialist in content (68), was published in early 1976 and the debate took place throughout the summer, with an unprecedented degree of freedom of expression and criticism being permitted to ordinary citizens both in meetings and the columns of the national press. The final draft was submitted for ratification to a referendum on 27 June 1976 (69). It had been amended on numerous points of detail and many suggestions from the public had been incorporated but no substantial alteration to its political content had been made. Thus the ideological and programmatic framework within which the deliberations of the National Assembly would proceed had been clearly defined in advance. Elections for the new legislature were held on 25 February 1977 and it was formally opened a few days later. One of its first acts was the election, as its President, of Rabah Bitat, one of the four survivors from the original leadership of the FLN in 1954 (the so-called 'nine historic chiefs') and the only one to have retained a – largely formal – place in the regime, as Minister of State for Transport, since 1965. The changes which had occurred since 1971 made it unlikely that the Assembly would be as bourgeois in character as it would have been had it been reconvened five years earlier. Among the eleven deputies from the wilaya of Constantine we may note the return to the political stage of the veteran trade unionist, Mouloud Oumeziane, whom the Assembly promptly elected to the Presidency of its Commission for Economic Affairs.

An eminent feature of the process of political change since 1971 had been the growth in Boumediène's personal power and the degree of autonomy which the presidency had acquired in relation to the rest of the government. In sharp contrast to the rigorous self-effacement which had accompanied his largely mediating role within the regime from 1965 to 1971, Boumediène emerged during the 1970s as the architect of government policy, an increasingly confident and effective public speaker and a statesman of international stature, in all three respects conspicuously dominating his ministers. This process was consecrated by the presidential election of 1976 and thoroughly consolidated in the government reshuffle which followed it. As a counterweight to the National Assembly, Boumediène had announced, also on 19 June 1975, that an election for the Presidency of the Republic would be held. In this way he might obtain the popular legitimisation for his position as Head of State which the manner of his accession to power in 1965 had denied him. His official designation prior to this election was *Chef de l'Etat, Président du Conseil de la Révolution et du Conseil des Ministres*; he was never referred to as *Président de la République*, the title enjoyed by Ben Bella, until after the election, in which there was one candidate and which was held in December 1976, preceding by several weeks those for the National Assembly. The reconvening of the latter thus presented few dangers for Boumediène: on the contrary, it enabled him to shunt a number of ministers out of the government and into the legislature and undertake the most thorough-going reconstruction of the government since 1965. In addition to Bitat, returned, for no discernible reason, from the wilaya of Bouira (70), five other deputies had exchanged portfolios for order papers: Mahmoud Guennez, Minister of War Veterans since 1970, returned from Tebessa; Layachi Yaker, Minister of Commerce since 1969, Abdelkader Zaibek, Minister of Public

Works and Construction since 1970 and Abdelmalek Temmam, Minister of Finance since February 1976, all three returned from Algiers (71), and Abdallah Fadel, Minister of Youth and Sport since 1970, returned for Annaba. The ensuing reshuffle reinforced Boumediène's position and the socialist orientation of the government in several respects.

First, four posts were filled by former presidential aides. Mustapha Lacheraf and M'Hamed Hadj Yala, both until then counsellors to the President, became Minister of Primary and Secondary Education and Minister of Commerce respectively. Mohamed Amir, General Secretary of the Presidency, became Minister of Labour and his former assistant, Smail Hamdani, became General Secretary of the Government. Second, Boumediène assumed direct personal control of the *Sûreté nationale* and the *Gendarmérie nationale*, having shunted their former commanders, Ahmed Draia and Colonel Ahmed Bencherif, both known for their conservative outlook, into the minor ministries of Transport and of Water Supply and Environment respectively. Third, two other notably conservative ministers, Mouloud Kassim Nait Belkacem and Dr Ahmed Taleb Ibrahimi had their wings clipped by being attached to the Presidency. Kassim retained his portfolio of Traditional Education and Religious Affairs but lost his former comparative independence and capacity to dispense patronage; Taleb Ibrahimi became a Minister-Counsellor, losing the portfolio of Information and Culture in the process. His replacement was Redha Malek, a left-wing intellectual who had been a member of the FLN delegation at the independence negotiations at Evian in 1961 and 1962 (72) and had helped to draft the famous Tripoli Programme of July 1962 (73), later serving as ambassador to Paris, and from October 1970, Moscow. Fourth, Dr Omar Boudjellab, who as Minister of Health since 1970 had presided most inconspicuously over the introduction of the 'free medicine' system, was replaced by a noted confidant of Boumediène, Said Ait Messaoudène, who as commander of the Air Force had played a key role in suppressing the Zbiri coup in 1967 and had run the Posts and Telecommunications ministry since 1972 (74). The latter was now taken over by another loyalist officer and veteran of the Zbiri crisis (75), Colonel El Hadj Mohamed Zerguini, commander of the Third Military Region (Bechar) from 1969 to 1975 and since 1975 Inspector of the Army. Finally, the Ministry of Industry and Energy, empire since 1965 of Belaid Abdessalem, the architect of Algeria's hydrocarbons and industrial development strategy, was broken up into three new ministries. The Ministry of Energy and Petrochemical Industries was taken over by Sid Ahmed Ghozali, who had succeeded Abdessalem as Président-Directeur-Général of SONATRACH (the state oil and gas company) in 1965, and that of Heavy Industry by Mohamed Liassine, the Directeur-Général of the *Société Nationale de Sidérurgie* (SNS: the state steel company), while Abdessalem became Minister of Light Industry. At the time, this was not necessarily much more than a formal change, although one involving a measure of demotion for Abdessalem, since both Ghozali and Liassine had already enjoyed considerable power before becoming ministers and their responsibilities did not change very substantially thereafter. However, it did emphasise the government's intention to expand the state's role in light industry and gave industry in general three votes inside the government instead of one. Moreover, the appointment of Liassine, like those of Hadj Yala, Lacheraf and Redha Malek, reinforced the socialist tendency within the regime (76).

With the assumption of their functions by the new government and the National Assembly, the Council of the Revolution which had been constituted on 19 June 1965 ceased to exist. Originally composed of 26 members, it had shrunk to ten (77) by 1977. Its disappearance also testified to the changes which had taken place in the balance of forces within the regime. Throughout the twelve preceding years, the government had been composed of two tiers, the Council of the Revolution and the Council of Ministers. The most powerful figures were those who belonged to both, namely Boumediène himself and the Oujda clan. The existence of these two bodies had given Boumediène a certain room for manoeuvre from the start, despite his initial unpopularity and the constraints on his capacity for decisive action to which we have referred. The Council of the Revolution functioned as a convenient receptacle for political opponents: by including them in it, Boumediène was able to neutralise them without having to allow them the real power which would come from control over a government department and the patronage which went with it. Once they had been kicked upstairs, so to speak, into essentially honorary posts, it became possible to detach them from their original social base and clientele and incorporate the latter into the regime through more reliable political channels; this done, the former adversaries could with safety be evicted from the regime, as most were in 1967. From 1968 onwards, the Council of the Revolution essentially consisted of Boumediène and the Oujda clan and the commanders of the defence and security apparatus. In the meantime, Boumediène filled as many ministries as possible with non-political 'technocrats' (Belaid Abdessalem, Layachi Yaker, Smail Mahroug, Abdallah Fadel (78), Abdelaziz Maoui (79), Abdelkader Zaibek, Kamel Abdallah-Khodja (80), Abdallah Arbaoui (81),) but in order to limit the development of the personal power and political ambitions of the latter, he maintained the Council of the Revolution in being with the role of supervising the activities of the Council of Ministers. By 1977, the change in the complexion of the regime and the reinforcement of the presidency vis-à-vis the rest of the government made this kind of double-decker chess unnecessary, while the conservative outlook of the regional army commanders made their exclusion from the national political stage desirable from Boumediène's point of view. Within two years, however, a new dual power structure had been established, but with potentially very different implications from its predecessor.

FROM BOUMEDIENE TO CHADLI : THE RISE OF THE PARTY 1977-1979

No national party congress was ever held during the 13 year presidency of Houari Boumediène and only one during that of his predecessor, in April 1964. In a speech to the 'cadres of the Nation' on 30 October 1969, Boumediène had spoken of his intention to convene a congress:

as soon as the necessary conditions are fulfilled.

Some people have not failed to pose questions concerning this Congress. But we have already had occasion to say it was necessary for us to proceed without precipitation, particularly since a first Congress has already taken place without any concrete result.

To convene a Congress composed of four or five hundred cadres would not have been a task beyond our means, and if we have not done it up until now, it is because the conditions do not yet lend themselves to it. For as long as they are not all met, any edifice that we may erect will be fatally flawed, for we believe that the Party Congress should be the last act of the operation of reorganisation which has been undertaken from the base to the summit (82).

Boumediène fell ill in the autumn of 1978 and died at the end of December. The congress for which he had been working took place, as scheduled, in January 1979. It not only selected the party's candidate for the vacant presidency in the person of Colonel Chadli Bendjedid, but also passed two detailed resolutions concerning future government policy at home and abroad (83) and elected a Central Committee of 160 members as its supreme instance. The latter, in turn, elected a Political Bureau of 17 members as its executive (84). Two months later, in March 1979, the formation of eleven permanent commissions and two permanent councils of the Central Committee was announced and the Statute of the FLN – the party's constitution – was published.

In order to gauge the significance of these developments it is necessary to recall the extremely marginal role of the FLN in the politics of the Boumediène regime from 1965 onwards. We have already noted that, as a result of the disintegration of the wartime FLN in the summer of 1962, the government of the independent state lacked a crucial instrument of political mobilisation. In addition, the initial shortage of trained personnel meant that anyone with the barest qualifications was assured of an administrative post, so that the party apparatus was reduced, by and large, to precisely those ex-guerrillas and militants who were not competent to perform any other functions. Accordingly, the party was quite incapable of orienting or controlling the activities of the Executive (both government proper and administrative and security apparatuses). Moreover, in so far as membership of the party was *de rigeur* for ambitious functionaries, its ideological complexion was as heterogeneous as that of the executive bodies it was supposed to 'lead'. In addition, consciousness within even the left-wing of the FLN as to the implications of the party's leading role was by no means clear at the time. As Gerard Duprat has pointed out, 'when the (Tripoli) Programme...fixed the goal of the vanguard as being to "elaborate a social and political doctrine faithfully reflecting the aspirations of the masses", this vanguard seriously risked being, again, no more than a rearguard' (85). From 1965 to 1971 the weakness of the party, while officially deplored, was not of substantial concern to the government. Perfunctory attempts were made to revive it, notably in 1968 (the 'Year of the Party') and in early 1970, when the party was reorganised at local level. Little came of these efforts, at most formal modifications to its structure and internal functioning. They did not lead to the revitalisation of the FLN to any appreciable extent. The reason for this was that, for as long as the government was preoccupied with laying the foundations of the state through the construction of the administrative apparatus on the one hand and the progressive nationalisation of foreign capital on the other hand, its policies were essentially elitist in concept and bureaucratic in method and in no way required the mobilisation of popular energy or enthusiasm for their success. In consequence, the party had no role to play other than mouthpiece - one among several, moreover - of the Executive. At the local level, it also acted as an arena for the interplay of competing parochial interests, notably during the elections for the communal and departmental assemblies, but, playing no role of substance in the policy-making process at the national level, since it was not where power lay, it completely failed to attract the active participation (as opposed to purely formal membership) of the vigorous and ambitious elements of the younger generation, all of whom could aspire rather to the more influential and rewarding positions available in the burgeoning bureaucracy.

And that is how matters have stood until recently, with the corollary that access to the bureaucracy has been far more important to ordinary Algerians than participation in the party. As Jean Leca observed in 1968:

> the weakness of the party is largely due to its former strength: its character of representative of the struggle of the people against colonial alienation. To the demands which it expressed in the past (national liberation and independence, construction of an egalitarian economic order) only the State can respond for the time being (86).

Thus it was the administrative apparatus which functioned as the transmission belt both of popular aspirations and governmental decisions, while the party was reduced to accessory after the fact, symbol of national unity and of continuity with the Revolutionary period and so guarantor of the legitimacy of the regime, while simultaneously masking the latter's heterogeneity behind a facade of monolithicity and serving as a standing pretext, by its mere existence, for the ban on all rival political formations. The FLN formally monopolised the political arena, therefore, without being able to fill it in reality, and in the meantime serious politics were conducted within the bureaucracy and the army.

That this state of affairs was largely satisfactory to the Boumediène regime during its first six years is clear from the fact that the party was denied the deliberative prerogatives and organisational attributes necessary for it to play a more positive role. No party congress was held at any stage and no policy debates of substance occurred, for the party's role was to explain decisions taken elsewhere, not to reason why. Similarly, the central apparatus was meagre in the extreme: there was no Political Bureau, let alone a Central Committee, and the departments which did exist were explicitly limited to the functions of propaganda (*'Orientation et Information'*), control (*'Organisation de Masse'*) and parallel diplomacy (*'Affaires internationales'* and *'Mouvements de Libération'*) (87). There was not a single committee or commission concerned with particular areas of government policy such as industry, agriculture, education, health, and so forth. Thus the changes which had taken place by early 1979 were quite considerable. How had they come about?

If the regime had tolerated, or even connived at, the incapacity of the party prior to 1971, this weakness began to pose a serious problem with the launching of the agrarian reform in December of that year. The controversial nature of the reform, given that it was at the expense of an influential sector of the population, meant that the party had, in principle, a major role to play, in countering hostile propaganda and bureaucratic inertia not to mention corruption and attempts at evasion, and in mobilising popular enthusiasm in general and that of the new beneficiaries of the reform in particular in order to ensure the success of the new systems of production and marketing. The government had decided, in 1972, to establish a National Union of Algerian Peasants (UNPA) to mobilise the members of the new cooperatives and raise their awareness of both their rights and their responsibilities; it was clearly the party's task to get the new union off the ground. As numerous commentators have noted, however, the party was completely incapable of assuming such unfamiliar duties. It is likely, moreover, that it was largely unwilling to do so. The political outlook of the full-time officials was predominantly conservative and often strongly religious, in consequence of their wartime role as 'fighters for the faith'. In the countryside, they were frequently closely linked by ties of blood or clientele to the local notables, both the landowning families and the influential administrators; they thus had little incentive to act against the interests of either of these categories of the population, let alone mobilise the latter's erstwhile dependants against them. As we have seen, this conservative outlook was faithfully reflected in the person of Kaid Ahmed. His eviction was preceded, it will be remembered, by Boumediène's proclamation of the need for a radical transformation of the party. There was no immediate follow-up to Boumediène's speech, however, and he himself did not give the matter much further emphasis until his speech at Constantine in June 1974. The likely reason for this is that there was very little that could be done to transform the party in the short run; it could not be revitalised by fiat. Instead, Boumediène appears to have counted upon the gradual awakening of popular enthusiasm as the new policies – the agrarian reform, the introduction of 'free medicine', the partial democratisation of industrial relations, the reform of higher education and so forth – entered into practical application and gradually dispelled the apathy and disillusionment which had set in during the 1960s. In the absence of an effective party none of these policies could be completely successful, but the struggle to secure their implementation itself would lead to the emergence of a new generation of committed socialists from whom the cadres of a reformed party could eventually be recruited. Thus Boumediène appears to have counted upon the revival of the various mass organisations, the UGTA, the student Volontariat, the UNFA and so on as the precondition for the transformation of the party (88). In the short run, therefore, the FLN itself was largely by-passed and ignored. Following Kaid's departure, no successor was named, routine party functions being shared between the head of the Orientation and Information department, Mohamed Cherif Messaadia (89), the Minister of State without Portfolio, Cherif Belkacem, until the latter's dismissal in 1975, and Boumediène himself. The decision to name no successor to Kaid was very likely due to Boumediène's recognition that, until the social basis and political outlook of the party had been thoroughly transformed, it was necessary to deny to the conservative forces it embodied any independent representation in the regime, since the various policies embarked upon since late 1971 were all bound to evoke opposition from precisely these forces.

It was not until these policies had had six years in which to bear their political fruits, notably in the rallying of the Left, previously in disarray if not opposition, the eviction of conservative figures, the promulgation of the National Charter and the reinforcement of his personal power, that Boumediène seriously set about the transformation of the party along the lines that he had indicated at Constantine in June 1974. On 30 October 1977, a new coordinator of the party was finally appointed, Colonel Mohamed Salah Yahiaoui (90), a veteran of the guerrilla war, a close personal follower of Boumediène, who had been a member of the Council of the Revolution throughout its existence and had occupied since 1969 the strategic post of Director of the Combined Services Academy at Cherchell. The following spring, a number of party commissions were set up and prominent personalities drafted in from outside the old central party apparatus to staff them, namely Abderrazak Bouhara (91), Salah Goudjil (92), Slimane Hoffman (93), Abdellatif Benachenhou (94) and Abdelhak Bererhi (95). The essential function of these appointments was to prepare for the holding of the Party Congress, initially expected for summer 1978 but subsequently scheduled for early 1979, which was to consummate the transfusion of younger and explicitly socialist blood into the party apparatus and launch the party upon its new role at the centre of national political life. The Party Congress was preceded by those of the other mass organisations, the UGTA in March 1978 (96), the UNPA in April, the War Veterans in May, the UNFA (National Union of Algerian Women) in September and the UNJA (National Union of Algerian Youth) (97) in December. It was, thus, in prospect, to be the climax of the process of radicalisation and mobilisation begun with the promulgation of the Charter of the Agrarian Revolution on 8 November 1971. It was in the last approaches to this climax, on the eve of the UNFA congress in September, that Boumediène fell ill.

As we have seen, Boumediène's incapacitation did not prevent the Congress from taking place and establishing major new party bodies. (The resurrection of the constitutionally defunct Council of the Revolution, comprising now only eight of its original 26 members, to act as caretaker during his long agony had no long term implications and with the election of the FLN Central Committee and Political Bureau at the Congress it once again ceased to exist). For all the official insistence on continuity, however, Boumediène's death produced a fundamental change in the political situation. For the functioning of the new party institutions was now to be determined, not by the perspectives of an established president resolved to use the party as an instrument with which to curb and control the bureaucracy, but by the concern of the new incumbent to assert his personal authority vis-à-vis, above all, his own colleagues in the political leadership.

TOWARDS 'L'APRES-BOUMEDIENE': CHADLI'S NEW COURSE, 1979-1981

As Boumediène lay dying, two tendencies within the regime emerged to contest the succession. Both addressed themselves, at least by implication, to the central issue, namely the problems posed by a sprawling bureaucracy riddled with patron-client relationships and increasingly incapable of assuring a rational management of the economy (98), and both had proposals for dealing with this, although their policies were diametrically opposed. The first tendency was that which formed around the candidature of Mohamed Salah Yahiaoui, the party coordinator. Yahiaoui advocated tighter political control of the bureaucracy and sought to establish the primacy of the party over the administrative apparatus of the state. In this he saw himself very much as the standard-bearer of 'Boumediènism' and as such enjoyed the support of elements of the officer corps, the UGTA, the student left and most of the UNJA leadership, a section of the *arabisant* lobby, the clandestine PAGS and sections of the press. The second tendency was that associated with the candidature of Abdelaziz Bouteflika, the Foreign Minister, who favoured calling a halt to the left-wing policies pursued since 1971 and advocated a measure of liberalisation in government economic policy. As such, Bouteflika was the candidate of a substantial proportion of the administrative and technocratic elite and also of the private bourgeoisie and liberal professions, but possessed little support in the party or mass organisations or the armed forces. In the event, neither tendency was strong enough to secure the victory of its champion and the army emerged as the arbiter of the situation, by supporting the claims of its most senior regional commander, Col. Chadli Bendjedid, chief of the Second Military Region (Oran) since 1964. With 600, that is nearly 20 per cent, of the 3,298 delegates at the party congress coming from the armed forces (99), and with only one nomination to vote on, ratification of Chadli's candidature was a formality. In addition, however, the congress approved the appointment of Chadli to the new post of General Secretary of the Party, which implied a major qualification of Yahiaoui's authority in this sphere, as subsequent events were to confirm.

Chadli's election as President of the Republic on 7 February 1979 formally completed a succession which had proved far more orderly and peaceful than many observers had expected. However, it also constituted the point of departure for the most profound reshuffle of the national elite to have occurred since 1965. All branches of the state apparatus have been affected by this process, from the Cabinet, the bureaucracy and the party to the banking system, the press and the armed forces themselves. At the same time, an important modification has been taking place in the nature of the relationship between state and society in Algeria. For the changes in the apparatuses of the regime since 1979 have been accompanied by the development of a number of autonomous social movements articulating specific cultural or economic demands and acting independently, if not in outright defiance, of the authorities.

The reshuffle got under way with the naming of Chadli's first government (100) at the end of the first meeting of the FLN Central Committee held from the 6 to 8 March 1979. Only six of the ministers in Boumediène's last Cabinet retained their portfolios and 16 of the government's 28 members (26 ministers and two secretaries of state) were newcomers, including two army officers, two deputies from the National Assembly, three former walis, three senior party figures and three former advisers to President Boumediène. Of the eleven ministers included in the new 17-man Political Bureau announced at the party congress in January, five were now shunted out of the government and into Presidencies of the various new Party Commissions, but two others, Mohamed Tayebi Larbi and Ahmed Draia, both former members of Boumediène's Council of the Revolution, were for practical purposes eliminated from the political stage, retaining now largely honorary places in the Political Bureau but nothing more. In addition, Abdelaziz Bouteflika, with whom both Tayebi and Draia had been associated, was removed from the Ministry of Foreign Affairs, over which he had reigned since 1963, to be replaced by Mohamed Seddik Benyahia. The five members of the Political Bureau who left the government to take up party posts were Belaid Abdessalem, Ahmed Bencherif, Mohamed Amir, Boualem Benhamouda and Mohand Said Mazouzi. For Benhamouda and, to some extent, Mazouzi, this was to prove of tactical significance only. For Abdessalem and Bencherif, who had dominated economic policy and the national gendarmerie respectively for most of the 1962–1978 period, as for the lesser figure of Mohamed Amir, it was a further step towards political oblivion. Two other notable casualties were Redha Malek and Mustapha Lacheraf, appointed by Boumediène in 1977 to the Ministries of Information and Culture and of Primary and Secondary Education respectively, and noted for both their socialist leanings and their moderation in matters of cultural policy. They were replaced by Abdelhamid Mehri, a noted *arabisant* intellectual, and Mohamed Cherif Kharroubi, the zealously *arabisant* wali of Greater Kabylia (101). A third prominent casualty was Sid Ahmed Ghozali, who had run Algeria's oil and gas industry since 1965, first as PDG of SONATRACH and then, since 1977, as Minister of Energy and Petrochemical Industries, and who now suffered the indignity of demotion to the minor Ministry of Water Supply and Environment, where he replaced the evicted Ahmed Bencherif, being himself replaced at Energy by a former adviser to Boumediène, Belkacem Nabi. This fate, which was clearly linked to that of his former mentor Belaid Abdessalem, was to prove too much for Ghozali. Accused of intertering in affairs which no longer concerned him, he was unceremoniously sacked from his new post seven months later, on 14 October 1979, his eviction being announced with unprecedented, indeed brutal, bluntness in the official press (102).

In terms of the struggle between Left and Right, it was definitely the Bouteflika group which had sustained the heavier losses at this stage, Bouteflika himself technically remaining in the government, but only as a supernumary Minister-Counsellor to the President, while three of his allies in the Political Bureau, Abdessalem, Draia and Tayebi, had lost their portfolios. But Yahiaoui and the Left had also had their wings clipped, for not only had Redha Malek and Mustapha Lacheraf been dropped but two important potential allies, Abderrazak Bouhara and Salah Goudjil, had been lured out of their party role (and thus Yahiaoui's sphere of influence) by the offer of ministries. More important, perhaps, was the fact that, while Presidencies of five of the eleven new Party Commissions and one of the two new Party Councils had been appointed, the other six commissions and one council remained unstaffed. Moreover, the Central Committee decided to entrust Chadli rather than Yahiaoui with the power to designate their Presidents, a power he proved in no hurry to exercise.

Having achieved this initial restructuring of the government, one which gave him ample room to manoeuvre, moreover, in that, while all factions were represented, none was preponderant, Chadli began to frame his policies. In general, the watchword was 'continuity'. No major departures in economic strategy or foreign policy were contemplated. In particular, Chadli surprised many observers with his commitment to Boumediène's line on the Western Sahara. In internal affairs, however, he made two important gestures, the first to the population in general, the second to the old anti-Boumediène opposition. For the former, the unpopular exit visa was suppressed, thus facilitating travel abroad, a measure particularly appreciated by the new middle class. For the latter, Chadli spoke of reconciliation and soon matched words with deeds. In April 1979 eleven former opponents of the regime, most of them in exile (103), were pardoned and in July Ahmed Ben Bella was at last released from prison and permitted to live in the qualified freedom of *résidence surveillée* at M'Sila, 150 miles south-east of Algiers, on the edge of the Sahara. This latter move proved generally popular, and Chadli was eventually able to grant Ben Bella complete liberty of movement in October 1980, at the same time pardoning the exiled leader of the 1967 putsch, Tahar Zbiri (104). In the summer of 1979, Chadli also announced a big campaign to clean up Algiers and slyly saddled Yahiaoui with the thankless task of supervising this.

Before long, however, the new regime was overtaken by autonomous movements of social protest, which the new liberal tone of Chadli's rhetoric had unwittingly encouraged. First off the mark were the *arabisant* high school and university students, who mounted a long strike in the winter of 1979/80, together with numerous public demonstrations, to protest at the incoherence of the government's Arabisation policy. Numerous subjects in secondary and higher education had been arabised in recent years, yet few posts in the state administration were, in practice, open to *arabisants*, who tended, in addition, to come from humbler backgrounds than their *francisant* compatriots. The protesters had no doubt been encouraged by the replacement of moderates at the Ministries of Information and Culture and of Primary and Secondary Education by doctrinaire *arabisants* in Chadli's first government and the authorities responded sympathetically to their protests. The ensuing prospect of further substantial measures of arabisation was viewed with alarm, however, by the intelligentsia of the two-million strong Kabyle community, the largest and much the most important of the Berber-speaking populations of Algeria, inhabiting the rugged mountains of Greater and Lesser Kabylia to the east of Algiers but also heavily represented in Algiers and the other coastal towns, in the Algerian community in France, and, above all, in the administrative apparatus of the state. Kabyle students and intellectuals were strongly opposed to the policy of compulsory arabisation and, in particular, sought official recognition of the Berber language as a second national language alongside Arabic (105). When on 10 March 1980, Kabylia's most distinguished intellectual, Mouloud Mammeri, was banned from addressing a conference at the University Centre at Tizi Ouzou (the capital of the wilaya of Greater Kabylia) on the seemingly innocuous subject of traditional Berber pottery, the students went on strike, occupied the university buildings, and organised demonstrations in Tizi Ouzou and Algiers (106). Very soon all high school students in Greater Kabylia had gone on strike and the movement had evoked echoes as far afield as Sétif, Oran and Paris. The official reaction contrasted sharply with the sympathetic hearing given to the *arabisants* a few weeks earlier. Vague promises that the students' grievances would be considered at the next meeting of the FLN Central Committee in May were not enough to persuade them to call off their strike, and as the movement stiffened its protest and broadened its social base with a highly effective general strike at Tizi Ouzou on 16 April, the government decided to break it by force, using riot police to clear the university buildings at Tizi Ouzou on the night of 19-20 April. The following day, Tizi Ouzou witnessed the most serious rioting seen in Algeria since independence, with several public buildings, including the party offices and a luxury tourist hotel, being put to the sack.

These events, promptly baptised by the protesters as the 'Tizi Ouzou Spring' by explicit analogy with Prague 1968, received extensive international press coverage and were a severe shock to the government. Nonetheless, Chadli was able to turn them to advantage in his struggle with rival factions in the regime. The Left, in particular, emerged from the affair in disarray, its secular and libertarian wing sympathising with the Kabyles' grievances, its radical nationalist and Arabist wing being utterly hostile to them. At the May meeting of the Central Committee, which vigorously proclaimed the government's continuing commitment to the Arabisation policy, the ineffectual performance during the crisis of the FLN Political Bureau, paralysed as it was by the struggle between Yahiaoui's supporters and those of Bouteflika on the one hand, and the advocates of conciliation and those of exemplary repression on the other, came in for sustained criticism. Yahiaoui himself was violently attacked and although his offer to resign as Coordinator was not accepted, the Central Committee voted full powers to Chadli to restructure the leading organs of the party. It also decided that the extraordinary congress of the party to be held in June to consider and adopt the new Five Year Plan would have the additional task of revising the party statutes. The two commissions set up to prepare this congress were placed under the direct authority of Chadli and neither contained any members of the Political Bureau. Still nominally Coordinator of the party, Yahiaoui played no part whatsoever in the organisation of the congress.

The extraordinary congress of the FLN met from 15 to 19 June. Of its 3,993 delegates, 800 (just over 20 per cent) came from the armed forces (107). Having approved the new Five Year Plan, (1980-1984), which contained several marginal modifications but no major revisions of the development strategy pursued since 1967, the congress debated the question of strengthening party control over the 'mass organisations' and particular emphasis was placed on Arabo-Muslim values, with Marxists in general and the PAGS in particular being attacked by certain delegates. The upshot was that Chadli was given the power to choose (and not merely, as before, to propose) the members of the new Political Bureau and to allot their responsibilities, prerogatives which formerly belonged to the Central Committee, and henceforth the Political Bureau would meet only once, not twice, a month and would be answerable to the President. The congress thus marked a further stage in the subjugation of the party to presidential control, with Chadli adroitly using both Central Committee and Congress to emasculate the Political Bureau.

The new Political Bureau, announced on 30 June 1980, contained only seven members in place of its original 17. Yahiaoui and Bouteflika were retained, but neither now had any influence to speak of. Apart from Chadli himself, the other members were Rabah Bitat, the President of the National Assembly, Abdallah Belhouchet, the Inspector-General of the Armed Forces, Boualem Benhamouda, noted for his strong Arabist and religious convictions and soon to return to the government as Minister of the Interior, and Mohand Said Mazouzi, President of the Organisation Commission of the Party and the token Kabyle. For several prominent figures, notably Abdessalem, Bencherif, Draia, and Tayebi, their exclusion from the Political Bureau was the end of the road. For others, such as Mohamed Benahmed Abdelghani, the Prime Minister, and Mohamed Seddik Benyahia, the Foreign Minister, their exclusion was a temporary affair, a necessary part of a manoeuvre designed above all to reduce the Political Bureau to a very secondary role within the structure of the regime.

Two weeks later, on 15 July 1980, Chadli announced a new government reshuffle (108). Four new secretaries of state were appointed, in addition to the two existing ones and the 26 ministers. Of the latter, 17 were confirmed in their existing posts, but four were sacked outright (109) and two were shunted out of government and into party responsibilities. Contrary to certain expectations,

Abdelghani remained as Prime Minister but lost his Interior portfolio to Benhamouda. The controversial Minister of Education, Kharroubi, whom many observers expected to be sacrificed as a sop to Kabyle opponents of his doctrinaire Arabisation policies, was also retained, but, on the other hand, a token concession to the 'Berberists' was made in the creation of a new Secretary of State for Culture and Popular Arts and the appointment of a Kabyle, Mohamed Larbi Ould Khalifa, to this post. In all, the government contained twelve newcomers, of whom three were former general-secretaries of ministries, four were deputies in the National Assembly and only one was an officer in the armed forces. However, it was without doubt in the Ministry of Defence that the most significant changes took place.

The fundamental political constant of the period from 1962 to 1978 had been Boumediène's personal control of the armed forces. Ben Bella had made two attempts to undermine this, first, by appointing Col. Tahar Zbiri as Chief of the General Staff during Boumediène's absence in Moscow in October 1963, and, second, by creating a Popular Militia in July 1964 under the command of Cdt. Mahmoud Guennez but answerable to the presidency instead of the Ministry of Defence (110). Both attempts failed, Boumediène easily winning over both Zbiri and Guennez to his side and pointedly employing them in person to arrest Ben Bella on the night of 19 June 1965. The failure of Zbiri's subsequent attempted coup in December 1967 gave Boumediène the opportunity to suppress the General Staff altogether. Henceforth the armed forces possessed no institutional expression of their collective interests outside Boumediène's Ministry of Defence. Within the ministry, three key posts staffed by picked men assured Boumediène's political control: the Political Commissariat of the ANP, directed since 1967 by Cdt. (subsequently Colonel) El Hachemi Hadjerès, saw to the ideological and political education of the armed forces, while Military Security, directed by Lt. Col. Kasdi Merbah, kept all potential sources of unrest, whether inside or outside the armed forces, under effective if largely discreet surveillance. Finally, the running of the ministry itself was assured by the Secretary-General, a post filled from 1962 by Col. Abdelkader Moulay, more generally known as Chabou, a close confidant of Boumediène until his death in an accident in 1971, and from 1971 onwards by Lt. Col. Abdelhamid Latreche. Thus, if substantial concessions had necessarily to be made to the five commanders of military regions, to whom large powers were delegated by Boumediène within the limits of their respective fiefs, at the national level the political loyalty of the army to Boumediène's regime was assured, and its capacity for independent initiatives nullified, a point that was of especial importance from 1971 to 1978, in view of the radical and controversial nature of many of the policies which Boumediène pursued during this period.

One of Chadli's moves on becoming President had been to reshuffle the commanders of military regions. He himself abandoned his own military fief at Oran, but he took care to coax his counterpart at Blida, Col. Abdallah Belhouchet, out of that post and into the Ministry of Defence, as Inspector of the Armed Forces. The other major move at this stage concerned Lt. Col. Kasdi Merbah. A native of Kabylia, Kasdi was a key, if extremely discreet, figure in the power structure of Boumediène's regime; in view of the character of his responsibilities and the degree of his power as head of Military Security, he was undoubtedly loyal to the late president's policies. He is rumoured to have played a central and very influential role in the struggle for the succession in 1978-9 and was named to the Political Bureau in January 1979. Although the matter remains shrouded in mystery, it appears that he was subsequently winkled out of his power base in Military Security, for from mid-1979 onwards references to him in the press described him only as Secretary-General of the Ministry of Defence, a post which he had assumed at the expense of Lt. Col. Latreche. In June 1980, he was one of the ten men dropped from the Political Bureau. Now, in the government reshuffle, both he and Col. Belhouchet were named to the new posts of Deputy Minister of Defence, but whereas Belhouchet retained his functions as Inspector of the Armed Forces, as well as his seat in the Political Bureau, Kasdi was replaced as Secretary-General of the Ministry by Colonel Mustapha Belloucif, formerly Director of Personnel at the Ministry and a native, like Chadli, of the Annaba region of eastern Algeria (111). Thus, step by step, Chadli was establishing his control over the defence establishment as well as the party at the expense of Boumediène's former confidants. Finally, together with these changes it was announced that the General-Staff was to be re-established. While this move represented a concession on Chadli's part to the officer corps, it also underlined the essential conservatism of the new regime: if the armed forces could now be permitted this institutional expression of their collective interest outside the Ministry of Defence, this was because Chadli, unlike his predecessor, had no intention of promoting radical changes in the society.

The government reshuffle was immediately followed, at the first meeting of the new Political Bureau on 16 July 1980, by Chadli's measures to restructure the party. The number of party commissions were reduced from eleven to five and the two Party Councils were abolished. Thus the prospect, which had existed in 1979, that the party would develop the technical and institutional capacity to orient and control the activities of the various government departments was finally dead and buried. Appropriately enough, moreover, the post of Coordinator of the Party held by Yahiaoui since October 1977 was also abolished. Instead, Mohamed Cherif Messadia, who had exercised routine party functions prior to 1977 but who had abandoned these in exchange for government office as Minister for War Veterans in 1979, now returned to what were in effect his old duties under the new title of Head of Permanent Secretariat of the Central Committee. Thus Yahiaoui now found himself on exactly the same footing as Bouteflika in the Political Bureau, without function or influence of any kind. As for the party, the wheel had come full circle. The only change from the pre-1977 situation which had survived the vicissitudes of the factional struggle was the existence of the Central Committee. However, the Central Committee was not really an emanation of the party, but rather a national level assembly of notables, comprising

37

the senior figures from all branches of the state apparatus, a forum for debate, certainly, but performing essentially the function of sounding board for the President and without the slightest interest in asserting party control over either ministers or administrators. Henceforth, the notion of party control was to be applied in a different direction altogether.

This new direction was made clear by Chadli himself in a speech to the National Assembly on 30 October 1980, in which, echoing the sentiments of several speakers at the Party Congress in June, he made a barely veiled attack on the PAGS as well as the Muslim Brethren and the Kabyle 'Berberists' (112). A few weeks later it was announced that three officer cadets and two civilians who had been arrested in November 1978 for having attempted to organise a Trotskyist cell would be tried for conspiracy against the state. On 27 December it was announced that sentences of from three to ten years imprisonment had been handed down, a clear warning that henceforward Marxist agitation would not be tolerated, least of all within the army. A related theme dominated the discussions of the Central Committee meeting of 29-31 December, where apart from government health and energy policy the main item on the agenda was the controversial question of the relationship between the party and the 'mass organisations'. Despite the opposition of the UGTA and UNJA leaderships, the Central Committee decided to apply Article 120 of the revised FLN statutes, which stipulates that all officials of the 'mass organisations' must be members of the FLN. The principal target of this measure was the clandestine PAGS, many of whose members held responsible posts in the UGTA in particular but also in other organisations, and who were now confronted with the choice of abandoning these posts or joining the FLN and abandoning the PAGS. But the measure was aimed not only at the Communists, but at independent spirits in general. Previously it was not necessary to be a party member in order to get elected to the Workers' Assemblies within the *sociétés nationales* or the Popular Assemblies at communal, wilaya or even national levels. It was sufficient that one's candidature had the approval of the relevant party instance. Henceforth, the FLN was to have a total monopoly of political representation. The party which Boumediène and Yahiaoui had intended to ensure a degree of popular control over the state apparatus was now launched on the opposite role of ensuring popular subordination to that apparatus. The same meeting of the Central Committee ratified Chadli's nominees for the posts of party secretaries at the wilaya level, replacing Yahiaoui's followers in the process, and elected a Disciplinary Commission under Chadli's personal authority as General Secretary. 1980 had been a disastrous year for the Left.

The same pattern of, on the one hand, moves by an increasingly conservative regime to tighten its political control and on the other hand, outbreaks of autonomous and frequently violent agitation and social unrest continued throughout 1981. With strikes by the oil workers at Hassi Messaoud and by the employees of *Air Algérie* in January following that of the Customs Officers in December (113), industrial action in the public sector was becoming, despite legal prohibition, a frequent occurrence. Wages and conditions were at issue in all of these instances, as in the strike of public health service doctors in March, but such grievances were increasingly overshadowed by agitation over cultural issues. The government had promised, after the events at Tizi Ouzou in 1980, to subject the whole question of cultural policy to intensive review and to draw up a framework for the future in the form of a Cultural Charter to be adopted after a public debate conducted under the aegis of the party. To this end, the *arabisant* Minister of Information and Culture, Abdelhamid Mehri, had abandoned his government post in the reshuffle of July 1980 to take up the Presidency of the Party Commission for Information and Culture, with the task of producing the initial draft of the Charter and animating the debate. Mehri's appointment did nothing to raise the expectations of the Kabyle Berberists, however, who continued to organise their own activities outside official channels. In August 1980, they held a 'seminar on Algerian popular culture' at Yakouren in Greater Kabylia, which the authorities made no attempt to prevent - the first event of its kind in the history of independent Algeria. On 15 March 1981, they organised a successful one-day general strike at Tizi Ouzou and a large meeting at the university centre there (as well as a smaller meeting at the Faculty of Algiers and on the 19 and 20 April the anniversary of the Tizi Ouzou Spring was celebrated with meetings and a gala at Tizi Ouzou and a debate attended by 1500-2000 students and teachers at the university in Algiers, the authorities making no move to interfere with these activities on either occasion. These developments soon took a violent turn, however. The activities of the Berberists were viewed with particular hostility by many *arabisant* students and Muslim extremists, two categories which have tended to overlap in recent years, and serious fighting broke out at Algiers on 19 May, when a meeting organised by the UNJA to commemorate the 'Day of the Student' was attacked by Arabist-Muslim extremists, forcing the temporary closure of the Algiers Faculty (114). Even worse clashes occurred at Annaba, where 30 odd people were injured, (two of whom required surgery), the Faculty was closed for four days and 19 Muslim extremists were expelled and subsequently arrested. Worst of all were the events at Bejaia, the capital of Lesser Kabylia, where 50 arrests were made after the Town Hall had been stoned and cars and the state-owned chain-store had been set on fire in extensive rioting involving workers and unemployed as well as students (115).

The rise of Muslim extremism assumed alarming proportions during 1981. Inspired partly by the the Islamic Revolution in Iran but more directly by the doctrines of the Muslim Brotherhood, groups of radical Muslims (usually referred to as *intégristes* in Algeria) had been visibly, if intermittently, active since January 1980, when a hotel was burnt down, stocks of alcohol destroyed and the inmates of a brothel attacked in the oasis town of El Oued (116). A few weeks before the events of 19 May 1981, a number of arrests had been made in Sidi Bel Abbes following an armed attacked on the wilaya offices (117). Attacks on young women deemed to be improperly dressed became frequent and in a number of localities unofficial mosques, outside the ambit of the Ministry of Religious Affairs, were set up for brief periods. Despite a speech by Chadli attacking 'fanaticism' on 20 May, incidents continued to occur throughout the summer, culminating in a pitched battle between *intégristes* and the police at Laghouat on 28 September, in which one policeman was killed (118).

It was against this background of accumulating social tension and unrest that the government launched a campaign to clean up the administration in the autumn of 1980. By December 1980 arrests of officials in SONACOME and OFLA had been announced (119). In January 1981, the PDG of SONACAT was arrested together with one of his deputies (120). By March, several dozen officials were under arrest (121). By mid-summer the campaign was beginning to reach bigger fish. At its meeting of 30 June – 2 July, the Central Committee suspended four of its members, namely Ahmed Bencherif, Mohamed Tayebi Larbi, Mahmoud Guennez and Mustapha Bouarfa (122). Deprived of their immunity in this way, they were now open to criminal proceedings on corruption charges. The same meeting of the Central Committee saw the consummation of Chadli's drive to eliminate his opponents of the Left and the Right. A new ten-man Political Bureau was announced, to which the Prime Minister, Abdelghani, now returned, but from which Yahiaoui and Bouteflika were at last excluded, their seats being taken by the men who had succeeded them in their other functions in the party and the Ministry of Foreign Affairs, Mohamed Cherif Messaadia and Mohamed Seddik Benyahia. Of the original 26 members of the Council of the Revolution which had taken power under Boumediène in June 1965, only three now retained places in the Political Bureau: Chadli, Abdelghani and Belhouchet, the men who, under Boumediène, had commanded the three most important military regions, Oran, Constantine and Blida. Of the perspective which Boumediène had outlined in his speech at Constantine on 6 June 1974, nothing now remained.

CONCLUSION

The relationship between state and society in Algeria has gone through four distinct phases in the 20 years since independence. After a period of romantic incoherence under Ben Bella and incessant factional turmoil which was not finally brought to an end until after the abortive Zbiri coup of 1967, this relationship was one of authoritarian and technocratic elitism in which the construction of state institutions and the public sector of the economy had no place for popular participation. This second phase lasted until late 1971, when the Boumediène regime suddenly and unexpectedly embarked upon an audacious strategy of popular mobilisation around an extremely ambitious programme of radical social policies. During this later period, the state was able to communicate a considerable sense of purpose to the society, and demonstrated the ability to realise many of its projects. The public in general was divided between those who were susceptible to this mobilisation and those who remained sceptical – those who positively resisted the state's policies were a very small minority – but it is striking, at least in retrospect, that no conflicts of substance took place outside the formal structures of the regime during the Boumediène period. In particular, cultural and religious differences were of negligible political significance to a population to which rapid economic development offered the prospect of generalised social mobility.

Since the death of Boumediène, the state has settled down into an essentially conservative role in relation to society. Boumediène's followers have been purged and his successors are content to administer the system in routine fashion, having no changes of substance to propose. Neither of the lines of development advocated by Left and Right in 1978-1979 has been followed. Bouteflika's proposals to deal with the problem of bureaucratic inefficiency by measures of economic liberalisation suffered the same fate as Yahiaoui's perspective of continued popular mobilisation to impose political control on the administrative apparatus through a genuinely vanguard party. Instead, Chadli and his colleagues have opted for a third and much less ambitious course - utilising the impatience of the younger generation of technically qualified Algerians to bring about a rejuvenation of the administrative apparatus without thereby substantially altering the manner in which it functions. Individuals are being removed on charges of corruption, but the system of patron-client relations and its roots in the wider relationship between the bureaucracy and the public remain undisturbed. In consequence, the state has lost the capacity it possessed under Boumediène to capture and canalise the political reflexes of the underprivileged sections of the population and, with the loss of *élan* in the regime's economic development strategy, popular discontent has tended increasingly to surface in the form of competing claims to representation in the state apparatus expressed in terms of cultural identity and legitimacy, and a growing disposition to contest the prerogatives and legitimacy of the state apparatus when these claims are frustrated. To the claims of the Berberists are counterposed those of the *arabisants* and the Islamic radicals. Both the first and the last of these groups comprise elements disposed to contest the entire basis of the political system, the former inspired by Western democratic and pluralist models, the latter by the message from the East. It remains to be seen whether the Chadli regime will be able to contain this ferment, or whether it will develop into a coherent and sustained challenge to the state.

NOTES AND REFERENCES

1. Brendan Clifford, Russia (unpublished article, roneo, London 1978).
2. Bruno Etienne, L'Algérie, Cultures et Révolution (Editions du Seuil, Paris, 1977), p.205.
3. Pierre Bourdieu, The Algerians (Beacon Press, Boston, USA, 1962), chapter 7. passim.
4. Ibid., p.160.
5. Jean Leca, 'Algerian Socialism: Nationalism, Industrialisation and State-Building' in: Helen Desfosses and Jacques

Levesque, (eds.) Socialism in the Third World, (Praeger Publishers, New York, 1975), p.123.

6. Literally provinces or regional governorates. The term has been retained with this sense in the independent state.

7. Harbi was one of the principal authors of the Algiers Charter of 1964 and the group he led, distinct from the Algerian Communist Party, provided the main left-wing support for Ben Bella. He was its sole Algerian member of note, his principal collaborators being a Greek Trotskyist (Michael Raptis alias Pablo) and an Egyptian Marxist (Lotfallah Soliman). The Harbi group was accordingly baptised les pieds rouges. Ferhat Abbas, leader of the évolué assimilationist tendency in Algerian politics in the 1930s, adopted a separatist perspective in the 1940s and finally rallied to the FLN in 1956, serving as President of the GPRA (Provisional Government) from 1958 to 1961, in which capacity he was used by the FLN as a moderate front man in much the same way as the Armed Forces Movement used Spinola during the Portuguese Revolution. He was briefly President of the National Assembly after Independence.

8. That is, the Union Générale des Travailleurs Algériens (UGTA). The UGTA leadership in no way sought to overthrow Ben Bella's government, merely to preserve the union's freedom of action. This was intolerable to Ben Bella and Khider, then allied, who rapidly asserted the party's control over the union, reducing the latter to an adjunct of the former. The best account of this question is that of François Weiss, Doctrine et Action Syndicales en Algérie (Editions Cujas, Paris, 1970), especially chapters IV-VI.

9. The dispute between Ben Bella and Khider was over whether the party should control the government or vice-versa. Khider found himself outvoted in a meeting of the FLN Political Bureau on 16 April 1963 and resigned the next day.

10. As President of the National Assembly, Abbas protested that instead of framing the Constitution of the independent state, the Assembly was expected merely to ratify a draft presented to it by the Party, now a simple tool of Ben Bella. He resigned on these grounds on 14 August 1963 and was expelled from the FLN two days later.

11. That is, the Front des Forces Socialistes (FFS) led by Hocine Aït Ahmed. I have discussed the nature and significance of this rebellion in my doctoral thesis: 'Political Development in Algeria: the Region of Greater Kabylia', unpublished D.Phil. thesis, Oxford University, 1980, chapter 5.

12. That is, the group of politicians so called because of their wartime role as staff officers at the Moroccan HQ of the 'army of the frontiers' at Oujda, namely Cherif Belkacem, Ahmed Medeghri, Abdelaziz Bouteflika, Kaid Ahmed and Mohamed Tayebi Larbi.

13. Weiss, Doctrine et Action Syndicales. pp.272-279.

14. Mohamed Lebjaoui, Vérités sur la Révolution Algérienne (Editions Gallimard, Paris, 1970), pp.204-210. Lebjaoui provides a detailed account of these negotiations, in which he acted as one of the principal intermediaries between Ben Bella and the FFS.

15. William Quandt, Revolution and Political Leadership: Algeria 1954-1968 (M.I.T. Press, Cambridge, Mass., and London, 1969),

p.234; Jean Leca and Jean-Claude Vatin, L'Algérie Politique: Institutions et Régime (Fondation Nationale des Sciences Politiques, Paris, 1975), p.416.

16. Lebjaoui, Vérités sur la Révolution Algérienne, p.210.

17. That is, the army of the independent state as distinct from the Armée de Libération Nationale (ALN) of 1954-1962.

18. Ben Bella's view of the role of the army was expressed obliquely when he spoke of the economic and social role which the army might play (cited by Quandt, Revolution and Political Leadership, p.211). The omission of political speaks for itself.

19. Chaabani was commander of wilaya VI (Sahara) by 1962 and thereafter commander of the 6th Military Region (Eastern Sahara). Having been named to the Political Bureau of the FLN in April 1964, he apparently entered into rebellion against the regime. Captured shortly afterwards, he was sentenced to death by a military tribunal presided by Colonel Ahmed Bencherif and executed on 3 September 1964. The affair has never been elucidated.

20. Quandt, Revolution and Political Leadership, pp.230-231.

21. Commander of wilaya II (Nord-Constantinois) 1956-1958; with Belkacem Krim and Abdelhafid Boussouf, formed the 'triumvirate' which dominated the GPRA from 1958 to 1962. President of Société Nationale de Sidérurgie since the mid-1960s.

22. Commander of wilaya II 1958-1959; ambassador to Syria 1966(?)-1970, Libya 1970-1975 and Tunisia 1975-1979; member of the FLN Central Committee 1979.

23. Played leading role in wilaya IV (Algérois) till 1958; Secretary of State in GPRA 1958-1960; deputy commander of the Zone Autonome d'Alger, April-July 1962; noted for his left-wing views, he was appointed ambassador to Moscow in October 1966.

24. Commander of wilaya II 1959-1962; opposed Ben Bella-Boumediène faction July 1962; arrested for opposition activities in July 1963, released November 1963 and appointed Algerian representative on the 'United Arab Command' in Cairo. Member of the Council of the Revolution 1965, evicted December 1967.

25. Commander of wilaya III (Kabylia) 1959-1962 and of the 7th Military Region (Kabylia) 1962-1963; reluctantly supported Ait Ahmed's revolt in 1963, then rallied to Ben Bella. Member of the FLN Political Bureau April 1964; member of the Council of the Revolution 1965, evicted December 1967; died December 1972.

26. Commander of wilaya III 1956-1957 and of the Tunisian HQ of the 'army of the frontiers' 1958-1960; Minister of State in GPRA 1960-1962; member of Ben Bella's Political Bureau July 1962 and of 2nd Political Bureau April 1964; Minister for War Veterans 1962-1963; 2nd Vice-President of the Republic 1963-1965; member of the Council of the Revolution June 1965, evicted December 1967.

27. Commander of wilaya IV 1961-1962; led internal guerrilla opposition to Boumediène's army July-August 1962; member of the National Assembly 1962-1964; member of the Political Bureau April 1964; member of the Council of the Revolution June 1965; evicted December 1967, accused of complicity in Zbiri's coup.

28. The Aurès region, although predominantly Chaouia and fairly uniform in cultural terms, differs markedly from Kabylia in the lack of cohesion of its population. Following the death in 1956 of Mustapha Ben Boulaid, the first commander of wilaya I, the wilaya command was rent by internecine feuds for the remainder of the war.

29. Notably the Chief of the General Staff, Zbiri himself, the editor of the army review El Djeich, Capitaine Ferhat, and the commander of the 1st Military Region (Blida-Algérois), Col. Said Abid, Zbiri's brother-in-law, who died in the course of the coup and whose role in it has never been clarified.

30. Head of the Constantine region of the UGTA 1956-1958 and 1962-1965; General Secretary of the UGTA 1965-1968, he was forced out of office in the context of the deteriorating relations between the UGTA and the FLN under Kaid's control.

31. Philippe Herreman, in Le Monde, 21-22 June 1970.

32. Hubert Michel, 'Chronique politique: Algérie' in: Annuaire de l'Afrique du Nord 1970, (Editions CNRS, 1971, Aix-en-Provence), p.299. Michel suggests that the postponement of the reconvening of the National Assembly in 1971 was due to the government's pre-occupation with the difficult nationalisation of the hydrocarbon industry in that year. If this was the main reason, it remains to be explained why the Assembly was not reconvened in 1972 instead of 1977.

33. Etienne, L'Algérie, Cultures et Révolution, p.215.

34. Etienne argues that, because the launching of the agrarian reform was decided on the basis of the same pragmatism which had enjoined its earlier repeated postponement, it did not involve a change in policy, still less a radical one. The same could be said, of course, of the Bolsheviks' decision to reject Preobrazhensky's prescriptions in 1923-1924 but to implement them in 1929.

35. For example, Kader Ammour, Christian Leucate and Jean-Jacques Moulin, La Voie Algérienne, (Maspero, Paris, 1974), pp.76-77; Etienne, L'Algérie, Cultures et Révolution, p.216 (but see also page 220 where he substantially qualifies this). There is no room for a full discussion of this question. I can only report that the view that this was the principal objective of the agrarian reform was emphatically and categorically rejected by one of President Boumediène's advisers in an extended interview with me in October 1975.

36. Lars Jönsson, La Révolution agraire en Algérie: historique, contenu et problèmes, (Scandinavian Institute of African Studies, Research Report No.47, Uppsala, 1978); Etienne, L'Algérie, Cultures et Révolution, pp.219-223; Keith Sutton, 'The Progress of Algeria's Agrarian Reform and its Settlement Implications' The Maghreb Review, vol.3, nos.5-6 (January-April 1978), pp.10-16.

37. The full membership of the CNRA was published in the Party weekly Révolution Africaine, no.412 (14-20 January 1972).

38. Jönsson, La Révolution agraire en Algérie, p.33.

39. The PAGS had called upon its members to support the regime's economic and social policies on 8 January 1971, a year before the Volontariat was set up.

40. Interviews in February 1974, upon which my account of the formation of the *Volontariat* is largely based.
41. For example, in Terre et Progrès (review published by the Ministry of Agriculture and Agrarian Reform: MARA), no.4 (November 1973), pp.21-52.
42. As I was able to observe personally, so far as the villages in the wilaya of Bouira are concerned, in September 1975.
43. Lacheraf is one of Algeria's most distinguished socialist intellectuals. The son of the *qadi* of Sidi Aissa in central Algeria, he was arrested and imprisoned with Ben Bella and his companions in October 1956. He was one of the authors of the famous "Tripoli Programme" of July 1962 and later published a major collection of essays: L'Algérie, Nation et Société (Maspero, Paris, 1965).
44. El Djeich, nos.111, 112 (August and September 1972).
45. A point emphasised by Boumediène in his speech to the IVth Congress of the UGTA in April 1973 (Le Monde, 4 April 1973).
46. Only one of the 15 original wilayat was unaffected by the change, that of Saida, the native region of the then Minister of the Interior, Ahmed Medeghri.
47. John Dunn, Modern Revolutions (Cambridge University Press, 1972), p.171.
48. Speech of 2 February, cited by Etienne, L'Algérie, Cultures et Révolution, p.313, (my translation).
49. Paul Balta, 'Le Tournant Socialiste en Algérie' Le Monde, (28 December 1974).
50. David and Marina Ottaway, Algeria: the Politics of a Socialist Revolution, (Berkeley, 1970), pp.296-298, 300.
51. Oujda was, in addition, the birthplace of Bouteflika, arguably the chief political brain of the 'clan'.
52. Tayebi's role in wilaya V had been such as to cause a nervous breakdown on his part in 1959, whereafter he was given a staff post at Oujda. (D & M Ottoway, Algeria, the Politics of a Socialist Revolution, p.300).
53. Leca and Vatin, L'Algérie Politique, p.99.
54. La République, 3, 4 August 1972 (but see also 9-10, 16-17, 27, 28 July 1972).
55. Le Monde, 2 November 1972.
56. According to the terms of the official announcement (Le Monde, 22 December 1972).
57. In which he told the assembled faithful that 'verses from the Koran will not fill an empty stomach', amongst other choice observations (cited by Etienne, L'Algérie, Cultures et Révolution, p.28).
58. El Moudjahid, 8 June 1974 (in which the speech was published in full).
59. Etienne, L'Algérie, Cultures et Révolution, p.34.

60. Révolution Africaine, no.536 (31 May-6 June 1974); the article was entitled, somewhat euphemistically, 'La Vertu du Dialogue'.

61. Ibid., p.8.
62. Etienne, L'Algérie, Cultures et Révolution, p.35.
63. Particularly since he was suffering from a wasting illness by this time, if usually reliable sources are to be credited.
64. Since at least 1967 (D. & M. Ottaway, Algeria, the Politics of a Socialist Revolution, p.306).
65. El Djeich is edited by the Central Directorate of the Political Commissariat of the ANP.
66. Mohamed Harbi, Le FLN, Mirage et Réalité (Editions J.A., Paris, 1980), p.423.
67. The text of this speech was published in El Djeich no.146 (July 1975).
68. Projet de Charte Nationale (FLN: Imprimérie El Moudjahid, Algiers, April 1976).
69. Receiving the approval of 98.51 per cent of a 91.36 per cent poll, according to the official figures (cited in Wilfred Knapp, North West Africa: a Political and Economic Survey, Oxford University Press, 1977), p.173.
70. He is from Ain Kerma, in the Constantinois, by origin.
71. In the case of Temmam, formerly Director of the Banque Nationale d'Algérie until he took over the Finance portfolio in 1976, the motive for the change was his failing health; he died not long afterwards, in 1978.
72. Quandt, Revolution and Political Leadership, pp.142, 146.
73. Henry F.Jackson, The FLN in Algeria: Party Development in a Revolutionary Society (Greenwood Press, Connecticut USA, 1977), p.62.
74. Having meanwhile served as PDG of Air-Algérie, the civil airline, from 8 January 1968.
75. Quandt, Revolution and Political Leadership., p.260.
76. Liassine had been noted for his support for the new socialist management system; as we have seen, the SNS was among the first state companies in which this was introduced.
77. Or perhaps only nine. It is not clear whether Colonel Benhaddou Bouhadjar (alias 'Si Othman') was still formally a member; he had ceased to be an active participant some time before (Etienne, L'Algérie, Cultures et Révolution, p.36) but then so had Chadli.

78. Deputy for Bône (Annaba) to National Assembly in 1962; Minister of Youth and Sport 1970-1977; Deputy for Annaba since 1977.
79. Minister of Tourism 1965-1977.
80. Secretary of State for Planning 1970-1979.
81. Secretary of State for Hydraulics 1970-1977.
82. The text of this speech is available in AAN 1969, pp.927-939.
83. Published in El Djeich no.190, (March 1979).
84. The 17 members of the Political Bureau were: Chadli Bendjedid, Mohamed Benahmed Abdelghani, Belaid Abdessalem, Dr. Mohamed Amir, Colonel Abdallah Belhouchet, Ahmed Bencherif, Dr. Boualem Benhamouda, Mohamed Seddik Benyahia, Rabah Bitat,

Abdelaziz Bouteflika, Ahmed Draia, Guezzane Djilali Affane, Dr. Ahmed Taleb Ibrahimi, Lt. Colonel Kasdi Merbah, Mohand Said Mazouzi, Mohamed Tayebi Larbi, Mohamed Salah Yahiaoui.

85. Gerard Duprat, Révolution et Autogestion Rurale en Algérie, (Armand Colin, Paris, 1973), p.54, footnote.

86. Jean Leca, 'Parti et Etat en Algérie' in Annuaire de l'Afrique du Nord, 1971, (Editions CNRS, Paris, 1972, p.36).

87. There was also a Département d'Etudes et de Conceptions; its head, Ali Ammar, has given occasional interviews in Révolution Africaine.

88. Etienne, L'Algérie, Cultures et Révolution, p.38.

89. An *arabisant* and regarded as a relatively conservative figure; he is the son of Cheikh El Hadj Tahar Messaadia of Souk Ahras (El Moudjahid, Carnet, 20 October 1973); served in ALN in Tunisia; head of the FLN Orientation and Information Department since at least 1968; he abandoned his Party functions on becoming Minister of War Veterans in Chadli's government in 1979.

90. From locally notable family of Barika in south-eastern Algeria; fought in *wilaya* I throughout the war; Assistant Director of Cherchell Academy 1963-1965; Member of FLN Central Committee April 1964; Commander of 3rd. Military Region (Bechar) 1965-1969; Director of Cherchell Academy 1969-1977.

91. Officer in ALN; military attaché at Paris 1965; commanded ANP brigade sent to Suez zone in 1967; military attaché in Moscow 1968; Ambassador to North Vietnam 1970-1974; *wali* of Algiers 1975-1978; President of the Commission for Internal Organisation of the FLN 1978; Minister of Health 1979.

92. Fought in *wilaya* I 1955-1962; party secretary (commissaire national du Parti) for the *wilaya* of Annaba, then Setif; President of the Commission for the Mass Organisations of the FLN 1978; Minister of Transport 1979.

93. Saint-Cyr graduate; commander of armoured battalions in ANP; instrumental in stopping Zbiri coup 1967; Director of the Bureau of International Studies at the Presidency 1969; *wali* of Algiers 1970-1974; President of the Commission for International Relations of the FLN 1978.

94. Marxist intellectual; Director of the Centre de Recherches en Economie Appliquée (CREA); President of the Commission for Economic and Social Affairs of the FLN 1978; not to be confused with, although undoubtedly related to, Professor Abdelhamid Benachenhou, Director of the Journal Officiel.

95. Born Khenchela 1940; Professor of Medicine; Rector of the University of Constantine 1972-1977; Vice-President of the Commission for Economic and Social Affairs of the FLN 1978; Minister of Higher Education and Scientific Research 1979.

96. At which Abdelkader Benikous, the tame General Secretary imposed on the UGTA, at Oumeziane's expense, by Kaid Ahmed at the 3rd Congress held in camera in 1969, was finally replaced. His successor was Abdallah Demene Debbih, reputed to be much further to the Left in his outlook.

97. UNJA is an extremely recent creation, the heir to the old Jeunesse FLN and to the Union National des Etudiants Algériens (UNEA), which had been dissolved in 1971. In 1976-1979 UNJA was equipped with an extremely left-wing leadership, much of it recruited from the Volontariat activists.

98. For a further discussion of the nature of these problems, see Hugh Roberts, 'The Algerian Bureaucracy', Review of African Political Economy, no.24 (May-August 1982), pp.39-54.

99. The Guardian, (1 February 1979).

100. Details of this were given in Le Monde, (10 March 1979).

101. Kharroubi is himself a Kabyle, but, having been educated in the Middle East (University of Baghdad), he achieved notoriety in Greater Kabylia for his refusal, as wali from 1975 to 1979, to speak in his native tongue. His appointment to the Ministry of Education was badly received in Kabyle intellectual circles.

102. Le Monde, 16 October 1979. The sacking of Ghozali followed shortly after the resignation of his protégé, Nourredine Ait Lahoussine, from the post of Secretary-General of SONATRACH, where he was replaced by one of Nabi's protégés, Youcef Yousfi.

103. But not all: one of those pardoned was Amar Mellah, who had been sentenced to death, commuted to life imprisonment, for having organised an attempt to assassinate Boumediène in 1968.

104. Le Monde, (1 November 1980).

105. For a full discussion of the Kabyle question and the complexity of the issues involved in the events of Spring 1980, see Hugh Roberts, 'Towards an understanding of the Kabyle question in contemporary Algeria' The Maghreb Review, vol.5, nos. 5-6, (September-December 1980), pp.115-124 and 'The unforeseen development of the Kabyle question in contemporary Algeria' Government and Opposition, vol.17, no.3 (Summer 1982), pp.312-334.

106. Le Monde, 19 March and 9, 10, 11, 12, 15, 18, 22, 23, 29 April 1980.

107. Le Monde, (20 June 1980).

108. Details of this were given in Le Monde, (17 July 1980).

109. Two of the sacked ministers, Mohamed Zerguini (Posts and Telecommunications) and Abdelmadjid Aouichiche (Construction), were former senior army officers and old Boumediène loyalists. The other two, Lahcene Soufi (Justice) and Abdelghani Akbi (Commerce) were former *walis* and proteges of the Prime Minister, Mohamed Benahmed Abdelghani. Since the latter also lost the portfolio of the Interior in the reshuffle, he had very thoroughly been reduced to Chadli's poodle.

110. Leca and Vatin, L'Algérie Politique, pp.387-388.

111. Le Monde, (17 July 1980).

112. Le Monde, (1 November 1980).

113. Le Monde, (30 January 1981).

114. Le Monde, (21, 22 May 1981).

115. Le Monde, (24 May and 1, 2 June 1981).

116. Le Monde, (6 October 1981).

117. Le Monde, (1 June 1981).

118. Le Monde, (6 October 1981).

119.   Le Monde, (20 December 1980). SONACOME is the state mechanical construction company, OFLA the National Office for Fruit and Vegetables.
120.   Le Monde, (30 January 1981). SONACAT is the state marketing company dealing in electrical consumer durables (radios, televisions, refrigerators, domestic appliances etc.).
121.   Le Monde, (28 March 1981).
122.   Le Monde, (2 July 1981). Bouarfa had been the director of the Commissariat National à l'Informatique, a satellite body of the Planning Ministry; Guennez had been Minister for War Veterans 1970-1977.

Chapter 2.

MODERN MOROCCO : POLITICAL IMMOBILISM, ECONOMIC DEPENDENCE

Peter Sluglett and Marion Farouk-Sluglett

If history is 'what men need to remember of the past' (1), the rulers of modern Morocco have succeeded in pressing the country's history into service as an essential part of the mechanism of the state, a function which it is peculiarly well fitted to perform. Morocco's past, assiduously refurbished and regularly presented for current reference, provides a permanent framework and means of justification for the political apparatus which governs the country today. The dual notion, of Islamic state and Moroccan empire, is constantly invoked and publicly recalled by the ruling institution, ultimately in order to explain and vindicate its continuing existence. As well as being completely different from its neighbours in never having been part of the Ottoman Empire, Morocco is unlike other contemporary or recently defunct 'Islamic' monarchies; it is not of obviously recent creation, or imposed on the society from above or from outside, like Iran or Jordan, and it lacks the intensity and reforming traditions of Saudi Arabia, partaking of a longer and generally more creative tradition. No other Maghreb state - indeed no other Arab state - is in a position of being able to appeal to centuries of independent government, and an unbroken and apparently entirely orthodox combination of *imam* and *amir* (2).

How far this interpretation of history corresponds with reality is of course another matter, since those in power are well placed to control the way in which the past is projected for present consumption. One contention of this chapter will be that much of the state apparatus of modern Morocco is as much the creation of Lyautey and his successors as of the 'Alawite monarchy. Thus the French administrators' version of their role as an essentially static one, approximating simply to that of game wardens in a 'national park', to adapt a phrase of Jacques Berque, is an over-simplistic description of the colonial period (3). Since the French neither abolished the traditional institutions in Morocco nor introduced permanent replacements for them, the institutions were able to survive the colonial period more or less intact, and indeed greatly strengthened, while their Algerian or Tunisian equivalents were either abolished or so enfeebled as to perish shortly after independence (4).

More generally, since the national movement developed out of an essentially Islamic reaction to French rule, the cooption of the sultan, the embodiment of Moroccan Islam, was a vital precondition for its ultimate success. Although Muhammad V had maintained an attitude of complaisance rather than defiance towards the French authorities for much of the early part of his reign, the moment he took up the stance of the 'rebel sultan', his continuing legitimacy was assured. Paradoxically, therefore, instead of being absorbed by 'Allal al-Fassi and the Istiqlal, Muhammad V was himself able to absorb and thus to neutralise the independence movement and turn to his own advantage what might elsewhere and in other circumstances have developed into a serious threat to his authority.

MOROCCO IN 1912

In spite of a long history of political and commercial interaction with Europe (5), Morocco had become relatively isolated both from the rest of the Arab world and from the northern shore of the Mediterranean by the beginning of the nineteenth century (6). The rulers of the country in the eighteenth century had been forced to concentrate most of their efforts on securing the throne for themselves and their descendants, and the country had become divided *de facto* between those areas which did, and those areas which did not, submit to the fiscal and administrative authority of the 'Alawite sultan, respectively the *bled al-makhzan* and the *bled al- siba'*. The precise meaning of these terms, 'one of the most profound, yet most flexible divisions in Morocco over the centuries' (7), is still a matter of some controversy. Germain Ayache, perhaps thinking as much in terms of the present as of the past, considers the function of the *makhzan*, the ruling institution, to have been arbitral rather than primarily coercive, while Charles-André Julien, concerned to demonstrate 'la fiction du protectorat', holds that the bled al-siba' did not 'contest the authority of the sovereign, but tried to escape from the authority of the makhzan' (8). Since the French administration claimed to be reintegrating the bled al-siba' into the bled al-makhzan on the sultan's behalf, and indeed justified their *reconquista* in those terms, the discussion is not, as we shall see, entirely academic (9).

Morocco's isolation, and the general weakness of its diplomatic, political and economic structures rendered the country particularly vulnerable to European colonial expansion (10). The repercussions of the French invasion of Algeria in 1830 were almost immediately felt in Morocco, as the leader of the Algerian resistance, the Amir 'Abd al-Qadir, sought and obtained vital if somewhat grudgingly granted aid from the Moroccan Sultan Muhammad Ibn 'Abd al-Rahman. However, after the decisive defeat of 'Abd al-Qadir by the French at Isly in 1844, Muhammad was forced to declare him an outlaw, and this failure on his part 'to defend the country against the Christians' (11) was the signal for widespread tribal rebellions, which in their turn served to facilitate economic and political penetration by France, Spain and Britain.

Modern Morocco: Political Immobilism, Economic Dependence

Although foreigners were largely confined to the ports of Larache, Mazagan (el-Jadida), Mogador (Essaouira) and Tanger, European trade grew very considerably throughout the nineteenth century. Here Britain, largely represented by British subjects from Gibraltar, enjoyed a brief period of paramountcy, controlling some 80 per cent of foreign trade in 1856, although her share had fallen to only 29 per cent by 1905 (12). In 1832, there were only 250 Europeans in the whole country; by 1894 this figure had increased to 9,000. During the same period Casablanca rapidly grew into the country's most important seaport, growing from a town of 9,000 inhabitants in 1850 to 21,000 in 1900 (13). Britain, France's traditional rival, viewed the conquest of Algeria with some misgivings, especially when Morocco, and thus the Straits of Gibraltar, seemed threatened. Sir John Drummond-Hay, British representative in Tanger between 1845 and 1886, negotiated a special Anglo-Moroccan commercial treaty in 1856, and tacitly supported Morocco's attempts to assert her sovereignty in the face of pressures from France.

This treaty, and other evidence of increased British interest in Morocco, encouraged Spain to try to regain some of her former influence in the country, particularly in the north. Spain had been in continuous occupation of the *presidios* (fortified towns) of Ceuta, Melilla and Alhucemas since the sixteenth century (1497 in the case of Melilla), and now sought to extend her influence further into the Rif. A *casus belli* was established, and Spain sent an army to lay siege to Tetouan in 1859. As a result of this war, a major watershed in nineteenth century Moroccan history (14), Morocco was forced to pay an indemnity of three million *douros* for the evacuation of Tetouan, and to make other humiliating concessions to Spain. Borrowing the money to pay the settlement set Morocco off on the road to enormous and ultimately crippling indebtedness, which reached 62 million francs in 1904, and 101 million in 1910 (15). Debts had to be paid in foreign exchange, and as a result it was no longer possible for the Moroccan authorities to place any effective limitations on European economic penetration. The markets were flooded with cheap imports, and European 'protection' — an arrangement similar to the capitulations in the Ottoman Empire — was extended to hundreds of Moroccans, who were thus removed from the jurisdiction of the sultan. The special status of the *protégés* was enshrined in the Treaty of Madrid (1881), by which time the Moroccan state 'had ceased to be anything but a fiction maintained for reasons that were by no means purely diplomatic' (16), for the benefit of the European powers.

The decline continued in spite of, though perhaps partly because of, the accession of the vigorous Sultan Hasan I (1873-1895). Like his Tunisian and Egyptian contemporaries Muhammad al-Sadiq (1855-1882) and Khedive Isma'il (1863-1879), Hasan's attempts at financial, administrative, and military reform (17) led inevitably to further crippling loans. The fundamental flaw in these reforms was their limited scale; no overall reorganisation of the structures of government was ever envisaged (18). Furthermore, the economic chaos which they brought had important domestic repercussions, in that the reforms were also rejected as impious, un-Islamic innovations, the same kinds of criticism that had been levelled at the reforms of the Ottoman sultans Mahmud II, 'Abd al-Majid, and 'Abd al-'Aziz (19).

However, while a combination of internally generated reform and European communications technology did in fact considerably improve the administrative efficiency of the Ottoman Empire in the latter half of the nineteenth century, Hasan's reforms had no such positive effects. In the first place, the laisser-faire economic policies forced on Morocco by the Powers only benefitted a certain number of wealthy urban families, who gained considerable leverage over the fortunes of the makhzan, and formed the nucleus of an emergent comprador bourgeoisie. Secondly, the political uncertainty and lack of order in the countryside under Hasan, and more particularly under his successor 'Abd al-'Aziz (1894-1908) permitted a number of relatively insignificant local chiefs, notably the Mtouga, Glawa and Goundafa, to extend their authority over vast populations and territories, to the extent that they developed into a powerful counterweight to the 'Alawite throne, a process in which they were aided and abetted by the Powers (20).

In 1894 Hasan died and was succeeded by his youngest son 'Abd al-Aziz, then aged 14. Hasan's vigorous chamberlain, Ba Ahmad, acted as regent until his death in 1900, the year in which French forces operating from Algeria began to annex Touat and other oases in southern Morocco. Ba Ahmad knew that the Moroccan state was quite incapable of resisting such attacks, but his counsels of restraint towards the French, however well-grounded, inevitably 'undermined the legitimacy of the government in the eyes of many Moroccans' who could not understand why the makhzan should be prepared to let parts of the Dar al-Islam fall into Christian hands (21). The groundswell of discontent thus created was further fuelled by 'Abd al-Aziz' apparent incapacity to rule, although the sultan's well-known passion for the gadgets and toys lavished on him by his European and Moroccan 'advisers' was by no means the sole cause of the disasters which followed, as is sometimes alleged.

In 1901, a new form of taxation, the *tartib*, was introduced. The new tax was meant to remove the many different kinds of exemption enjoyed by the Europeans and various privileged groups of Moroccans, notably the religious brotherhoods and the *jaysh* tribes, who provided soldiers for the makhzan. As the tartib was meant to replace the traditional Qur'anic taxes, and had clearly been introduced in response to promptings from 'Abd al-'Aziz' European advisers, it was easy to rally opposition to it on the grounds that it was un-Islamic. Failure to collect the tartib, and the shortages of food caused by poor harvests in 1901-02 and 1904-05 led to an ever widening financial abyss, accompanied by signs of popular discontent, which eventually broke out into open revolt.

During the first few years of the twentieth century, somewhat shaken by her defeat at Fashoda in 1898, France embarked upon a cautious policy aimed at the *pénétration pacifique* of Morocco. She attempted to placate her European rivals by trading off some of her less prized colonial territories in return for a free hand in Morocco, while gaining political and economic ascendancy over the makhzan through loans and support for 'reforms'. In 1904, the *Entente Cordiale* was signed with Britain; its main provision was that Britain agreed to abandon all political claims to Morocco in return for a similar declaration of French disinterest in Egypt. Also in 1904, a Franco-Spanish agreement gave Spain a conditional grant of territory in northern Morocco, which was later formalised in the *convenio* following the Treaty of Fez (22). At the same time, the *Banque de Paris et des Pays Bas* negotiated another huge loan to the makhzan, for which part of the proceeds of the Moroccan customs were to be held forfeit in repayment. When these arrangements became public knowledge in Morocco, opinion was outraged but helpless; the makhzan endeavoured to obtain the support and sympathy of Germany, herself anxious to stake out claims in Morocco (23), and succeeded in convincing the signatories of the Treaty of Madrid to call another international conference, which met at Algeciras in 1905-6. Here again French pre-eminence was resoundingly confirmed, and the pénétration pacifique continued.

More vigorous French intervention was facilitated by widespread rural revolt, and also by attacks upon Europeans, the latter culminating in the murder of Dr. Mauchamps, a French medical missionary in Marrakech in 1907. As a reprisal, General Lyautey, the officer commanding French troops on the Algerian border with Morocco, crossed into Morocco and occupied Oujda, exacting ignominious terms from the sultan as the price for evacuation. From 1902 to 1912, but particularly after 1907, a series of local rebellions provided the pretext for a further escalation of French military activity (24). The earliest of these, led by the 'pretender' (al-Rugi) Bu Himara, was a less successful version of the provincial dissidence initiated by the Glawa, Mtouga and Goundafa some 20 years before (25). However, the risings around Casablanca in 1907, in which Bu Himara was also indirectly involved, led to the landing of a French military expedition in August of that year; this precipitated a further crisis of confidence in the Moroccan government, which in its turn encouraged 'Abd al-'Aziz' brother, 'Abd al-Hafidh, to take to the field against him. 'Abd al-Hafidh managed to secure the backing of some of the *grands qa'ids*, notably Madani al-Glawi, 'Abd al-Malik al-Mtougi and Moha ou Hamou, and ultimately of the *'ulama'* of Fez, which gave greater authority to his own designation of his revolt as a *jihad*. By August 1908, in spite of several reverses, 'Abd al-Hafidh had defeated 'Abd al-'Aziz in battle, and had forced the latter's abdication (26). However, although the new sultan at first gained considerable prestige from his independent stand, and even more from his defeat of the rebel Bu Himara in 1909, he too gradually found pressures from France and Spain impossible to withstand, and soon attracted much of the 'collaborationist' criticism previously levelled at his brother. His attempts to play off France and Spain against other Powers, notably Germany and Italy, also foundered on the rock of French political, diplomatic and economic pre-eminence; 'Abd al-Hafidh was forced to sign a humiliating agreement with France in March 1910 which provided for a new loan, an enlarged military mission, and 'temporary' French occupation of the Chaouia and a strip along the Algerian frontier, as well as a similar agreement with Spain the following September.

The last years of 'independent' Morocco were marked by further outbursts of rural dissidence, directed both against increasing French penetration and the sultan's apparent inability to withstand it. Such events, particularly the long revolt of al-Hiba, the son of the saintly Mauritanian leader Ma' al-Aynayn, which took place in the Souss, and that of the Ait Ndhir tribe, which actually marched on Fez and threatened the sultan with the siege of the city in the spring of 1911, resulted in 'Abd al-'Aziz being forced to make even more desperate appeals to France and led ultimately to his abdication. By March 1911 a more interventionist government had come to power in France which showed itself eager to establish French hegemony in Morocco once and for all; French troops were sent to raise the siege of Fez, much to the irritation of Spain and Germany, who also sent military detachments to the north and south of the country respectively. The Germans were eventually bought off with an agreement ceding parts of the Congo to Germany in return for a promise of German non-intervention in Morocco, while Spain was also assured that her own stake in the country would not be overlooked.

The raising of the siege of Fez signalled the beginning of a full scale French occupation, and indeed of the Protectorate, which was enshrined in the Treaty of Fez, signed by the sultan in March 1912. A new government was to be set up, parallel to but independent of, the makhzan, and foreign and financial affairs were to be controlled by the French Resident-General. By April 1912 the makhzan army had mutinied at the threat of French military 'reforms', and as a result over 60 French civilians and 47 Moroccan Jews were massacred in Fez. This event was sufficient to convince the French that the Resident-General would have to be a soldier, and Lyautey, who had served in Indo-China and Algeria, was despatched to Morocco in May to commence a 14 year governorate. Savage reprisals were exacted for the mutiny (27) in the form of executions, long prison sentences and collective fines. In spite of this there were more attacks on Fez and other cities by alliances of tribes immediately after Lyautey's arrival; as was to be the case over the next 20 years, the extent and efficiency of the resistance took the French by surprise.

'Abd al-Hafidh was finally bribed into abdicating in August 1912 in favour of his more pliant brother Yusuf, a sovereign, in Julien's words, who was 'ready to exercise honorific functions with exemplary discretion' (28). 'Abd al-Hafidh's 'defection' occasioned the last major revolt of this transition period, that of al-Hiba, which was a form of fundamentalist religious rebellion very similar to that of Muhammad ibn 'Abd al-Wahhab in the Arabian peninsula in the middle of the eighteenth century, or perhaps to that of the Sudanese Mahdi. al-Hiba proclaimed himself sultan, alleging that both Yusuf and 'Abd al-Hafidh had so to speak disqualified themselves by having submitted to the French. He gained a considerable following among the tribes of the south, who eagerly threw off the authority of the grand qa'ids, which the French had forced the makhzan to impose upon them. The qa'ids themselves actually sided with the movement in its early stages, but prudently dissociated themselves from it when it became clear that the French would not adopt al-Hiba in the way that they had accepted 'Abd al-Hafidh in 1908 (29). Although al-Hiba entered Marrakech in triumph in August 1912, and even had himself proclaimed sultan there, his army was heavily defeated and he was forced to retreat to the south, where he continued his resistance on a smaller scale until his death in 1926.

POLICY AND PRACTICE: LYAUTEY AND THE PROTECTORATE

After the signature of the Treaty of Fez, Morocco became a Protectorate, divided between France and Spain under another treaty signed in November 1912. Theoretically, both powers ruled their respective zones in the name of the sultan, whose court was now permanently established by the French at Rabat (30). The Spanish zone, with its capital Tetouan, was only one twentieth the size of the French, and contained some ten per cent of the population at independence. The north had no mineral resources and offered little scope for profitable investment, with the result that its economic development lagged sharply behind the south.

In French Morocco, the principles introduced by the first Resident-General, Lyautey (April 1912–October 1925), although in practice substantially ignored by many of his successors, remained a touchstone for the whole of the colonial period:

> The Sultanate survived if indeed it was not revived, the traditional state bureaucracy was left largely untouched and a calculated effort to preserve (or even aggrandise)traditional leadership is discernible in the *écoles des fils des notables* and the policy of working through the *grands caïds* (31).

Lyautey himself insisted that *'Tout en représentant ici le Gouvernement de la France, je m'honore d'être le premier serviteur du Sidna'* (32), and certainly made every effort to preserve his own version of the traditional structures in a kind of timeless suspended animation. Thus he attempted to restrict European agricultural colonisation, forbade missionaries to proselytise and used his extensive powers to prevent the circulation of subversive ideas from the outside world (33). In fact, of course, by insisting on 'the sultan's theoretical sovereignty as a rationale for local autonomy (Lyautey) assured his own freedom of action' vis-à-vis both the Quai d'Orsay and, for the time being at least, the *colons* (34).

As we have already suggested, the apparently anachronistic political and social structure of contemporary Morocco owes much to the work of Lyautey and his more vigorous successors, who provided the essential foundations on which the rulers of the independent state were subsequently able to build and consolidate their authority. In the first place, it is undoubtedly the case that, at whatever cost in lives and human misery, the French authorities and their Spanish counterparts actually unified the Sharifian Empire, in the sense of extending the authority of the sultan to the remotest corners of the country (35). In traditional pre-Protectorate Morocco, the essence of the sultan's authority was spiritual rather than temporal, or, to put it another way, the sultan's capacity to impose his authority was in direct proportion to the authenticity of his spiritual claims (36). Thus 'Abd al-'Aziz' collaboration with the Europeans, and allegations that he was acting against Islam, could be used as powerful ideological weapons to justify unseating him by his brother 'Abd al-Hafidh, who in his turn forfeited his own authority by being defeated in 1912. In addition, *siba'*, dissidence, usually in the form of a tribe's refusal to pay taxes, was generally conceived as an act of defiance against the temporal authority of the makhzan and not, except in the fairly rare kinds of circumstance just described, as any questioning of the sultan's spiritual capacities. The long term consequence of the French 'pacification', which was not completed until 1934, was ultimately to deliver the country intact into the sultan's hands, and thus greatly to strengthen his power and authority.

Two other policies which were ultimately to be of considerable benefit to the monarchy – although these benefits were, admittedly, most unlikely to have been perceived as such at the time – were the use of 'traditional' provincial notables as local administrators, and the attempt to drive a wedge between Arabs and Berbers which came to a head with the promulgation of the Berber *dahir* in 1930. As Laroui observes, 'throughout the Maghrib the policy was to make the old elites collaborate in the work of colonialism by transforming them, into a ruling class' (37). In the towns, the old families would work for the administration, while in the countryside local grands qa'ids like the powerful Mtouga, Glawa and Goundafa, with lesser leaders beneath them *'constituent une sorte de féodalité politico-agraire sur laquelle le régime (du Protectorat) s'est constamment appuyé depuis ses origines jusqu'à sa chute'* 38). In Morocco, as in other colonial territories, official support for 'traditional' leaders often gave these individuals powers which were in fact quite alien to the system of authority from which they were alleged to derive (39). Another long term consequence of this policy was, that particular individuals were thereby promoted and 'frozen' in positions of authority in a society where leadership was normally a far more fluid concept, a development which in its turn meant that an individual's political power gradually came to depend less on the number of followers he could muster than the strength and efficacy of his ties with Rabat or Tetouan (40). This ever increasing pressure towards centralisation eventually redounded to the benefit of the monarchy, since the countryside gradually became inextricably and permanently linked with the government.

The other cornerstone of Lyautey's policy was the notion, which had very little foundation in fact, that 'Arabs' and 'Berbers' were discrete historical entities, and could be treated separately. Although this policy may at first sight seem to contradict the other aim, of incorporating the local notables, the two were in fact perfectly compatible. The French wished to make the local notables, and the Berbers, dependent upon the new administration which the

French themselves ran, and in particular to detach the Berbers from the more sophisticated population of the cities. An important element of the theory was that the Berbers were not really Muslims at all, and that they would welcome the opportunity offered to them by the French to throw off the Arab/Muslim yoke. The theory is aptly summarised as *'une conception manichéenne de la société marocaine, opposant le bon Berbère à l'Arabe pervers'* (41), inspiring a whole school of colonial ethnographic studies, perhaps most notably Robert Montagne's *Les Berbères et le Makhzen dans le Sud de Maroc* (42). The general principle was, as far as possible, to prise the Berbers away from the control of the makhzan, a process which began with Lyautey's proclamation of Berber rights in 1914. Since Berber has no written form, it was decided to teach the Berbers French and administer them in French, and a series of schools were set up for the purpose, perhaps most notably the *collège* at Azrou, which was intended to produce *'une pépinière d'intellectuels désislamisés'* (43).

It must be said that this policy failed almost entirely, largely because it was grounded on a series of misconceptions. Certainly, there were and are cultural differences between Arabs and Berbers, and it is more than probable that in the first quarter of this century many Berbers were as little acquainted with 'orthodox' Sunni Islam as the inhabitants of Central Arabia had been in the period before the advent of Muhammad ibn 'Abd al-Wahhab in the mid-eighteenth century, but it might have been more realistic to think in terms of an opposition between town and country rather than between Arabs and Berbers. The former categorisation makes some geopolitical sense, while the latter bears little relation to twentieth century realities. Apart from incidents which were very largely manufactured by the French, notably the 'descent on Rabat' and other cities by the tribesmen in 1951 and 1953 (44), the Berbers exhibited a profound loyalty to the Shariflan throne and ultimately threw their weight against rather than behind the colonial power.

To complete this review of the policies inspired by Lyautey, mention must be made of the attitude of the Marshal and his successors towards education. Here too attitudes can be seen as a logical extension of the stated desire to preserve rather than interfere: only 503 Moroccans passed the *baccalauréat* during the whole Protectorate period - in comparison with the 2,355 who did so in the single school year 1965-66 (45). Such educational provision as was made was almost entirely in French or at least conceived in French cultural terms. Ironically, although this was rightly seen by many as a denial of Morocco's Arab-Islamic past, it is undeniable that the French curriculum was a crucial catalyst in the formation of nationalist, patriotic and western notions among those who did go to school in the 1920s and 1930s (46). Again, although numbers were small, those Moroccans who were able to study in France had the chance to make contact with other North Africans in Paris, particularly those attached to the *Association des Etudiants Musulmans de l'Afrique du Nord*, founded in 1927. In this way they also became associated with students from the Arab East, especially Syrians, who introduced them to the currents of Arab nationalism which the Résidence generally managed to divert away from Morocco itself until much later (47).

An important by-product of the lack of widespread educational facilities – only about 3 per cent of Moroccan children were attending state schools in 1940, for example (48) – and the heavy French bias of what was in fact provided, was the foundation of the so-called 'free schools' after 1921 (49). Those who encouraged the spread of such schools were generally associated with the *Salafiyya* movement, whose members also came to play an important role in the national movement. The *salafis*, who favoured Islamic reform on lines similar to those advocated by the Egyptian Muhammad 'Abduh and his circle, had long been active in Morocco, acting particularly as a bastion of opposition to what they regarded as the heterodoxy of the Sufi orders. They were given new impetus by the French occupation and the imposition of the Protectorate, especially as the French authorities tended to favour the Sufi orders as a kind of counterweight to the prestige and authority of the makhzan. The '*Neo-Salafiyya*' who emerged after the First World War were concerned to establish a political and social order in which Muslims would be able to practise their religion freely according to orthodox precepts. In this context Jamil Abun-Nasr has made the valuable point that the imposition of foreign, Christian, rule in Morocco actually facilitated the reformers' task, since they were now at liberty and in fact almost bound, to criticise the infidels who had taken over the country. Previously, it had been difficult for the salafis to criticise the various manifestations of the decline of Islamic orthodoxy in Morocco without explicitly or implicitly implicating the sultan if he did not join in their criticism; after 1912 they could attack the government without 'forsaking their allegiance to the Muslim head of the community' (50). Allal al-Fassi, a *salafi*, emerged as the leader of the national movement in the 1930s, and attempted to combine within it – not always harmoniously – the twin strands of the French cultural legacy of economic and political liberalism, patriotism and equality before the law with the Islamic themes of the *shari'a* as the ultimate source of all legislation, Arabic as a lingua franca linking Morocco with other Arabic-speaking Muslims, the need to rediscover the true Islam of the pious generation (*al-salaf al-salih*), and finally the notion that attacks on the prerogatives of the Moroccan state were attacks upon the Islamic religion, and should be resisted as such. As we shall see in the context of the reaction to the Berber *dahir* in 1930, 'in the Moroccan context it was Islam, with its many symbols, that acted as the midwife of nationalism' (51).

CONQUEST AND RESISTANCE: THE GROWTH OF THE NATIONAL MOVEMENT

The final conquest of Morocco took the French over 20 years, and the very length of this period is sufficient indication that a successful outcome for French arms was not always a foregone conclusion. The Rif war, the most serious challenge to European penetration, lasted more than five years and at one stage involved over 700,000 French and Spanish troops (52). Urban protest and resistance developed more slowly and was given particular impetus under the aegis of Lyautey's immediate successors, Steeg (1925-1929), Saint (1929-1933) and Ponsot (1933-1936) and also after the accession of Muhammad V in 1927 (53). The Marshal's successors were less careful of Moroccan sensibilities than the Marshal himself had been, and also permitted, or at least did little to prevent, a very considerable increase in the European population:

Year	1921	1926	1931	1936
Muslims	4,162,000	4,682,000	5,068,000	5,881,000
Jews	,91,000	107,000	125,000	162,000
Europeans	,81,000	105,000	172,000	202,000
Total	4,334,000	4,894,000	5,365,000	6,245,000

(54)

A particularly important feature of the period was the immense increase in agricultural colonisation by Europeans on land sequestrated or confiscated from Moroccans. Between 1918 and 1931, 270,000 ha were distributed to 1,800 *colons officiels*, and a further 358,000 ha in *colonisation privé* by 1932 (55). In 1925, only about 500 colons actually lived on the land; by 1934 their number exceeded 4,000 (56). One third of all Moroccans were completely landless in 1931; these either became day labourers or left the land in search of work in the cities. The demoralisation, *déracinement* and pauperisation involved in this process can easily be imagined.

In the cities, the first major manifestation of opposition to French rule took place in the summer of 1930, following the promulgation of the Berber dahir. An earlier dahir, issued in 1914, assuring the Berbers that their customary rights would be protected, had passed almost unnoticed, but by 1930 there had been a decisive change of mood. In brief, the new law proposed to transfer the Berbers from the jurisdiction of the shari'a to French criminal law, or perhaps more relevantly, to remove them from the jurisdiction of the sultan (57). As we have stated earlier, that such an edict could be promulgated at all reflects a French belief, assumption or policy that the Berbers somehow were not really Muslims. Moreover, the dahir was certainly in contravention of the Treaty of Fez, since it effectively limited the 'traditional' prerogatives of the sultan.

Out of the furore produced by reactions to the dahir the Moroccan national movement suddenly came to life. Kenneth Brown has provided a vivid description of the way in what was perceived, or could be represented, as an attack on the fundamentals of Islam was seized upon by educated young people and their parents and grandparents as a rallying point for opposition to the Christian invader. To the economic upheavals caused by massive European economic penetration, the effects of the world recession of the late 1920s and the bewildering social and cultural changes brought about by colonisation was added a major assault on the religious sensibilities of the population (58). On a wider scale, the substantial publicity which the demonstrations and the cause in general received in other Arab countries was instrumental in bringing Morocco into the larger sphere of Arab and pan-Arab politics (59).

In the 1930s, the major figures in the nationalist movement were divided into those whose intellectual formation originated in the Islamic roots of the free school system and those who had been educated in the French system. For the time being, the Arabophone and Islamic cultural influence predominated, although this situation was to change markedly after the Second World War. Muhammad Ghazi, 'Allal al-Fassi, Ibrahim al-Kattani, Mukhtar al-Susi, Ahmad Balafrej and Ahmad Sharqawi had either studied or taught in the free schools, while Muhammad al-Wazzani and Muhammad Lyazidi (al-Yazidi) had received their education in French. al-Fassi, born in 1907 into a wealthy religious family of Fez, soon emerged as the principal figure in the movement. By 1934, he and al-Wazzani, as founders of the *Comité d'Action Marocaine*, had formulated a *Plan de Réformes Marocaines*, which they presented to the sultan, the Resident General and the French Prime Minister. This document, which runs to 134 printed pages, was subsequently given wide distribution in both France and Morocco. It is significant that although it proposed a gradual Moroccanisation of the administration, and ultimately the exclusion of the French from public life altogether, the reform plan did not specifically demand the abolition of the protectorate. Instead, the authors stressed that the original terms of the protectorate as laid down in the Treaty of Fez should be more scrupulously adhered to, and that tendencies towards direct rule should be checked. They also called for a single Islamic legal system for the whole country, a clear reference to the response to the Berber dahir.

Although the plan was rejected out of hand by the Residency, the Moroccan nationalists, like their counterparts in other French colonies had high if short-lived hopes of the good intentions of the Popular Front government under Leon Blum when it came to power in June 1936. al-Fassi organised public meetings in the main towns calling for the granting of fundamental democratic liberties, but the French authorities disbanded the *Comité d'Action Marocaine* in March 1937; the Popular Front government fell in June, and al-Fassi himself was sent into exile in Gabon in November, largely as a result of extensive riots and demonstrations in Meknes, Fez, Marrakech, and Khemisset during the summer and early autumn. Other nationalist leaders were either banished to remote parts of the country or went into voluntary exile. In view of the rifts which were to develop between the two men later, it is worth remarking that while Muhammad V seems to have shown a rather lukewarm sympathy for the nationalist movement, 'Allal al-Fassi was zealous 'in his efforts to promote the prestige of the king in the eyes of the Moroccan people' (60).

The national movement, deprived of its leaders, now entered a period of quiescence and despondency. At the same time, General Noguès (Resident 1936-1943) sought to ease the situation by embarking upon a programme of modest reforms, and also seems to have succeeded in convincing Muhammad V that al-Fassi represented a threat to the authority of the throne, since the palace made no public allusion to his deportation (61). Similarly, Muhammad V gave his consent to a dahir submitted to him in 1938 forbidding Moroccans to join trade unions, perhaps 'seeing in union membership a grave threat to the authority of the Makhzan' (62). The outbreak of war and the rapidity with which the Germans overran France, Belgium and the Netherlands encouraged some of the nationalist leaders to make tentative overtures to the Axis, but such contacts do not seem to have met a particularly ready response, and in any case events moved too quickly. The Americans landed in Morocco in November 1942, and Muhammad V received President Roosevelt on 22 January 1943 in an interview which is considered to have been particularly influential in the formation of his political awareness (63). Six months later Noguès left for exile in Spain, and de Gaulle appointed Gabriel Puaux as his successor. A diplomat rather than a soldier, Puaux had shown little flexibility or imagination in his dealings with nationalists in Syria and Lebanon in 1939-1940 (64), and the choice was an unfortunate one.

The American landings marked the end of active hostilities in North West Africa, and the Americans, following their President's lead, made no secret of their general support for the notion of Moroccan independence. Thus encouraged, the nationalists began to resume their activities, and were joined by a growing body of supporters from all social strata (65). The movement itself shifted its centre of gravity from the traditional cities of the interior to the coastal towns of Rabat-Salé, Kenitra and particularly Casablanca, where an urban working class was emerging as a result of the rapid development of industry during the war years (66). In January 1944 the nationalists announced the formation of a political party, the Istiqlal, led by Ahmad Balafrej, with 'Allal al-Fassi, who was still in Gabon, as honorary president.

The manifesto of the Istiqlal demanded the independence of Morocco under Muhammad V, for which the sultan was asked to obtain international guarantees, while safeguarding the legitimate interests of foreigners residing in Morocco. It also asked the sultan to place himself at the head of the reform movement and to establish 'a democratic régime comparable with the form of government adopted in the Muslim countries of the East' (67). The French authorities took some time to react to the manifesto, but the effect on the Moroccan population was electric. The sultan, apparently convinced of the strength of the new nationalist organisation, lost no time in taking the initiative, by asking the Resident-General to comment on the manifesto. Eleven days later the Istiqlal clarified and somewhat moderated their demands by acknowledging that the French and other foreigners had legitimate rights in Morocco which would be safeguarded, and stressing that they had no intention of resorting to violence. For its part the French government was apparently determined to make no concessions whatever and in February 1944 the principal signatories to the manifesto, including Balafrej and Lyazidi were arrested on trumped up charges of collaboration with the Germans. This provoked widespread indignation throughout the country, and large demonstrations in Rabat, Salé and Fez in which several hundred were killed and thousands arrested. The sultan was forced to pledge his support for the Protectorate authorities and to dismiss his Ministers of Justice and Education (68).

In spite of this setback the Istiqlal and the national movement gradually won new adherents. The small Moroccan Communist Party, whose membership was originally almost entirely European, was at first wary of throwing itself into the national struggle – preferring to agitate for the democratisation of the political system – but by the end of 1945 it too had placed itself unreservedly at the service of the national movement. It also made strenuous efforts to recruit Moroccans, notably through the trade unions, which were legalised in 1945. Under the more liberal Resident Erik Labonne (1946-1947) 'Allal al-Fassi was permitted to return from Gabon in the spring of 1946, and was immediately installed as leader of the Istiqlal. All seemed set fair for a period of greater flexibility and compromise in Franco-Moroccan relations.

In April 1947 Muhammad V had planned a visit to Tanger, which had by that time regained its international status. His journey from Rabat was to take him through the Spanish zone, which neither he nor his father before him had ever visited officially. On 7 April, in circumstances which strongly suggest the intervention of *agents provocateurs*, a body of Senegalese troops ran amok in Casablanca, killing and wounding hundreds of Moroccans without encountering any response from the army or police authorities. On the following day the sultan was given an enthusiastic welcome by his subjects in both zones, and on 10 April delivered a speech to the diplomatic corps in Tanger which is generally held to mark the beginning of the nine year 'crise franco-marocaine'. The speech stressed Morocco's links with the Arab world, and in particular the sultan's admiration for the newly created Arab League, but it did not make the customary genuflexion towards France which had appeared in the version previously approved by Labonne.

Precisely why Muhammad V chose to throw down the gauntlet to France at this particular moment is not clear. His son states unequivocally that the Casablanca massacre made it impossible for him to act differently (69), but other considerations may also have played an important role. The French had just released 'Abd al-Krim, the veteran hero of the Rif, who would almost certainly have developed into a serious rival to the sultan if he had in fact returned to Morocco. More immediately, the growing appeal of al-Fassi and the Istiqlal might, if not checked, render the monarchy almost superfluous. By speaking out at Tanger, the sultan placed himself at the head of the national movement, and steered the monarchy clearly and firmly to the centre of the political stage (70).

After Tanger, the battle lines were drawn; in France, right wing public and press opinion seized upon the speech to mount a violent and often hysterical opposition campaign. The liberal Labonne was replaced by the soldier and pied-noir Juin, and a long period of confrontation began. The sultan had already shown some signs of non-cooperation by refusing to sign the 1946 budget without the scrutiny of a committee of his own choosing. Further afield, 'Abd al-Krim had jumped ship in Egypt on his way back from Réunion, and had formed a

Committee for the Liberation of the Arab Maghreb in Cairo with Arab League support (71). With him in Cairo were 'Abd al-Khaliq Torres, leader of the nationalist movement in the Spanish zone, and 'Allal al-Fassi, who began a period of voluntary exile in Egypt in May 1947. Meanwhile, in Morocco itself, the Protectorate authorities were mustering their supporters, especially the grand qa'ids of the south and the heads of the religious orders; all 'forces of the past' (72), but extremely powerful nevertheless. As well as favouring this group, Juin tried to strengthen the ties binding Morocco to France by encroaching further on the prerogatives of the makhzan. He invented the principle of 'co-sovereignty' which was a denial of the residual rights remaining to the Moroccan throne under the Treaty of Fez, and resolutely refused to consider the reforms which Paris pressed him to carry out, arguing that the Moroccans were incapable of being given any major responsibility. The sultan visited France in the autumn of 1950 hoping to be able to initiate serious Franco-Moroccan discussions, but was unable to do so.

By December 1950, on the occasion of the discussions of the following year's budget, matters reached a head. Juin quarrelled with the Moroccan members of the budget commission, mostly moderate Istiqlalis, who immediately appealed to the sultan for support; this episode occasioned al-Glawi's famous remark to Muhammad V, so comically inept, as future events were to prove: 'You are not the sultan of Morocco; you are the sultan of the Istiqlal'. Finally, on the eve of his departure for military talks in the United States, Juin threatened the sultan with deposition if he did not publicly disavow his attachment to the Istiqlal. On Juin's return in February 1951, Muhammad V was forced to make a general condemnation of the Istiqlal to prevent the French sending the tribes of the south to devastate the cities (73). The general attitude of the tribes at this stage indicates both the extent to which the French had succeeded in maintaining the grands qa'ids in power and the wide disparity in political consciousness between town and country.

By April 1951 the nationalist parties of the French and Spanish zones, together with the Committee in Cairo, formed a Moroccan National Front, pledging support for the sultan, seeking cooperation with the Arab League, and, significantly, stressing that they were not prepared to negotiate before the declaration of independence. Partly as a result of the continued rebuffs administered by the French (74) to the sultan, the Istiqlal gained growing numbers of adherents, particularly in the towns, and militancy continued to increase. Even at this stage, some of the basic contradictions of the Istiqlal had begun to emerge, which were to threaten and ultimately to fragment it in the early post-independence period.

Like its counterparts the National Bloc and the Wafd in Syria and Egypt, the Istiqlal was more a coalition of interest groups than a political party in the Western European sense. It was composed of three main elements: the traditional bourgeoisie of the northern cities, particularly Fez, who had ruled the country themselves together with the sultan, until the installation of the Protectorate; the emerging national bourgeoisie, whose activities were greatly restricted by the weight of the colonial economy and by the colons themselves, and finally the 'leftists' from petty bourgeois and professional backgrounds, generally with Western education, who formed a vanguard of militants. The latter, a group also familiar to us from other parts of the Arab world, generally rejected the Communist Party's internationalism and the radical nature of its socio-economic programmes, but was unable to remain intellectually and politically comfortable within the Istiqlal after independence, eventually breaking away to form the *Union Nationale des Forces Populaires* (UNFP) in 1959.

Meanwhile, in August 1959, the replacement of Juin by Guillaume, another soldier, did not herald any changes of policy, since Guillaume was if anything even more obdurate than his predecessor. Muhammad V had now adopted the tactic of refusing to sign the dahirs presented to him, and the signatories to the National Front were determined to boycott the elections, planned for the late autumn, in which some 220,000 carefully selected Moroccans were to be given the franchise. During these months the national leaders made strenuous efforts to gain international support, pressing for a United Nations debate on Morocco which eventually took place late in 1952. The French authorities, both in Paris and Rabat, continued to set themselves firmly against any concessions in the direction of independence, in spite of a further series of overtures by Muhammad V in the spring of 1952, and the recognition by the Istiqlal in its own paper *al-Istiqlal* on 29 March 1952 that *'La France a des interets et des droits dont les marocains reconnaissent la légitimité,'* but the concept of co-sovereignty, which the French now insisted on putting forward, was totally unacceptable both to the sultan and to the political parties (75). Early in December 1952 a major trade union demonstration in Casablanca in protest against the assassination of the Tunisian trade unionist, Farhat Hached, rapidly erupted into a major disturbance which was brutally repressed by troops and police. Political parties were banned, and political and trade union leaders arrested (76).

Attitudes hardened over the following months. Guillaume, now acting virtually independent of Paris, was busily working for Muhammad V's deposition, with the support of most of the European community. Public opinion in France was deeply divided, especially after an article by François Mauriac in *Le Figaro* comparing French crimes in Morocco with wartime Nazi atrocities (77). Guillaume now began a policy of attempting to convince Moroccans, especially the tribes, that al-Glawi and al-Kittani were the defenders of Islamic orthodoxy, while Muhammad V was the associate of Christians and the enemies of Islam. His efforts proved successful to the extent that some of the tribes did in fact respond to the call to arms, although it seems that not all those who took part on the marches on Rabat in 1951 and 1953 really understood what they were doing (78). Early in August 1953 some quarters in Paris and Rabat were toying with the idea of a separation of religious and temporal powers, making the sultan into a constitutional monarch and devolving his spiritual powers upon his cousin Moulay 'Arafa, but this expedient came too late. The tribesmen began to move towards the cities of Fez, Marrakech and Rabat, and the idea of a double imamate was hurriedly abandoned. *'Il faut aller vite'* comments Montagne at the end of a highly partisan account *'pour sauver la dynastie et éviter que l'opposition du Palais et les tribus ne conduise à l'anarchie'* (79). 'Arafa was hastily proclaimed sultan, and Muhammad V and his family arrested and sent into exile.

By this summary action, Guillaume and his supporters in Paris and Rabat, as well as the grands qa'ids and the *chefs de confréries*, probably thought that they had settled matters once and for all, and that the authority of France could be reasserted in Morocco. The enormity of this miscalculation soon made itself clear, since, following the principles that have been outlined earlier, a sultan who owed his position so directly to foreign support could not function as a meaningful object of religious or political loyalty. As Muhammad V's period of exile lengthened, the nationalists became increasingly confident that their cause would triumph, the tribes increasingly doubtful of the propriety of their action, and mosques throughout the country were deserted because the *khutba* was pronounced in 'Arafa's name. The absent sultan became a martyr, the principal symbol, of the struggle for independence, which now began to focus around his person and his return, thus giving the Sharifian throne a degree of sanctity and legitimacy which might, in different circumstances, have evaporated almost entirely.

Meanwhile in Cairo, 'Allal al-Fassi stated unequivocally that Muhammad V was the sole legitimate ruler of Morocco, and encouraged his fellow countrymen to avenge the indignity to his person and to struggle for his return (80). With all political parties suspended and any opposition to the French made illegal, the urban population took to the streets. There were sporadic outbreaks of violence against the supporters of the new regime, and the 'pretender' himself was the object of a number of assassination attempts. A campaign of bombing and assassination claimed large numbers of victims, notably informers and policemen. The French authorities responded with such violence that their activities became the object of a parliamentary enquiry. Public opinion in France remained divided, although increasingly aware of the futility of a hardline policy, while in Morocco an ultra conservative grouping, *L'Union pour la Présence Française* began to take power into its own hands. Terrorism and counter terrorism continued throughout the period between 1953 and 1955 under the aegis of four residents, Lacoste, Grandval, Boyer de Latour and Dubois. Arms found their way to the resistance from Tanger through the Spanish zone.

By mid-1955 it had become clear in Paris, if not yet in Rabat, that the only way out of the impasse was the recall of the sultan from exile. In August, negotiations with members of the Istiqlal began at Aix-les-Bains, while General Catroux was despatched to Madagascar for discussions with Muhammad V. The sultan agreed to accept assurances that French policy would faithfully respect 'the principle of Moroccan sovereignty and lead Morocco to the status of a free, modern sovereign state, linked to France by the permanent ties of an interdependence freely entered into in the spheres of strategy, diplomacy, politics, economics and culture' (81). Moulay 'Arafa was induced to leave Rabat for Tanger on 1 October 1955, and an interim Council of the Throne was appointed.

Even after having conceded the substance of victory to the sultan and the nationalists, the actual timetable, and the precise form, of the handover had still to be negotiated. For this and other reasons, including, as Waterbury suggests, a ban on labour migration from the Rif to Algeria imposed by the French in the summer of 1955 (82), sporadic fighting broke out in the Middle Atlas mountains along the borders of the French and Spanish zones on 1 October. On 4 October, 'Allal al-Fassi announced from Cairo that the 'Army for the Liberation of the Arab Maghreb' was taking over to free both Algeria and Morocco from the French. By the end of October, the *pashas, qa'ids* and *chefs de confréries* who had been Moulay 'Arafa's most vigorous supporters had taken fright, had announced a change of heart, and were petitioning for the restoration of Muhammad V to the throne. Meanwhile the sultan himself had been flown back to France for meetings with Pinay, the French Foreign Minister; on 6 November 1955 a communiqué was published, promising the eventual independence of Morocco (83), and ten days later Muhammad V returned to Morocco to celebrate the anniversary of his accession among his people in Rabat.

In the speech from the throne which he delivered on 18 November, the sultan was careful to stress an important aspect of the policy which he and his son were to follow sedulously in the future:

> The independence to which our people aspires should not be taken to imply a relaxation of our links with France, because the friendship between our two countries is solidly rooted and goes back a long way in history. Furthermore, we have not lost sight of the fact that thanks to this friendship and to the achievements of France in different spheres, Morocco has been able to take vital steps along the road of progress. We count upon the support of France to inaugurate a new era of interdependence between our countries (84).

This speech has been described as showing 'remarkable moderation' (85), but it also displays shrewd political sense. Muhammad V seems to have lost no time in realising that the maintenance of his position required active acquiescence by France in the new political situation if he himself were not be supplanted, or rendered obsolete, by other elements who favoured major social and economic reforms in addition to formal political independence.

THE MOROCCAN ECONOMY, 1912-1956

One of Morocco's primary attractions before the discovery of its rich phosphate deposits was the prospect held out for large scale agricultural settlement. In a sense, the French penetration of Morocco was a 'natural' consequence of the country's proximity to Algeria, and settlement had begun well before the Protectorate was actually declared (86). The process of land acquisiton was entirely uncontrolled until 1918, when the so-called *colonisation officielle* was inaugurated, under which lots of between 200 and 400 ha were sold to French colonists on favourable terms. In 1912, 73,000 ha were in European hands; this figure rose to 628,000 in 1932 and to just over one million in 1956. In the latter year, 60 per cent of the million ha were divided between 900 large holdings, the property of individuals or agricultural companies (87). Most of these lands were situated in the most fertile regions of the country, notably the Fez-Meknès plain, the Gharb, the Chaouia, the Souss, and the Haouz of Marrakech. Large scale irrigation projects, both canals and barrages, particularly in the Gharb were built for the benefit of the colons and their Moroccan successors (88). New legislation facilitated the transfer of land from traditional or customary owners, who were normally unable to furnish sufficient proof of their own claims to it, although European acquisition of land was often fiercely resisted (89). By 1952 there were nearly 400,000 Europeans in Morocco, mostly 'poor whites', but with a powerful minority of about 5,000 very large landowners and businessmen who had the ear both of the Resident General and of his superiors in Paris (90).

Before 1912 there was no significant industry in Morocco apart from the traditional handicraft sector (91). In the first years of the Protectorate some light industry was established, but little was achieved before the Second World War, in spite of tax and other concessions held out by the makhzan. The Act of Algeciras of 1906 had stipulated an open door economic regime, under which France could not claim the status of most-favoured nation. However, after the abolition of the capitulations in 1937 (92) and the introduction of wartime controls in 1939, the Act of Algeciras was tacitly abandoned, and for the time being French capital no longer had to fear foreign competition. The textile industry in particular underwent a boom during the war years and the profits from this and other sectors were reinvested in various new industries after 1945. In the immediately post-war years French capital was attracted by low wages and low taxation, and much of Morocco's basic industrial structure was constructed between 1949 and 1955, including the chemical, cement, milling, canning and sugar refining industries. However, Amin puts this period of growth in perspective:

> Despite the appearance created by the 'Moroccan industrial boom' over the years 1948-1953, by 1955 the country did not seem noticeably better off than her Algerian neighbour, though enjoying a clear lead over Tunisia...The only truly industrial areas of production were the agricultural and food-stuffs industries, a few mechanical engineering industries and building materials...No proper basic industry yet existed when colonial rule came to an end (93).

Morocco's main source of foreign earnings, and indeed the Moroccan government's main source of income, are its phosphate deposits, which were discovered after the First World War. Their exploitation should have been put out to international tender under the terms of the Act of Algeciras, but this was neatly circumvented by Lyautey, who nationalised the phosphates in 1920, creating the *Office Chérifien des Phosphates*. 'In this way, not only were foreign interests kept out, but the government gained...a major source of revenue...that had the advantage of being outside the control of the French Parliament' (94). Exports of phosphates rose from a few thousand tons in 1921 to nearly two million tons in 1930, nearly four million in 1952, and currently average about 18 million tons per year; Morocco is the third largest producer of phosphates in the world, after the United States and the Soviet Union.

Towards the end of the Protectorate, when the uncertainties surrounding Morocco's political future began to increase, the flow of foreign investment began to slow down, and was gradually reversed, with capital outflow reaching some 35 billion francs in 1955. In spite of this, the period immediately before independence saw a rapid growth in public expenditure, at the rate of 9 or 10 per cent per annum, due mainly to the increase in the numbers of Moroccan children receiving education, improvements in health and welfare services and the general expansion of the administration, tendencies which continued unabated after 1956. It will be clear from this brief account that although the Protectorate had seen considerable growth in most sectors of the economy, the baseline was so low that this development had little general impact. In 1956, large-scale agriculture, foreign trade, and virtually all industry, was almost entirely in foreign hands, so that when Morocco obtained its political independence from France it remained, and indeed still substantially remains some 27 years later, bound hand and foot to the French economy.

THE EARLY YEARS OF INDEPENDENCE, 1956-1960

The declaration of the ending of the Protectorate in 1956 marked the formal termination of the struggle for Moroccan independence, but it also signalled the beginning, or perhaps the resumption, of a profound internal power struggle. Exceedingly desperate urban and rural forces had joined together to force the French to return the sultan to 'the Moroccan people', and to withdraw their soldiers and administrators from the country. This temporary alliance, or *unité de façade*, as one commentator puts it, was concentrated almost entirely around the single issue of the sultan's return, and began to founder almost as soon as this objective was achieved (95).

In socio-political terms, a great gulf still divided the city from the countryside in the middle 1950s, a situation which Muhammad V showed consummate political skill in exploiting. Much of the urban population, particularly in the cities of Fez and Casablanca where the national movement had begun in the 1930s, looked beyond the person of the monarch to the Istiqlal Party, whose programmes seemed to embody many of their aspirations for political and socio-economic 'modernisation'. For their part the rural population had a less coherent vision of the future, and saw their destiny most safely, and of course most properly, entrusted to their sultan and *amir al-mu'minin*. Although both urban and rural populations were equally vigorous in their demands for the Moroccanisation of the economy and the administration, the latter were generally readier to show blind and unquestioning loyalty to the monarch himself, and to display varying degrees of indifference or hostility to less trusted and inevitably less 'legitimate' aspirants to political power. Hence, while Muhammad V had eventually consented to play a leading role in the independent struggle directed by the urban bourgeoisie and their allies, he countered what he perceived as a serious potential threat to his own position from that same quarter after 1956 by pursuing policies which were likely to ensure the more secure if less creative support of the rural masses, or more specifically, the rural notables. Although the monarchy's continuing reliance on these forces has probably been responsible for much of Morocco's social and economic stagnation, this policy has almost certainly been instrumental in ensuring its own survival (96).

These years, between the declaration of independence and Muhammad's assumption of direct personal rule in 1960, were to be crucial in the determination of the future course of the country's political and socio-economic development. In the first place, the sultan, who now assumed the title of *malik*, king, managed simultaneously to make use of the skills of the Istiqlal, whose members were effectively running much of the civil service (97), and to deflect the potential threat posed by the party's claim to be recognised as sole legitimate representative of the Moroccan people (98). There was as yet no constitution, and no elected chamber; the first constitution was promulgated in 1962, and the first elections held in 1963. The first two post-independence cabinets, although containing several members of the Istiqlal, were headed by Mubarak Bekkai, an 'independent' or royal nominee, and the resistance army ('for the Liberation of the Arab Maghreb') was gradually absorbed into the new national army, called significantly, *Les Forces Armées Royales*, commanded by the Crown Prince, the future Hassan II, which, like the *sûreté nationale*, has always remained under palace rather than governmental control.

Apart from having the effect of asserting his own supremacy within the political domain, two other important consequences followed from the king's effective refusal to allow the Istiqlal to take its place as 'sole party'. In the first place, sections of the rural population took advantage of the king's ambiguous attitudes first to stage rural revolts, and then to form political groupings to challenge the Istiqlal and its allies, and secondly, the membership of the Istiqlal, which, as we have already indicated, was extremely heterogeneous, began to raise serious questions about the nature, ideology and future strategy of their party.

The rural revolts of the late 1950s, the most potentially serious being that led by the governor of Tafilelt, Addi ou Bihi in 1958 (99), seem at first sight rather puzzling phenomena, in that the 'rebels, always claimed to be acting in the interests of rather than against the political status quo. They probably had their origins partly in reaction to the new local administrative system, which replaced the dual system of a (normally French) centrally appointed district official alongside the 'traditional' tribal/rural leader by a single administrative hierarchy in which local interests, or more accurately the interests of the rural elite, were not so clearly represented, and partly in the fact that the 'national political battle had not yet been fought', and some testing of the water from time to time was thought to be a risk work taking (100).

These rural revolts eventually died out, but they were gradually replaced, or perhaps institutionalised, by the *Mouvement Populaire*, a Berber/rural party which played an important if somewhat ambiguous role in the politics of the late 1950s and 1960s. In October 1957, during a rising in the Rif, two Berber politicians, Dr. Ahmed Khatib, the mayor of El-Jadida, and Mahjoubi Aherdane, the governor of Rabat, announced the formation of a new loyalist party, which was to promote the cause of the disaffected 'rural masses' and to bring their plight to the urgent attention of the disdainful urban elite of the court and the Istiqlal. The Mouvement Populaire had a wide appeal, both to those whose immediate political past had perhaps been less than entirely respectable, in that they had not seen through the grands qa'ids and Moulay 'Arafa as early as they ought, and to the *anciens combattants* of the rurally based Liberation Army, as well as to those who feared that the Istiqlal would eventually take over as sole party; 'we have not acquired independence in order to lose our freedom', as Aherdane remarked (101). Aherdane and Khatib were briefly arrested because of their involvement in the revolt, but released in November 1958 after the promulgation of a new code of civil liberties which enabled them to register the Mouvement Populaire as a political party.

By early 1958, it had become clear that the divisions inherent in the structure of the Istiqlal (102) were gradually finding their way to the surface. The main issue, which led to the formation of a breakaway group in January 1959, was whether the party should continue to acquiesce in, or take a more vigorous stand against, the seemingly ineluctable extensions of the royal prerogative which had been the most notable feature of politics in the immediately post-independence period. A crisis in April 1958 precipitated the resignation of the nine Istiqlal cabinet ministers, and a month of negotiations followed over the composition of the new government. The King insisted on his right to appoint the two key ministers of defence and interior from outside the party if he so wished; the 'right wing' of the Istiqlal was prepared to accept this, and thus by mid May Ahmed Balafrej had been appointed Prime Minister with a largely Istiqlal cabinet.

In the course of the next few months, friends and members of both Mouvement Populaire and the *Union Marocaine du Travail* made clear, either by rural risings or labour disturbances, that they did not wish to accept the Istiqlal as then constituted as the party of the government. Thus the party itself split; Belafrej resigned, and the eft wing of the Istiqlal, led by Abdullah Ibrahim, was invited to orm a government, to prepare for municipal elections and to prepare a Five Year Plan for the period 1960-64. In January 1959 the two wings of the party formally separated; the left wing under Ibrahim formed *L' Union Nationale des Forces Populaires* (UNFP) in September that year, in an attempt to gain support for their efforts to strike out in a more radical direction. The new Prime Minister and his team duly prepared the Five Year Plan, the most thorough and ambitious attempt made by any Moroccan government before or since to make fundamental structural changes in the economy (103). In particular, the plan advocated substantial changes in the pattern of landholding, which pushed other political groups into a position of united opposition; while generally anti-French, members of the rural elite were anxious to take over the farms of the colons themselves, and did not wish to be reformed out of existence by the UNFP.

Waterbury, who has carried out a minute analysis of the 'scission' in the Istiqlal, concludes that 'it is extremely difficult to generalize about the basic causes... or to categorize the actions of the various participants', but specifically warns against any simplistic formulation of a movement of 'Young Turks' against 'vieux turbans' (104). The secessionists took with them the Istiqlal's main link with the urban working class, the *Union Marocaine du Travail* and its leader Mahjoub ben Siddiq; other prominent members of the new party included Mehdi ben Barka, Muhammad al-Basri, Abdurrahman Bouabid and Abdullah Ibrahim.

Although the UNFP has always claimed to be a radical and progressive party, it has always been plagued with internal contradictions, which were to be responsible for the eventual split in its own ranks which took place at the end of 1974. In the first place, when it was first founded it had come straight from the Istiqlal, and retained important links with those who had been activists in the pre-independence period. However, their general sympathy for the aims of the UNFP did not extend to condoning its opposition to the dominating role played by the monarchy in Moroccan politics. Secondly, many UNFP adherents, especially the Soussi traders, were drawn to the party more because they opposed the dominance of the Istiqlal by the Fassi bourgeoisie than because they actively supported the political initiative which the new formation had taken. Finally, the UNFP throughout its existence has never resolved the important question of whether it wishes to participate within the political arena as that arena is actually constituted, or whether, given what have turned out to be the almost suffocating constraints inherent in the Moroccan political system, the political and socio-economic goals for which it has stood could ever in fact be achieved without a fundamental transformation of Moroccan society. As a result, although most UNFP members have been 'moderate' leftists in any sense of the term, the party's reputation as a potentially disruptive and divisive force has resulted in its constant harassment, repression and even persecution throughout the 1960s and early 1970s (105).

Ibrahim's cabinet lasted 18 months, but signs of strain began to appear within a year. In December 1959 the UNFP newspaper *al-Tahrir* published an article questioning the basic premises of the monarchy's function in the Moroccan state; its joint editors, Abderrahman Yusufi and Muhammad al-Basri, were arrested, and two months later four other prominent party members were arrested on a charge of 'plotting' against the life of the Crown Prince. Meanwhile, in this highly charged atmosphere, preparations for the country's first local and municipal elections were under way. Sensing, perhaps, that the results were not going to turn out to his liking (106), the King dismissed the Ibrahim cabinet on 20 May 1960, and took over effective control himself, appointing the Crown Prince as 'deputy' Prime Minister, claiming that circumstances made it impossible to constitute a truly representative government, and also promising a constitution, and a referendum upon it, by the end of 1962 (107). Until this point, the monarchy had 'always maintained the fiction of its neutrality; now, for the first time, it moved to the front of the political stage' (108). This step has so far proved to have been irrevocable; apart from the brief period of constitutional government between 1963 and 1965, the monarchy has continued to rule, as well as reign over, Morocco. The results of the elections at the end of May 1960 showed that the King's fears of the increasing popularity of the parties was well founded; the newly formed UNFP secured 23 per cent of the vote (including overall control of the municipalities of Casablanca, Rabat, Kenitra, Tanger, Safi and the rural communes in the Souss), the Istiqlal 40 per cent, the Mouvement Populaire 7 per cent, and independents, or loyalists, only 30 per cent (109).

THE 'CONSTITUTIONAL EXPERIMENT' 1961-1963

It is a considerable tribute to the tenacity with which Muhammad V had established, or re-established, the position of the monarchy, and to the veneration in which the office itself was traditionally held in Morocco, that his sudden and early death in February 1961, at the age of 50, while occasioning profound national grief, did not cause a crisis, and that the succession of his son Hassan II, then aged 32, proceeded smoothly. Hassan continued to govern the country directly, but pledged his determination to carry out his father's promise to promulgate a constitution (110). The threat from the UNFP, the only political formation to offer any serious challenge to the propriety of the status quo, had been somewhat blunted by a series of disagreements between the party and its labour wing, the UMT, and the Istiqlal's establishment of a rival organisation, the *Union Générale des Travailleurs Marocains.*

Hassan refused to accept UNFP participation in government, and chose his first cabinet from the Istiqlal and the Mouvement Populaire. In the face of this affront the UNFP called for a boycott of the constitutional referendum in 1962, but it could no longer carry the UMT with it, and this, together with an astute campaign conducted by Hassan's Richelieu, Ahmed Rida Guédira, who was Minister of Interior and of Agriculture, ensured the overwhelming acceptance of the new constitution. Immediately after the referendum, the Istiqlal cabinet ministers, who had campaigned vigorously for the constitution, were surprised and insulted to find themselves demoted to minor posts; this obvious affront caused the Istiqlal to enter the forthcoming elections in opposition to the government (111). The party's 'Manifesto for Economic Liberation', published in January 1963, is an interesting expression of the change of direction which the new circumstances had forced upon it, and its appeal to those holding UNFP sentiments is unmistakeable; the Manifesto called for an

> equitable division of the national revenue...the purpose of this is to lead the country out of underdevelopment and to construct a classless society where social justice reigns... the Istiqlal Party realises that these developments and trends will not be possible unless Morocco achieves economic independence, which implies the liberation of the country's economy from the mortgage of the consequences of colonialism.

The manifesto called for the nationalisation of credit, insurance, energy, transport, mines and basic industries, and urged that the land shall be given 'to those who work it' (112).

It goes without saying that the King had no intention of allowing either of the 'ideological' parties to gain power. Working through Guédira, he set up a 'monarchist', or apolitical party, the *Front pour la Défense des Institutions Constitutionelles* (FDIC), a coalition of loyalists who were joined by the Mouvement Populaire. The situation was further complicated for the 'political' parties by the fact that the King decided to announce the elections, to be held on 17 May 1963, on 18 April, allowing them the minimum legal period to prepare for the campaign. The Istiqlal accused the FDIC of being 'un nouveau parti du Glaoui en service du néo-colonialisme'; 'Allal al-Fassi referred to the necessity for 'une nouvelle bataille de la libération', but, after a fashion, the tactic worked, in that the FDIC and the MP secured 69 seats in the new Assembly, against 41 for the Istiqlal and 28 for the UNFP (113).

The FDIC, the *Parti Socialiste Démocratique*, another Guédira-inspired grouping which appeared in 1964, and the more recent *Rassemblement National des Indépendants* can be seen as coalitions of the 'real' Moroccan ruling class; the landowners, senior civil servants, technocrats and businessmen from Rabat-Salé and Marrakech, the modern, western-educated bourgeoisie, which was and is the mainstay of the monarchy, and whose presence round the throne is in direct proportion to its capacity to keep others out. This group profits enormously from its position in such matters as contracts and land purchases, but it is also faced with the uncomfortable truth that major structural changes are almost bound to be required, particularly in the economy, if the country is to be able to develop at a speed which will keep pace both with rapid population growth and the rising expectations of those whom it has generally managed to exclude from the political system. If these reforms are not undertaken, the possibility of some form of violent rebellion is always going to be present, although, again, this threat has generally been contained by such diversions as the war in the Sahara. Hence the 'independents' and their allies tend to take refuge under the wings of the monarchy.

preferring the certainties of a form of immobilism to the uncharted waters of change. However, as more recent events have shown, this elite has difficulty in maintaining its unity, since its political and economic philosophies range from the 'enlightened despotism' of the planner/technocrat via the laisser-faire of the comprador bourgeoisie to the intense conservatism of the Mouvement Populaire (114). In 1963, the election results also indicated that while the supporters of the throne could be called out to validate a referendum of the *'Faites respecter votre Oui'* kind (115), the throne could not be assured of victory in a free electoral contest between 'political' and loyalist parties (116).

In the next two years, the so-called 'Constitutional Experiment', reflected some of the major tensions in the political situation. Repression of the UNFP increased severely, particularly after July 1963 when another alleged plot against the state was discovered; three of those implicated, Muhammad al-Basri, Mehdi Ben Barka and Hamid Berrada (then Secretary General of the student union, UNEM), left the country secretly and began a campaign of denunciation of the monarchy in a number of Arab and European capitals. At the beginning of 1964 there were waves of strikes in all higher educational institutions; in March 1964, several of those inculpated in the 'plot' of the previous July were condemned to death, including Muhammad Al-Basri *in absentia*. At the end of June an 'attempted invasion' of Moroccan guerrillas from Algeria was foiled by the authorities, and the participants swiftly executed. In March 1965 Ben Barka was also condemned to death in absentia, for fomenting illegal opposition; demonstrations of students and unemployed workers in Casablanca against the government's (that is the crown's) apparent inability to cope with the deteriorating economic situation and widespread bureaucratic corruption turned into bloody riots, brutally repressed by the security forces, and according to some sources over 200 people were killed (117). In June, after several ineffectual attempts to persuade the political parties to join him in government on terms which they could not possibly accept, Hassan declared a state of emergency, and took full powers into his own hands (118). The whole constitutional episode illustrates the contradictions inherent in the coexistence of a parliamentary system with a more or less unreconstructed absolute monarchy (119).

DIRECT RULE FROM THE THRONE: THE FIRST PHASE, 1965-1974

At least for the next five years, formal political life remained at a virtual standstill. In October 1965 Ben Barka disappeared in Paris in circumstances which have never been satisfactorily explained, an episode in which the regime's strong man, General Oufkir, was clearly implicated. Although he had lived outside the country for some time, and was always something of a political maverick, Ben Barka remained the symbol of the most serious challenge to the continuation of the monarchy in the form that it had to come to assume. For Hassan II, the news of his removal from the scene at a time when the popularity of the regime was at a particularly low ebb, cannot have been entirely unwelcome, perhaps a modern 'Murder in the Cathedral'. The affair caused a temporary rupture in Franco-Moroccan relations, since neither Oufkir nor Colonel Dlimi appeared in court in Paris to answer the charges against them.

Meanwhile, the economy continued to stagnate, since no fresh initiatives were taken to reduce the country's heavy dependence on trade with France or to regenerate agriculture. In 1966 the average standard of living fell by 7.5 per cent, while the population continued to rise inexorably. In 1967, it was estimated that about 85 per cent of the country's 14 million inhabitants gained their livelihood in the 'traditonal' sector of the economy, and that two-thirds of those in the 'modern' sector (workers in small factories, wage-earners and lower grade civil servants) were only marginally integrated into it (120). A study by two economists in 1970 concluded, that:

> the extent of the transformations which have taken place in Moroccan economy and society since independence reveal that there has been no fundamental change in the structure of the economy and its external relations. Rather, they indicate that a part of national revenue and national capital - which used to be under foreign control - has now passed into the hands of Moroccan nationals, as a result of the Moroccanisation of the administration and certain sectors of the economy (121).

The author of a wide-ranging socio-geographical study of Rabat concluded that in 1970, the city was:

> suffering from the kind of urban economic involution that we have come to consider 'classical' in third world cities ...the combination of capital city, which by definition implies heavy emphasis on service and administrative occupations, and the complete abortion of the movement towards industrialisation, left the city without a generative economic base (122).

In August 1969, it was announced that local and municipal elections would be held in October. This seems to have been an attempt on the King's part to see how far his efforts to depoliticise public life had been successful, since the vigorous interference of the government on behalf of its own nominees made it almost impossible to draw any meaningful conclusions from the results. 'Non-political' candidates gained 82 per cent of the votes, the Mouvement Populaire 12 per cent, with the Istiqlal and the UNFP sharing the remaining 6 per cent, amply demonstrating the *'caractère superficiel du jeu politique'* (123). *'Le fiction démocratique'* (124) was taken to even more absurd lengths in July 1970, when a referendum on a new constitution was held: although both the Istiqlal and the UNFP instructed their supporters to say 'no', they had no access to the media (because of the state of emergency), and the new constitution was accepted by 98.7 per cent of those who voted. Four weeks later, national elections were held in which 219 of the 240 deputies elected declared themselves supporters of the government. Perhaps rather more significantly, the Istiqlal and the UNFP decided to establish a National (opposition) Bloc in August 1970.

Until 1971, political life continued in a state of suspended animation. In contrast to the situation in most other Arab countries, there had been no post-independence revolution in Morocco, partly because of the peculiar circustances in which independence had been achieved, and partly, as will have become evident, because of the monarch's consummate skill in ensuring that no such development took place. It is significant too that both the attempted coups, when they came in July 1971 and August 1972, can be traced to the disaffected right rather than the revolutionary left, since both were organised from within the armed forces whose loyalty to the throne had always been taken for granted (125).

Early in 1971, a major political trial of some 180 UNFP members began, on self-evidently trumped up charges of endangering the security of the state. The trial ended after the Skhirat coup in July; the comparative leniency of the verdicts seemed to indicate an attempt on the part of the authorities to mollify the political parties and there were reports of renewed contacts between the king and the leaders of both the UNFP and the Istiqlal (126). In addition, following revelations of a major scandal involving widespread corruption in high places, another trial began in Marrakech in November; although this was somewhat overshadowed by the Kenitra coup attempt the following summer, the fact that it took place at all served as further evidence of the king's apparently serious intention to reform some of the more outstanding abuses which the system had encouraged.

The two coup attempts clearly shook Hassan and his entourage, especially the extent to which highly placed officers and officials, notably the sinister Oufkir, were involved. In spite of this, no major changes in political style followed; it seemed that the king had in some sense become the prisoner of the 'tradition' which he and his father had created, and could not bring himself to relax his grip on the reins of power. Another constitution had been announced in 1972 before the Kenitra coup, but once more the terms proved neither attractive nor even remotely acceptable to the political parties.

By early 1973, however, there was a perceptible change of atmosphere. Two major economic reforms were introduced, presumably with the intention of taking some of the wind out of the sails of the opposition. First, those lands still remaining in the hands of foreigners – some 260,000 ha – were to be appropriated by the state and then to be distributed to small farmers. In a similar vein, all major businesses were to be 51 per cent Moroccanised. Both measures were clear attempts to broaden the base of the regime's support, as will be described below.

In March 1973 a new plot was discovered. This time, armed militants of the UNFP, allegedly under the direction of Muhammad al-Basri, now apparently at the court of Colonel Qadhafi, had invaded the country across the Algerian border and had regrouped in the Middle and High Atlas in an attempt to foment an insurrection. At first the government denied that anything irregular had taken place, but then seems to have realised the propaganda value that could be extracted from the incident. A wave of arrests of UNFP members followed, on the grounds that they were still loyal to al-Basri, and the Rabat branch of the UNFP was suspended. In the course of the trials which followed, allegations of police brutality and torture were almost routine, but an important feature of the proceedings was the role played by the Rabat branch secretary, Abderrahman Bouabid, who seems to have been determined to disassociate his own members from the subversive and revolutionary image which the authorities were casting for the UNFP as a whole. Eventually, after two separate sets of trials, 22 of the accused were executed for their part in the plot.

The long term importance of this event lies in the fact that it caused a final split in the UNFP. Bouabid and those who may be called the moderates left to form the *Union Socialiste des Forces Populaires*, (USFP), while Abdullah Ibrahim stayed in command of the more militant, or at least more uncompromising, left. As future events were to show, this represented the division between those who were, and those who were not, prepared to play the political game according to the rules and within the parameters set by the king, and to a certain extent resolved the paradoxes and contradictions which had always surrounded the UNFP since its foundation in 1959, in that it institutionalised the two tendencies once and for all.

In spite of their wide ranging nature, the essential inadequacy of the economic measures of 1973 soon became apparent, particularly after the poor harvests of 1974, which also coincided with the beginning of the world oil price rise. The rate of inflation, and thus prices of basic essentials, began to rise alarmingly, revealing the considerable vulnerability of the economy to outside pressures. By 1074, the combination of political frustration and socio-economic dissatisfaction reached a new peak. In the face of these major challenges, the Sahara issue provided the king with an almost miraculous diversion, an efficacious cement to cover the widening gaps in the fabric of the national consensus that he had somehow managed, however shakily, to preserve.

THE WESTERN SAHARA

The uncertainties over the precise extent of the territory of the Moroccan state derive essentially from the vagueness of the text of the accords of Saint Cloud, the instrument under which Morocco gained its independence from France in March 1956 (127). Since the accords did not define the precise geographical extent of the state, and the Sharifian Empire which had preceded the Protectorate had no internationally recognised frontiers, the possibilities for territorial irredentism were virtually unlimited. As the question of the physical extent of the Moroccan state is inextricably linked to its supposedly theocratic raison d'être, it will be clear that the issue has considerable potential mileage both for 'government' and 'opposition' in the broadest sense: the monarchy could assert that it was pursuing its religio-political duties by extending or simply stating the country's territorial claims, while the opposition could rebuke the monarchy for any suspicion of lukewarmness over the issue and maintain a 'more-legitimist-than-thou' stance simply by extending the area at issue. Hence 'Allal al-Fassi, in part, his biographer confesses, out of naivety and unfamiliarity with the ways of international diplomacy, was particularly vigorous in pressing such demands (128). Thus al-Fassi and the Istiqlal made it their business to claim substantial areas of what were even at the time fairly long established sovereign states as integral parts of Morocco, basing their claims on highly questionable historical evidence. As well as Tarfaya, which was acquired by Morocco in 1958. Moroccan irredenta included Mauritania, the whole of Spanish Sahara, Sidi Ifni, the northern corner of Mali, the western part of the Algerian Sahara and the Spanish presidios of Ceuta and Melilla (129). Needless to say, such demands have been the cause of considerable conflicts with Morocco's neighbours, notably Algeria and Mauritania; Mauritania's existence was only recognised (by the king and not by the Istiqlal) in 1969, ten years after it had become an independent state. In a characteristic speech on the 'stolen territories', Allal al-Fassi stated that 'French neo-colonialism has alienated a part of Moroccan territory which it calls the Islamic Republic of Mauritania'. Even after Ould Daddah and Hassan had been formally reconciled at the Islamic Conference in Rabat in 1969, al-Fassi continued to insist that Moroccan independence had been 'mutilated' and that it was shameful and unworthy of the nation to accept this state of affairs.

More serious, because of the nature of the conflict which it has caused, has been the more acrimonious dispute over the Western Sahara (130). In the late 1880s, Spain occupied much of what later became the Spanish Sahara, placing a small garrison at Villa Cisneros, now Dakhla. As part of the Franco-Spanish agreement of 1904, which was confirmed by the Treaty of Fez, France recognised the area as a zone of Spanish influence. For its part Spain took little serious interest in the area until after the Second World War, although the coastal settlements, like the Spanish presidios in the north, became free ports and thus attracted a relatively considerable volume of trade. As had been noted earlier, Spain played a comparatively restrained role in the independence struggle, apart from showing a certain stubbornness in giving up Tarfaya, which was only ceded to Morocco in 1958.

Spain's renewed interest in the Sahara, which was manifested by considerable infrastructural and welfare investments in the territory in the 1960s, was prompted by the discovery, in 1947, of an enormous vein of phosphate near Bou Craa, estimated to contain some 10,000 million tons. It should be mentioned here that phosphates are Morocco's main source of foreign exchange and that Morocco is the third largest supplier of phosphates in the world, which largely accounts for Moroccan interest in acquiring or 'liberating' the territory. As well as developing the Sahara economically, and building a new capital at al-Aioun, Spain set up a national assembly in 1967 and embarked upon a policy of 'lavish paternalism', which seems to have won fairly widespread support in its early stages from among a largely illiterate population of between 70,000 and 100,000 people, nearly a third of whom lived in the capital. By 1963 a multinational consortium, Fosbucraa, was formed to exploit the phosphates, and the first exports began to leave the territory in 1972.

Until 1970, Spain encountered little serious resistance to her presence from the inhabitants of the Western Sahara, although occasional anti-colonial petitions were submitted to the United Nations. However, in that year violent nationalist demonstrations took place, and the Spanish authorities began to organise their departure in a manner which would be both orderly and conducive to the preservation of their economic interests. In 1974, Spain announced that she was seeking to create an independent state in the area 'under Spanish guidance', but this solution was not acceptable either to Morocco or Mauritania, both of whom claimed parts of the territory as their own. In the autumn of 1974, King Hassan proposed to refer the matter to the Permanent Court of International Justice at The Hague; for its part Spain founded a local pro-Spanish political grouping, but this soon faded into insignificance with the rise of *El Frente por la Liberación de Seguia al-Hamra y Río de Oro, Polisario*, a movement founded in 1973, with its headquarters at Tindouf in the Algerian Sahara. On 16 October 1975, the World Court delivered a judgement worthy of Solomon, stating that the territory had had ties with both Morocco and Mauritania before the Spanish arrived in the late nineteenth century. On the same day, Hassan II announced that the northern part of the territory would be taken over by a vast body of unarmed Moroccans: this was the celebrated Green March, almost a national act of faith, in which some 350,000 Moroccans participated. On November 14 a pact was signed in Madrid, dividing the territory between Morocco and Mauritania and splitting the shares in the Bou Craa mine between Spain and the other two countries. Both the Green March and the Madrid pact were fiercely opposed by Polisario and the Algerian government, who made no secret of their distaste for this kind of neo-colonialism. Relations between Morocco and Algeria, which had always been difficult, deteriorated rapidly; the Moroccans occupied Dakhla in January 1976, and the southern part of the territory, Tiris al-Gharbia, was 'absorbed' into Mauritania. On 28 February, Algeria and a few other states recognised the Sahrawi Arab Democratic Republic. The war in the Sahara has been going on ever since.

POLITICS AND SOCIETY SINCE 1975

For some considerable time, the Saharan issue generally had the effect of diverting the attention of most of the population of Morocco from the more glaring social and political problems of their country (131). The Istiqlal Party, headed by Muhammad Boucetta after 'Allal al-Fassi's sudden death in 1974, immediately threw its weight behind the Green March and the king's policy generally, as did the USFP and the *Parti du Progrès et du Socialisme* (PPS), led by 'Ali Yata. The leaders of all the political parties (with the exception of the UNFP, which no longer participates in the 'conventional' political and parliamentary process) were sent on tours of various parts of the world in an attempt to publicise and gain international support for Morcco's case. The political leaders probably hoped to be able to wrest some concessions from the king in return for their support, although they may also have feared the consequences of being judged to be running against the almost instinctive nationalism of their fellow countrymen if they demurred (132).

By the end of 1974, the 'moderate' wing of the UNFP had finally seceded from the rest of the party to form *L'Union Socialiste des Forces Populaires* under Abderrahman Bouabid. The new party held its inaugural congress at Casablanca in January 1975, and put forward a wide ranging analysis of the political situation, appealing for 'democratic socialism', major structural reforms in the economy, full democratic liberties, a genuinely representative parliament, the nationalisation of the commanding heights of the economy and the introduction of comprehensive economic planning. However, in spite of a certain degree of liberalisation, the hope that the new national consensus might lead to major reforms was not to be fulfilled; what one commentator has called 'le resacralisation de pouvoir', rather than any democratisation, has taken place (133). This may well be because all the political actors have tacitly consented to participate in politics according to ground rules which have been devised and maintained by the king, whose essential feature is that his own supremacy must be assured. Thus, for the politicians, 'although the regime may not win their approval,...their destiny is nevertheless entirely bound up with its own' (134).

Hence in the local elections in 1976, the 'independents' gained 74 per cent of all seats (13,362 out of 17,975) and the Istiqlal 14 per cent, with the remaining 12 per cent being shared among the USFP, the MP, the UMT and PPS (135). A similar pattern emerged in the elections to the Chamber of Deputies in June 1977, in which the 'independents' gained 141 out of 264 seats, the Istiqlal 51, the Mouvement Populaire 44, the UMT 7, the remaining 6 being shared by three smaller parties including 2 to the PPS (136). Immediately after the elections the Istiqlal consented to join the government: Boucetta was made Minister of Foreign Affairs and Laraki Minister of Education. This effectively left the USFP and the PPS as the sole 'opposition' parties.

Meanwhile, and indeed until the present time, the war in the Sahara continues. In 1977, defence costs absorbed over 30 per cent of the budget; economic growth stood at 0.8 per cent, partly because of poor harvests but also because of a combination of the strains of the war, higher oil prices and mounting food deficits. The price of phosphates continues to stagnate, with the result that although the amount of exports increased by 7.6 per cent, their value dropped by 5.4 per cent (137). In the south, Polisario managed to contain the Moroccan army and ambush its units in Mauritania, as well as launching a daring raid on Nouakchott in July 1977. In general, Mauritania's economic vulnerability proved a major constraint on her effective participation in the conflict; this was effectively terminated after a coup in August 1978 and a truce with Polisario a year later, in which Mauritania renounced its claim to Tiris al-Gharbia.

In spite of the material and moral costs of the war, the political parties in Morocco have shown no sign of softening their attitudes. Whether this is due to genuine conviction, or whether they have in fact simply manoeuvred themselves into a cul-de-sac from which only victory or defeat will deliver them, is a matter for speculation. In 1978, the Istiqlal and USFP party congresses reaffirmed their determination to stand by Moroccan national rights in the Sahara; the USFP ridiculed the notion of a Saharan 'people' or 'state', and vowed 'à ne pas ceder le moindre arpent' (138). The grave economic consequences of this intransigence were substantial with enormous rises in the cost of living in 1978 and an increase in the country's trade deficit forcing Morocco to introduce major austerity measures. These produced waves of strikes in April and May 1978, but in addition seemed to act as a brake on almost all levels of economic activity; commentators noted the gradual emergence of a widening fissure between the economic powerholders associated with the palace and the 'modernising bourgeoisie', whose attempts to realise their own development potential were being constantly frustrated by the regime's policies. Thus:

> La politique économique poursuivie a freiné la croissance des forces productives sans, pour autant, entraîner une stabilisation réelle. Les politiques sectorielles reproduisent la structure déséquilibrée du forces productives. Les sources de financement internes se tarissent et incitent à l'endettement extérieur. Les distortions sociales se renforcent par le fonctionnnement à rebours les transferts sociaux. L'inflation devient un mode regulateur de l'économie... (139)

Although there has been no sign of any fracturing of the national consensus on the Sahara, the hardships which have been forced upon the country have occasioned mounting opposition. A number of strikes took place in the winter of 1978-79 and the spring of 1979; textile, banking, dock and railway employees, as well as some 60,000 teachers, all came out for higher wages, and managed to organise demonstrations which were dispersed with considerable brutality. In response to these demands, industrial and agricultural minimum wages were raised by 30 per cent and 40 per cent respectively on 1 May 1979, but these gains were very quickly cancelled out by huge rises in the costs of basic foodstuffs later in the year and in 1980. By the end of 1979, Morocco's diplomatic isolation was further emphasised by an overwhelming vote in the United Nations calling on Morocco to end its attempts to occupy the Sahara and demanding the recognition of Polisario as the representative of the 'people of the Sahara' (140).

In an attempt to break out of this isolation, the King and his ministers made a further series of efforts to rally their remaining friends in the outside world to more vigorous support for the Moroccan cause. Thus in February 1980, Hassan paid a state visit to Saudi

Arabia, in the course of which he obtained a $235 million loan; in his speech from the throne in March the same year he depicted the Saharan issue as part of a world-wide policy of destabilisation and disruption, of which events in Zaire, Tunisia, Mecca and Afghanistan were further examples. However, such efforts were not particularly successful, since, in the Arab world only Saudi Arabia and Iraq (141) declared their outright support for Morocco. In Africa, a majority of the members of the Organisation of African Unity (OAU) had come to recognise Polisario by 1980 (142), and in 1981 this diplomatic defeat for Morocco was heightened by military losses during a successful Polisario attack on Guelta Zemmour. Under pressure from the US, Morocco agreed to a referendum on the future of the Western Sahara, although a timetable has yet to be announced, and at the same time launched a new diplomatic initiative. The admission of the Sahrawi Arab Democratic Republic to the OAU led to a boycott by Morocco of the OAU meeting in Tripoli in August 1982. Morocco succeeded in securing the support of 18 other African states which refused to attend the meeting, thus making it inquorate. Under President Reagan the USA increased military assistance to Morocco and in May 1982 the US Airforce was offered transit facilities in Morocco. King Hassan undoubtedly benefited politically from the success of the twelfth Arab Summit held in Fez in September 1982. By the end of 1982 Morocco had strengthened its international diplomatic position concerning the Western Sahara, and in February 1983 King Hassan and President Chadli of Algeria met to begin negotiations on the Saharan issue. At long last there are some signs that Morocco and Algeria are seeking a compromise solution to the dispute.

Although the Moroccan government's handling of the Saharan issue seems to have evoked little, if any, opposition within the country itself, the costs of the conflict, in both human and economic terms, have exacerbated many of the contradictions inherent in Moroccan society. Whatever political capital the regime may once have been able to make from the war has now been exhausted, and it seems imperative that it should be brought to an end. The government's main problem will be to find a suitably face-saving formula to enable it to cloak its retreat from the Sahara with some semblance of dignity. The following section is an attempt to relate recent political developments to the changing fortunes of the Moroccan economy between 1956 and the early 1960s.

THE MOROCCAN ECONOMY SINCE INDEPENDENCE

By the time the country became independent in 1956, the Moroccan economy had already begun to pass through a period of decline and stagnation. Investment had fallen to about 12 per cent of GNP (143), and remained at this level until 1962. In the latter years of the Protectorate, as mentioned earlier, foreign capital had begun to leave the country, and this process continued during the uncertainties of the immediately post-independence years. The economic policies pursued during these years represent a continuation of trends in the late 1940s and early 1950s, in the general direction of laisser-faire and non-intervention.

Even when the outflow of capital began to act as a serious drain on the economy, the government did nothing to stop it (144). Instead, it chose to increase taxation to sustain both the outflow and the rising cost of the administration. Income from taxation actually produced a surplus, which was deposited abroad, and the substantial foreign reserves thus accumulated enabled the government to continue along the same path until 1964, when the folly of the previous policies began to take deeper effect, and it was forced to liquidate its foreign assets to finance current deficits.

Ironically, economic stagnation, the contraction of imports (145), and the decline in purchasing power had kept the balance of payments in equilibrium for many years, and this too enabled the government to ignore the deterioration which was taking place. Hence it managed to muddle along until 1964, when it was forced to introduce an austerity programme and exchange controls (146). However, the more interventionist policies of the kind advocated by the UNFP in 1959-60, and its Five Year Plan for the quinquennium 1960 to 1964, were rejected by all subsequent governments. In very general terms, the social and economic policies promoted by almost all post-independence governments have tended to operate primarily in the interests of the old loyalist strata in Moroccan society, particularly merchants, landowners and manufacturers, which like those of the monarchy itself, lay in the maintenance and perpetuation of the economic and social structures inherited from the protectorate. This group also became the main beneficiary of the Moroccanisation programmes introduced in later years, acquiring the businesses, hotels, restaurants and above all land sold by French colons over the years, earning themselves the soubriquet 'Moroccan colons' in contemporary political writing. Between 1956 and 1965 alone some 500,000 ha were bought by Moroccans, mainly tribal shaikhs, bureaucrats and members of the royal family (147).

The sale of colon land had begun long before independence, so that while the settlers owned approximately one million ha in 1950, this figure had fallen to some 646,000 ha in 1956. Sales and transfers continued until 1973, by which time the area remaining was less than 260,000 ha. Moreover, the government itself contributed directly to the process of private appropriation; between 1963 and 1965 it took over nearly a quarter of a million ha of *domaine privé*, which was initially to be managed by a state company, SOGEA, but which was in fact sold privately on very favourable terms in 1966. Although this land was supposed to have been distributed to peasant communities, the actual beneficiaries were the top 15-20 per cent of rural households. Over the period between 1956 and 1972, 11,101 individuals obtained 181,197 ha in this way; only one per cent of these had previously owned less than two ha (148). In fact, it 'was not until 1973, 17 years after independence, that the government, in a desperate attempt to increase its popularity after the abortive army coup in 1972, finally nationalised the remaining 300,000 ha of foreign owned land' (149). Part of this land was allocated to peasants, who were regrouped into commercial cooperatives, while the rest was to be managed by the two state corporations SODEA and SOGETA (150). In spite of these more thorough-going attempts at wider distribution, a very high proportion of the rural population still has insufficient land for its own subsistence, and most rural households have holdings of less than four ha (151).

Naturally, conditions vary considerably from region to region. In the fertile Sebou Basin for instance, 31 per cent of households owned no land at all in 1972, a further 31 per cent owned less than 2 ha and 21 per cent owned between 2 and 4.99 ha. In other words, at least four fifths of households in the area either had no land at all or insufficient land for their own subsistence. At the other end of the scale, less than one per cent of households owned holdings of more than 500 ha, or just over 36 per cent of all available cultivable land (152). Landlessness was equally pronounced elsewhere in the Gharb away from the irrigated perimeter; here 92 per cent of all households owned less than 8 ha, 10 ha being the minimum viable dry-farming holding, while one per cent of households own 58 per cent of cultivable land (153). The high degree of social differentiation and inequality which characterises rural Morocco is also reflected in the fact that agro-businesses in the Gharb own over 30 per cent of the land, while the owners of such businesses account for less than a quarter of one per cent of this population. Most of the landless population work as share croppers, *khammès*, or shepherds, or as permanent seasonal wage labourers (154). Although most of these figures refer to the period 1972 to 1973, there is little evidence to suggest that the situation has changed substantially in the last ten years. Thus a high proportion of rural households have very little agricultural income and eke out a living from wage labour, traditional artisan crafts, and, most importantly, remittances from family members living abroad (155).

Another important feature of Moroccan agriculture is the almost absolute division into a modern capitalist sector and a traditional sector (156). Out of a total cultivable area of about seven million ha, only one million (the former *Maroc utile*) are worked with modern machinery and modern production methods, producing 85 per cent of the country's cash crops (157). The remaining land is worked in the traditional way with primitive equipment, much of its produce never reaching the market as it constitutes all or most of the food consumption of poor peasant households (158). However, the very low and uncertain income of peasant households does not mean that the countryside is totally excluded from the domestic market. The landlessness and poverty which we have already mentioned results in many peasants being unable to engage in subsistence cultivation, and hence being forced to buy their food and other requirements. Nevertheless, the low and fluctuating income of the bulk of the rural population acts as a severe constraint to the penetration of market relations into these regions. As Wilfred Knapp comments 'The picture of the *bour* (dry-farming area), with its 40 per cent landless...or its estimated 70 per cent owning 2 ha or less, is a daunting one' (159).

In general, the dual character of Moroccan agriculture, together with a highly unequal structure of landownership constitutes a serious obstacle to the development of more coordination and integration in agriculture and thus in the economy as a whole. Despite the urgent need for a more radical agrarian reform, the monarchy's activities in this direction have always been confined to policies which have avoided transforming existing property relations, with the result that 'traditional' social structures in the countryside have survived largely unscathed (160). Hence agrarian reform has been confined primarily to efforts to improve agricultural productivity, through the construction of large hydro-electric schemes and the provision of credit facilities for large landowners. Much progress has been made in this respect, and the agricultural sector has received priority in government planning in the years since independence. Most of the investment undertaken, however, has gone to the modern sector, that is, the irrigated commercial sector, while comparatively little has found its way to the traditional cereal lands, representing about 85 per cent of the cultivated area, where the majority of the rural population lives. Given the existing structures of landownership, it is clear that these infrastructural investments have tended to benefit the already privileged owners of agro-businesses and large and medium landowners, while a 'poor and unemployed peasantry hungry for land continues to wait for social justice' (161).

As well as making the rich in the modern agricultural sector richer, the construction of barrages and new irrigation schemes has also reinforced the dualism already mentioned (162). The majority of rural producers continues to be completely dependent on the vagaries of the weather, and frequent crop failures due to bad harvests have had devastating effects on the country's food supplies. Dependence on food imports has been further aggravated by the failure of the reform and modernisation programmes to direct agricultural production away from 'luxury' cash crops, such as early vegetables, grapes and citrus fruit, to basic foodstuffs. In fact, the continuing subordination of agricultural production to the private interests of agro-business, coupled with the promotion of export cash crops, has led to stagnation in grain production (163), and thus inevitably to even higher food imports to feed a population of over 20 million (164). Between 1974 and 1980, for example, the cost of wheat imports alone rose from DH 587 million to DH 973 million (165).

In these circumstances, the general lack of prospects and growing poverty among the rural population have encouraged many either to seek employment in the overcrowded cities or to migrate abroad; as the official rate of unemployment in the cities is 14-16 per cent, the attraction of working abroad is hardly surprising (166). Government planning itself has placed great emphasis on migration, and remittances have come to play a central role in the economy, comparable only with that of phosphates. In 1979, when the international market for Moroccan labour had already begun to contract, some 530,000 Moroccans were working abroad, 300,000 in France alone (167), and income from remittances had risen from DH 200 million in 1968 to DH 2,417 million in 1976, and to DH 3,600 million in 1979. In comparison phosphate earnings fluctuated between DH 2,836 million in 1976 and DH 2,034 million in 1979, while tourism brought in DH 1,650 million in 1979 (168).

As food imports - particularly of cereals, sugar and vegetable oils - have increased substantially in both volume and cost over recent years, the standard of living would have deteriorated even further had the government not decided to subsidise basic foodstuffs (169). However, despite the fact that food subsidies cost the government DH 977 million in 1974 and DH 2,000 million in 1981, food prices have continued to rise inexorably over the past decade (170).

Industry
Until 1973, the government concentrated most of its efforts on extensive public works programmes, and had left manufacturing industry almost entirely in the hands of the private capital. Manufacturing industry today still contributes less than 20 per cent of GNP, and most existing factories were established in the years shortly after the Second World War. Apart from food processing and the production of relatively unsophisticated consumer goods for the domestic market, Moroccan industry is primarily involved in import substitution, which accounts for about 63 per cent of all industrial production. The overall linkages between this sphere of the Moroccan economy and foreign capital are difficult to determine, as the necessary data is not available. However, as almost all the components required have to be imported, the indigenous contribution is fairly minimal. The extent of association with foreign capital can be seen from the names involved; for example, in the vehicle industry, Fiat, Chrysler-Simca, Opel and Austin produced 24,500 cars in 1975, and Berliet, Volvo, Mercedes and Fiat produced 5,000 trucks in the same year (171). The Moroccanisation laws of 1973 stipulated that the amount of foreign investment in any one enterprise must not exceed 50 per cent, but the actual scale of foreign investment is difficult to determine with any accuracy; Eikenberg estimates that it forms at least 41 per cent of all 'known' investment, and suggests that the true figure is probably much higher (172).

Overall, Moroccan industry grew steadily in the 1970s; the index of industrial production rose from 100 in 1969 to 132 in 1974, and to 170 in 1979, albeit from a very low original base line. Much of the manufacturing sector is sensitive to fluctuations in supplies of raw materials, particularly from agriculture, and as it is primarily directed towards the domestic market it is also vulnerable to the fluctuations in and the limitations upon the purchasing power of the population, with the result that it is often forced to work at as much as 50 per cent below capacity for long periods.

In the early 1970s, partly to stimulate the economy, and partly out of a desire to widen his social base, the king began to adopt some of the measures for which the opposition parties had been campaigning. The non-interventionist stance was tacitly abandoned, and the state became gradually involved in most of the main sectors of the economy (173). As is generally characteristic of such state involvement in Third World countries, the government concentrated on building up those basic capital intensive industries which require a higher investment than indigenous private capital is able or willing to invest. Hence the state controls all of *Maroc Chimie*, the iron and steel complex at Nador, most oil and sugar refining, and about half of all cement production and car assembly (174). In contrast, private capital dominates in light industry, notably textiles, plastics, electrical manufacture and food processing (175), although, again, the electrical and mechanical industries are largely engaged in assembling imported components. In general, private capital prefers short-term projects, and apart from commerce, light industry and construction is largely invested in traditional manufacture. While industry employed 163,900 in 1971, the traditional sector, *artisanat* and small workshops, employed about a quarter of a million (176).

Apart from a small minority of wealthy owners, who control most of the artisanat, the artisans generally live in miserable conditions and are totally dependent on their employers with regard to wages and working hours (177). Again the picture in Morocco seems very typical of many Third World countries; the state invests in capital intensive basic industries which do not usually generate very high employment, but is unable to stimulate a comprehensive or integrated take-off of industry. Thus there is a proliferation of small workshops and businesses, which although easing some of the pressures, are unable to absorb the increasing numbers of those seeking employment (178). Although migration has functioned as a safety valve in the past, the recession in the EEC means that the whole question of employment will become an increasingly crucial factor in Moroccan politics.

As in other spheres, foreign trade has not undergone any fundamental transformation since independence. Phosphates continue to be the main currency earner, and the government has devoted considerable efforts to increasing production. As we have seen, the whole issue of the Western Sahara is closely linked with Morocco's phosphates (179). Despite substantial price fluctuations, Morocco has generally maintained its place as the world's third largest producer, although the value of exports fell sharply from DH 3,400 million in 1975 to DH 2,200 million in 1976. This level was continued until 1980, when world prices recovered and exports reached DH 3,000 million (180).

While the cost of essential imports, particularly oil and cereals, has increased very considerably, the overall value of exports has remained low, amounting to DH 6,200 million in 1975 and increasing slightly to DH 7,300 million in 1979. In contrast, imports increased from DH 10,440 million to DH 14,300 million over the same period (181). Thus, as we have seen, the balance of payments has become heavily dependent on transfer payments, especially remittances, as well as aid and loans (182). As a further result, debt service payments are devouring more and more of export earnings, rising from DH 700 million in 1976 to DH 2,500 million in 1980 and an estimated DH 5,000 million in 1983 (183).

Hence, although Morocco has potentially a more favourable base for economic development than many other Third World countries because of its well developed infrastructure, the size of its internal market and its geographical location, this potential has only been exploited to a very limited extent. The monarchy's programmes of agrarian reform and agricultural modernisation have contributed little towards reducing the country's dependence on food imports, agricultural production has generally been subordinated to the economic interests of individual private landowners, and the majority of the rural population have become landless labourers, without access to sufficient land for their own subsistence requirements. In addition, industry continues to play a subordinate role in the economy, and employment in this sector has been unable to keep up with the growth in the size of the labour force. Thus Morocco seems to have become imprisoned within the logic of the economic policies pursued by the monarchy, which have resulted in increased food imports, a substantial and expanding trade deficit, and rising dependence on foreign capital and international financial institutions.

CONCLUSION

Inevitably much of this chapter has been concerned with the development of the role of the monarchy before and after independence. The combination of a number of different factors has helped to ensure that the monarchy has remained the principal, in some sense the only, political institution in the country (184). Through the alliances it has forged, principally with the rural elite but also with the urban comprador bourgeoisie and the technocrats, it has generally managed to keep claims for a more genuinely democratic political process at a safe distance. At times of national crisis, perhaps most notably over the last nine years of fighting in the Sahara, it seems able to retain its legitimacy in the eyes of most of the population. Although it is possible to imagine circumstances under which the monarchy might be destroyed by force, a republican *movement* would make little headway in Morocco; even the leaders of the two coups in 1971 and 1972 wanted to replace Hassan II by another member of his family rather than destroy the institution altogether (185).

For a variety of reasons, the constraints on the political process as a whole have prevented the development of a 'genuine' multi-party system. The Istiqlal, which might in other circumstances have emerged as the 'natural' party of government after independence, was cleverly frustrated in its attempt to play this role by Muhammad V, who rightly recognised it as the most serious challenge to his own authority. After the brief constitutional experiment of the early 1960s, the parameters of the political arena have been clearly delimited; specifically, no party, unless created by the king and his entourage, can be allowed to wield significant power.

Here the experience of the UNFP is instructive. While in government between January 1959 and May 1960, Ibrahim's cabinet put forward a series of radical proposals, notably on the economy, whose implementation would have involved major structural changes, of a kind that would have alienated the monarchy's principal supporters both inside and outside Morocco. Muhammad V found it necessary to intervene personally, making his son deputy Prime Minister. Over the next few years allegedly extremist supporters of the UNFP were rounded up imprisoned and in some cases condemned to death, often after long periods of detention without trial. In the mid 1960's, just before Hassan's declaration of a State of Emergency in 1965, leading UNFP figures were condemned to death *in absentia* and in 1965, Ben Barka, the most dangerous challenge to the throne, was eliminated in Paris. By the early 1970s it was intimated to the surviving UNFP leadership that it would only be able to return to a legal political existence if it confined itself to acting within the limits set by the king. The result was a split in the UNFP ranks, the more moderate opting for 'respectability' with Abderrahim Bouabid in the USFP, while the more radical remained with Abdullah Ibrahim and thus outside the *'jeu politique'*. At the same time, however, Hassan introduced a major reform programme, including agrarian reforms and the 'Moroccanisation' laws, both of which had been major planks in the UNFP platform.

Part of the reason for the apparent immutability of this system undoubtedly lies in the monarch's position as *grand patron*, the nexus of a complex system of informal clientage extending into all aspects of public life (186). Perhaps equally important has been the monarchy's evident capacity for flexibility, the combination of intimidation and bounty, repression and liberalisation. Above all, however, as we have suggested at the beginning, it seems that the monarch's deft manipulation of his theocratic and traditionally validated role is the main key to the survival of the monarchy as an institution. Although events in other parts of the Islamic world have undoubtedly had echoes in Morocco (187), Hassan II's success in presenting himself as the religious leader of the nation and the leading defender of its traditional territorial prerogatives has made the task of any 'full-blooded' opposition a daunting one.

NOTES AND REFERENCES

1. Albert Hourani, Arabic Thought in the Liberal Age 1978-1939 (London, 1970) p.8.
2. For further details of the genealogy of the Sharifian dynasty, see C.E. Bosworth, Islamic Dynasties, (Edinburgh, 1967), pp.38-40.
3. Rémy Leveau, Le Fellah Marocain, Défenseur du Trône (Paris, 1976), p.84:- 'le type idéal du parc national berbère évoqué par Jacques Berque'; cf. Jacques Berque, French North Africa: The Maghrib Between Two World Wars, trs. Jean Stewart, (London, 1967), pp.123, 219.
4. cf. Tunisia, where 'the logical outcome of the Neo-Destour victory was the abolition of the monarchy'; Jamil Abun-Nasr, A History of the Maghrib (Cambridge 1973), p.354. The constituent assembly abolished the monarchy on 25 July 1957.
5. Charles-André Julien, History of North Africa from the Arab Conquest to 1830, trs. J. Petrie, ed. C.C. Stewart, (London, 1970), which has a very full bibliography (pp.353-321).
6. See Lucette Valensi, On the Eve of Colonialism : North Africa before the French Conquest, 1790-1830, trs. K.J. Perkins, (New York, 1977) passim; and 'at the death of Mulay Sliman (1822) Morocco

was taking virtually no part in the economic life of a world where commercial exchanges were developing with increasing speed'. Julien, History of North Africa, p.270.

7. John Waterbury, The Commander of the Faithful; the Moroccan Political Elite (London, 1970), p.69.

8. Charles-André Julien, Le Maroc Face aux Impérialismes 1415-1956, (Paris, 1978), p.98; G. Ayache, 'La Fonction d'arbitrage du Makhzen', in Actes de Durham: Recherches Récentes sur le Maroc Moderne (public- du Bulletin Economique et Social du Maroc, Rabat, 1979), pp. 5-22.

9. Julien, Le Maroc Face aux Impérialismes., pp.95-128. For two classic statements of the colonial case, see H. Terrasse, Histoire du Maroc des Origines à l'Etablissement du Protectorat Français, (2 vols. Casablanca, 1949-50), and Robert Montagne, Les Berbères et le Makhzen dans le Sud du Maroc; essai sur la Transformation Politique des Berbères Sédentaires (Paris, 1930). For the way in which the theory was used, see Germain Ayache, 'Histoire et Colonisation; l'Exemple du Maroc', Hespéris-Tamuda, vol.17, (1976-77), pp.47-67.

10. The period 1830-1912 is summarised in Abun-Nasr, History of the Maghrib, pp.284-303; the standard European source is Jean-Louis Miège, Le Maroc et l'Europe 1830-1894 (4 vols, Paris 1961-63).

11. Abun-Nasr, History of the Maghrib, p.288.

12. In 1858, imports at Essaouira, the port of Marrakech, consisted mainly of cotton and other textiles; British imports, some 82 per cent of the total, were valued at £268,102. Exports, also mainly to Britain or 'British ports' (presumably mostly Gibraltar), were largely olive oil, almonds, goatskins, gum, sheepskins, beeswax, and wool. Consul Elton, Mogador, to Consul-General Drummond Hay, Tangier, No.8, February 1858: FO 830/2.

13. J. Brignon et al., Histoire du Maroc (Paris and Casablanca, 1967), pp.293-313; André Adam, Histoire de Casablanca (des Origines à 1914), (Aix-en-Provence, 1968).

14. See Edmund Burke III, Prelude to Protectorate in Morocco : Pre-Colonial Protest and Resistance, 1860-1912 (Chicago, 1976), p.30, and Germain Ayache, 'Aspects de la Crise Financière au Maroc après l'Expédition Espagnole de 1860', Revue Historique (1958), pp.271-310.

15. Abdulla Laroui, The History of the Maghrib : an Interpretative Essay, trs. R. Mannheim (Princeton, N.J., 1977), p.325.

16. Ibid., p.322.

17. See Brignon, Histoire du Maroc, pp.314-321.

18. Ibid., p.318.

19. See Bernard Lewis, The Emergence of Modern Turkey (London, 1968), pp.74-128.

20. 'The development of dissidence and widespread rebellions on the eve of the protectorate can be traced directly to colonial intrigue whose purpose was to facilitate the conquest of the country'. Brignon, Histoire du Maroc, p.313.

21. Burke, Prelude to Protectorate, p.45. The following paragraphs are based substantially on Burke's account.

22. For Franco-Spanish relations, see the useful archival and bibliographical guide by V.M. Lezcano, 'Quelques Observations sur le Protectorat Espagnol au Maroc', Revue d'Histoire Maghrébine Nos. 13-14, (1979), pp.95-104, and H. Marchat, 'La France et l'Espagne Pendant la Période du Protectorat (1912-1956)', Revue de l'Occident Musulman vol.10, (1971), pp.81-110.

23. For a full discussion of Germany's role in Morocco, see P. Guillen, L'Allemagne et le Maroc de 1870 à 1905, (Paris, 1967).

24. See Ross Dunn, Resistance in the Desert: Moroccan Responses to French Imperialism 1881-1912, (London and Madison, 1977).

25. For Bu Himara see Ross Dunn, 'Bu Himara's European Connection: the Commercial Relations of a Moroccan Warlord', Journal of African History, vol.21, (1980), pp.215-253.

26. See the useful discussion on baraka and deposition in R. Jamous, Honneur et Baraka: les Structures Sociales Traditionelles dans le Rif (Cambridge and Paris, 1981), p.224.

27. See the photograph in Julien, Le Maroc Face aux Impérialismes, pp.92-93.

28. Ibid., p.90.

29. Burke comments that 'the qa'ids chose to defect at an opportune moment, thereby guaranteeing themselves a prominent place in the new order of Morccan politics that was just beginning', Prelude to Protectorate, p.209.

30. See Janet Abu Lughod, Rabat: Urban Apartheid in Morocco, (Princeton, 1980), p.135: 'It was to Fez's lack of submissiveness that Rabat owed her new destiny'. David Seddon has summarised the conquest of the north in 'Local Politics and State Intervention: North East Morocco from 1870-1970' in Ernest Gellner and Charles Micaud (eds) Arabs and Berbers: from Tribe to Nation in North Africa, (London, 1973), pp.109-139.

31. L.C. Brown, 'The Many Faces of Colonial Rule in French North Africa', Revue de l'Occident Musulman, vol.13-14, (1973), pp.171-191.

32. Robin Bidwell, Morocco under Colonial Rule: French Administration of Tribal Areas 1912-1956, (London, 1973), p.68.

33. 'Décriant la démocratie, il refusait aux Français, et à plus forte raison aux Marocains, les libertés de la presse, de réunion et de participation'. Le Maroc Face aux Impérialismes, p.106.

34. Abu Lughod, Rabat, p.137.

35. For a rather overstated version of this case, see John Halstead, Rebirth of a Nation: the Origins and Rise of Moroccan Nationalism, (Cambridge Mass., 1969), pp.29-31.

36. See Jamous, Honneur et Baraka, p.228, and L.Duclos, 'The Berbers and the Rise of Moroccan Nationalism' in Gellner and Micaud, Arabs and Berbers, pp.217-229.

37. Laroui, History of the Maghrib, p.340.

38. Brignon, Histoire du Maroc, p.345; Leveau, Le Fellah Marocain, passim.

39. cf. Hanna Batatu, The Old Social Classes and Revolutionary Movements of Iraq... (Princeton, 1978), pp.63-152.

40. David Hart, 'The Tribe in Modern Morocco: two Case

Studies', in Gellner and Micaud (eds), Arabs and Berbers, pp.25-58, especially pp.39-41; David Seddon, 'Local Politics and State Intervention' in ibid., pp.109-139.

41. Julien, Le Maroc Face aux Impérialismes, p.99; Bidwell, Morocco under Colonial Rule, Ch.IV.

42. See here Ayache, 'Histoire et Colonisation' (note 9 above); Edmund Burke III, 'La Mission scientifique au Maroc', Actes de Durham; Recherches Récentes sur le Maroc Moderne (Bulletin Economique et Social du Maroc, Rabat, 1979), pp.37-56; 'Our interests oblige us to help the Berbers, evolve outside the framework of Islam' (extract from one of Lyautey's circulars, quote by Halstead, Rebirth of a Nation, p.71.

43. Charles-André Julien, L'Afrique du Nord en Marche, (Paris, 3rd edition, 1972), p.128. The first edition of this powerful indictment of French colonial rule was published in 1952, an act of very considerable courage on its author's part.

44. Halstead, Rebirth of a Nation, p.74; Robert Montagne, Révolution au Maroc, (Paris, 1953), p.186.

45. Julien, Le Maroc Face aux Impérialismes, p.103.

46. Roger Le Tourneau, Evolution Politique de l'Afrique du Nord Musulmane, 1920-1961, (Paris, 1962), pp.192-194.

47. Berque, French North Africa, p.268.

48. Bidwell, Morocco under Colonial Rule, p.253.

49. John Damis, 'The Origins and Significance of the Free School Movement in Morocco, 1919-1931', Revue de l'Occident Musulman, 19 (1975), pp.75-100.

50. Jamil Abun-Nasr, 'The Salafiyya Movement in Morocco: the Religious Base of the Moroccan Nationalist Movement', St. Antony's Papers, no.16 (London, 1963), pp.90-105.

51. Kenneth Brown, 'The Impact of the Dahir Berbère in Salé' in Gellner and Micaud (eds), Arabs and Berbers, pp.201-215.

52. 'La virulence, du combat n'a d'égal que l'acharnement avec lequel les tribus défenderent leurs territoires'; Brignon et al., Histoire du Maroc, p.339. For a scholarly study of the Rif war, see C.R. Pennell, The Opposition of the Rifi Confederation Led by Muhammad bin 'Abd al-Karim al-Khattabi to Spanish Colonial Expansion 1921-1926, unpublished Ph.D. thesis, University of Leeds, 1979; and the same author's 'Ideology and Practical Politics: a Case Study of the Rif War in Morocco, 1921-1926', International Journal of Middle East Studies, 14, (1982), pp.19-33.

53. An interesting eye-witness account of the accession of Muhammad V is given by J. Luccioni, 'L'Avènement de Sidi Mohamed ben Youssef au Trône du Maroc (1927)', Revue de l'Occident Musulman, no.12, (1972), pp.172-179.

54. C.F. Stewart, The Economy of Morocco 1912-1962, (Cambridge, Mass., 1964), pp.60-63.

55. Brignon et al., Histoire du Maroc, p.356; Berque, French North Africa, pp.47-50, 142-144; N. Bouderbala, M. Chraïbi, P. Pascon, La Question Agraire au Maroc, (Publications du Bulletin Economique et Sociale du Maroc, Rabat, 1974), p.12.

56. Halstead, Rebirth of a Nation, p.84.

57. Halstead gives an account of the legal system in Rebirth of a Nation, Chapter V.
58. Brown, 'The Impact of the Dahir Berbère'
59. See Jacqueline Bessis, 'Chekib Arslan et les mouvements nationalistes au Maghreb', Revue Historique, vol.119, no.2, (1978), pp.467-489.
60. Le Tourneau, Evolution Politique, p.202; A. Cohen, 'Allal al-Fassi: his ideas and his Contribution towards Morocco's Independence', Asian and African Studies, no.3, (1967), pp.121-164.
61. Julien, Le Maroc Face aux Impérialismes, pp.187-188.
62. Europeans in Morocco had been granted the right to form trade unions in 1936. For a concise account in English see R.D. Forst, 'The Origins and Development of the Union Marocaine du Travail' International Journal of Middle East Studies, no.7, (1976), pp.271-287.
63. Le Tourneau, Evolution Politique, p.206; Hassan II of Morocco, The Challenge, (trs. Anthony Rhodes), (London, 1978), pp.29-32.
64. For Puaux, see Albert Hourani, Syria and Lebanon: a Political Essay, (London, 1946), pp.225-231.
65. Albert Ayache, Le Maroc, Bilan d'une Colonisation. (Paris, 1956), pp.343-354.
66. Ibid.
67. The French text is given in Claude Palazzoli, Le Maroc Politique: de L'Indépendence à 1973 (Textes), (Paris, 1974), pp.140-142.
68. Douglas E. Ashford, Political Change in Morocco, (Princeton, N.J., 1961), pp.59-60.
69. Hassan II of Morocco, The Challenge, pp.37-38.
70. Le Tourneau, Evolution Politique, pp.219-221; Julien, Le Maroc Face aux Impérialismes, pp.199-201.
71. It is interesting to note that 'Abd al-Krim advised the French to part from the Moroccans as friends; 'vous conserverez alors toutes vos positions'. Julien, L'Afrique du Nord en Marche, p.318.
72. For a convincing description of the rapacity, cruelty and unscrupulousness of al-Kittani and al-Glawi, see Julien, Le Maroc Face aux Impérialismes, pp.222-230.
73. Ashford, Political Change in Morocco, p.69.
74. In general, Spanish policy during this period was considerably less repressive than the French, and although the Spanish were apparently unprepared for France's 'capitulation' in 1956, Spain's relations with the national movement were far less acrimonious than those of France. Furthermore, the Spanish authorities never recognised Ben Arafa as sultan. See Ashford, Political Change in Morocco, pp.51-55.
75. 'The years of relative inertia (until 1950) were succeeded by a period of crisis in which successive (sc. French) governments, caught as they were between the two opposing forces of nationalism and the French settlers, followed a policy which was vacillating and incapable of becoming stabilised. Whereas the official declarations sometimes gave the impression that real autonomy

was in the offing, the government's actions for the future were directed to the concept of an imposed co-sovereignty'. Henri Grimal, Decolonisation, (trs. S. de Vos), (London, 1978), p.341.

76. See Forst, 'Origins and Development of the Union Marocaine du Travail'; Julien, Le Maroc Face aux Impérialismes, pp.261-276.

77. For an opposing view, see Robert Montagne, Révolution au Maroc, (Paris, 1953), pp.231-236.

78. Bidwell, Morocco under Colonial Rule, p.59.

79. Montagne, Révolution, p.250.

80. Attilio Gaudio, Allal el-Fassi ou l'Histoire de l'Istiqlal, (Paris, 1972), pp.253-254, quoting al-Fassi on 20 August 1953, half an hour after the announcement of the sultan's deposition.

81. Julien, Le Maroc Face aux Impérialismes, p.442, quoting Muhammad V's letter to General Catroux of 3 September 1955.

82. Waterbury, Commander of the Faithful, p.205.

83. The text is in Le Tourneau, Evolution Politique, p.247.

84. For the full text, see Palazzoli, Le Maroc Politique, pp.60-63.

85. Le Tourneau, Evolution Politique, p.246.

86. See Bouderbala, Chraibi and Pascon, La Question Agraire au Maroc, p.10. Land purchase by foreigners was authorised by the Madrid Convention (1880) and the Act of Algeciras (1906).

87. See notes 54-55 above, and Stewart, The Economy of Morocco, pp.75-79, and André Adam, 'Maroc: Chronique Sociale et Culturelle', Annuaire de l'Afrique du Nord, 1977, pp.647-658.

88. M. Benhlal, 'Politique des Barrages et Problèmes de la Modernisation Rurale dans le Gharb'; A. Benhadi, 'La Politique Marocaine des Barrages' both in Bruno Etienne (ed), Les Problèmes Agraires au Maghreb, (Paris, 1977), pp.261-274, 275-294.

89. Brignon, Histoire du Maroc, p.354.

90. For an interesting account of French business activities see William Hoisington, 'Commerce and Conflict; French Businessmen in Morocco, 1952-1955,' Journal of Contemporary History, vol.9, no.2 (April 1974), pp.49-68, which is concerned with the career of Lemaigre Dubreuil. See also Réné Gallissot, Le Patronnat européen au Maroc 1931-1942, (Rabat, 1964), and L. Cerych, Européens et Marocains 1930-1956; Sociologie d'une Décolonisation, (Bruges, 1964).

91. The information on the Moroccan economy under the Protectorate is taken from Stewart, The Economy of Morocco, and Samir Amin, The Maghreb in the Modern World, (London, 1970), pp.25-59.

92. For the abolition of the capitulations, see M. Kenbib, 'Protections, Protectorat et Nationalisme 1904-1938', Hespéris-Tamuda, vol.18, (1978-1979), pp.173-198.

93. Amin, The Maghrib in the Modern World, pp.42-43.

94. Stewart, The Economy of Morocco, p.119.

95. J-J. Regnier, 'Monarchie et Forces Politiques au Maroc', in Werner Ruf (ed), Introduction à l'Afrique du Nord Contemporaine, (Paris, 1975), pp.341-359.

96. See the excellent study by Leveau, Le Fellah Marocain, passim, and Jean Claude Vatin, 'Revival in the Maghreb; Islam as an

Alternative Political Language' in A.H. Dessouki (ed), The Politics of Islamic Resurgence. (New York, 1982), pp.221-250.

97. The 'Istiqlalisation' of the local administration in the late 1950s is described in David Hart's paper 'The Tribe in Modern Morocco: two Case Studies' in Gellner and Micaud (eds), Arabs and Berbers. pp.25-58.

98. 'La Nation marocaine n'a pas besoin de multiplier les tendances politiques dans le circonstances actuelles'...Speech of Allal al-Fassi, 18 March 1956, quoted in Palazzoli, Le Maroc Politique. pp.157-158.

99. See Waterbury, Commander of the Faithful, pp.235-238; Ashford, Political Change in Morocco, pp.211-218.

100. See Ernest Gellner, 'Patterns of Tribal Rebellion in Morocco' in P.J. Vatikiotis (ed), Revolution in the Middle East and other case studies. (London, 1972), pp.120-145.

101. A. Coram, 'A Note on the Role of the Berbers in the Early Days of Moroccan Independence', in Gellner and Micaud (eds), Arabs and Berbers. pp.269-276.

102. See above. pp.64-65.

103. The agricultural section of the plan is reproduced in Bouderbala, Chraïbi and Pascon, La Question Agraire au Maroc, pp.59-83; its generally pioneering nature is applauded by H el-Malki, L'Economie Marocaine: Bilan d'une Décennie (1970-1980), (Paris, 1982), p.150; for a fuller assessment, see Samir Amin, L'Economie du Maghreb, vol.II; Les Perspectives d'Avenir, (Paris, 1966), pp.105-152.

104. e.g. Gaudio's statements on p.46 of Allal el Fassi; Waterbury, Commander of the Faithful, pp.169-195.

105. See Palazzoli's useful comments on the UNFP and the selection of key party documents in Le Maroc Politique, pp.229-290.

106. Waterbury, Commander of the Faithful, pp.219-220; cf. the rather misleading account in William Zartman, Government and Politics in Northern Africa. (London, 1963), pp.23-24.

107. Muhammad V's speech is reproduced in Palazzoli, Le Maroc Politique, pp.67-71.

108. Regnier. 'Monarchie et Forces Politiques...', p.347.

109. For further details see Paul Chambergeat, 'The Moroccan Communal Elections', in William Zartman (ed), Man, State and Society in the Contemporary Maghreb. (London, 1973), pp.260-266.

110. Muhammad V had formed a Constitutional Council in 1960; see Jacques Robert, La Monarchie Marocaine. (Paris, 1963), pp.105. ff. Wilfred Knapp notes that all three Moroccan constitutions (1962, 1970 and 1972) contain a clause expressly prohibiting a single party system. North West Africa: a Political and Economic Survey. (London, 1977), p.287.

111. See Stuart Schaar, 'King Hassan's Alternatives', in Zartman (ed), Man, State and Society, pp.229-244.

112. Reproduced in Palazzoli, Le Maroc Politique, pp.142-147.

113. See O. Marais, 'L'Election de la Chambre des Répresentants du Maroc', Annuaire de l'Afrique du Nord, 1963, pp.85-106. The Istiqlal and the UNFP together obtained 37 per cent of the

popular vote, while the FDIC gained only 24 per cent. Knapp, North West Africa, p.300.

114. See J. Waterbury, 'Endemic and Planned Corruption in a Monarchical Regime', World Politics, 1973, pp.533-555.

115. Marais, 'L'Election de la Chambre...', p.87.

116. Leveau, Le Fellah Marocain, p.9.

117. See J. and J. Aubin, 'Le Maroc en Suspend', Annuaire de l'Afrique du Nord, 1964, pp.73-89; B. Munier, 'L'Economie Marocaine,' Annuaire de l'Afrique du Nord, 1964, pp.284-302; B. Munier, 'L'Economie Marocaine en 1965', Annuaire de l'Afrique du Nord, 1965, pp.334-361, especially p.361 : 'Dix ans d'indépendance suggèrent bien que la stratégie adoptée, si même il en est une, est bien loin d'être satisfaisante... de vastes zones d'ombre subsistent; péril démographique, misère endémique, faiblesse de l'investissement'.

118. Schaar, 'King Hassan's Alternatives', pp.236-239.

119. M. Camau, 'Institutions Politiques des Etats Maghrébins post-Coloniaux', in Ruf (ed), Introduction à l'Afrique du Nord Contemporaine, pp.255-281; see also Paul Chambergeat, 'Bilan de l'Expérience Parlementaire Marocaine', Annuaire de l'Afrique du Nord, 1965, pp.101-116.

120. B.Munier, 'L'Economie Marocaine en 1966', Annuaire de l'Afrique du Nord, 1966, pp.401-415; A.A. Belal and A.Agourram, 'L'Economie Marocaine Depuis L'Indépendance', Annuaire de l'Afrique du Nord, 1969, pp.145-168; J.P. Mockers, 'L'Economie Marocaine en 1967', Annuaire de l'Afrique du Nord, 1967, pp.445-461.

121. Belal and Agourram, 'L'Economie Marocaine...', p.168.

122. Abu Lughod, Rabat, p.272.

123. J. Gourdon, 'Les Elections Communales Marocaines du 30 Octobre 1969, Annuaire de l'Afrique du Nord, 1969, pp.329-338.

124. J. Despois, 'Constitution et Consultations Populaires au Maroc', Annuaire de l'Afrique du Nord, 1970, pp.163-194.

125. For the 1971 coup, see John Waterbury, 'The Coup Manqué', in Gellner and Micaaud (eds), Arabs and Berbers, pp.397-424; for the role of the armed forces, generally see the useful analysis by J.-J. Regnier and J.C. Santucci, 'Armée, Pouvoir et Légitimité au Maroc', Annuaire de l'Afrique du Nord, 1971, pp.137-178, written after the second (Kenitra) coup attempt.

126. Gourdon, 'Maroc: Chronique Politique 1970, Annuaire de l'Afrique du Nord, 1970, pp.322-334.

127. For a historical and geo-political survey of the question within the context of international law, see F.E. Trout, Morocco's Saharan Frontiers, (Geneva, 1969).

128. Gaudio, Allal al-Fassi..., 195-198. See also Allal al-Fassi, La Vérité sur les Frontières Marocaines, (Tangier, 1961).

129. Zartman, Government and Politics in North Africa, p.37.

130. For full details, see V. Thompson and R. Adloff, The Western Saharans, (London, 1980) on which much of the following account is based. John Damis, Conflict in Northwest Africa : the Western Sahara Dispute, (Stamford, 1983) appeared after this chapter had gone to press.

131. J. Dessaints, 'Maroc: Chronique Politique', Annuaire de

l'Afrique du Nord. 1975. pp.457-476.
   132.   M. Rousset. 'Changements Politiques et Equilibre des Forces Politiques au Maghreb; un Essai d'Interprétation', Annuaire de l'Afrique du Nord. 1977. pp.195-197.
   133.   J-C. Santucci. 'Chronique Politique Maroc 1976', Annuaire de l'Afrique du Nord. 1976. p.357; cf. J. Waterbury. 'La Légitimation de Pouvoir au Maghreb; Tradition, Protestation et Répression', Annuaire de l'Afrique du Nord. 1977. p.417; 'La Marche Verte, avec tout son côté religieux, réunit la dynastie avec l'histoire de la nation et les sources de l'Islam'.
   134.   Rousset. 'Changements...' p.198.
   135.   Santucci. 'Chronique Politique Maroc 1976'. pp.372-378.
   136.   Dessaints. 'Chronique Politique Maroc 1977'. Annuaire l'Afrique du Nord. 1977. pp.215-242.
   137.   L. Jaïdi and H., el-Malki. 'Chronique Economique Maroc 1977', Annuaire de l'Afrique du Nord. 1977. pp.593-614. In 1982-83, military expenditure reached 40 per cent of the budget. Le Monde. 25-26.2.83.
   138.   Santucci. 'Chronique Politique Maroc 1978', Annuaire de l'Afrique du Nord. 1978. pp.385-409.
   139.   L. Jaïdi. 'Chronique Economique Maroc 1978'. Annuaire de l'Afrique du Nord. 1978. p.524.
   140.   Santucci. 'Chronique Politique Maroc 1979'. Annuaire de l'Afrique du Nord. 1979. p.539.
   141.   Iraq supplies most of Morocco's crude oil. King Hassan has also thrown his weight behind Iraq's irredentist claims in Iran. See Economist Intelligence Unit, Quarterly Economic Report. 1st quarter, 1981.
   142.   See the list of countries recognising the SADR on 1 April 1980 in Annuaire de l'Afrique du Nord. 1979. pp.968-969; and Simone Nasse and Raoul Weexsteen. 'Sahara Occidental; Chronologie 1980'. Annuaire de l' Afrique du Nord. 1980. pp.911-922.
   143.   Amin, The Maghreb in the Modern World. p.169.
   144.   Ibid., p.171.
   145.   Ibid., p.173.
   146.   Ibid., p.173.
   147.   Christian Eikenberg, Marokko - Rahmenbedingungen und Struktur der marokkanischen Wirtschaft. Afrika Industrieberichte 21, (Hamburg. 1977). p.189; R.I. Lawless, 'Progress and Problems in the Development of Maghreb Agriculture'. Maghreb Review. no.3, 1976, pp.6-11, 22.
   148.   Knapp. North West Africa, pp.321-322.
   149.   Lawless. 'Progress and Problems', p.10.
   150.   Eikenberg, Marokko, p.188.
   151.   Ibid., p.177; see also the table in N. Bouderbala, M. Chraïbi, P. Pascon. La Question Agraire au Maroc (Publication du Bulletin Economique et Sociale du Maroc, Rabat, 1977). vol.II, p.221
   152.   Eikenberg, Marokko, p.178. 6.2 per cent of households owned between 10 and 49.99 ha, 26.8 per cent of the cultivable area.
   153.   Benhlal, 'Politique des barrages', p.269.
   154.   Ibid., p.271.

155. Eikenberg, Marokko, p.165.
156. Only 11.4 per cent of households use modern machinery; see Bouderbala, Chraïbi, Pascon, La Question Agraire, vol.II, p.217.
157. 80 per cent of wine, 80 per cent of citrus fruits, 33 per cent of vegetables and 15 per cent of cereals. Economist Intelligence Unit, Morocco, Annual Supplement, 1981, p.8.
158. 80 per cent of milk, 70 per cent of grain, 65 per cent of olives and about 37 per cent of all vegetables produced are consumed on the spot. Eikenberg, Marokko, p.183
159. Knapp, North West Africa, p.323.
160. 'After 1960, judicious use of agricultural credits enabled the Ministry (of Interior), through governors and qa'ids to consolidate its control over the countryside... and to build up clienteles of provincial notables'. Lawless, 'Progress and Problems', p.11. See also Leveau, Le Fellah Marocain.
161. Lawless, 'Progress and Problems', p.11. The 1973-76 plan allocated DH 1,586 million to the irrigation zones and DH 574 million to the traditional sector.
162. Benhlal, 'Politique des barrages'.
163. Thus: Wheat   Barley (Tons)
         1974   1,853,000   2,389,000
         1980   1,800,000   1,800,000
Economist Intelligence Unit, Morocco, Annual Supplement, 1981, p.10.
164. Bank of Morocco, Annual Report 1979, p.19. The same source makes the general point that the rate of agricultural expansion has failed to keep up with population growth over the last 15 years.
165. Economist Intelligence Unit, Morocco, Annual Supplement, 1981, p.19.
166. See Anne Findlay, Allan R.Findlay and R.I. Lawless, The Kingdom of Morocco, International Migration Project, Country Case Studies, (Durham, 1978), p.30. The Muslim urban population increased from 1.9 million in 1956 to 5.5 million in 1971 and 8.1 million in 1979. Annuaire Statistique du Maroc, 1979, p.21.
167. Economist Intelligence Unit, Morocco, Annual Supplement, 1980, p.4.
168. The sharp rise in remittances was also encouraged by preferential exchange rates introduced by the Banque Populaire. Bank of Morocco, Annual Report, 1979; table A 36; Economist Intelligence Unit, Morocco, Annual Supplement 1981, p.18. See also A. Adam, 'Chronique Sociale et Culturelle Maroc', Annuaire de l'Afrique du Nord, 1980, pp.693-700.
169. Imports of foodstuffs cost DH 2,500 million in 1975 and DH 2,100 million in 1979. Bank of Morocco, Annual Report 1979, table A 32. The austerity measures recently recommended by the World Bank encouraged the government to cut some of the food subsidies; this led to 'violent riots and strikes all over the country'. Economist Intelligence Unit, QER Morocco, 3rd Quarter 1981, p.6. See also El-Malki, L'Economie Marocaine, pp.80-81.
170. Eikenberg, Marokko, p.43; cereal prices rose by 48 per cent between 1970 and 1974, and the cost of living doubled between 1973 and 1979. Economist Intelligence Unit, Morocco, Annual

Supplement 1981, p.18.
171. Eikenberg, Marokko, pp.280-284.
172. Ibid p.122. Moroccanisation has now been abandoned : see Le Monde, 25-26/2/83.
173. El-Malki, L'Economie Marocaine, p.164.
174. Lawless, 'Industrialisation in the Maghrib', Maghreb Review, no.2, (1976), p.9.
175. Ibid., p.9.
176. Eikenberg, Marokko, pp.150, 161. 34,800 were employed in mining and 154,000 in construction, in addition to these figures.
177. Eikenberg, Marokko, p.161.
178. See Findlay, Findlay and Lawless, International Migration Project, pp.19-27. The authors note that migration to the Arab World seems 'the only ray of hope'. (p.51).
179. See above, pp.78-80.
180. Economist Intelligence Unit, Morocco, Annual Supplement, 1981, p.18. However, citrus exports increased by 35 per cent between 1979 and 1980.
181. Bank of Morocco, Annual Report for 1979, table A 32.
182. Foreign borrowing amounted to DH 4,795 million in 1979, and DH 48,485 in 1982-83. The main lenders are the World Bank, the IMF and the Arab oil states. See Economist Intelligence Unit, QER, Morocco, 3rd quarter, 1981, p.7, and Le Monde, 25-26 February 1983.
183. Economist Intelligence Unit, Morocco, Annual Supplement, 1981, p.16; Le Monde, 25-26 February 1983.
184. cf. Waterbury, 'La Légitimation du Pouvoir...', p.413; Jean Leca, 'Réformes Institutionelles et Légitimation du Pouvoir au Maghreb', Annuaire de l'Afrique du Nord, 1977, pp.1-15.
185. At least in the eyes of the principal actor; King Hassan, The Challenge, pp.149-155.
186. See Waterbury, Commander of the Faithful, passim, and the same author's 'Endemic and Planned Corruption in a Monarchical Regime', World Politics, 1973, pp.533-555.
187. See Vatin, 'Revival in the Maghreb', and two useful articles in Annuaire de l'Afrique du Nord 1979: Rémy Leveau, 'Réaction de l'Islam Officiel au Renouveau Islamique au Maroc,' pp.205-218, and M. Tozy 'Monopolisation de la Production Symbolique et Hiérarchisation du Champ Politico-réligieux au Maroc', pp.219-234.

Chapter 3.

TUNISIA : CONTEMPORARY POLITICS

Werner Ruf

The political situation in Tunisia in the 1970s, and the likely course of future developments, can only be understood in the context of the political, economic and social history of the country over the last 100 years. This brief attempt to highlight the principal forces at work in Tunisian society will help to provide an interpretation of political events since 1978 as well as serving as a base for projections into the future. A survey of the country's past is particularly relevant at the time of writing, since there are increasing signs that certain traditional characteristics of the political situation which have been a feature of the past 25 years are undergoing at least partial dissolution.

THE SOCIAL AND POLITICAL TRANSFORMATION OF TUNISIA UNDER THE FRENCH PROTECTORATE

From the beginning of the eighteenth century, Tunisia began to participate increasingly in the emergent mercantile capitalism of the Mediterranean basin. The ruling family and the *grande bourgeoisie* of the city of Tunis were the main beneficiaries of this trade. Here it must be said that the use of the term *bourgeoisie* must remain problematic in the context of an essentialy pre-capitalist society. In this chapter the term *grande bourgeoisie* designates a narrow urban stratum deriving its surplus from rent, tenure and foreign trade. In the nineteenth century this *grande bourgeoisie* was strong enough to force the enactment of political reforms, including the introduction of a liberal constitution in 1861 and radical reforms in the judicial, educational administrative systems (1). These reforms were generally directed towards the liberalisation of politics and the economy to facilitate their greater integration into wider economic relationships, especially with France. They were also intended to make the state apparatus a more efficient instrument to bring about the necessary political and economic 'modernisation' (2). The result of this policy was that the state incurred substantial foreign debts, a trend which was given added impetus by the activities of European finance capital in the region as a whole (3), which led eventually to military occupation by the main creditor, France, and the creation of the Protectorate under the treaties of 1881 and 1883.

For the Tunisian *grande bourgeoisie*, the occupation meant the loss of its economic and political power. As well as seeking to exploit the country's raw materials (particularly phosphates, iron, zinc, and lead) and to develop agricultural colonisation with the assistance of French finance houses, France also sought to control the country's foreign trade and administrative apparatus (4). The achievement of the two latter objectives struck at the jugular vein of the *grande bourgeoisie* which had initially come forward as the ally of France, with its pro-French attitudes and its identification with the norms and values of the colonial power (5). In contrast, the petty bourgeoisie, the Beylical administrators, small traders from the Sahel and Jerba, and the richer farmers from the Sahel saw that the new educational system provided an opportunity for the social advancement of themselves and their families, and sent their sons to French or Franco-Arab schools.

The Policy of the Neo-Destour Party in Colonial Tunisia

Disappointed with the protecting power, which had failed to respond to their political and ideological overtures while simultaneously ruining their economic base, the *grande bourgeoisie* began to develop nationalist ideas. After the First World War, nationalist forces joined together in the Destour (Constitution) Party. The choice of this name for the party underlined its main political objective, a return to the fundamental principles of the Tunisian constitution of 1861.

In time, the Destour Party was also joined by other groups, who although originating from the lower middle classes, and having had their education at French schools or even at French universities, found themselves discriminated against in their own country because of their nationality. In many ways, Habib Bourguiba is sociologically representative of this group: born in Monastir in the Sahel in 1903, the son of an officer in the Beylical Guard, educated in French at the Lycée Carnot, continuing to higher education at the Faculté de Droit and the Ecole des Sciences Politiques in Paris, married to a Frenchwoman, and establishing a legal practice in Tunis. The origins and training of this younger generation of party members not only made the party more appealing to wider strata among the petty bourgeoisie and the emerging working class, but also differentiated them quite clearly from its *grand bourgeoisie* membership who were not confronted so immediately by the discriminatory practices of the Protectorate. As a result their demands were more radical, inspired particularly by the socialist ideals of the Third Republic (6).

In 1934 the progressive petty bourgeoisie grouping around Bourguiba and Materi split away from the 'Old Destour' as it now became, and founded the Neo-Destour Party. The Party deliberately sought conflict with the Protectorate authorities over issues which it knew would mobilise the mass of the population. It formed an alliance with the CGTT (*Confédération Générale des Travailleurs Tunisiens*) which had split away from the French CGT, supported the demands of pupils and students and put forward generally progressive demands for universal compulsory education, academic freedom, the development of irrigation, the application of French labour and social security laws to Tunisians, the nationalisation of key industries, equal pay for equal work without distinction between Tunisians and Europeans, equal rights for Tunisians and Frenchmen in land distribution, and unrestricted access for Tunisians to all administrative posts etc (7).

In the years which followed, the party's skillful espousal of burning social and national issues gradually had the effect of making it the main mouthpiece of petty bourgeois, peasant and worker interests (8). Various incidents led to the frequent arrest of party leaders. In contrast to the Old Destour and some circles within his own party, Bourguiba did not favour an alliance with the Axis Powers during the German occupation of Tunisia, which enabled him to present himself to the Allies after the war as a negotiator with a certain degree of legitimacy. The intransigeance shown by the French government towards nationalist demands in its colonies and the not inconsiderable contacts between the Neo-Destour (and especially the CGTT, later to become the *Union Général des Travailleurs Tunisiens* (UGTT) and the USA, gave the party even greater importance (9).

THE STRUGGLE FOR INDEPENDENCE AS THE STRUGGLE FOR POLITICAL POWER IN TUNISIA

From 'Internal Autonomy' to Independence

As well as escalating existing conflicts in a number of its colonies, notably Indochina, Tunisia, Morocco and Algeria, the contradictory policies pursued by the various cabinets of the Fourth Republic (10) also led to the gradual success of the skillful decolonisation tactics of the Neo-Destour Party. After two years of armed resistance and the arrest or enforced exile of leading members of the party (11), Pierre Mendès-France offered the Tunisian nationalists 'internal autonomy' which however implied the gain of only a small proportion of their demands (12). Bourguiba, who had most probably been consulted by the French Government before the proposal was made public, agreed to the offer immediately (13).

Bourguiba's acceptance led to a fundamental conflict between himself (as president of the party) and the Secretary-General of the party, Salah ben Youssef. The latter and the majority of the guerrilla units who had been in contact with the Algerian FLN felt betrayed by the 'autonomy' compromise and demanded the continuation of the armed struggle (14). Bourguiba managed to secure the agreement of the Politburo to the Secretary-General's expulsion from the party. The party immediately split into the followers of Bourguiba and the followers of ben Youssef. Bourguiba relying mainly on the membership in the Sahel and the UGTT, while ben Youssef relied on the traders of his native island of Zarzis, a large part of the Old Destour and the guerrillas of south and west Tunisia. It is difficult to assess how much this split owed to ideological differences and how much to personal rivalry (15), but it is a fact that different sections of the petty bourgeoisie were ranged against one another.

Here it is significant that vestiges of this conflict are still visible today. The new government, led by the Bourguiba wing sent French troops against the guerrillas of ben Youssef (16), and after the discovery of a number of more or less implausible 'plots', the followers of ben Youssef were sentenced in a number of show trials. Ben Youssef himself was murdered in Frankfurt/Main by Tunisian agents in 1961. Brahim Tobal, the leader of the ben Youssef faction, which still has supporters in Tunisia, lives in exile in Algiers.

This conflict with the followers of ben Youssef played into the hands of Bourguiba and his supporters, in the sense that the colonial power quickly sided with them as the more evidently 'moderate' of the two. In order not to discredit Bourguiba, and in order to ensure that the nationalists were not driven into the arms of ben Youssef, France was forced to make further concessions, beyond the promised 'internal autonomy'. This combination of circumstances enabled Bourguiba to achieve independence on 20 March 1956, only nine months after the granting of 'internal autonomy'.

The Second Political Force : The Trade Union Federation (UGTT)

The industrialisation of Tunisia in the colonial period speeded up the formation of a Tunisian working class, especially in the phosphate industry, the ports and the railways. Parts of this working class were initially organised in the French CGT, but in 1924 the CGTT constituted itself as an independent trade union federation, whose main demand was equal treatment for Tunisian and European workers (17). Discrimination against Tunisian workers under the colonial regime made all trade union demands take on nationalist overtones and thus become political. Hence there has always been close cooperation between the Neo-Destour and the unions, and many trade union members also became members of the party.

After numerous bannings of the CGTT, the UGTT was founded in 1946. This body gave more and more support to the Neo-Destour within the framework of the anti-colonial alliance. Here the party benefitted particularly from the UGTT's good relations with the AFL/CIO in the United States (18). The alliance which Bourguiba had concluded with the UGTT in the summer of 1955 was of decisive importance in his power struggle with ben Youssef. The then Secretary-General of the UGTT, Ahmed ben Salah, was consistent in his support for the Bourguiba wing, and the votes of the party delegates who were members of the UGTT were decisive in expelling ben Youssef and his supporters at the Party Congress in November 1955.

PARTY AND STATE IN INDEPENDENT TUNISIA

Although the party has always maintained its position as the leading political force in Tunisia since independence, it has pursued a variety of often contradictory political lines in the course of the past 25 years. It seems useful to attempt an analysis of its role with respect to the changing economic and development goals set in this period, because the economic policies pursued inevitably had far-reaching repercussions for the social, and thus the political, development of the country.

Economic Liberalism and the Monopoly of Political Power, 1956-1962

Bourguiba's style, both in leadership and in government, is best illustrated in the President's own words:

> Notre stratégie suppose donc un peuple uni et discipliné, un chef jouissant d'une confiance totale, ce qui lui permet d'avoir les coudées franches, un grande liberté de manoeuvre...C'est au chef, je le répète, qu'il appartient de prendre ses responsabilités, de juger la valeur des solutions politiques et de leur opportunité. Quand par mon refus j'engage le peuple dans une lutte à mort, c'est moi qui porte la responsabilité du sang versé (19).

Apart from the victory over the suporters of ben Youssef, the first internal conflict after independence resulted in a largely successful attempt to weaken the UGTT and to bring it into line. Bourguiba's government had attempted to bring the trade union under its control as early as the autumn of 1965; when the Secretary-General, Ahmed ben Salah, resisted, the party created a split in the trade union organisation, and ben Salah was relieved of his functions while on a journey abroad. The union subsequently reunited under Ahmed Tlili, and the instigator of the split, Habib Achour, became his deputy (20). The conflict had arisen because the UGTT congress had unanimously demanded the transition to a planned economy, nationalisation and agrarian reform (21).

In contrast, the Bourguiba government was pursuing a form of economic liberalism which in the last analysis had the effect of maintaining the integration of the Tunisian economy within the French economy. French settlers and businessmen were able to continue their activities in the country and to bring pressure to bear on the government. Sections of the Tunisian petty bourgeoisie were active in the economic sectors controlled by the French, and Tunisia remained linked to the franc zone.

Apart from controlling the trade unions, the party also brought other professional associations and organisations into line, or actually founded such organisations itself. These are UNAT or UGAT, the peasant organisation, UTICA, the industry and trade organisation, UGET, the student organisation, and UNFT, the women's organisation. In 1957 the monarchy was abolished; Bourguiba permitted himself to be elected President. After having been re-elected twice, the constitution was amended to allow him to remain President for life.

The concentration of all political power in the hands of the party, combined with a policy of economic liberalism especially in the period before the country's departure from the franc zone in 1958, resulted in political leaders viewing politics increasingly as a means of self-aggrandisement. Furthermore, the liberal economic policy led to an almost complete disruption of state finances and the economy, as French settlers and businessmen transferred all their profits home.

The Planned Economy Phase, 1961-1968

In 1958, after Tunisia's departure from the franc zone and the evacuation of French troops, Ahmed ben Salah, the former Secretary-General of the UGTT who had been trained at the ICFTU in Brussels, became Minister of Health. In 1959 he began to formulate an economic plan, and in 1960 took over the newly created Ministry of Planning. The outline of a ten year development plan, the *Perspectives Décennales*, was drafted, substantially based on the resolutions of the UGTT congress of 1956. The main goals of the plan were (22):

> Economic decolonisation: the commanding heights of the Tunisian economy were to be removed from the control of French capital.
> Raising the standard of living: the establishment of a minimum wage and the urgent improvement of health, education, nutrition and housing standards.
> Structural reforms: the creation of structures to promote increases in productivity.
> The development of self-sufficiency: the reduction of dependence on foreign capital and its replacement by increased self-sufficiency and the creation of a national market.

This programme was self-evidently political and thus a challenge to the political stratum from which the Neo-Destour drew its support. Although this stratum was beginning to suffer from the ruin of the economy, it was not prepared to endorse such a programme wholeheartedly. However the introduction of the planned economy in 1961 was ushered in with a major propaganda campaign and at its congress at Bizerte the party changed its name to the Socialist Destour Party. However, Bourguiba's second marriage to Wassila ben Ammar, from one of the richest families in Tunis, can be seen as a gesture of reassurance to the bourgeoisie.

In fact ben Salah's plan envisaged setting up state and cooperative sectors which would not threaten the continued existence of private capital. Thus while 'profitable' private Tunisian businesses remained largely unaffected, the public sector would set up economic and social infrastructures such as the educational system which would form the basis for industrial development, while 'unproductive' businesses, particularly agricultural small holdings, were to be grouped together in cooperatives. The practical effect of this was that the Tunisian bourgeoisie emerged virtually unscathed from the transition to 'socialism', which was introduced to the sector with the least capacity to resist, the small peasant farmers (23), who were grouped together in cooperatives, occasionally by force. The former land of the French settlers was nationalised and also transformed into cooperatives, many of which were worked by agricultural labourers under the aegis of the UGTT. Ben Salah also pursued a policy of control and supervision of the trade unions, by making them responsible for the negotiation of wages and working conditions while actually forcing them to check or even suppress the demands of the workers (24). The half-hearted and inconsistent application of the reforms and their considerable cost meant that they were far less successful than had been expected.

Thus instead of developing towards self-sufficiency, Tunisia's debts in particular to the World Bank, the USA and the Federal Republic of Germany, now beginning to replace France as Tunisia's banker, meant that the country was becoming increasingly integrated into the world market (25). Thus in 1969 ben Salah, who had by this time managed to accumulate the portfolios of Planning, the Economy, Finance,Agriculture and Education, was forced to pass a law encouraging investments, which offered foreign investors fabulous opportunities for profit (26). Finally, also in 1969, the World Bank and US-AID presented their account, and forced a re-liberalisation of the economy (27). In this period ben Salah also attempted to collectivise the land of the larger peasants, particularly in the Sahel, many of whom occupied important positions in the party (28). A revolt, apparently of small peasants who had been collectivised for some time, began in the Sahel, which finally led to ben Salah's dismissal and conviction for treason and 'thirst for power' in 1970. In 1973 he fled abroad via Algeria, and has led the social democratic opposition movement MUP (Mouvement d'Unité Populaire) ever since.

Economic Reliberalisation since 1970 and its Social Consequences
Within a very short time the parliamentary legislative apparatus of the Neo-Destour destroyed the entire system which ben Salah's policies had attempted to construct. In particular, the cooperatives were abolished and foreign trade liberalised. A 'land reform from above' was inaugurated which gave even the very smallest plots back to their former owners. Since the peasants concerned no longer owned any means of production, either draught animals, tools, fertiliser or seed, they were obliged to indebt themselves to the larger landowners in the neighbourhood. Thus in a very short time, in three or at most five years, tens of thousands of small peasants had to sell their land to the larger landowners and migrate to the cities. The ensuing concentration of agricultural production not only encouraged the import of agricultural machinery, which had been facilitated by the liberalisation of foreign trade (29), but also permitted a further rationalisation of agricultural production and the release of more of the labour force. This open door policy had the further effect of encouraging the increased production of speculative export goods, sold directly on the world market, such as fruit, early vegetables, citrus fruit and flowers. This process, combined with the policy of encouraging tourism which had already begun under ben Salah, had the effect of causing serious shortage of basic foodstuffs which resulted increasingly in nutritional deficiencies (30).

The policy of privatisation at home was complemented by measures which favoured foreign capital, notably the law for the promotion of exports of 27 April 1972, and the law for encouraging processing industries of 3 August 1974 (31). These laws were in fact extensions of the investment law of 26 June 1969, which offered fabulous profit and investment opportunities for foreign and international capital, in close cooperation with a narrow stratum of the Tunisian comprador bourgeoisie (32). Here the World Bank, acting together with the National Bank of Tunisia and its President, Hedi Nouira, later Prime Minister and a leading exponent of the open door policy, played a key role. It is more than likely that the suddenly negative reports of the World Bank and the freezing of its credits contributed substantially to the fall of ben Salah (33).

Thus ben Salah's planning phase can be regarded as the means by which the infrastructure of Tunisia was built up at public expense, for the use of private capital, which could then develop without further risk to itself. At the precise moment when this stage was reached, the process was halted and turned back in the opposite direction. The cost was borne by the small peasants and artisans, and especially by the working class; the omnipresence of the party, and especially its control over the trade unions, the absence of any opposition, and the close links between the interests of capital and a handful of leading party families combined to turn Tunisia almost overnight into an ideal location for low wage production and a model of dependent capitalist underdevelopment (34). Poncet's diagnosis is therefore accurate:

> The kind of growth which we have seen in Tunisia over the past few years is that of petty local capitalism entirely subordinated to the interests of the major monopolies. Tunisia is modernising, in the sense that both towns and countryside are witnessing the disappearance of all that has remained of the 'traditional' sectors, for the benefit of a type of expansion which is concentrated in both a sectoral and geographical sense, from which elements of the bourgeoisie have profited...Tunisia is completely dependent on external supplies of industrial plant, aid, investments and loans, exploiting a labour force which is compelled either to emigrate or to work within the country for extremely low wages (35).

Social and Political Resistance

This abrupt transformation of the economic and political situation led to a massive aggravation of social antagonisms, accelerated by the brutal installation of capitalist interests already described and accompanied by pauperisation of the mass of the population. Large sections of the former rural population were turned into a *lumpenproletariat*, and wages frozen (36). However, during a period of impoverishment in which basic rights which had long been fought for were now under threat, it became clear that the trade union infrastructure had by no means been destroyed; it was in fact capable of standing up to exploitation and attempts to deprive it of its rights. This was evident in the outbreak of a number of 'wild-cat' strikes. Eventually the strike movement in individual factories and trade unions grew to such proportions that the government promulgated an anti-strike law in December 1973, prohibiting all strikes and threatening strikers with large fines and prison sentences of between one and five years (37). In spite of this, the number of strikes increased. The trade union leadership under Habib Achour, who as member of the Party's Politburo was supposed to contain the union's activities, became increasingly responsive to pressures from below and began to support the demands of the working class. A large number of political trials, particularly of students and workers, particularly between 1973 and 1975, and the widespread use of torture (38) were not sufficient to damp down a swelling social protest.

Eventually, in the autumn of 1977, the strikes reached such proportions that whole sectors of the economy were effectively brought to a standstill, and the regime finally ordered troops out against the striking workers (39).

In response the UGTT called a general strike for 26 January 1978, which was observed throughout the country. The 'hawks' in the cabinet, who were also closest to major commercial and industrial interests, notably Hedi Nouira, Muhammad Sayyah and Abdullah Farhat, voted for a massive repression of the strike movement, in an attempt to destroy the trade union. Thus on 26 January 1978 there were major disturbances in Tunis. It is still not clear to what extent these were the result of the work of *agents provocateurs* employed by forces within the party which wanted to ensure the intervention of the army at all costs. At any event, the army did intervene (40), and as a result of its brutal activities some 800 people were arrested and a large number killed. Estimates vary between 46 and 200 (41). What acutally happened in the provinces,in Sousse and especially in Gafsa and the surrounding mining region, will probably never be known.

The most reactionary group within the regime seemed to have achieved its aim, since the entire trade union leadership was arrested, and several thousand trade unionists were sentenced by summary courts (42). The whole leadership was sentenced to long prison terms after farcical trials (43) and the party foisted a new and opportunistic leadership on the UGTT. Although severely weakened by mass arrests, the determination of the rank and file was not broken. Habib Achour, a supporter and executive of the Bourguiba regime for decades, became the symbol of resistance. Since the social and political situation did not change, the 'wild-cat' strikes soon began again.

One particular event shook the regime exactly two years later. According to the official version, a band of about 40 or 50 'terrorists' took over the mining centre of Gafsa, and occupied the city, with a population of some 50,000, for about a week (44). The situation was considered sufficiently grave for France to despatch three warships,- including the modern missile carrier Colbert – with helicopters and beach assault troops to the Gulf of Gabès (45) with logistical support from the Sixth Fleet (46). From this incident, and the support on which the attackers were able to draw from the population of Gafsa, it became clear both in Tunisia and in the world at large how fragile the regime in Tunis had become. Furthermore, even the official claim that the capture of Gafsa was simply a manoeuvre of the Libyan government which had been met with the unanimous resistance of the local population (47) could hardly conceal the fact that at least in the south of Tunisia, where the population was almost entirely dependent on remittances from Libya, the very foundations of the Bourguiba regime were threatened.

Political Liberalisation or Total Repression

All Tunisian political organisations, especially the UGTT, made a point of declaring that they had nothing to do with the forces behind the occupation of Gafsa, which is most probably true (48). The relative political isolation of the attackers from the rest of the spectrum of opposition forces - with the possible exception of the Youssefists (49) can be deduced from the harshness of the sentences and the fact that they were carried out immediately (50). However the attack on Gafsa and popular reaction to it revealed the weakness of the regime, while foreign interest and foreign readiness to intervene also showed the true neo-colonial character of the ruling clique in the Neo-Destour. This clique now had two alternative means of retaining power in the medium term: it could either increase repression in an openly fascist direction or attempt some degree of political relaxation which might bring parts of the bourgeois opposition, especially the trade unions, back to legality. As the trade unions had shown that they could not be cowed in spite of brutal repression, the second method seemed the logical choice.

The different opposition forces in Tunisia will be discussed later; our concern here is to show the way in which the system attempted to broaden its base once more through a series of cautious steps towards political liberalisation, with the ultimate objective of ensuring its own survival. Considering that the government had already embarked upon a policy of economic liberalism, the new measures can only be seen in terms of a gesture towards the remaining fragments of the bourgeoisie. As any analysis of the new 'opening' will also contribute to a more informed understanding of the likely course of future developments in the country, it is useful to give an account of the present state of the new policy. The critical illness of Hedi Nouira, the former Prime Minister, who was the main exponent of the economically liberal and politically repressive policies, provided a suitable opportunity for his replacement by the 'more liberal' Muhammed Mzali on 23 April 1980. The 'open government' (51) proclaimed by the new Prime Minister also found favour in European financial circles (52).

A bourgeois-democratic opposition to the Socialist Destour Party had in fact been in existence for some time. Led by Ahmed Mestiri, this group had split away from the party in the 1970s but although constitutionally entitled to do so, had in practice been unable to establish itself in the prevailing political climate (see below). However, the main problem now facing the regime in its attempts to make gestures towards political liberalisation is the unsolved problem of the trade unions, particularly the fact that the rank and file of the UGTT has always refused to accept the new leadership which the Party foisted upon it in the aftermath of 'Black Thursday' (26 January 1978). This new leadership has also been unable to gain international recognition from bodies such as the ICFTU, which is particularly important for the regime. Thus the regime must first broaden its own now too narrow class base by attempting to recruit other fractions of the bourgeoisie to the government (and the distribution of the spoils). It must also try to break the resistance of the trade unions which have managed to restrict its manoeuvrability since January 1978. However, the creation of an openly fascist government would not necessarily have encouraged the confidence of foreign capital.

The first measure towards 'open government' was to permit the UGTT to hold a congress, and to pardon all the trade union leaders who had been sentenced after 26 January 1978, with the exception of Habib Achour (53). Ahmed Mestiri and his Democratic Socialists were eventually given permission to publish a weekly newspaper (54). Finally, an extraordinary congress of the Socialist Destour Party in April 1981 declared itself in favour of a multi-party system, although within certain defined limits: the person of the President for life, Habib Bourguiba in whom total competence has been vested, remains sacrosanct, and immune from all criticism. Equally, all organisations advocating sectarianism, fanaticism, preaching class struggle, or having ideological or financial ties with other countries are banned from legal political activity (55).

Two things emerge. The Islamic integrationists are not served by the new national charter, but Ahmed Mestiri's Social Democratic Movement certainly is. Whether the other political groupings will comply with the vague provisions of the Charter, or whether their own political muscle will permit them to assert themselves, still remains to be seen. The outcome will certainly depend as much on the strength of these groupings as on the readiness to compromise shown by the ruling fraction of the bourgeoisie and its tactical flexibility. In order to make an informed prognosis, however, it is first necessary to look briefly at the existing political forces within the country.

POLITICAL FORCES IN TUNISIA IN THE 1980s

The UGTT
In the long run the Tunisian trade unions have emerged strengthened from the conflict which has been going on since 1978. The fact that Gafsa, the stronghold of the Mineworkers' Union, and the scene of the 'events' of 1980 was chosen in April 1981 as the location for the first congress to be held since January 1978, shows the extent to which the union has become politicised. This is also reflected in the results of the election to the executive committee; eleven members of the thirteen man committee were part of the former leadership which had been arrested and sentenced after the 26 January 1978, and had now to be released from prison (56). For the first time since 1944, the new Secretary-General, Taieb Baccouche, was not a member of the party. As Habib Achour remains under house arrest, the executive committee has been mandated to explore every possibility of setting him free and to give him the opportunity to resume his civil, political and trade union rights (57). The congress also demanded a general amnesty for all trade unionists still in prison, for all political prisoners and permission for political exiles to return (58).

Thus the UGTT not only set out its political objectives, but also expressed its support for a socialist option for Tunisia. It defined itself clearly as a political force which had severed its links with the Party, and which is determined to have its own say in the future development of the country. If the regime sticks to its promise of introducing a multi-party system it is difficult to forecast which political force the UGTT would support.

The Mouvement d'Unité Populaire (MUP)

The MUP is a social democratic movement opposed to the Bourguiba regime, led by Ahmed ben Salah since his escape from prison in 1973. As most of the MUP's supporters seem to live in Europe, it is difficult to estimate its influence, and it is also dependent upon the support it receives internationally from socialist and social-democratic parties in Europe. After the 'Liberalisation congress' of the Socialist Destour Party in April 1981, the MUP seems to have become somewhat divided; its supporters in Tunisia seem inclined to accept the conditions laid down by the congress, while the MUP in exile does not appear to be prepared to constitute itself as a party and contest the Tunisian elections, at least for the time being (59). The relatively narrow base of the Movement in Tunisia itself probably derives from the fact that the role of ben Salah in Tunisian politics is considered somewhat ambivalent by many progressives, and that many of those who might join the MUP regard the UGTT as a more powerful means of furthering their own interests.

The 'Democratic Socialists' around Ahmed Mestiri

This bourgeois-democratic opposition group plays an ambivalent role in Tunisia. Its leader, Ahmed Mestiri, had several ministerial posts in the 1960s, and he and his group belong to well-to-do local families. The Mestiri wing set itself up as a political grouping outside the Socialist Destour Party mainly because of political differences and the increasing influence of parvenus within the party structure (the role of Muhammad Sayyah is significant here). The 'Democratic Socialists' have published a weekly paper *al-Ra'i* (Opinion) since 1977, with the agreement of the party, although it too was banned after the events of January 1978.

The 'Democratic Socialists', who are also supported by right-wing social democrats abroad, and by bourgeois-progressive forces, are prepared to set themselves up as an opposition party on the basis of the 'open government' resolutions of the Socialist Destour Party Congress, which seem quite congenial to them. It remains to be seen how far the Democratic Socialists would cooperate with elements in the MUP, or whether they would be able to join forces with right-wing opportunist groups within the UGTT.

Muhammad Masmudi

Another representative of the bourgeois-democratic forces is Muhammad Masmudi, who has so far not cooperated with the Mestiri group. As one of the supporters of UGET, the student movement, in the pre-independence period, Masmudi held several ministerial posts, and always fought for the independence of the bourgeois press; he himself built up a substantial economic and newspaper empire (60). Masmudi also maintained generally cordial relations with the Algerian FLN and was responsible for the project of a union between Tunisia and Libya at the end of 1974, which occasioned his downfall at the hands of the clan of the Prime Minister, Hedi Nouira. Like Habib Achour, Masmudi regarded Libya as a valuable potential partner which would export raw materials to Tunisia and provide a market for highly qualified members of the Tunisian labour force. In order to establish themselves as a political force, Masmudi and his supporters may wish to form a coalition, either with the ruling Party, the 'Democratic Socialists', the MUP, or the UGTT.

The Youssefists
The Youssefists movement still has a fair number of supporters in France as well as in Tunisia (see above), but systematic political repression has made its real influence difficult to estimate. So far it has not responded positively to the official declarations of reform, because it considers that only parties and movements prepared to play along with the existing system would in fact be permitted, and that the reform measures are simply a diversionary move aimed at preventing any fundamental change.

The Communist Party
Since 18 January 1963 (62) the Tunisian Communist Party has played no role on the political stage. Although it was never officially banned, it was forced to suspend its activities as a result of pressures from the ruling party. However, the communists never had a wide influence, and always had a limited membership. This was partly because of their close links with the French-dominated CGT, which was primarily concerned to represent the interests of European workers in Tunisia. Nevertheless, it may be assumed that the Communist Party has gained influence, especially in the 1970s, and has played an important role within the UGTT. The party hopes for a class alliance with other progressive movements (63). Given the conditions on which parties are allowed to operate in Tunisia (64), it seems unlikely that it will achieve legality under existing circumstances.

The Islamic Movement
This movement, generally referred to in the Middle East under the umbrella term 'Muslim Brothers', has gained considerable strength in Tunisia over recent years. The main support of the movement, as indeed of almost all fascistoid movements, comes from those sections of the petty bourgeoisie which have been ruined by foreign capital and its local bourgeois partners, and from among the lumpenproletarian masses. Petty traders and small businessmen whose livelihood seems threatened, many of whom are *'ulama* and *fuqaha*, see the root of all evil in the growing influence of the West. They fear the disruption of their customs by tourism, but are also opposed to propaganda and rules of the party with regard to the emancipation of women, its campaign against the veil and the observance of the fast of Ramadhan, the education of girls, women in the professions, the legalisation of

abortion and birth control etc. All this must be fought against by returning to a strictly Islamic way of life. This ideology accords with the traditionally rooted and backward looking value system of the numerous small peasants who have lost their plots over the last decade, and who see their salvation in terms of the re-establishment of some fictitious 'old order' which will arrest the continuing economic, social and cultural decline of themselves and their families. For these urban and rural dwellers the enemy to be fought against is the West and its 'modernist' satraps in Tunis.

The growing influence of the Islamic Movement, as the Tunisian integrationists call themselves, is evident when cafes and restaurants are sacked during Ramadhan because they serve alcohol and/or serve meals during the day. At the end of April 1981 there were disturbances and numerous arrests at the University of Tunis of supporters of both the Islamic Movement and the Ba'th Party (65). The regime has so far refused to recognise the Islamic Movement as a party under the terms of the conditions laid down at the party congress (see above) (66). In view of the considerable strength of the movement it is unlikely that this will have been the last word, and its legalisation under another name cannot be excluded.

The Army

In contrast to almost all countries in the area, indeed in the continent of Africa as a whole, the army has played an insignificant role in the 20 years of Bourguiba's rule. Bourguiba personally distrusts the army, and for many years balanced it against the National Guard, both of which were relatively badly equipped. However in the face of growing social antagonisms in the reliberalisation period under Hedi Nouira, the need for a functioning and efficient instrument of repression became more urgent. The first test of its capacity to suppress a popular rising presented itself on 26 January 1978, when it attacked demonstrators in Tunis and in other parts of the country. In this way the party confirmed that, as in all other countries in the area, the army is the ultimate means of upholding the power of the rulers. It is difficult to say whether forces will emerge from within the army itself who no longer consider it the army's duty to preserve the status quo, but will use it for their own purposes. The personal links between the army and the petty bourgeoisie of the Sahel are well known.

SUMMARY: TUNISIA IN THE 1980s

The rapid polarisation of the social and political situation is a direct consequence of the various political and economic experiments which Tunisia has undergone since Independence. In fact these phases are only superficially contradictory, since ultimately they have had the effect of consolidating the economic power of an ever narrower comprador bourgeois clique, consisting of parts of the old *grande bourgeoisie*, and in particular of petty bourgeois groups who have obtained political power through the party. The party itself, which was once the vanguard of a broad anti-colonial movement, has now lost its base in the population as a whole and has become the hierarchical instrument of power of a narrow stratum which participates in the exploitation of the country.

In spite of bloody repression, the trade union movement has been able to assert itself as a broad and progressive opposition to these comprador bourgeois forces, and has even managed to consolidate itself because of the determination of the rank and file. However the trade union must also be seen as a sort of portmanteau of all the opposition forces, stretching from ultra-left elements, through the Communist Party to the Social-democratic reformist and quasi-bourgeois-liberal camp. From the other side the regime is opposed by the growing power of the Islamic Movement, whose actual influence is difficult to assess but which should certainly not be underestimated.

In these circumstances the regime had to choose between adopting an openly fascist system through a major increase in repression, to be carried out by the army, which was not prepared, either ideologically or materially, to assume such a role, or to attempt the policy of liberalisation which is now being tried. This is simply an effort to revitalise the legitimacy of the system by legalising bourgeois-liberal and social-democratic reformist forces, permitting them a certain degree of participation in the exercise of power.

This attempt to restabilise the internal political situation naturally has its own limitations. No significant transformation of the social, economic and political system are to be expected. Neither the country's integration into the world economy nor the question of ownership of the means of production are under debate. Hence the old conflicts between the government and the newly legalised and politically stronger trade union remain on the agenda. The pauperisation of the broad mass of the population will continue and the revenues from oil earned over the last few years and the generally precarious hard currency earnings from tourism will probably decline as oil reserves fall and the economic crisis in Europe sharpens. This will mean that the pressure of debts and debt service will weigh more heavily on the Tunisian economy than before. The attempt to integrate the forces of the political centre, which is the main objective of the open government policy, will not last long. Awareness of the continuing weakness of the political system explains the cautious response of most political groupings, including reformist movements such as the MUP, to the regime's offer of open government. Hence all opposition groups, whether legal or not, except for Mestiri's Democratic Socialists, will keep a certain distance from the regime, and in consequence its overtures are most unlikely to bring about the results they hoped for. This is particularly the case with the UGTT, because if the regime were to give in to the demands of the unions, these would strike at its roots and at its essentially comprador bourgeois function.

However, as the events of Gafsa have clearly indicated the development of the country will be less of an internal Tunisian affair in the future. It would certainly be in the interest of this small and barely economically viable country to find a Maghrebi solution, in terms of an association with one of its richer neighbours, either

Algeria or Libya. This however would not only be against the nature of the regime, as the attempts at a union with Libya in 1974 indicated. It would also not be permitted by the United States and the Western European powers, whether the Federal Republic of Germany, which has substantial interests in Tunisia, or the new Socialist government in France. At a time of increasing militarisation, and the importance of military and strategic considerations, Tunisia's key geographical location in the Mediterranean has taken on a significance beyond pure considerations of profit on the part of foreign capital interests, which also coincide with a desire to stabilise the present regime. Thus the tranquillity in Tunisia is unlikely to last, but its future development will be watched more than ever before by the United States with a degree of attention which may well constitute a serious danger for the region as a whole.

NOTES AND REFERENCES

1. W.Ruf, Der Burgibismus und die Aussenpolitik des unabhängigen Tunesien, (Bielefeld, 1969), pp.19-23.
2. The aims of these reforms were set out by the nineteenth century Tunisian Prime Minister, Khair al-Din in his book, now translated into French, Réformes nécessaires au Etats musulmans (Paris, 1975).
3. cf. similar developments in Egypt, Morocco, Turkey etc.
4. see Ruf, Burgibismus, pp.22-26, and R.E.Germann, Verwaltung und Einheitspartei in Tunisien, (Zurich, 1968), pp.30-39.
5. see Ruf, Burgibismus, pp.26-31; for a representative sample of this attitude, see the book probably written by Abd al-'Aziz Taalbi, La Tunisie Martyre, (Paris, 1920).
6. For more details see Ruf, Burgibismus, pp.32-43.
7. Ibid., especially pp.38-40, with references to original documents.
8. loc. cit., see also Ruf, Tunesien: Gewerkschaften - Potential für eine demokratische Entwicklung, Friedrich-Ebert-Stiftung, (Bonn, 1978), pp.1-5.
9. Ruf, Burgibismus, pp.47-50.
10. Ibid., pp.47-60.
11. Speech of Pierre Mendès-France, 31 July 1954, in La Documentation Française, Série Articles et Documents, no.088, 2 August 1954.
12. L. Noé, Les Conventions Franco-Tunisiennes du 3 Juin 1955, (Tunis, 1955).
13. Ruf, Burgibismus, pp.61 f.
14. Ibid., pp.61-68.
15. Whether Bourguiba's alliance with the UGTT, which was probably more of a tactical manoeuvre, can be interpreted as identifying him as the more progressive, or even as a man of the 'left' and ben Youssef as a man of the right, is doubtful. See here B. Chabbi, La Crise Youssefiste, (Mémoire, Fac. de Droit et des Sciences Politiques, Paris, 1963). It is also doubtful, as Tibi claims - with no evidence- that Bourguiba represented a more

progressive policy. See B. Tibi, 'Die tunesische Unabhängigkeitsbewegung und ihr Werdegang im Dekolonisationsprozess. Vom Antikolonialismus zum konstitutionellen Sozialismus' in G. Grohs and B. Tibi (eds), Zur Soziologie der Dekolonisation in Afrika, (Frankfurt/Main, 1973), p.92, esp. note 42.

16. Ruf, Burgibismus, pp.66f.

17. For the history of the Tunisian trade unions, see especially W. Plum, Gewerkschaften im Maghreb, (Hannover, 1962), and the same author's Chronik der tunesischen Gewerkschaft, Friedrich-Ebert-Stiftung, (Bonn, 1969). cf. also Ruf, Tunesien-Gewerkschaften, and the sources cited there.

18. In 1951 the UGTT joined the International Confederation of Free Trade Unions. The then Secretary-General, Ferhat Hached, murdered by the French terrorist organisation The Red Hand in 1952, had visited the United States in 1951.

19. Speech of Bourguiba, 2 March 1959, published by the Ministry of Information.

20. For further details, see Ruf, Burgibismus, pp.82-84.

21. Rapport économique au VIe Congrès de l'UGTT, 20-23 September 1956, (Imprimerie La Presse, Tunis, 1956).

22. M. Nerfin, Entretiens avec Ahmed Ben Salah, Maspéro, (Paris, 1974), pp.15-19.

23. Ibid., pp.80-96.

24. Ruf, 'Le Socialisme Tunisien: Conséquences d'une Expérience Avortée', in Ruf et al., Introduction à l'Afrique du Nord Contemporain, (CNRS, Paris, 1975), pp.399-411.

25. Nerfin, Entretiens, pp.126-143, especially the notes.

26. R. Bolz, Tunesien - Wirtschaftliche und soziale Strukturen und Entwicklung, (Institut für Afrika-Kunde, Hamburg, 1976), pp.146-151 and 427-432.

27. J. Poncet, La Tunisie à la recherche de son avenir, (Paris, 1974), pp.147-158. See also Bolz, Tunesien, pp.44-56 and 209-252.

28. It is indeed remarkable that the mass of the small peasantry did not demonstrate at the time of the collectivisation of its own lands, but only years later, at the time when the land of the great landowners of the region was to be handed over for collectivisation. The Farhat family is the most prominent in the region, and Abdullah Farhat had been a member of all Bourguiba's cabinets since independence. His brother Muhammad took care of the family's land and other properties. On this Bourguiba wrote "On 20 March 1970 I had to intervene and bring ben Salah before the civil court, presided over by Muhammad Farhat, who had himself been his victim". L'Action (the newspaper of the Socialist Destour Party), 1 August 1973.

29. see 'Chroniques Economiques' in Annuaire de l'Afrique du Nord, (Paris yearly). The consequences of the liberalisation may be illustrated by the threefold increase in the import of tractors and other agricultural machinery in 1970, almost all of which was intended for use in extensive agriculture. See for example the figures given by Poncet, La Tunisie, p.106.

30. Ruf, 'Tourismus und Unterentwicklung', Zeitschrift

fur Kulturaustausch, vol.3, (1978), pp.108-114.
31. See here the analysis in Bolz, Tunesien, pp.166-226.
32. Ibid.
33. Ibid., pp.220f., and Nerfin, Entretiens, pp.132-136, and the Tunisian press during March and April 1970.
34. 'Arbeitskreis Tunesien', Tunesien Dokumentation, (Bonn, 1976), pp.10-19, Deutsche Gesellschaft für wirtschaftliche Zusammenarbeit, Produzieren in Tunesien, (Koln, 1973).
35. Poncet, La Tunisie, pp.147ff.
36. Ruf, Tunesien - Gewerkschaften, p.11.
37. Ibid.
38. 'Arbeitskreis Tunesien', Tunesien Dokumentation, pp.28-33, and the Annual Report of Amnesty International.
39. Le Monde, 15 and 19 October 1977.
40. Ruf, Tunesien - Gewerkschaften, pp.12f.
41. Ibid., p.13; Le Monde, 28, 29, 30, 31 January 1978,3 February 1978.
42. Le Monde mentioned 3000 convictions; Le Monde, 30 April - 2 May 1978.
43. See especially Le Monde, 21, 22, 28 July, 1, 6-7, 13-14, 17 August and particularly between 28 September and 11 October 1978. The conduct of the trials and the sentences were severely criticised by the ICFTU and a number of human rights organisations.
44. Le Monde, 29 January 1980 ff.
45. Ibid., 31 January 1980.
46. Ibid., 8 February 1980.
47. L'Action, 1-10 February 1980.
48. The attackers were certainly given at least tacit support by Libya; this can be deduced from the establishment of a 'Radio Free Gafsa' in Tripoli (Le Monde, 6 March 1980). However the Tunisian claim in the course of the trials that the event was solely masterminded by Libyan agents is hardly credible given the evident support of the local population.
49. It is probably the case that the attackers reached Gafsa via the Algerian border; Ben Tobal is in exile in Algiers. No mention of any connection with the Youssefists was made during the trials.
50. Of the 53 defendants (5 were tried in abstentia) 13 were sentenced to death. All sentences were carried out on 17 April 1980. See Le Monde, 13, 14 and 19 April 1980.
51. For the Mzali cabinet see Le Monde, 26 April 1980.
52. This is reflected in the creation of a Franco-Tunisian Investment Bank. See Le Monde, 27 October 1980.
53. Le Monde, 18 December 1980 and 15 January 1981.
54. Ibid., 6 December 1980.
55. Le Monde, 14 April 1981, 15 May 1981, Die Neue, 18 June 1981.
56. Le Monde, 3 and 4 May 1981.
57. Ibid.,
58. Ibid.,
59. Le Monde, 3 March 1981 carries a report on the split in the party and ben Salah's harsh criticism of the 'opportunists'.

60. Masmudi was originally the publisher of the Party's paper L'Action, which was banned at the end of 1957 because of its sharp criticism of Bourguiba's authoritarian style of government. He then became publisher of the weekly Afrique-Action, which was the fore-runner of Jeune Afrique, now published in Paris. After his second political demise in 1961 (he was appointed ambassador to Paris in 1965 and later foreign minister until 1975) he became head of Le Moteur, a motor vehicle importing company.

61. Le Monde, 10-11 May 1981.

62. Bourguiba's speech of 18 January 1963 (published by the Ministry of Information). He once again condemned the Yousefist 'plot' and also banned all opposition activity.

63. Akademie für Gesellschaftswissenschaften beim Zentralkomitee der Sozialistischen Einheitspartei Deutschlands, Entwicklung und Kampf der kommunistischen Bewegung in Asien und Afrika, Berlin (East), 1980, pp.293-295.

64. Ibid., especially the condition laid down at the 'liberalisation' congress, in which parties which 'preach class struggle' are expressly excluded.

65. Le Monde, 10 and 11 May 1981.

66. Ibid.

Chapter 4.

STATE AND LABOUR IN LIBYA*

Pandeli Glavanis

INTRODUCTION

An examination of recent contributions to the study of economic and political realities in the Socialist People's Libyan Arab Jamahiriya (Libya) indicate that they tend to be confined within the development/underdevelopment problematic (1). This approach, however, has been effectively questioned by many scholars working in other area studies (2) as well as by Ruth First in her contribution to the study of Libyan society (3). As Ruth First points out the inadequacy of such studies stems from the fact that 'development is handled as an ostensibly neutral, technical, non-class process...[and an] uncritical acceptance of the concept of "national development"' (4). Such studies fail to integrate into their analyses the diverse aspects of the socio-historical specificity of the Libyan social formation and so fail to situate structural changes in the context of an evolving international division of labour. Instead of a critical analysis of class forces and politics we are presented with indeterminate and unspecific economic evaluations of 'Islamic Socialism' and the 'critical discussion of the philosophy and recommendations of the *Green Book*' (5). These two elements have been analysed and criticised on the assumption that they constitute the two cornerstones of a new order which was introduced by Muammar al-Qadhafi.

It is beyond the scope of this contribution to present a more detailed critique of such interpretations which remain at the level of describing changes of the phenomenal and institutional structures. It suffices to point out that their major limitation is that they rest on a voluntarist and highly subjective view of policies and their limitations (6) implying, of course, that the situation can be remedied through a change of state personnel. Instead this contribution to the study of Libyan society is located at the point of intersection of two contemporary debates - that on the origins, contradictions and nature of the state in Third World societies, and the other on the nature of the evolving international division of

*Dedicated to the memory of Ruth First for her life and work and for the uniqueness of her understanding of class and state in Libya.

labour (7). For it is necessary, as Ruth First points out, 'to probe the character of the Libyan state, itself arising out of the nature of the Libyan social formation, the balance of class forces and the class struggle, and the social forces on whose behalf the state acts' (8).

The character of the Libyan state needs to be explained in the context of an articulation of domestic class alignments and an evolving international division of labour. For Libya is above all else an oil state and the oil industry is a central component of the international division of labour — especially since 1973. This study, therefore, will advance from a brief summary of the main theoretical parameters, through an analysis of the socio-historical specificity of the Libyan social formation in an evolving international division of labour, finally to take up the characterisation of the contemporary Libyan state. It should be pointed out that the lengthy exposition of conceptual and substantive material which preceeds the main concern of this study is necessary if we are to attempt a new reading of the Libyan state. A reading, it might be added, which is in much need given the limitations of the existing interpretations.

This proposed reading of the nature of the Libyan state will argue that state policies during the last decade exemplify an attempt to meet the contradictions generated by the disarticulation of the economic and political structures, contradictions which were ultimately due to an articulation of the specificity of her social formation and her location in an evolving international division of labour as a producer of oil. Islamic Socialism and *The Green Book* are but moments in this historical process which at one and the same time centralised economic resources and decentralised political culture. Political radicalism and economic conservatism, therefore, constitute the institutional parameters for the containment of class contradictions and contribute to the apparent balance of domestic class forces. It is the nature of these class forces, however, which represents the key to an understanding of the nature of the contemporary Libyan state.

STATE AND THE INTERNATIONAL DIVISION OF LABOUR

It was once possible to study and analyse the economic structure of any one part of the world in complete isolation from the rest of the world. Scarcely anywhere is this true today. A truly international world economy with a specific international division of labour and world economic order started to emerge from the sixteenth century — with the expansion of trade into world trade and the rise of the world market. During the one hundred years preceeding the First World War, during the days of European colonial expansion, the international world economy was well established and clearly reflected in the fact that world trade and international transfers of capital increased far more quickly than population and production (9). A most important feature of the internationalisation of the world economy has been the development and expansion of capitalism. Unlike other modes of production, capital has a tendency to expand without limit and consequently to break down barriers and borders. Its long-term trend has been towards the increasing international division of labour, towards foreign investment, and international markets in commodities, financial assets, and some forms of labour.

The starting point for the historical constitution and for the growth dynamic of the international economy, lies in the historically changing needs of the reproduction of capitalism which originated in certain European metropoles. With the spread of capitalism's dominant reproduction dynamic, via the structures of an international economy, the previously self-centred development of Third World societies was dramatically transformed. Third World economies were integrated into the international economy where they occupied a subsidiary, complementary and peripheral role to the dominant dynamic of the metropolitan centres.

> The result of this interweaving is the development of the capitalist and peripheral-capitalist social formations, the development of the metropolis and the underdevelopment of the periphery as 'two sides of a common, universal process', 'accumulation on a world scale' (10).

This international economy has characteristics which, though derived from the particularities of specific metropolitan and peripheral social formations, can be said to identify a specific form of economy which is not the sum total of each particular economy that has been incorporated. It is necessary, therefore, to outline the principal elements which constitute the unique structures of the international economy. Of several elements this study considers that the following six are the most pertinent (11):

(i) The world market is an international production relation 'derived' from the reproduction of the metropolis;

(ii) The world market is a production relation on a higher level;

(iii) The derived, international production relation is an augmented force of production, for the extended reproduction of the metropolis;

(iv) The economic structure of the peripheral social formations is characterised by 'derivative' not original relations of production and overlaid by the derived international relation of production;

(v) The extent and form of the peripheral dependent reproduction depends on the internal structural elements; and

(vi) The peripheral societies are the social formations of the relatively stagnating transition from pre-capitalist social formations to capitalism.

It is within such parameters that the general characterisitics of a peripheral economy can be analysed. In particular, however, these characteristics can be derived from the distinctive feature of the peripheral economy, in the international economy – the 'unity of reproduction dependent on the world market and structural heterogeneity' (12).

On the basis of the above discussion it is now possible to outline the economic role of the peripheral state in the evolving international division of labour. Initially, it is important to emphasise that the 'inherent assumption of any theory of the state regarding the congruence of the "national" political and the economic spheres is ruled out' (13). For it is evident from the above discussion that the parameters of the economic sphere (world market) and the political sphere (national state) no longer coincide. The peripheral state, therefore, is located in between two spheres whose conditions of reproduction do not coincide, and it is this dialectical contradiction which constitutes the locus of its historical evolution. In other words, it is the preconditions for reproduction of the world market which constitute the logic and parameters for the 'economic intervention' of the peripheral state in the national economy. This can be highlighted when a periodisation of state intervention in Third World societies is outlined. From the nineteenth century to the present three distinct phases may be observed:

(i) <u>The export phase</u> characterised by state-promoted organisation of the relations of production designed to ensure the reproduction of 'the factors of production' necessary for the export-based economy, e.g. public works such as the transport network linking the productive sectors to the ports.

(ii) <u>The transition from oligarchic to industrial state</u> the state moves to reorganise the labour force (e.g. through corporativist trade unions) and carries out a redistribution of surplus value from the agro-export sector to the industrial sector. Furthermore, it begins to invest in the productive sector, thus making the internal circuit of capital more profitable.

(iii). <u>The phase of industrial accumulation</u> the economic activity of the state which had earlier expressed the needs of industrial capitalism, rapidly becomes related to the process of expansion of monopoly capitalism. The role of the state is expanded with regard to infrastructure provision, the extension of financial institutions adequate to monopolistic expansion and an increased degree of participation in education, health and housing to cater for the expanded reproduction of the labour force (14).

The above periodisation hints at two important, structurally speaking, transition phases, each of which has preceeded a new phase in the international division of labour and a new world economic order. The first transition phase was initiated with the world economic crisis of 1929, and was greatly enhanced by the Second World War and the post-war period of decolonisation and economic boom. The second transition phase was initiated in the early 1970s (15) and is in the process of introducing a new international division of labour and a new world economic order. It is beyond the confines of this study to elaborate further on any of the above indicated phases, but given the central concern under consideration it is necessary to outline briefly some of the primary features of the two transitional phases and especially as they relate to the transformations experienced by peripheral-capitalism in Libya.

The period following the Second World War has been one of enormous extension of the international interpenetration of capitalist economies. Once more this has been reflected in the fact that world trade grew at a much faster rate (8.6 per cent per annum) than world production (4.9 per cent per annum) between 1950 and 1970 (16). An important factor contributing to this development was the marked increase in foreign investments. In 1946, for example, the United States' foreign investments were equivalent to 3.4 per cent of its GDP, while in 1970, the foreign assets of American enterprises had reached 8 per cent of GDP (17). This world capitalist boom also had profound effects on the colonial and semi-colonial countries of the Third World. The post-war boom had raised the prices for primary commodities so that from 1945 to 1951 the terms of trade between primary commodities and industrial products improved by about 30 per cent (18). In fact, on average, Third World economies experienced a faster rate of growth of production than the advanced capitalist countries - 2.7 per cent and 2.5 per cent respectively for the decade of the 1950s. It was a growth, however, which took place within the confines of a world economy whose order and division of labour had been created by and for the advanced capitalist countries.

In the aftermath of the 'Korean boom' the position of the newly established Third World nations, in a rapidly expanding world economy, was dramatically affected. From 1954 to 1962, for example, the terms of trade between primary commodities (oil being no exception) and industrial products deteriorated by 10-15 per cent (19). This sharp decline was of particular significance when it is recalled that during the same period some 70-90 per cent of the exports of all Third World countries consisted of primary products while 50-60 per cent of their imports consisted of industrial products (20). Furthermore, the decline in the terms of trade was followed by an absolute reduction in the demand for primary commodities in the world market. Industrial production was increasingly concentrated on highly processed products in which raw material costs were only a minor part and technological changes permitted a more effective utilisation of raw materials.

The deteriorating position, in the international economy, of the 'primary products' producers coincided with the emergence of liberation movements and the consequent process of decolonisation. From 1945 to 1960 in Africa and Asia alone some 40 countries with a combined population of 800 million inhabitants became independent (21). In most of these newly created nation-states the political elites took advantage of the international economic boom and their relative autonomy from the international economy and embarked on a strategy whose aim was the consolidation of their reconquered political independence by strengthening their economic independence. Invariably, this entailed a programme of rapid industrialisation aimed at replacing manufactured products that had previously been imported - so-called import substitution.

The crisis of the early 1970's has initiated a new transition phase in the international economy with a growing tendency towards 'transnational production' – national and multinational companies move parts of the production process out of high-wage economies, into countries where there is a virtually unlimited industrial reserve army to keep wages down. For example, trousers are cut out in Germany, then flown in air-containers to Tunisia, where they are sown together and packed and then flown back for sale in Germany. Or, an American electronics company produces masks and wafers for integrated circuits in the USA (a highly automated process) flies them to S.E. Asia, where they are soldered into capsules (labour intensive) and then brings them back to the USA for testing and marketing (22). It is the newly acquired centrality of this tendency in the international economy which has been seen by social scientists as the initiation of a 'new international division of labour' which is characterised by a world market for labour, a world wide industrial reserve army and a world market for production sites (23).

In the new international division of labour the production process is split into sub-processes which are carried out anywhere in the world, according to where the most profitable combination of capital and labour can be found. Furthermore, it is not an exaggeration to note that for the first time in the 500 year history of the world economy, manufacturing plants producing for the world economy can be profitably situated in the Third World. There are several 'technical' reasons which have facilitated the introduction of this new international division of labour of which three have been isolated as being central:

1. The breakdown of traditional economic and social structures in underdeveloped countries (The Green Revolution being the most recent form of this process) has led to an inexhaustible industrial reserve army, which is cheap and available at all times for any kind of work.
2. The fragmentation of the production process makes it possible for most sub-processes to be carried out by unskilled workers after very short training periods.
3. The development of transportation and communication technology makes it possible to carry out complete or partial production processes at any site throughout the world without prohibitive technical, organisational or cost problems (24).

There are several important implications derived from the introduction of this new international division of labour of which three are particularly relevant to this study. *First*, it suggests that the 'crisis' in the advanced industrial societies is merely a symptom of a major shift in the organisation of capitalism as a world system towards a new international division of labour. *Second*, it indicates that although it is for the first time that the periphery is becoming the location of manufacturing, yet this merely perpetuates a previous international inequality in a new form and also reproduces dependence in a new form and does not indicate any 'real' development of the Third World (25). *Third*, and possibly the most relevant for this study, is the greater emphasis placed on *the role of the peripheral state in the internationalisation of production and the introduction of the new international division of labour accompanied by a new world economic order* (26).

There is, of course, no mechanical relation between tendencies in the international economy or the introduction of a new international division of labour and peripheral state intervention in the national economy. For it is not possible to specify theoretically the specific nature of changes in any one peripheral social formation outside of concrete analysis, and it is for this reason that this study now moves on to an examination of the internal transformations experienced by the Libyan economy and the nature of the state.

SOCIO-HISTORICAL FORMATION OF THE LIBYAN STATE

The preceeding discussion challenges approaches which attempt to locate the characterisation of Third World states at the level of the 'centrality of the state'. The subjective nature of these interpretations permits the creation of illusions about the 'effectiveness' of Third World states and thereby attributes the failure of economic and socio-political development to the character of state officials. Such voluntarist approaches dismiss a socio-historical examination of state formation and instead focus on an analysis of the social origins, attitudes and behaviour of the holders of prominent state posts. The Socialist People's Libyan Arab Jamahiriya, of course, more so than other Third World states, lends itself to the use of a behavioural approach to deal with what is essentially a socio-historical problem. The writings of Omar El Fathaly and Monte Palmer, for example, are but one illustration of an attempt to examine political institutions in contemporary Libya by reference to a critical discussion of the writings and activities of one prominent state official – Muammar al-Qadhafi (27). This study, however, suggests that the problem of characterising the state in any Third World society should start from 'an analysis of the economic structure of the production process, the process of circulation and of mystification, and an analysis of class relationships' (28).

Pre-oil

On the 24 December 1951 the United Nations granted Libya her independence thus bringing into existence a state which was imposing in the extent of its territory, but lacking in natural resources and containing a population of just over one million. The imposition of a Federated Kingdom, comprising the three autonomous regions of Cyrenaica, Fezzan and Tripolitania, reflected both the external influences and the nature of Libya's class alignments and economic structure. Given that it was the articulation of this socio-economic structure with the discovery of oil in the mid-1950s which constituted a central factor in bringing about the Revolution of 1969, it is necessary to isolate the main features of Libya's economic and societal structures at the time of independence. The physical make-up of the country consists of a discontinuous mosaic of better-watered and settled territory, embedded in a wide expanse of arid or semi-arid land. A more productive zone lies along the Mediterranean coast, but this is by no means continuous, being broken by expanses of semi-desert and steppe land which reach the sea. It is in this coastal strip, comprising the Tripolitanian coastal plains, the Jebel, and the Cyrenaican plateau, that 95 per cent of the Libyans lived in 1951 (29). The eastern extremity of the Tripolitanian zone is separated from the western end of the Cyrenaican by 650 km of desert and semi-desert. Zuara is 400 km from Sfax in Tunisia; Derna, 700 km from the Nile valley. The nearest oases of the Fezzan lie 450 km south of Tripoli across broken and arid plateaux; those of Kufra lie 700 km south of Benghazi, ten days journey by truck. On the other hand, Syracuse in Sicily is only 500 km across the sea from Tripoli; and from Derna, in Northern Cyrenaica, the distance to Crete is 300 km and to southern Greece 400 km. Finally, the port of Tripoli is about 280 km south of the main shipping line running from the Suez Canal to the western Mediterranean (30).

An examination of Libya's natural resources in 1951 suggests that even agriculturally she was one of the marginal or sub-marginal land areas in the world. Nevertheless, agriculture was the mainstay of the Libyan economy, and in 1951, at least 80 per cent of the population were engaged in this branch of economic activity (31). Potential productive land amounted to just over 14 million ha; that is, less than one per cent of the total area of the country (32). This land was further subdivided into three categories: land under static farming, land under shifting cultivation, and grazing land. Of this land 11.6 million ha were used only for grazing leaving just over two million ha as potential area for cultivation of subsistence crops (33). Cereals were the most important crop and especially barley which is best suited to the climate. In fact, barley formed both the staple diet of the population and constituted the principal item in Libyan exports (34).

Other chief crops were wheat and millet. Olives were approaching maturity at the time of independence and provided an important item of food in the north, while in the south dates were and still are a staple, with consumption averaging about 500 grammes per day (35). Figs, peaches, apricots, pomegranates, and citrus fruit, introduced just before independence, were also important crops. The quality of citrus fruit is unusually high so that in 1950 5,000 tons were exported (36). Vines were introduced under the Italian regime and in 1951, there were an estimated 20 million plants (37). A fair quality of wine was produced and some of it exported. At independence, however, viticulture was prohibited (38) and whole areas of vines were left to waste. Finally, almonds thrived in Libya, supplying an intermediate planting in the olive groves. Vegetables were important in most localities, and because their quality was distinctly higher than in some of the neighbouring countries, an export trade could have developed, especially since in some cases the maturing season is ten to 15 days earlier than the rest of the Mediterranean (39).

Animal husbandry, the most important single source of income in 1951, played an integral part in the economic life of Libya, particularly in Cyrenaica where life tended towards pastoralism. Besides providing them with many of the necessities of life - milk, milk products, some meat, and wool and hair for clothing and tent-making - animal products formed a significant proportion of the export trade of Libya at that time. Cattle were also kept in gardens in Tripolitania and were primarily used as draught animals. The dromedary camel was the principal means of transportation in the interior of the country and camel milk and meat were also items of the local diet.

At the time of the Italian conquest (1911) the country had not proceeded beyond a primitive handicraft economy producing simple consumption goods for domestic use. Italian industrialisation in its limited scale never affected local industry and was only rarely in competition with the local crafts. Most of the Italian industry centered around capital goods: buildings, construction, timber, mechanical engineering; and public utilities, transport, electricity, and telephones. The investments were largely the results of needs created by economic growth itself. In addition, limited capital was invested in the processing of agriculture and fishing products and light consumption goods such as leather, textiles, printing, and paper.

With the withdrawal of the Italian community in Cyrenaica during the Second World War industry almost disappeared and Cyrenaica reverted to village crafts. In Tripolitania, on the other hand, a considerable part of the plants installed remained to the day of independence. Fishing, largely in Italian and Greek hands, supplied the raw materials for an important local processing industry. There were also extensive spongo-beds off the coast of Libya. This industry was, however, entirely in the hands of Greek firms, most of which were registered in Greece. Several food processing factories for local consumption, two tanneries, and two shoe factories completed the picture of modern industry. Textiles were still manufactured by the old handicraft methods in a great number of small shops or in homes. Finally, there was an English-American Tobacco company which produced 389.6 million cigarettes and 120 tons of tobacco in 1950 (40).

Due to the limited size of the internal market and the predominance of subsistence agriculture and a basic pastoral economy money wages were infrequent. An idea of labour conditions prevailing at that time in some areas can be obtained by focusing on the *Jebbad* (drawers of water) in the Fezzan. This category of labour was not paid money wages, but had long-established rights to a certain share of the crops produced (41). Their income was usually so low that they were constantly in debt to the landowners who advanced dates and barley to them, resulting in their loss of freedom to move.

In Tripolitania the greatest employer of labour in 1951 was the government. For managerial, professional, supervising, secretarial and clerical staff, monthly wages began at below MAL 4,600 (42) and went up to MAL 11,000. The minimum daily wage for an eight hour day was MAL 80 for unskilled workers and up to MAL 104 for skilled labour.

Unskilled agricultural workers were paid MAL 50 to MAL 70 a day (43). A comparison of wages and the costs of commodities reveals the purchasing power of wages in 1951. The monthly cost of food, including soap, fuel, and cigarettes, on the 31 May 1951, for a family of urban Libyans (four persons) was MAL 3,233.74 (44). On the basis of 25 day working month an adequate diet would require a daily wage of about MAL 130; note, of course, that the above does not include rent, clothing, etc. British administration officials in Tripolitania and Cyrenaica – Fezzan was under French tutelage – reported that a national income per capita of 30 to 40 US dollars per annum represented a reasonable figure (45).

Such an economic structure had prevented the emergence of a more conventional social structure with a characteristic peasantry and landlord economy; as witnessed in other Arab countries such as Egypt. Similarly, as surplus generation was marginal it inhibited the emergence of dominant classes based on an economic control over resources and instead favoured the continuation of tribal and clan alliances. That is, a decentralised political culture where power was derived from control over the ideological and mystification process in the society. The viability of this geographical/physical and socio-political decentralisation was severely tested by the Italian occupation of the country from 1911 to 1932, but Italian colonisation had to restrict itself to the coastal plains with minimal control over the hinterland. It is not surprising, therefore, that in the nineteenth century it was a religious order, The Sanussi of Cyrenaica, that took advantage of the segmentary tribal political system to exercise hegemony in the land. The Sanussi developed into a political movement and came to 'provide a system of authority over and above the segmentary tribal system, and the Sanussi notables, by virtue of their control over land and water resource allocation and long-distance trade in the interior, constituted a ruling class' (46).

The expansion of European commercial capital in the Mediterranean during the nineteenth century had produced a concomitant development of an indigenous commercial bourgeoisie in the coastal towns. Italian colonisation, however, brought an early end to this urban-based class and inadvertently reinforced the hegemonic authority of the Sanussi in the whole country. That the Italians fought the Sanussi for 21 years (1911 – 1932) before they could excercise minimal control over the whole country was but a moment in the reproduction of tribal and religious hegemony in Libyan political culture.

Sanussi hegemony was maintained despite the emergence of a Libyan working class and elements of an urban-based middle class in the coastal towns during the period of Italian colonisation. This was due to the fact that the tribal/religious political authority had now taken on a proto-nationalist character in its struggle against the Italian occupation. This proto-nationalist character was further reinforced during the Second World War when the Sanussi cooperated with the allied armies and eventually formed a political organisation, *al-Jabha al-Wataniya* (National Front), that sought complete and immediate independence. The main opposition to this political demand came from Tripolitania where, especially the working class and petty-bourgeoisie was developing at a fast rate during British control of the economic and political life. The Tripolitanian-based political movements, however, had no control over any of the country's meagre resources and their source of livelihood derived entirely from their employment in British army bases and administrative structures. Furthermore, as will be shown later, the working class organisations had been tainted with communist ideology and so were harshly restricted in their activities by the victorious British army.

It was within such a socio-political and economic background that Libya was granted her independence and the head of the Sanussi order was installed as monarch of a federated kingdom in 1951. This political system reflected both the nature of the internal class alignments, derived from Libya's socio-historical specificity, and an attempt by external forces to insulate the country from the radicalisation of Arab nationalism that was taking place in the region after the Second World War. The effect, of course, of granting the Sanussi and their tribal alliance political power was that for a second time in Libya's modern history the urban-based classes were prevented from sharing in the hegemonic control of their society. For the Sanussi regime derived its legitimacy from two principal sources which reflected the traditional socio-economic structure of Libya in 1951:

> the claim to religious authority exercised over the lodges of the Sanussi order and the tribal notables who presided over the allocation of grazing and water rights within traditionally defined areas. They were joined by townsmen and business families picked for their complicity with the system of political patronage (47).

Post-oil
The discovery of oil in 1955 brought about a massive inflow of capital and also generated a series of socio-political contradictions which ultimately led to the Revolution of 1969, and the emergence of a new political culture. It is beyond the scope of this section of the study to outline the dramatic transformations experienced by the Libyan economy during the oil era, especially as they are dealt with in some detail in the economic section of this volume. It is necessary, however, to indicate some of the characteristic changes which articulated with the traditional political structures and thereby generated important dislocations in the political culture. It is important to note, for example, that the initial impact of oil exploration and production, from 1955 to 1963, was to increase further the deficit in the balance of payments, so that in 1960 it stood at 56 million Libyan Dinars (LD) (48). This was primarily due to the fact that following the initiation of the oil industry there followed a concommitant increase in the demand for consumer goods which had to be imported given Libya's primitive productive economy at the time. As the oil concession revenues increased the deficit in the balance of payments decreased to 45 and 23 million LD in 1961 and 1962 respectively, but still constituted an important problem (49). A

problem, of course, which reflected the dramatic transformation in consumption and quality of life in the coastal towns of Libya.

For the first time in Libya's recent modern history an urban-based bourgeoisie was emerging, developing and relying on surpluses that were not derived from the traditional economic structures. If not politically, but at least socially and culturally this newly-emerged class posed the first serious challenge to the hegemonic control of political power that had been held by tribal leaders. It should also be noted that this early phase of Libya's oil boom coincided with the tail-end of the second phase of the evolving international division of labour that was discussed in section one of this study. Whereas, Egypt under Nasser and many other newly independent Third World nations were taking advantage of the international economic boom to consolidate their economic base, Libya was increasing her dependence on the international economy. This dependence can be seen from the nature of the transformations experienced by the economy during the 1960s. The dominance of the oil sector in the economy, for example, increased to such an extent that in 1969 it represented 74 per cent of gross national income (50).

The increased flow of capital in the economy, however, did not enhance Libya's sound economic development. The productive sectors of the economy, agriculture and industry, experienced important declines in output. Agriculture, for example, though receiving 4 per cent and 10 per cent of state investment in the years 1962 and 1972 respectively contributed 10 per cent and 3 per cent to national production for the same years. During the same years, industry received 3 per cent and 12 per cent and contributed 6 per cent and 2 per cent to national production. It was the service sector, of course, which received the largest investments, produced the highest and ever-increasing outputs and attracted an increasingly larger proportion of the work-force - 72 per cent in 1972 (51). By the end of the 1960s Libya had established itself as a service-economy, par excellence, and the commercial bourgeoisie in the coastal towns was accruing the benefits in partnership with the traditional tribal notables. For it is important to note that though national revenue was increasing dramatically it was not followed by similar increases in real per capita income. In fact, per capita income increased only half as much as real national income and this was primarily due to the high rate of inflation (52). An inflation, of course, that was fuelled by the deterioration in the terms of trade between primary commodities - including oil - and western-produced industrial consumer goods which was discussed in section one of this study.

It was within such a situation that the urban-based classes started to emerge as potential threats to the traditional political system. The merchants and entrepreneurs, however, had been fused with the tribal leaders on the basis of their common source of newly-found wealth - profits from the tertiary sector of the economy. Given that the productive sectors of the economy did not provide any surpluses it was the tertiary sector which provided the sole opportunity to accumulate wealth. The tertiary sector, however, was totally dependent on the expansion of the oil industry and so 'access to government now gave access to business and financial manipulations' (53). The urban-based commercial bourgeoisie was coopted into the dominant tribal political culture and saw its long-term viability in an alliance with Western oil interests. Politics of the tribe and patronage of the palace continued and prevented the emergence of class contradictions and their reflection in class-based politics. Instead, and similarly to other Third World nations, albeit a bit later, Libya was on the brink of a nationalist uprising. This was particularly so in the aftermath of the 1967 Arab-Israeli war where the government's attitude of non-involvement produced the first major indigenous nationalist challenge in the oil era. The hegemony of the tribal political system and its dominant class - composed of tribal leaders and urban-based merchants and entrepreneurs - was in question. The challenge, however, came from social strata that had not benefitted from the oil boom, but were themselves created by it; working classes and the petty-bourgeoisie.

THE REVOLUTION OF 1 SEPTEMBER 1969

The military coup which put an end to the hegemony of the tribal political system was led by junior army officers who came from the minor tribes, poorer families of the interior and the poorer social strata of the coastal towns (54). The code word for the coup was 'Palestine is ours', indicating the political direction of the new regime, and it was led by an adamantly Arab nationalist Revolutionary Command Council. Within a short period of time Libya had been transformed into one of the most staunchly anti-western regimes in the region and it directly challenged western control of its oil industry. This was but the start of the radicalisation of political culture which in the next decade passed through various institutional forms each of which was more radical than the preceeding one: Arab Socialist Union, the Popular Committees, the General People's Congress, the Revolutionary Committees and the militarisation of the whole society. These changes which perplexed outside observers who had grown accustomed to the Sanussi regime and Libya's traditional social structure constitute a central factor in the plethora of voluntarist, subjective and critical interpretations of the nature of the Libyan state after 1969. Nevertheless, this section of the study will argue that the apparent radicalisation of political culture had little to do with the social origins of the Libyan state officials or their eccentricities, but represented a logical development of Libya's socio-historical specificity and her location in an evolving international division of labour.

As indicated earlier the roots of the September 1969 Revolution have to be located in the articulation of Libya's historical socio-economic specificity and her role as a producer of oil for the international economy. In section two of this study the major characteristics of Libya's socio-economic specificity have been outlined. It is now necessary to draw out the nature of the internal and external class alignments which constituted the background of the September 1969 Revolution.

From the very start the Libyan oil industry took on a clear political role.

> Libya was seen by Western oil strategists as an alternative to the "unstable" political environment that characterized the rest of the Arab world in the '50s and '60s. Pre-production expenditures and activities climbed sharply in 1957 and 1958, after the nationalization of the Suez Canal and the political turmoil that extended through the American and British military interventions in 1958 following the revolution in Iraq. Similarly, Libyan crude exports skyrocketed in 1968 and 1969, following the 1967 June War and the closing of the Suez Canal (55).

As indicated in the previous section the oil boom had little effect on the productive sectors of the economy. It did, however, have a major effect on the lives of Libyans. In addition to experiencing high rates of inflation the bulk of the Libyan population was marginalised during the decade of the 1960s. Not only did the newly-found wealth find its way predominantly into the hands of tribal leaders and urban merchants and entrepreneurs, but the majority of the Libyans were unable to find jobs in the expanding economy. The oil boom had created demands for highly-educated or skilled and semi-skilled labour while the Libyan labour force was predominantly non-skilled and uneducated. By 1965, for example, 67 per cent of the professionals, 52 per cent of the technicians and supervisors and 22 per cent of all skilled labour were foreigners (56).

The allocation of the better-paid jobs to foreigners created much resentment amongst the indigenous labour force especially since the traditional economic activities were quickly disappearing. One of the ways in which many traditional economic activities were brought to an end was through the utilisation of Libyan labour for the oil exploration period. Exploration is the most labour-intensive stage of the oil industry and companies utilised unskilled Libyan tribesmen in the remote desert areas were oil was located. These tribesmen who received relatively high wages during the exploration period abandoned their livestock and subsistence agriculture. Once the exploration stage was completed, of course, they were unemployed and drifted to the coastal towns in search of jobs.

This period of the late 1950s and the 1960s, therefore, saw a tremendous urban migration of tribesmen so that the city of Tripoli, for example, doubled in size between 1954 and 1964 (57). As tribesmen abandoned their livestock and subsistence agriculture and the urban population increased the demand for food and other consumer goods so Libya had to rely more on imports.

> This process led to increased inflation and unrest among Libyan working class and petty bourgeoisie. Another problem adding to social discontent was the limited job opportunities for many of those who migrated into the cities in search for work. High levels of unemployment and under-employment developed, even as

oil revenues were doubling each year, and the shortage of housing led to the development of squatter slums around the major cities (58).

It was within such a socio-political climate that nationalist politics started to challenge the hegemony of tribal and patron-client political structures. The demand for an ever-increasing number of skilled and educated workers had also led to a rapid expansion of the educational system. The first generation of Libyan university students went to Egypt and became involved in Nasserist nationalist politics. Similarly, many of Libya's officers were trained in the Baghdad Academy and returned with Baathist nationalist politics. It is not surprising, therefore, that following the 1967 Arab-Israeli war Libyan oil workers and port workers went on strike and closed the industry for almost two months (59). Once the strike was defeated, however, it brought even greater surpluses to the Libyan economy. The closure of the Suez Canal after 1967 put a premium on Libyan oil and the gap between the few wealthy Libyans and the prosperous foreigners, on the one hand, and the increasingly impoverished Libyan population, on the other, increased. As indicated above the urban-based bourgeoisie had already been coopted by the tribal regime so it was left to the petty bourgeoisie and urban poor to challenge the hegemony of the state.

> The classes that moved in opposition to Idris in this period were the petty bourgeoisie (employees in the public sector, middle-level military officers), the impoverished peasants and unemployed city migrants, and some tribal elements - all of whose positions deteriorated under Idris. It was the contradiction between the increasing wealth of the Idris clique and the rampant poverty of the rest of the population plus the spread of Arab nationalist consciousness, that generated the *coup d'état* in 1969 (60).

NATURE OF THE STATE IN REVOLUTIONARY LIBYA

There has been a plethora of writings which analyse and discuss the philosophy of the Revolution and the political and economic activities of the Revolutionary Command Council and especially the thoughts and actions of its leader Muammar al-Qadhafi. It is not the intention of this section of the study to add to this literature. Instead, the study will focus on two aspects, one external and one internal, which might constitute the basis on which to evaluate the nature of the Libyan state after 1969: the oil industry and trade unions. It should also be pointed out that such an evaluation will have to be located in the historical socio-economic specificity of the Libyan social formation which was presented in section two and the theoretical discussion of section one.

Oil after the Revolution
Within two years of coming to power the Libyan Revolutionary Command

Council had acquired a reputation as an extremist government which would do all in its power to achieve full control over its oil resources. Libya was one of the first oil states to push for 51 per cent participation in its oil industry and within four years had achieved more than 70 per cent control over its oil resources. By 1974, Occidental Oil Company signed an agreement by which the profits were to be split 81-19 in favour of Libya (61). Similarly, Libya was in the forefront of the demand to increase oil prices from as early as 1971, and it was one of the first oil producing states to impose production cutbacks in order to conserve its natural resources. There are several ways of interpreting this 'radicalised' approach to the Libyan state. The present section of this study proposes to go beyond the confines of the Libyan case and locate the discussion at the more general level of the 'Primary Commodities Boom' in the evolution of the international economy in the early part of the 1970s.

One point about which there seems to be some form of general agreement is the rapid increase in the price of raw materials. Of particular importance is the suggestion that the producing nations have been able to increase substantially their share of profits through this rapid increase in prices. This is said to be particularly true for the oil industry.

> Oil is of course, the outstanding example with the under-developed countries having raised their share of profits on crude oil from 10-15 per cent in the 1920s to about 85 per cent in 1972... Oil is not an exceptional case. Copper, the second biggest field for US foreign resources investment, is clearly comparable...the copper producing countries too have substantially improved their rewards...Clearly, the situation has radically altered since the early days (62).

Although I recognise that there is a lengthy debate around these quantitative changes, regarding the rate of inflation - increases of industrial commodities - etc., I submit that the general trend indicated above is acceptable.

Along with these quantitative changes, important qualitative changes are said to have occurred. Such changes, it is argued, have permitted the producing countries to increase control over their own resources. Some of the qualitative changes cited are:

> the nearly universal trend towards processing, refining and fabricating raw materials in the country of extraction...pressure is now being exerted, on resource companies in general and petroleum ones especially, over pricing, the volume of production, investment policies, transportation and new supply sources. An important aim is to improve "backward linkages" of the resource industries...has led to the adoption of various policies and mechanisms of a general character to ensure such control, notably joint ventures or majority character, service contracts and outright nationalisation (63).

Furthermore, and as a corollary of the above, the same analysts suggest that there has been an 'overall improvement in the bargaining position of host countries vis-à-vis foreign resource companies' (64). Here again, although some of the aspects indicated above may be questioned, there is general agreement on the substantial improvement of the bargaining position of the producing countries which has occurred. As Emmanuel points out it...'is of course, an obvious fact of the contemporary world, and it would need a rather large dose of dogmatism to remain unaware of it' (65).

It is clear from the above, despite the inadequate and limited exposition, that sufficient changes have occurred in this particular part of the International Economic Order to permit some analysts to conclude that at least one of the demands of the new strategy, i.e. 'higher prices for raw materials and the control of natural resources', is in the process of being fulfilled. It is important, however, to draw attention to an important characteristic of these changes which is clearly reflected in the London-based International Institute for Strategic Studies Review for 1973:

> the greatest shock, the most potent sense of a new era of any event in recent years...change, drastic not only by recent standards but even in some respects by those of the two centuries since the Industrial Revolution...This was the first time that major industrial states had to bow to pressure from pre-industrial ones...(The Arab) victory upset the hierarchies of power long enjoyed, or resented, according to one's station, and opened up prospects of quite new political balances. By the same token, it was by far the biggest extension of the world's effective political arena since the Chinese Revolution (66).

This type of analysis which focusses on 'political aspects' is also developed by Angus Hone in his article entitled 'The Primary Commodities Boom' in which many of the price increases are ascribed to 'political crises' (67). Hone goes on to state that 'any break in OPEC's united front would have the very serious consequences of causing a steep decline from the present floor of "tax-plus-cost" towards a price based on the marginal cost of production' (68). Emmanuel also points out, with respect to the quantitative changes, that:

> This is not all that needs to be said, though. Current prices not only are not 'prices of production' (equilibrium prices); not only are they contingent and in part 'political' in character; they are also not even entirely *real*. To some extent, they are fictitious, for as Angus Hone admits "a significant portion of the boom" is a purely nominal reflection of the fall in the value of the pound and the dollar (69).

Emmanuel then goes on to raise certain questions with regard to the actual incomes derived by the producing countries from these price increases which are not 'real'. He notes that:

> We can now see that the increase in the prices of oil, and the fantastic profits made from it, will be largely illusory – manifested in mere alterations in book-entries in banks in Zurich, London and New York – for lack of adequate structures for the absorption, and so for the consumption, of commodities and services that could be imported by the oil-producing countries...Thus the rise in the price of oil will very probably remain formal, costing nothing to the consumer countries as a whole, and bringing no profit to the producing countries. The latter will continue to receive in real values, only the cost of production, some 10 or 20 cents per barrel...the rest of the price they will never receive, for lack of capacity to consume it. In other words, these countries, after having been for a long time too poor to be able to sell oil at a normal price, when at last they have the opportunity to unite and, nominally, dictate this price, turn out to be too poor to be able to ensure that they are paid it in real terms (70).

An important question emerges as a result of the above discussion, namely the extent to which the important changes, both quantitative and qualitative, reflect structural changes in the economies of the producing countries or the significance of 'political independence' that has so often been underestimated. Which is not to contrast 'political independence' with 'economic development', but to suggest that the former does not necessarily imply the latter. A fact which has been briefly, but adequately, emphasised above: producing countries are too poor to be able to take advantage of increases achieved by political pressure. What would, however, turn these illusory profits into *real* assets? A positive suggestion in this direction is made by Emmanuel when he notes:

> Let us imagine that the recent price-increases had been preceded by a wave of strikes in the Middle East which had resulted in a very substantial increase in wages. Let us further imagine that as a consequence, there had followed a rapid economic development of these countries, and intense urbanisations so that the price of a square metre of land in Saudi Arabia or Iraq had risen to the level of California or Texas; and that, as a result of all this, the real cost of extraction had risen from 10 cents to 10 dollars a barrel. It is clear that nobody, in *those* circumstances, would have vociferated about "blackmail" (71).

This is also emphasised by Amin when he indicates that these changes could have

> a different meaning when one proceeds in the opposite direction, i.e. when one *first* defines the internal objectives of a really self-reliant and 'popular' development and *then* considers the ways in which the world order must be acted on in order to promote the achievement of these objectives (72).

From the above discussion the major limitation of the price rises becomes clear. It is not that they were derived as a result of political pressures, but that they were achieved as a response to *external* stimuli rather than *internal* demands. As such, they reflect a situation which though different in form from the previous historical stage is not different in substance. External dependence cannot be said to have been reduced as a result of the considerable gains which the producing countries achieved through political pressures.

Trade Unions
The Socialist People's Libyan Arab Jamahiriya (Libya) is a capital-rich oil exporting state whose economic and political structures have experienced a dramatic transformation during the last two decades. Two aspects of this transformation, respectively in the economic and political spheres, are of particular significance to the discussion of trade-unions and need to be highlighted.

In the *economic* sphere Libya's pattern of development is similar to that experienced by other oil-rich Gulf states. In 1961, when oil exports were first initiated, Libya's per capita income was £71.85 (73). By 1978, the per capita income had risen to £1684.50 and the economy had experienced a dramatic transformation (74). Along with this increase in her per capita income Libya experienced a considerable increase in the proportion of expatriates employed in the national labour force. By 1978, the figures for legal migrant workers indicated that the expatriates constituted 32 per cent of the total labour force (75). As with the Gulf states, Libya has accumulated a super-abundance of money while experiencing a drastic shortage of manpower, and in order to sustain rapid growth in the economy she has had to import ever-increasing numbers of foreign workers. It is a policy, however, which has serious ramifications on the very process of development, in general, and the trade-union movement, in particular. The tendency, for example, for expatriate labour to enter the productive sectors whilst Libyan nationals monopolise the service and government sectors has created an important division within the trade-union movement (76). A situation, it might be added, which gains in significance when it articulates with the major political changes experienced during the last decade.

In the *political* sphere, Libya's pattern of development during the 1950s and 1960s also resembled that of the oil-rich Gulf states, a paternalistic/clientelistic monarchial regime, with strong pro-western tendencies, dominated the political culture. On September 1969 however, the monarchy was replaced by a Revolutionary Command Council (RCC), under the leadership of Muammar Al-Qadhafi. This had an important effect on the development of an independent trade-union movement in Libya. Whereas under the monarchy trade-union activity had increased during the 1960s, albeit in political rather than labour-relations direction, the RCC promulgated a new law outlawing student and industrial strikes (77). As to the labour policy of the new regime it was encapsulated in the statements made by Qadhafi himself when he noted that 'labourers and the revolution are an indivisable entity', labour organisations would be for 'ordinary administrative purposes', and 'we do not accept intermediaries between the revolution and its working forces' (78). Furthermore, on March 3 1977, the RCC was replaced by the General Secretariat of the General People's Congress, headed by Muammar Al-Qadhafi who declared that 'there are no wage-workers in the socialist society, only partners' (79). The articulation of these political changes with a labour force that is already divided along national/sectoral lines was of paramount importance to trade-union activity in modern Libya. This is particularly so, as the 400,000 plus expatriates, who are vital to the growth of the productive sectors of the economy, are excluded from the revolution and denied the right of becoming 'partners'.

The two instances, economic and political, mentioned above, constitute the parameters which determine current labour relations and trade-unionism in Libya. In order to highlight, however, the nature of the changes experienced by Libyan trade-unionism during the last decade it is necessary to situate them in a historical context. This is particularly so, as the history of Libyan trade-unionism is integrally tied to particular economic and political realities. The first trade-unions, for example, were established during the period of Italian colonisation and were closely linked to the Fascist regime of Mussolini. Furthermore, given that the bulk of the Libyan population was organised on tribal lines and involved in 'traditional' nomadic and semi-nomadic economic activities it is not surprising that the membership of these early unions was predominantly Italian settlers. During this period Italian labour not only dominated in the 'modern' sectors of the economy, but also actively participated in the discriminatory policies pursued by the colonial regime regarding Libyans. There was, however, an attempt to organise Libyan workers, who were employed in unskilled occupations by Italian entrepreneurs, but it was suppressed. This effort, it might be noted, was led by Rajab Neihum who was to later lead a federation of unions that were opposed to the pro-western policies of the monarchy. It was not until the defeat of the Axis forces and the establishment of the British administration in the 1940s that Libyans started to join trade-unions. Nevertheless, these unions were still controlled by Italians, albeit Communists, who used them as a base for attacking the British presence in Libya and the Middle East. Their activities were predominantly political and their goals were national liberation rather than labour relations. As to the Libyan participation in these unions it was drawn from the large number of workers employed by the British military authorities, and in particular from those Libyans who had been hired to replace Italian workers in the docks and military bases.

This particular character of the first successful attempts to organise Libyan labour was to be significant for the further development of trade-unionism. With independence in December, 1951, the Italian communists were deported and the first Libyan controlled unions were established. From the start, however, the 'Libyan General Labour Union', which was formed in 1952, was dominated by two opposing political ideologies rather than labour concerns. Salem Shiteh, who was to become a member of parliament during the monarchy, was appointed as its president in an election campaign that was funded by the Ministry of Interior (80). Shiteh maintained close contacts with the CIO-AFL leadership and affiliated his union to the ICFTU. He used his position to try and establish a federation of unions from the Maghreb to Egypt, as a counter to the Arab Labour Federation (81). This policy received the support of the regime, but was firmly opposed by the most important sectors of the Libyan labour force. The petroleum, dock and tobacco workers broke away and formed a second federation whose politics were opposed to the regime. This new federation was dominated by Nasserist and Baathist political ideologies and was primarily concerned with the current issues of local and regional Arab nationalism. It was led by such men as Rajab Neihum and Suleiman Maghrabi, who later became the first Prime Minister after the September 1 1969 Revolution.

A major consequence of the political character of Libyan trade-unionism during the period 1952-1969 is that the labour movement was divided in terms of political affiliations. By 1969, there were three major labour federations in the kingdom. By far the most important, due to its close links with the regime, was the 'National Federation of Trade Unions' which was based in Tripoli. Its forerunner had been the 'Libyan General Labour Union', and it was established as a result of the split mentioned above. It is important to note that one of the largest groups of workers affiliated to the federation was the waged and salaried workers from the American Wheelus Air Force Base in Tripoli. The second federation, the 'Professional Workers Federation', was also based in Tripoli and had adopted a pro-government approach. The third federation, 'The Federation of Libyan Trade Unions', was based in Benghazi and it followed a strong-anti-regime policy which was motivated by an allegiance to Nasserist Arab Nationalism type politics.

Given that the three federations were primarily concerned with political rather than labour issues it is not surprising that they did not attract a large proportion of the Libyan labour force. In 1965, for example, the total union membership, for all three federations, was estimated at 37,000. This membership was divided between the three federations in the following manner: NFTU=12,700, PWF=6,000; and FLTU=18,300. This low level of labour organisation is further emphasised when it is noted that, according to the 1964 census there were 218,099 Libyan male workers in the non-agrarian sectors of the economy; i.e. the trade-unions attracted only 17 per cent of the workers most likely to join. If the total labour force is considered then the percentage drops down to nine (82). This low level of labour organisation existed despite the fact that the Libyan labour law recognised the right of waged and salaried workers to organise, and prohibited employers from adopting discriminatory practices against union members. This labour policy had been enshrined by royal decree in 1962 and had superseded the earlier labour law of 1958. A further indication that it was the political nature of the unions that inhibited many workers from joining is exemplified in the following example. Whereas the labour law of 1962 provided for collective bargaining. by 1968, the sole bargaining agreement was between bakery employees and employers concerning working conditions.

In a context where the primary concern of trade-unions is national and regional politics it is not surprising that labour relations were determined as a result of government initiatives. Enforcement of labour legislation and the resolution of disputes was the responsibility of government officials from the Ministry of Labour. Similarly, strikes and other forms of trade-union activity were subject to government regulations. A further indication of government involvement in labour relations may be grasped from some of the provisions of the 1962 labour law. Formal hiring, for example, in any enterprise, had to be carried out through government employment offices. The determination of wages, working hours, holidays and other benefits were also the responsibility of the government. In effect, the government during the period 1952 to 1969 was not only the largest employer – approximately 25 per cent of the total labour force – but also the main initiator and guarantor of labour relations (83).

As the government had co-opted what is traditionally seen as the primary concern of the trade-unions this left the path clear for the latter to get involved in what is normally the arena for political parties. This was particularly so in the case of the 'Federation of Libyan Trade Unions' which, for all intent and purposes, functioned as an opposition political party. There were, however, two areas where the federation could be said to be acting as a trade-union, i.e. discrimination by Libyan and foreign employers in favour of expatriate workers, and in the case of oil field workers, food and housing at work sites. As a means of attracting much needed, expatriate labour, employers offered incentives which were not normally available to Libyan workers. Though this could have been handled as a labour-relations issue the 'Federation of Libyan Trade Unions' turned it into a major attack on the regime's pro-western policies. Furthermore, as employers in the oil fields were foreign companies this particular labour grievance was also used by the same federation to fuel its anti-regime attacks. Given that the foreign oil companies represented the most important single employer, after the government, it is not surprising that a casual glance at labour disputes during the 1960s would indicate that Libyan trade-unions were characterised by a strong anti-foreign feeling. The most serious strike of the 1960s, for example, took place in 1967, when the oil and port workers refused to accept government assurances that oil exports would not be shipped to countries that supported Israel following the events of the Six Day War. This particular strike was led by Suleiman Maghrabi who was subsequently arrested and was not released until after the September 1969 Revolution and named Prime Minister.

It should be clear from the above that the history of trade-unionism in Libya during the 1950s and 1960s is that of a confrontation between Nasserist-type Arab Nationalism and a paternalistic, pro-western monarchy. One particularly important aspect of this confrontation is that the radical trade-unions sharply opposed the regime's desire to import foreign labour. In 1965, for example, trade-union leaders successfully prevented the government from importing Moroccan workers. This policy of opposing foreign labour, which was to be dramatically overturned after 1969, had a very important implication. The 'Federation of Libyan Trade Unions', for example, was able to challenge successfully the government on several occasions despite its small membership. This was a direct consequence of the fact that Libyan labour pre-dominated in the productive sectors and especially in such areas as petroleum extraction (semi-skilled workers), ports and transportation. Expatriates tended to be Europeans or Americans and they occupied positions requiring technical expertise. As a result the politically motivated trade-unions had access to an important source of power; they could stop the flow of oil. It is possible, therefore, to suggest that despite the small membership and the over-extensive role of the government in labour-relations the Libyan trade-unions enjoyed considerable power during the 1960s. A power, however, that was used to pursue political aims rather than labour-related objectives. It is this background which helped determine the relationship between the government and trade-unions in the 1970s. A relationship which, as indicated above, led to the erosion of their power and the eventual redundancy of the trade-unions themselves.

The above discussion permits a re-examination of the significance of the September 1 1969 Revolution for the development of the trade-union movement in Libya. It may be suggested that the Revolution was but a moment in the historical development of trade-unionism, and that it only accelerated a process which had been initiated in the 1940s. One of the most visible indications of this suggestion is the case of Suleiman Maghrabi. As indicated above he had been jailed by the previous regime in 1967, and given a five year sentence. On September 8 1969 having served just over two years of his sentence he was invited by the Revolutionary Command Council to form the first government. This was the culmination of a protracted confrontation between Suleiman Maghrabi and his 'Federation of Libyan Trade Unions' and their nominal employers, the regime of King Idris. In trade-union terms this particular 'labour dispute' ended with the capitulation of the 'employers' and the achievement of the aims and objectives of the federation. It is not surprising, therefore, that Qadhafi was able to state that 'labourers and the revolution are an indivisable entity'. Furthermore, given the nature of the division between the two main federations during the old regime it was only to be expected that 'labour strikes' would originate from the 'National Federation of Trade Unions' which had always supported the monarchy. The prohibition of labour strikes, in such a situation, was but an attempt by one faction of the labour movement's leadership to safeguard itself; Suleiman Maghrabi had after all been imprisoned by them in 1967.

Clearly the above interpretation of the September 1 1969 Revolution in trade-union terms is highly simplistic. It does help emphasise, however, the political nature of trade-unions in Libya. One of the first acts of the new government was to encourage the trade-unions to form one federation. Given the historical background it is not surprising that the appeal failed, and the government was forced to take the initiative once more. On May 1 1970 Law 58 was promulgated. This law, which consisted of 186 articles and later partly amended by Law 22 in 1971, was quite comprehensive and it outlined the new government's views on labour relations. Of particular significance for the trade-union movement was the fact that the 1970-71 law created a single trade-union; thereby bringing together what had been bitter enemies by a legislative measure. Once more the government had taken the initiative and by decree had modified trade-union history. Given the importance of this law it is necessary to highlight some of its salient features.

> Not more than one trade union may be formed for the employees of a given occupation or industry. The Ministry of Labour and Social Affairs issues model rules to serve as a guide for the unions preparing their own rules. To become a member of a union one must be a Libyan national over 18, belonging to no other union, not unemployed for more than one year and not an employer in any type of occupation. The trade union has to be duly registered; it must have an executive board of not less than nine and not more than 15 members to be elected by secret ballot, serving for one year and without salary. The members must possess civil and political rights. Trade unions are not to have direct or indirect relationship with any other foreign union. Meetings of the trade unions are to be open at any time for representatives of the Minister of Labour and Social Affairs. The Ministry must receive notification of a meeting and the minutes of all meetings. A trade union can be dissolved at the request of the Ministry of Labour and Social Affairs by a decision of the Court of First Instance (84).

With the promulgation of the 1970-71 law the activities of the trade-unions had been drastically circumscribed. What is of importance, however, is that many trade-union leaders, who had confronted the monarchy on the very issue of trade-union freedom, strongly backed the new measures. In fact, it was men such as Suleiman Maghrabi who helped draft the legislation that destroyed the illusion of a free trade-union movement. They argued that the Revolution had come to power in order to defend the rights of the 'working forces' and as such it was necessary to prevent opportunists and politicians from abusing such rights. Of greater significance, however, is the fact that many trade-unionists saw the law of 1970-71 as their best opportunity of negotiating better working conditions for their members. For in addition to determining the structure of the trade-unions the law went further and attempted to regulate labour-relations. It defined, for example the rights and duties of workers, probation periods, minimum wages (were immediately doubled), compensation and pension funds, sick and maternity leave, over-time rates, minimum rest periods, the eight hour day etc. Similarly, the law legislated as far as the provision of housing (reducing company rents by half), local transportation, first aid facilities, recreation centres, etc. Given that the major employers in the private sector were the powerful multinational oil companies, who had resisted many of the provisions of the new law when they were pressed under the old regime, it is not surprising that trade-unionists welcomed the new law. For in effect this new law was in the nature of a very detailed agreement between workers and management that covered all aspects of labour-relations. In exchange, however, the trade-unions had surrendered many of their freedoms. This was particularly so in the area of labour disputes. The new law legislated as to what constitutes a labour dispute and how it should be resolved. Any dispute that came within the parameters of the law was to then be referred to a 'Conciliation Council' whose members were to be appointed by a decision of the Minister of Labour and Social Affairs. Trade-unions had both gained and lost a lot. What was of particular significance for the labour movement is that it was attained through governmental legislation and not trade-union activity. The result was that for all practical purposes the trade-unions had been co-opted by the new regime.

Having lost the traditional prerogative of negotiating working conditions the Libyan trade-unions also lost their political character. This was the result of a number of resolutions passed by the National Congress of the Arab Socialist Union, the only legal political party, in April 1972. The purpose of these resolutions was to define the nature of the relationship between the ASU and the trade-unions. Given their importance it is necessary to outline their major features.

> While the ASU is recognized as the only body that can undertake political activities, trade unions have the special duties of upgrading the social, cultural, technical and vocational levels of their members as well as raising adequate productivity. Furthermore, the ASU is given the right to supervise, guide and direct trade unions (85).

The nature of the relationship between the ASU and the trade-unions was further qualified by Qadhafi. Speaking at the April 1972 meetings of the National Congress of the ASU he stated:

> the ASU is political work, a popular political organisation. The trade unions have nothing to do with politics – at no time and at no place. Trade Unions and federations are professional organisations. It is ASU members who engage in politics. It must be clear that trade unions and federations are professional organisations which tackle the problems of their members. Politics must be confined to the ASU. It is impermissible to conduct politics outside the ASU in any union or profession. Otherwise, trade unions and federations would turn into political parties. Consequently, there would not be a single organisation for the people's working forces. There would be a group of political parties in the country (86).

The above indicated changes in the nature of the trade-union movement were at one and the same time a radical transformation and a logical conclusion of earlier developments. It is for this reason that the new regime was concerned to legislate both for the rights, regarding the conditions of work, that previous unions had failed to attain and the practice, functioning as opposition political parties, employed so successfully under the old regime: they supported the rights and outlawed the practice.

Nevertheless, and despite the emasculation of the trade-unions, Libyan workers still existed and there were labour problems, especially in the oil sector (87). This situation, however, was to be dramatically altered by Law 12 of March 14 1973 and the publication of the *Solution of the Economic Problem* by Qadhafi in 1977. The purpose of the 1973 Law was to allow labour's participation in administration and profit sharing of all industrial enterprises, with the exception of the petroleum companies. At this point the new regime embarked on a process which was ultimately to produce a radical transformation of the Libyan trade-union movement: it redefined the very conception of what is a worker. This redefinition of what is a worker, which has since been institutionalised in the case of Libyan nationals, had the effect of dissolving the very basis on which trade-unions are traditionally constituted. The decree which finally 'abolished' the working-class was preceeded by the joint workers-management councils in 1973. According to Law 12 workers were to be elected to councils by their fellow workers to participate in the administration and organisation of the establishment. Eventually the councils were renamed 'people's committees' and by 1977 Qadhafi declared that 'there are no wage-workers in the socialist society, only partners'. This finally abolished, for all practical purposes, the trade-union movement in Libya.

At this point it is necessary to return to the two instances, economic and political, that were mentioned above. The nature of the political instance has been elaborated in the preceeding discussion. What needs to be emphasised, however, is that whereas the trade-unions had opposed the importation of foreign labour in the 1960s, there was little resistance to the massive influx of predominantly unskilled and semi-skilled foreign workers during the 1970s. Furthermore, the bulk of these workers occupied positions in the productive sectors and Libyan nationals restricted themselves to the non-productive sectors. The magnitude of this change can be grasped when it is noted that in 1964 there were 17,300 expatriate workers and that by the late 1970s the figure had increased to over 400,000. An increase, it might be pointed out, that took place primarily after 1975 (88). It is this situation that has generated a labour market within which there does not seem to be any need for trade-unions. That is not to say, of course, that there are no labour grievances. It simply suggests that as the bulk of the productive workers are expatriates there does not seem to be a need to generate independent organisations that would defend their rights: after all they are 'guest-workers'. As to the Libyan nationals they see themselves as 'partners' and resolve their labour disputes through 'people's committees'. A system, it should be emphasised, that is entirely under the control of the government.

CONCLUSION

As indicated in the introduction the character of the state in the Socialist People's Libyan Jamahiriya needs to be explained in the context of an articulation of domestic class alignments and an evolving international division of labour. Libya is an oil producer and oil is an international commodity. It has been argued that despite radical transformations in form the oil producing states essentially respond to *external* stimuli and so external dependence; their location in a transformed international division of labour cannot be said to have been reduced. It is, in fact, this particular position in the international division of labour which also structured Libyan domestic class alignments and in particular the nature of the relationship between labour and the state in the Jamahiriya. A relationship, however, whose antagonistic and contradictory nature has been resolved by recourse to a 'radical' political culture and extended reliance on expatriate labour. In other words, 'political radicalism' is the ideological resolution of contradictions resulting from Libya's status as a peripheral and dependent economy in an evolving international division of labour.

The above reading of socio-political and economic transformations experienced by the Jamahiriya suggests that the logic of the State is to be grasped at the level of the reproduction of an internal social division of labour which is compatible with the requirements of an evolving international division of labour. Furthermore, the Libyan state and its apparatus is seen to perform a 'managerial' task of reconciling internal class contradictions and generating an equilibrium between exploiters and exploited. In fact, the supremely ideological nature of the state in the Jamahiriya of which *The Green Book* and *People's Committees* are but moments is but a political expression of the development of economic underdevelopment. The state and its functionaries, therefore, do not constitute a class as such and neither can Libya be characterised as a form of state capitalism. Instead, Libya's 'class-less' state derives its legitimacy and power through its location in a mediatory role between an internal social division of labour and the evolving international economy. It is precisely this role and nature of the state in the Jamahiriya which leads me to concur with Ruth First that:

> The rejection of any conception of the class structure of society and source of conflict has led, in turn, to a rejection of the independent role of dispossessed classes, and the assertion of a populist ideology which the state ideological machine projects as the interests of all Libyans (89).

NOTES AND REFERENCES

1. See J.A. Allan, Libya: The Experience of Oil, (Croom Helm, London, 1981); H.P.Habib, Politics and Government of Revolutionary Libya, (Le Cercle du Livre de France, Montreal, 1975); F.S.,Waddams, The Libyan Oil Industry, (Croom Helm, London, 1980).

2. See J.G. Taylor, From Modernisation to Modes of Production: A Critique of the Sociologies of Development and Underdevelopment, (Macmillan, London, 1979).
3. Ruth First, 'Libya: Class and State in an Oil Economy', in P.Nore and T.Turner (eds.), Oil and Class Struggle, (Zed Press, London, 1980), pp.119-142.
4. First, 'Libya: Class and State', p.121.
5. Allan, Libya, pp.17-18.
6. J.A. Allan, for example, notes 'it is possible therefore to examine whether a new government can affect significantly the direction and style of development'. In Allan, Libya, p.17.
7. See J. Holloway & S. Picciotto (eds.) State and Capital, (Edward Arnold, London, 1978); F. Fröbel, J. Heinrichs & O., Kreye, The New International Division of Labour, (Cambridge University Press, London, 1980).
8. First, 'Libya: Class and State', p.121.
9. 'At the beginning of the nineteenth century only about 3 per cent of production was circulated through international trade. By 1913 world trade was equivalent to about a third of the total world output' in Kenwood & Lougheed, The Growth of the International Economy, 1820-1960, (George Allen & Unwin Ltd, London, 1971), p.91.
10. W. Ziemann & H. Lanzedörfer, 'The State in Peripheral Societies', in The Socialist Register, (1977), pp.143-177.
11. Ibid., pp.155-159.
12. Ibid., p.159.
13. Ibid., p.160.
14. Ronaldo Munck, 'State and Capital in Dependent Social Formations: The Brazilian Case', Capital & Class, vol.8 (Summer 1979), pp.34-53.
15. Of course, the oil price increase of 1973 was not the basic cause of the capitalist crisis which began long before. See Y.Fitt, A. Faire and J-P Vigier, The World Economic Crisis, (Zed Press, London, 1979).
16. A. Glynn & J. Harrison, The British Economic Disaster, World Bank Development Report, (Washington, 1981).
17. L. Anell & B.Nggren, The Developing Countries and the World Economic Order, (Methuen, London, 1980), p.48.
18. Ibid., p.51.
19. Ibid., p.54.
20. Ibid.,
21. Ibid.,
22. Fröbel, New International Division of Labour
23. Ibid.,
24. Ibid.,
25. For an elaboration of this point see P. Glavanis, 'Historical Materialism or Imperialist Apologia? A re-evaluation of Industrialisation in the Third World', Sociology, vol.15, no.3, (1981), pp.431-435.
26. See Samir Amin, 'Self-Reliance and the New International Economic Order', Monthly Review, vol.29, no.3, (1977), pp.1-21.
27. M. Palmer & O. Fathali, 'The transformation of mass

political institutions in revolutionary Libya: structural solutions to a behavioural problem', in E.G.H. Joffé & K.S. McLachlan (eds.) <u>Social and Economic Development of Libya</u> (MENAS Press, London, 1982), pp.233-254.

28. Ziemann & Lanzedorfer, 'The State in Peripheral Societies', p.154.
29. United Nations Technical Assistance, <u>A General Economic Appraisal of Libya,</u> (New York, 1952), p.1.
30. Ibid.,
31. Ibid., p.932.
32. W.B.Fisher, 'Problems of Modern Libya', <u>The Geographical Journal,</u> vol.CXIX, no.2 (1953), p.189.
33. United Nations Technical Assistance, <u>Economic Appraisal of Libya,</u> p.9.
34. Fisher, 'Problems of Modern Libya', p.189.
35. Ibid.,
36. Ibid.,
37. Ibid., p.190.
38. The drinking of alcohol was restricted to Christians and Jews up to the 1 September 1969, and in theory an identity card was necessary before drinks could be served in public places. After the Revolution of September, 1969, no alcoholic drinks were allowed in the market.
39. Fisher, 'Problems of Modern Libya', p.190.
40. United Nations Technical Assistance, <u>Economic Appraisal of Libya,</u> p.17.
41. Ibid., p.30.
42. The British Military Authorities introduced in 1943 the Military Authority lira (MAL) whose rate of exchange in 1951 was MAL 480 to the British Sterling pound.
43. United Nations Technical Assistance, <u>Economic Appraisal of Libya,</u> p.30.
44. Ibid., p.31.
45. Ibid., p.32.
46. First, 'Libya: Class and State', p.125.
47. Ibid., p.126.
48. J. El-Jehaimi, A. Bubtana, A. Huni, Y. Kabir, P. Glavanis and A. Zlitni, <u>Labour Turnover in the Libyan Oil Industry,</u> (Research Centre, Garyounis University, Benghazi, 1980), p.9.
49. Ibid., p.9-10.
50. Ibid., p.10.
51. Ibid., pp.11-12.
52. Ibid., p.10.
53. First, 'Libya: Class and State', p.126.
54. Ibid., p.127.
55. C. Collins, 'Imperialism & Revolution in Libya', <u>MERIP, Reports</u> 27, (1974), p.13.
56. Ministry of Labour and Social Affairs, <u>The Occupational Patterns of Employment in Libya 1965,</u> (Tripoli, 1967), p.7.
57. Collins, 'Imperialism & Revolution', p.14.
58. Ibid., p.15.

59. Ibid., p.14.
60. Ibid., p.15.
61. Ibid., p.18.
62. B. Warren, 'Imperialism and Capitalist Industrialisation', New Left Review, vol.81 (1973), p.21.
63. Ibid., pp.22-23.
64. A. Emmanuel, 'Myths of Development versus Myths of Underdevelopment', New Left Review, vol.85 (1974), p.62.
65. Ibid..
66. International Institute for Strategic Studies, Strategic Survey, (London, 1973), p.1.
67. A. Hone, 'The Primary Commodities Boom', New Left Review, vol.81 (1973), p.80.
68. Ibid..
69. Emmanuel, 'Myths of Development' p.81.
70. Ibid., pp.73-74.
71. Ibid., p.74.
72. Amin, 'Self-Reliance', p.16.
73. El-Jehaimi, et al, Labour Turnover, p.10.
74. Ibid..
75. Ibid., p.12.
76. J.S. Birks & C.A. Sinclair, 'The Libyan Arab Jamahiriya: Labour Migration Sustains Dualistic Development', The Maghreb Review, vol.4, no.3 (1979), p.101.
77. Collins, Imperialism & Revolution, p.18.
78. Interview with al-Bataqh, 30 November, 1969.
79 Muammar al-Qadhafi, The Solution of the Economic Problem, The Green Book, Part II, (London, 1977), p.17.
80. Ruth First, Libya, The Elusive Revolution, (Penguin, London, 1974), p.85.
81. Ibid..
82. Stanford Research Institute, Area Handbook for Libya, (The American University, Washington, 1969), pp.220-221 and p.228.
83. Ibid., p.219-231.
84. Habib, Politics & Government, pp.48-49.
85. Ibid., pp.49-50.
86. First, Libya, p.131.
87. El-Jehaimi, et al., Labour Turnover.
88. Birks & Sinclair, Labour Migration, p.41.
89. First, 'Libya: Class and State', p.139. Also see P. Glavanis, 'Nature of the State with Reference to Social Classes: Peripheral Capitalism and Labour in the Socialist People's Libyan Arab Jamahiriya', in Joffé & McLachlan, Social & Economic Development of Libya; P. Glavanis, 'Libysch-Arabische Dschamahirifa' in Siegfried Mielke (ed.) Internationales Gewerkschafts - Handbuch, (Leske & Budrich, Opladen 1983); Centre de Recherches et d'Etudes sur les Sociétés Méditerranéennes, La Libye Nouvelle: Rupture et Continuité, (Centre Nationale de la Recherche Scientifique, Paris 1975); Mirella Bianco, Gadafi: Voice from the Desert, (Longman, 1975); Anne Marie Cazalis, Kadhafi: Le Templier d'Allah, (Gallimard, Paris, 1974).

PART TWO

THE ECONOMIES OF NORTHWEST AFRICA IN THE 1970s : INTRODUCTION

Allan Findlay

Analysis of the changing economic structures of the nations of NorthWest Africa during the 1970s is a complex but rewarding task. On the one hand, the countries of the Maghreb entered the decade with their imbalanced economies continuing to bear the marks of their similar colonial heritage, and with only relatively short histories of independent self-government. On the other hand, the economic policy makers of each country had declared by 1970 their intentions to pursue very distinct and highly contrasting development courses. In 1969 Libya had experienced a revolution, which in bringing to power the controversial figure of Colonel al-Qadhafi, would determine the country's politically radical economic course throughout the 1970s. In the same year the balance of power in Tunisia changed, ushering in a new era of economic liberalism which would encourage an export-led development policy, through the fostering of light manufacturing industry and the abandonment of the previous 'socialist experiment' in agriculture. Algeria in the 1970s maintained its position as a centrally planned economy, claiming to aim at the development of an independent socialist economy, while in Morocco economic policies remained conservative in almost every respect.

The chapters of this book which consider contemporary economic trends in the individual countries of NorthWest Africa show that, despite starkly contrasting economic policies, many common constraints on economic development were encountered. Agricultural production, whether under private or state management, continued to vary greatly from year to year and region to region in response to unpredictable environmental conditions. In all four countries the fundamental problem, which both governments and agriculturalists failed to solve, was how to supply sufficient food from the country's delicate agricultural resources to feed the rapidly growing population. In some sectors and in certain countries (such as the production of sugar beet in Morocco) progress was achieved, but these advances were outweighed by failures in other forms of agricultural production, resulting in a net shortfall in food production, and a trend in all four countries towards an increasing bill for food imports.

In the industrial sector all the NorthWest African nations have in some respect attempted during the 1970s to reduce their dependence

The Economies of Northwest Africa in the 1970s: Introduction

on the export of raw materials, such as phosphates from Morocco and Tunisia and oil and natural gas from Algeria and Libya, and to increase the level of processing of materials prior to export in order to add value to their exports and to provide wider employment opportunities within their economies. The growth of industry has, however, been severely constrained by a number of internal and external forces. Both private and state industries have encountered shortages of skilled local labour, while at the same time being unable (except in Libya) to provide sufficient unskilled and semi-skilled work to meet the massive demand for such work by the large stock of poorly trained or inadequately experienced labour in the work force.

One possible explanation for failure of nearly all of Tunisian, Algerian and Moroccan National Plans to achieve their targets during the 1970s was the growing significance of international economic trends in determining the economic courses of these countries. Tunisia and Morocco, with their self-avowed policy of favouring a certain level of integration with foreign capitalist economies, through the orientation of industrial production towards foreign markets and through the encouragement of foreign investment, have been most seriously affected by the depression in the industrial economies of Western Europe. The vulnerability of concentrating manufactured exports on the external market area is perhaps best illustrated by the case of the Maghreb's textile industry. In 1976 95 per cent of Tunisian textile exports were directed to the EEC. By the late 1970s textile production had been severely disrupted on a number of occasions due to the imposition by the EEC of stricter import quotas and higher tariff barriers against foreign producers. Furthermore, the expansion of the EEC to include Greece and possibly Spain and Portugal threatened not only industrial exports but the trade in agricultural produce between the Maghreb economies and Western Europe.

A further realm in which Maghreb-EEC relations turned sour during the 1970s was that of international labour migration. Morocco, Algeria and Tunisia had all been major labour exporters, particularly to France, in the late 1960s and early 1970s. From 1973 onwards not only did all significant migration of workers to France cease, but France sought determinedly to reverse the flow by encouraging North African migrants to return home. This policy was despite the unpreparedness of the Maghreb economies to receive a further inflow of workers to add to the existing surpluses of their labour market.

Algeria, while it avoided as great a dependence as its neighbours on European markets for sale of its products, was nevertheless technologically and financially indebted to the advanced capitalist states. Without foreign loans and large scale financial assistance it could not have implemented its ambitious public investment programme. Throughout the decade vast foreign credits were amassed to permit the establishment of the heavy industrial base outlined by the government's so-called socialist development plans. The slow rate of realisation of many of the projects, and the inability of state companies in many instances to implement complex investment programmes given their limited planning resources, forced many Algerian state companies to seek increasing assistance from foreign

The Economies of Northwest Africa in the 1970s: Introduction

and multinational firms.

Libya, unlike the rest of Northwest Africa, has faced no shortges of capital for investment during the 1970s, but ironically its economic course seems to have been just as dependent on external forces as capital-poor states such as Tunisia and Morocco. Nearly all new agricultural and industrial projects have been financed from income received from oil sales to the industrial nations, and implementation of the country's ambitious development plans has only been possible through the importation of foreign workers (both skilled and unskilled), foreign machinery and foreign technical expertise. It is difficult to evaluate the longterm impact of Libya's recent investment policies, but it seems highly unlikely that many of the projects will be sustainable once the oil runs out and capital subsidies are removed. With the exception of investments in oil refining and petro-chemical activities, it would seem that the country's natural resources and limited domestic market do not justify the types of industrial projects which have been undertaken. Even more questionable is the lavish use of unreplenishable fresh water resources in certain extravagant agricultural projects.

There can be no doubt that the economies of NorthWest Africa have changed very rapidly in the 1970s, but analysis of these changes indicates that it has seldom been in the form either predicted or desired by the national governments of the region. In the 1970s external economic forces appear to have been very significant, and have reinforced the extroverted nature of these economies in a new and more insidious fashion than during the colonial era.

Chapter 5.

ALGERIA : THE CONTRADICTIONS OF RAPID INDUSTRIALISATION

Richard I. Lawless

INTRODUCTION: THE COLONIAL INHERITANCE

Like its neighbours Morocco and Tunisia, Algeria experienced French colonial rule and settler colonisation. Algeria was the first Maghreb country conquered by France, and the last to receive its independence. Colonial rule began in 1830 and endured until 1962, (1) some 132 years during the last seven of which the country was plunged into a bitter war of liberation as the Algerian nationalists fought the French army for their independence. Algeria was ruled as an integral part of France, and by 1954 the European settlers numbered 1,042,000 or 11 per cent of the total population. They acquired over a quarter of the cultivated land mainly in the moister more fertile areas situated along the Mediterranean coast which were developed to produce cash crops (vines, soft wheat, citrus fruits, olives, tobacco and market garden products) for export to markets in metropolitan France. About four-fifths of the European residents lived in towns where they were mostly administrators, bankers, technicians, traders, professional men and skilled workers, though some had lesser jobs, and their influence was far in excess of their numbers. Their concentration was greatest in the big cities with Algiers, the capital and major port, containing over one third of all Europeans. The dualistic shaping of the economy with regard to agriculture, industry, mining and trade to serve the interests of the metropolitan power was accompanied by the polarisation of political, social and economic power. The settlers exercised power and enjoyed privileges and high incomes; the Algerian majority suffered loss of status, subservience and poverty. Few Algerians received any education or technical training, and few Algerian workers participated in industry or other non-agricultural activities. The country claimed only two Algerian engineers on the eve of independence. The vast majority of Algerians eked out a meagre existence on the land on small, fragmented holdings occupying the less productive land. Distinct from the modern European agricultural sector with its different techniques and structures of production, the traditional Algerian sector was nevertheless strongly influenced by it, providing a convenient source of cheap labour for the settler estates. After 1930, and particularly after the Second World War,

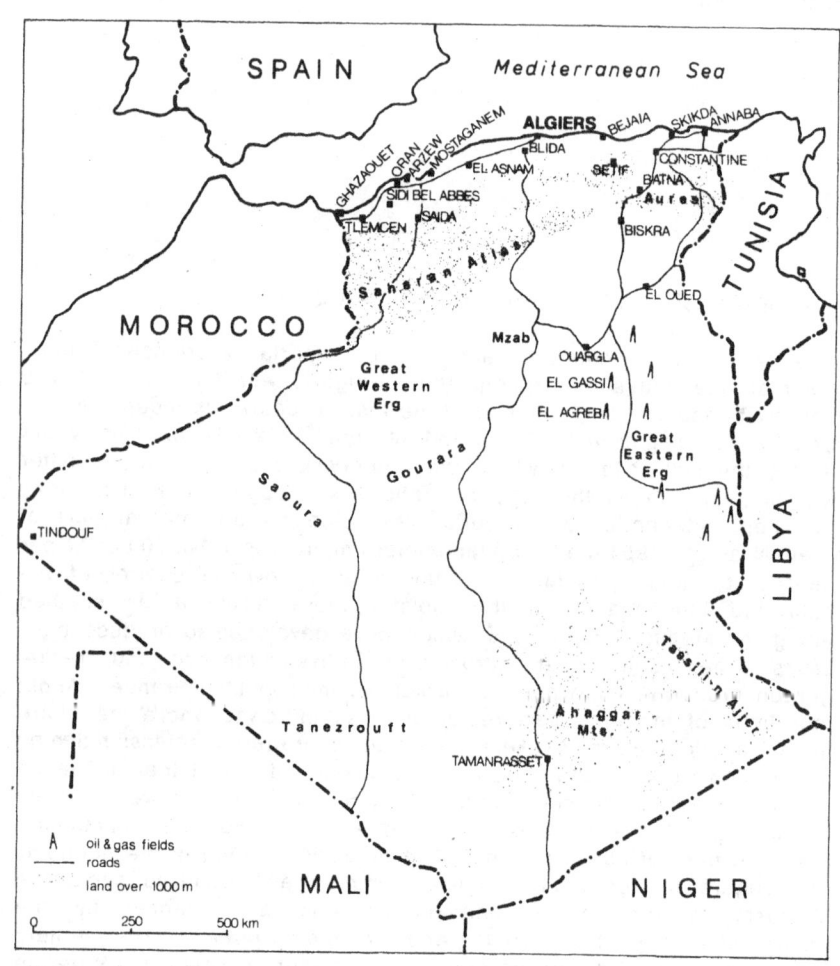

FIGURE 5.1   LOCATION MAP OF ALGERIA

the high rate of population increase among the Algerians further aggravated pressure of population on resources resulting in an increase in rural to urban migration, a quickening in the rate of urbanisation and massive proletarianisation. Few jobs were available in the urban economy for those new migrants, many of whom merely exchanged underemployment in the countryside for unemployment in the towns. Throughout the colonial period the two sectors of the economy, the modern and the traditional, and the two communities, European and Muslim, though distinct, were narrowly articulated one to the other in a relationship of dominance/dependence.

In the colonial economy agrarian capitalism was predominant and agricultural exports provided the motor for economic growth. Industrialisation was limited in spite of the favourable conditions created during the Second World War when imports of manufactured goods from France were severely disrupted. Heavy industry was absent and manufacturing mainly concerned the processing of primary products. The entire mining sector, transport and the banking system were controlled by French financial institutions. Integration between different sectors of the colonial economy was weak. In 1954 the industrial sector absorbed only 25 per cent of local agricultural production and in turn a mere 8 per cent of the value of industrial production was directed towards the agricultural sector. These figures demonstrate the strong extroversion of the Algerian economy. In 1954 80 per cent of commercial exchanges were with France. Exports were composed primarily of agricultural products; 40 per cent of cereal production, 90 per cent of the wine and 70 per cent of fruit and vegetables were exported. While local capital remained traditionally attached to agriculture and French capital was interested only in mines, banks and commerce there was little change in the structure of the Algerian economy or in the nature of its dependence on metropolitan France.

In 1958 in the middle of the War of Independence General de Gaulle, then President of France, announced a five year economic development plan for Algeria known as the *Plan de Constantine* (1959-64) (2). The plan was accompanied by a massive increase in state investment in Algeria at a time when insecurity resulting from the war had triggered off a flight of private capital from the territory. It aimed to reawaken the traditional countryside by means of an important effort to expand the training of agricultural technicians and extension officers, the construction of new villages, an extension of the irrigated area and a modest land reform programme to give small plots of land to several thousand landless peasants. The second major aim was the rapid industrialisation of Algeria. This was to be achieved through a policy of growth poles which favoured the concentration of investment in a few coastal locations and in certain privileged branches of industry which were given priority, namely iron and steel at Annaba, an oil refinery at Algiers, a petrochemical complex at Arzew and the construction of an oil pipeline from Hassi Messaoud to Bejaia and a gasline from Hassi R 'Mel to Arzew. In addition several import substitution industries were planned in order to create employment in the urban centres of the interior.

Algeria: The Contradictions of Rapid Industrialisation

Anticipating the end of the war, the plan sought to lay the foundations for a neo-colonial relationship between Algeria and France – the industrialisation of Algeria was envisaged as merely an annex of the French economy. Often ignored because it achieved little amidst an intensification of the war, the abortive Plan de Constantine nevertheless had a profound impact on the Algerian economy and influenced the direction and character of its later development. A number of key industrial developments undertaken after independence. eg., the gas liquefaction plant at Arzew and the iron and steel complex at El-Hadjar, were merely a continuation of French projects under the Constantine Plan.

THE FIRST YEARS OF INDEPENDENCE: BEN BELLA AND THE MYTH OF WORKER SELF-MANAGEMENT

When in 1962 at the end of a long and bitter struggle Algeria finally achieved its independence the country faced enormous political, economic and social problems. The war had claimed the lives of several hundred thousand Algerians and forced half a million to seek refuge in Morocco and Tunisia. Over two million people in rural areas had been uprooted from their homes by the French army as part of its pacification programme and resettled in *regroupement* villages. often under harsh conditions. Many more people had left the insecurity of the countryside and flooded into the towns and cities. Cornaton (3) has argued convincingly that half the Algerian rural population were displaced during the war in circumstances that Bourdieu and Sayad (4) describe as *'parmi les plus brutaux qu'ait connus l'histoire.'* In the major cities, principally Algiers and Oran, urban guerrilla warfare, murders and assassination had intensified during the last two years of colonial rule accompanied by the destruction of much public and private property. During the six months before independence some nine-tenths of the European minority representing almost all the administrators, technicians, teachers, doctors and skilled workers. left the country; some 328.000 Europeans departed during the single month of June 1962. Factories and shops were closed down and farms were abandoned. This exodus and the massive flight of private capital from the country paralysed the economy and merely intensified the already chronic problems of underdevelopment and unemployment. It has been estimated that the real value of production fell by 30 per cent between 1960 and 1963. The decline was particularly serious in the modern, export-oriented agricultural sector, mining and building and public works, while the remaining industries were operating at a very low capacity. Only the hydrocarbon sector survived these troubled years without any major setback. Unemployment in the new republic was estimated at a staggering 70 per cent of the active male labour force; four-fifths of Algerians were illiterate. Rapid population growth resulted in an extremely youthful population with 47 per cent under 15 years of age: a heavy burden for the new state to support.

Yet in spite of the failure of economic planning during the last years of colonisation, the new republic inherited an important technical, industrial and agricultural infrastructure and her economic potential was considerable. But as Samir Amin (5) put it, 'the national government inherited the material foundations laid during the colonial period but with no one to man them and no one to serve.' Furthermore the modern sector of the Algerian economy had been created to service the needs of the metropolitan power, not the Algerians themselves. The new republic remained heavily dependent on the former colonial power for its economic survival as indeed the Evian Accords which gave Algeria independence intended that it should. At independence agriculture made the largest single contribution to GDP (Table 5.1) and agricultural produce, notably wine, accounted for almost half of all exports. Almost all exports went to France which in turn supplied the bulk of Algeria's imports.

During the War of Independence the more activist elements among the nationalists had begun to formulate their ideas about the economic development strategy to be adopted by an independent Algerian state. These were articulated in the Tripoli Programme drawn up at the end of May 1961. The programme gave priority to the development of the agricultural sector to be achieved by radical land reform measures, the limitation of private property and the collectivisation of the land. A restructuring of the agricultural sector would increase the purchasing power of the Algerian population and create the necessary conditions for an industrialisation that was not oriented towards overseas markets. It favoured the nationalisation of large businesses in all sectors and the adoption of socialism as ideology and system. The programme emphasised the independence of the country economically as well as politically; the umbilical cord with France was to be neatly and decisively severed and economic sovereignty in the form of Algerian control of Algerian resources and economic life was to be asserted as an integral part of political independence. The Algiers Charter, a series of texts adopted by the first congress of the *Front de Libération Nationale (FLN)* in April 1964, went much further in detail and elaboration than the Tripoli Programme. It firmly rejected the capitalist path to development in favour of a socialist approach which it defined not only in terms of the nationalisation of the means of production but as a system of worker self-management.

In practice during the first years of independence the government's approach to economic matters was influenced by one primary factor - its own political survival (6). The authority of the President, Ben Bella, was weak. Challenged by different opposition groups, he was forced to make concessions, first to one faction and then to another. Furthermore, events marched faster than legislation or institutional arrangements. In the summer and autumn of 1962 many thousands of workers took over the management of farms and factories abandoned by the Europeans in order to keep these units in production and to protect their own jobs. When Ben Bella issued the famous March Decrees in 1963 legalising the position of these workers' committees it was essentially to gain their political support. Political expediency also determined the nationalisation of French-owned land at the end of 1963. By the beginning of 1964 the *secteur autogéré agricole* controlled 2.3million ha representing about a third of the

TABLE 5.1: SECTORAL COMPOSITION OF GDP 1963/1978
(in millions of Algerian dinars at current prices)

	1963	%	1969	1973	%	1978
Agriculture	2,680	19.8	2,560	2,477	7.9	6,750
Hydrocarbons	1,550	11.8	3,340	5,926	19	24,700
Other extrac- tive industries	70	0.5	90	177	0.5	370
Energy, water	250	1.9	270	394	1.2	1,250
Manufacturing industries	1,230	9.4	2,650	3,819	12.2	10,530
Construction and public works	600	4.5	1,160	3,422	10.9	12,800
Transport	440	3.4	740	1,075	3.4	
Commerce	2,960	22.5	4,850	6,910	22.1	30,450
Other non-govern- mental services	1,540	11.7	2,220	3,963	12.7	
Public services	1,910	14.5	2,540	3,000	9.6	10,950
Total GDP	13,130	100	20,529	31,163	100	97,800

Source: M.E. Benissad, L'Economie Algérienne Contemporaine, Presses Universitaires de France, Paris, 1980, p.28.

total cultivated area from which the bulk of the country's agricultural exports were produced and on which some 135,000 permanent workers and 50,000 seasonal workers were employed. By 1964 between 345 and 413 industrial units had passed under the control of self-management committees, although this sector never included more than 10,000-15,000 workers, 10 per cent of the total industrial workforce. The vast majority were small-scale units, even cafés, restaurants and hotels were included, and less than 5 per cent were factories employing more than 100 workers. Algerian worker self-management, which rapidly attracted international attention, therefore concerned essentially agriculture, and even here involved less than 200,000 workers -- together with their families probably about one million people out of a rural population of eight million. It was not a system of agrarian reform nor the answer to the Algerian peasants' land hunger and social stagnation. Yet autogestion monopolised the government's attention and financial means at the expense of traditional agriculture. In practice the majority of workers on autogestion estates did not fully understand the nationalisation decrees, and effective power within the worker self-management committees was exercised by the director appointed by the Ministry of Agriculture. The workers became simply state employees. The committees were also dependent on state organisations for credit and for marketing their produce which almost totally removed any possibility of independent action. During this period, Algeria's declared socialist approach to development was in fact a myth. Behind the rhetoric no real attempt was made under Ben Bella to make the self-management sector an organised political and economic force (7).

The only strong support for this system of economic organisation came from a relatively small group of intellectuals and trade unionists, and their position was weak within the party, the army and the administration. Another minority group within the Algerian political elite favoured private capitalism, but they were eliminated after the legislative elections in September 1963. In contrast, the position of the small and middle urban bourgeoisie was greatly strengthened after independence. They quickly penetrated and eventually established control over the state apparatus. They were responsible for bringing the self-management sector firmly under state control and were committed to building a powerful public sector.

The first steps towards the creation of an economic system dominated by state capitalism were taken under the Ben Bella regime. The Algerian Government acquired the French State's participation in certain industrial enterprises : in the oil company SN Repal, the Algiers' oil refinery, CAMEL *(Compagnie algérienne de méthane liquide d'Arzew)*, Caral-Renault, Sabab-Berliet and *Union industrielle africaine;* and a series of new state enterprises were created between 1962 and 1965: ONACO *(Office national de commercialisation)*, SNTA *(Société nationale des tabacs et allumettes)*, SNS *(Société nationale de sidérurgie)* and SONATRACH *(Société nationale de transports et de commercialisation des hydrocarbures)*. But Algeria remained heavily dependent on French aid, and internal sources of finance were strictly limited. At first therefore government economic policy was confined to the completion of certain projects initiated under the Constantine Plan, and it was only after 1964 that national development became oriented around two major projects, the El-Hadjar steelworks and the construction of a third oil pipeline from Haoud El Hamra in the Saharan oilfields to Arzew on the Mediterranean coast.

THE BOUMEDIENE ERA AND THE DOMINANCE OF STATE CAPITALISM

This trend towards state capitalism was substantially reinforced after Ben Bella was deposed by a swift and bloodless military coup in June 1965 which brought to power Houari Boumediène and the Oujda group and permitted the most active faction within the petty bourgeoisie to consolidate their power (8). At first the new regime sought to encourage private investment and invited the local private sector to participate in the construction of a modern and integrated national economy. The country's economy was still weak and all sources of investment were needed to strengthen it. As an incentive the government proceeded to return to private ownership certain small factories, transport companies, cafés and restaurants nationalised immediately after independence, and introduced a new Investment Code in 1966 which gave certain concessions and guarantees to the private sector. However the fundamental principle of the new code was that the state retained control over all vital sectors of the economy and private Algerian capital was restricted to those branches defined by the government.

At the same time the government set out to reduce the dominant position occupied by foreign enterprises in the country's economy and to regain control of the country's natural resources. Some progress had already been made, and a number of foreign enterprises had been nationalised and their activities placed under the control of state companies or national offices. For example in 1966 and 1967 foreign banks and insurance companies were nationalised; three state banks were created, the *Banque nationale d'Algérie*, *Banque extérieure d'Algérie* and the *Crédit populaire d'Algérie*. Nine foreign mining companies were nationalised in 1966 and their activities, which included the Ouenza iron mines and the Djebel Onk phosphate mines, were transferred to SONAREM. In May and June 1968 45 subsidiaries of foreign manufacturing companies (Cablaff, Neyrpic, ITT, Carnaud, Altairac, Eternit, Unilever, Lesieur and Lafarge) were nationalised. By 1970 of the 700 to 800 French-owned industrial enterprises which had existed in Algeria in 1963, less than 100 survived.

This wave of nationalisations culminated in the decision by the Algerian Government in February 1971 to declare unilaterally 51 per cent participation in *Elf Erap* and *Compagnie française de pétroles*, the two major French companies responsible for the bulk of Algerian oil production (9). Simultaneously all the natural gas reserves, among the most important in the world, were nationalised together with the transportation network of oil and gas pipelines. By this action the state oil company SONATRACH secured control over oil and gas production and over the national distribution system.

Algeria: The Contradictions of Rapid Industrialisation

By the early 1970 s all key sectors of the Algerian economy had been brought under state control which was effected through a network of major state companies, purchasing and marketing organisations. Although their ownership was vested in the state, these state companies were capitalist in their activity; Raffinot and Jacquemot have described them as *sociétés capitalistes sans capitalistes'* (10). Their capital was furnished by the state but they were governed by private commercial law which gave them operating autonomy and substantial financial independence. Each company was responsible for a specific branch of the economy and exercised a virtual monopoly over the whole of production, marketing and imports within that branch. By 1975 the public sector comprised 49 state companies involved in industrial production, 19 national offices and eight banking and financial organisations. There were no further additions to the self-management sector of the economy, and some industries formerly controlled by self-management committees were transferred to the new state companies.

Etatisation and regaining control over national resources were only a part of the economic programme adopted by the Boumediène regime. With a new found political stability and growing revenues from oil and gas exports (Table 5.2) the government embarked on an ambitious programme to restructure the Algerian economy through a newly created central planning system. Rapid industrialisation, integration and introversion became the main aims of the Algerian development strategy which was quickly recognised internationally as one of the most powerful attempts to break with the classic forms of economic dependence. The Algerian example of industrialisation was soon presented as a model for other oil-producing states to emulate.

Formulated between 1966 and 1967 the Algerian development strategy was strongly influenced by the theoretical work of economists such as F. Perroux, A.O. Hirschmann, E. Gannagé and notably G. Destanne de Bernis. In outline it seeks to ensure that national resources are utilised within the country in order to reduce progressively the extroversion of the economy. The long-term objective is to construct a 'complete' productive sector capable of satisfying the needs of consumption and at the same time the full utilisation of local resources, in particular manpower. The strategy is built around two basic priorities : that of capital accumulation over consumption and industrialisation over the development of agriculture. At the centre of Algeria's industrialisation strategy lies the so-called 'industrialising industries', a model developed by the French economist Gérard Destanne de Bernis in marked opposition to the partisans of industrialisation by import substitution. According to this theory some industries, particularly the power-producing ones, have stimulating capacities; that is to say, in the countries where they have developed they give rise to a series of associated industries, both up-stream and down-stream. The entire national economy is thereby stimulated. The industrialising industries include energy-related industries, petroleum and gas, which provide fuel, feedstocks and finance for the industrialisation process with petrochemicals representing the basis for a whole range of new

TABLE 5.2 OIL PRODUCTION AND REVENUES

	Production (thousand barrels)	Revenues (million US dollars)
1958	3,205	
1959	9,347	
1960	66,297	
1961	120,791	
1962	159,463	
1963	184,061	54.1
1964	204,140	61.2
1965	203,916	91.8
1966	262,308	128.6
1967	301,385	199.1
1968	330,992	261.8
1969	345,420	266.7
1970	375,622	271.9
1971	286,686	321.0
1972	388,802	613.3
1973	400,497	987.7
1974	368,139	3,299.2
1975	358,649	3,261.8
1976	393,487	3,699.0
1977	420,577	4,253.7
1978	423,824	4,589.1
1979	421,121	7,513.0
1980	373,211	10,787.0

Source: *Annual Statistical Bulletin 1980,* Organisation of Petroleum Exporting Countries, Vienna, 1981.

industries; iron and steel, metallurgical and mechanical industries and chemicals eg., phosphates. They are huge capital intensive projects based on Algeria's own natural resources and utilising the most modern production processes. They act as the 'motor' of the development process producing raw materials and machinery for other sectors of industry engaged in the production of finished goods such as vehicles, farm machinery, pumps and irrigation equipment, electrical goods and plastics thus strengthening the inter-industry matrix. In turn the products of the new industries will contribute to the modernisation of the more backward sectors of the economy, notably agriculture, forging new linkages that will eventually create an integrated economy reducing Algeria's dependence on the world capitalist market. But there was to be no immediate improvement in employment opportunities. The serious unemployment problem would only be resolved in the long-term. Not until the early 1980s would a sufficient number of new jobs be created in the non-agricultural sector to absorb the natural increase in the male labour force. Faced with one of the world's fastest-growing populations, rapid economic growth rather than birth control was seen as the most effective contraceptive.

A high rate of investment was essential to implement this ambitious development strategy and to finance the rapid expansion of the educational system to produce skilled workers, technicians and managers for the new factories. After 1966/67 priority was given by Algerian planners to capital accumulation and in order to maximise productive investment living standards already very low were held down by a deliberate policy of austerity in consumption. On average the rate of investment has exceeded 35 per cent since 1970, a level only surpassed in Japan and the Soviet Union. According to the official view *'Dans le développement planifié qui a été adopté par le pays, on peut dire qu'un investissement correspond à une renonciation de la population à des consommations immédiates au profit des consommations futures'* (11).

The first source of finance for public investment has been provided by revenues from oil and gas exports. Although Algeria's oil reserves and production are modest compared with the major Middle Eastern producers, the country possesses high reserves of natural gas which are among the most important deposits in the world. Since the mid 1970s oil and gas contributed over 95 per cent of all Algerian exports. Equally important Algeria has been able to raise large loans to finance development projects through European, American and Japanese banking consortia on the strength of future exports of oil and gas. In particular vast foreign credits have been essential to fund the massive installations for the liquefaction of natural gas. In some years servicing the outstanding debt has reached 15-20 per cent of all exports. Remittances from Algerians working in Europe have provided another source of revenue although their relative contribution declined from 34 per cent during the period 1967 to 1969 to 16 per cent between 1970 and 1973 (12). Together these three sources of capital accumulation, which are all dependent on Algeria's links with the advanced capitalist states, accounted for nearly 75 per cent of all investment funds between 1967 and 1973. Consumption stagnated during these years and for the mass of the population the austerity measures meant no wage increases, a limited range and quantity of even essential goods in the shops and delays in the provision of certain social infrastructures notably health and housing.

The framework of the recent development of the Algerian economy was set by the country's long term development objectives and strategy (1967-80) and by the development plans; the 'pre-plan' (1967-69), the First Four Year Plan (1970-73) and the Second Four Year Plan (1974-77). 1978 and 1979 were years of transition and reassessment before the introduction of a Five Year Plan (1980-84). Following the improved financial prospects resulting from the new oil prices in 1974 implementation of the long-term development strategy was speeded up, and this was reflected in the sharp increase in investments during the 1974-77 Plan. The annual volume of investment rose from 3,200 million Algerian dinars (AD) during the period 1967 to 1969 and 9,200 million AD during the First Four Year Plan, to 30,200 million AD during the Second Four Year Plan and 52,000 million AD during 1978. The composition of GDP underwent substantial changes, while the annual rate of growth of GDP has been at 7.5 per cent between 1967 and 1973, 6.6 per cent between 1973 and 1977 and 8.2 per cent in 1977 and 1978, an average of 7.2 per cent for the period 1967 to 1978 (Table 5.3). Since 1967 the industrial sector has been given priority in the allocation of investment funds. Industry was allocated 48.7 per cent of investment funds under the pre-plan (1967-69), 44.7 per cent under the First Four Year Plan and 43.6 per cent under the Second Four Year Plan (Table 5.4). This sector also proved capable not only of realising planned investment but of exceeding the targets assigned to it: industry absorbed 55.3 per cent of actual investment during the pre-plan, 57 per cent during the First Four Year Plan and 62 per cent during the Second Four Year Plan introducing serious distortions into Algeria's planning strategy. The level of industrial investment achieved was very high because project execution capacity developed more rapidly in industry than in the other sectors, industrialisation being at the centre of Algeria's development strategy. Industry was able to attract a large part of available management and technical resources because it offered more attractive employment conditions. As such resources were in short supply in the country, shortages already experienced by the other sectors could not be eliminated at the same pace as in industry. Industry also had more developed planning and project preparation capability than most of the other sectors. But in spite of the high rate of investment, output growth for industry as a whole has been much slower than expected, though there were marked differences in subsector development. Port congestion, inadequacy of maintenance, transport facilities, telecommunications and planning units impaired efficient plant utilisation and represented a major constraint on the growth of industrial value added. In particular the human aspect of industrialisation involved costly investment and long lead times that could not easily be reduced.

TABLE 5.3: RATE OF GROWTH OF GDP BY SECTOR 1967-78

Sectors	1967-73 %	1973-77 %	1977-78 %	1967-78 %
Hydrocarbons	6.9	1.5	9.3	5.2
Industry (excluding hydrocarbons)	9.7	7.5	20.8	8.8
Agriculture	1.2	2.3	9.8	2.4
Others	8.2	8.0	3.8	7.2
Total	7.5	6.6	8.2	7.2

Source: A. Benachenhou, Planification et Développement en Algérie 1962-1980, Presses de l' E.N. Imprimerie Commerciale, Algiers, 1980, p.266.

TABLE 5.4: PLANNED AND ACTUAL INVESTMENT 1967-1977

	1967-1969		1970-1973		1974-1977	
	Planned %	Actual %	Planned %	Actual %	Planned %	Actual %
Hydrocarbons	41.9	50.9	36.9	47.1	40.6	48.6
Capital and intermediate goods	47.0	40.6	48.9	46.2	47.6	44.5
Consumer goods	11.1	8.5	14.2	6.7	11.8	6.9
Total industry	48.7	55.3	44.7	57	43.6	62.0
Agriculture	16.9	16.4	14.9	13	13.2	4.7
Infrastructure	34.4	28.3	40.4	30	43.2	33.3
Total	100	100	100	100	100	100

Source: A. Benachenhou, Planification et Développement en Algérie 1962-1980, Presses de l' E.N. Imprimerie Commerciale, Algiers, 1980, p.49.

Algeria: The Contradictions of Rapid Industrialisation

The priority given to industrial investment since 1966 has aggravated the disparities and pressures existing between the development of industry and that of other sectors of the economy. For a long time the government was convinced that the infrastructures inherited from the colonial period, notably housing, transport and agricultural equipment, would support the early stages of industrialisation and that substantial investment in these sectors was unnecessary. In practice, agriculture, housing, health and education have all received inadequate investment resulting in acute shortages of housing and community facilities, stagnant agricultural production and a sizeable increase in imports of foodstuffs. The agricultural sector's share of planned investment fell from 16.9 per cent under the pre-plan, 14.9 per cent under the First Four Year Plan, to 13.2 per cent under the Second Four Year Plan. More important, actual investment fell from 16.4 per cent between 1967 and 1969, 12.5 per cent between 1970 and 1973, to a mere 4.7 per cent between 1974 and 1977; agriculture received only 6.5 per cent of actual investment during the planning period 1967 to 1978. Only 9.5 per cent of the urban housing units and 25.4 per cent of rural housing units planned for 1974 to 1977 were actually completed. Less than one third of planned investment in public health was achieved and only half in education during the same period. These sectors were not only allocated a low percentage share of investment but especially after 1974 were able to utilise only a part of the funds assigned to them. Housing problems adversely affected recruitment of management and supervisory staff and skilled workers to new factories, and the low level of investment in agriculture limited the consumption of industrial goods by that sector. The rapid increase in imports of agricultural products deprived other sectors of resources that could have been used for their development. These inter-sectoral imbalances have emerged as one of the most serious obstacles to economic growth, since they restrain the overall rate of development and cause serious problems in the industrial sector itself. These problems became more serious after 1974 when Algeria's revenues increased dramatically following the four-fold increase in oil prices. Between 1967 and 1974 the planning system, although experiencing certain structural weaknesses, had made some progress. After 1974 the rapid increase in the level of investment proved too ambitious for the planning system which was virtually overwhelmed by the scale of the tasks before it. The increased emphasis on non-industrial sectors and infrastructures envisaged under the 1974-77 Plan did not occur, and there was a further lengthening of the development lags between these sectors and industry which had appeared during the previous Plan. The distortions in the planning process which had begun to appear before 1974 were accentuated during the Second Four Year Plan. Escalating costs and long delays in the completion of development projects, many of which had to be carried over from one planning period to the next, restricted the ability of the planning system to adjust to these processes. At the end of 1978 projects to the value of 210,000 million AD remained to be completed - the equivalent of four years of planned investment at the 1978 level. Benachenhou has described these years as, *'la période du recul de la planification'* (13).

THE INDUSTRIAL SECTOR (14)

Within the industrial sector growth of investment has varied greatly from branch to branch. Investment has been particularly strong in hydrocarbons and heavy industry producing capital and intermediate goods, but well below planned levels in light manufacturing industries producing consumer durables, textiles, household goods, food and agricultural products. Between 1967 and 1977 hydrocarbons absorbed 49 per cent of total industrial investment, heavy industry 43 per cent and light industry a mere 8 per cent. Throughout this period actual investment in hydrocarbons consistently exceeded plan targets at the expense of the other industrial branches, but only a small proportion of this investment - some 10 per cent was devoted to strictly industrial projects eg., fertilizers, petro-chemicals and plastics. Within the heavy industrial branch actual investment favoured iron and steel, mechanical engineering, construction materials and electricity. The priority given to heavy industry was strongly defended by President Boumediène who pointed out that,

> *Il n'y a pas d'indépendance économique sans industrie lourde nationale... Vendre de la fonte, cela rapporte plus que vendre du mineral de fer; et vendre de l'acier rapporte plus que vendre de la fonte : voilà une vérité élémentaire dont nous avons tenu compte*(15).

Development in the hydrocarbon and heavy industrial branches have been strongly capital-intensive involving the construction of large scale plants using the most modern production techniques, a choice justified by Boumediène in these terms:

> *Nous avons voulu que notre équipement soit ultra-moderne parce qu' à échéance moyenne il est plus rentable. Nous ne pouvons accepter des machines datant de 1940, même si leur maniement permettrait de donner du travail à un plus grand nombre d'ouvriers... Je n'accepterai jamais le sous-équipement de mon pays* (16).

The rapid rise in the level of investment in the industrial sector since 1967 and especially after 1974 could not guarantee an equally rapid realisation of planned industrial capacity. The ambitious industrial programme was subject to long delays and to escalating costs. Unable to implement the investment programme using their own planning resources, the state companies quickly turned to foreign firms, often multinationals, who built and equipped complete factories under 'turnkey' and 'product in hand' contracts. Such formulas have considerably increased the cost of the industrialisation programme; they have strengthened Algeria's technological dependence on the advanced industrial economies (17), weakened national control over the planning process and restricted inter-industry integration and the technological coherence of the entire productive sector.

There have also been long delays in the effective utilisation of installed industrial capacity with marked differences in the level of utilisation between the various branches of industry (Table 5.5). By 1978 although a few industrial units were operating at close to full capacity others were utilising only a small part of installed capacity. The industrial sector as a whole suffers from a shortage of managerial, technical and skilled workers and is heavily dependent on foreign technical assistance. Given the choice of sophisticated imported technologies and the scarcity of appropriate skills among the Algerian labour force, recruitment of foreign workers, at least in the short term, was inevitable. In practice some branches of industry have been more successful than others in attracting trained manpower resulting in a sharp polarisation of skilled human resources in those branches possessing the necessary financial means to buy-in labour. In 1977 hydrocarbons employed 36.5 per cent of all managerial staff in Algerian industry and 30.5 per cent of all technicians and *agents de maîtrise*. These manpower problems represent one of the factors responsible for the low productivity of Algerian industry. Another factor is the size of wage increases which in recent years have been inversely proportional to the level of qualifications of the workers. Highly-skilled workers have received much lower wage increases than unskilled workers and labourers, increases which have not kept pace with inflation so that the purchasing power of highly-skilled workers has actually declined. Such policies have not encouraged high productivity.

Low productivity has been accompanied by high production costs, in some cases double those prevailing in Western Europe and Japan. Algeria's dependence on foreign technical assistance and a range of service agreements, maintenance contracts, licences and patents associated with the use of imported machinery and equipment have contributed to these costs.

With these reservations in mind it is possible to describe the anatomy of the state industrial sector in 1977 at the end of the Second Four Year Plan. Hydrocarbons remained the dominant element in the public sector, contributing about 40 per cent of GDP, 96 per cent of total exports and contributing 50 per cent of state revenues. Control was exercised through the state oil company SONATRACH which employed some 100,000 workers. Over the years its activities have diversified to include exploration and drilling, production and transport of crude oil and natural gas, gas liquefaction and petrochemicals. But exports of crude oil and to a lesser extent liquefied natural gas still represent its major source of revenue, revealing the strong extroversion of the Algerian economy and the country's continued dependence on raw material (commodity) exports.

The heavy industrial sector, which includes mining (except hydrocarbons), metallurgy and mechanical and electrical engineering, was controlled by five state companies SONAREM, SNS, SN Metal, SONACOME and SONELEC, responsible for 107 production units and 40 distribution units. This sector contributed 5 per cent of GDP and

TABLE 5.5: LEVEL OF UTILISATION OF INDUSTRIAL CAPACITY IN 1978

Production Unit	Level of utilisation	Production Unit	Level of utilisation
SNS		**SONACOME**	
El Hadjar complex	65%	Industrial vehicle complex, Rouiba	90%
Reghaia pipe factory	70%	Motor tractor complex, Constantine	75%
Metal sheets, Kouba	80%	Cycle and motorcycle complex, Guelma	90%
Steelmill, Oran	95%	Foundry, Berrouaghia	65%
Zinc electrolysis Ghazaouet	70%	Machine tools, Constantine	25%
		Agricultural machinery, Sidi Bel Abbes	10%
Metal sheets, Arzew	50%		
SN METAL		**SONELEC**	
Waggon construction, Annaba	60%	Domestic appliances, Tizi Ouzou	30%
Frames, Blida	85%	Electric cable, Algiers	90%
Cranes, Bejaia	30%	Telephone cable, Algiers	85%
Concretemixers, Algiers	30%	Batteries and accumulators, Setif	60%
Frames, Annaba 1	80%	Electronics complex, Sidi Bel Abbes	10%
Frames Annaba 11	5%	Refrigerators	80%
Frames Oran 111	20%		

Source: A. Benachenhou, Planification et Développement en Algérie 1962-1980, Presses de l' E.N. Imprimerie Commerciale, Algiers, 1980, p.62

employed some 106,000 workers. Finally the light industrial sector responsible for food processing, tobacco, textiles and clothing, leather and shoes, paper and construction materials was divided into eleven state companies – SOGEDIA, SN EMA, SN SEMPAC, SNTA, SONITEX, SONIPEX, SNIC, SNLB, SONIC, SNAT and SNMC. They managed over 300 production units, employed 120,000 workers and contributed 7 per cent of GDP.

Investment in public sector industry has been characterised by a strong spatial concentration along Algeria's Mediterranean coastline. The three major industrial development poles, Algiers, Oran-Arzew and the eastern triangle Skikda–Annaba–Constantine absorbed more than 75 per cent of investment between 1970 and 1973 and received over 60 per cent of the non-agricultural employment created during the First Four Year Plan – a trend that was reinforced during the Second Four Year Plan. The scale and speed of industrialisation experienced by these major growth poles provoked a number of profoundly negative effects on the physical and social environment. New industrial complexes were built on some of the country's best farmland; they deprived the agricultural sector of scarce water resources; while the disposal of industrial waste brought serious pollution problems. The prospect of industrial employment merely accelerated rural to urban migration, aggravating the already acute housing crisis in the major coastal cities to which the solutions were often hasty and ill-considered (18). Such problems have been identified elsewhere with the result that growth pole strategy has been subject to increasing criticism. Development of a regional growth centre, it is argued, may engender a sequence of growth leading to the decline of the surrounding regions as the growth centre attracts resources to itself. In this matter the growth centre becomes 'parasitic' with respect to the region it is supposed to aid in developing. That is, the 'backwash' effects may be stronger than the 'spread' effects to use Myrdal's terms. In the Algerian experience Raffinot and Jacquemot conclude

> *Aux "effets d'entraînement" supposés par ce type de développement industriel, on pourrait être tenté d'opposer les "effets d'enclaves" de zones privilégiées se développant pour elles-mêmes par ponction des ressources du milieu sans restitution d'aucun bénéfice* (19).

In an attempt to compensate for the strong concentration of development in the Mediterranean coastlands, the government launched a number of 'special programmes' between 1966 and 1973 to assist the country's most backward regions. Nine special programmes were introduced for the wilayat of Batna, Tizi-Ouzou, Médea, Tlemcen, Sétif, Saida, El-Asnam, Constantine and Annaba, involving a total investment of 10,000 million AD. But their implementation was narrowly constrained by the priority given to the major industrial projects; of the 3,700 million AD authorised for the three wilayat of Tlemcen, Sétif and Saida in 1972 and 1973 only 800 million AD was actually spent. The Second Four Year Plan called for a greater geographical dispersal of industrial investment and proposed the setting up of small and medium-sized industries in the mountains and steppelands of the interior, notably along an east-west axis linking Tiaret-Barika-Batna and Tebessa, a zone of strong outmigration. Some 500 small industrial projects were included in the plan, and following a further decentralisation of authority responsibility for their planning and execution was vested in the wilayat and communes. Unfortunately these local authorities proved incapable of carrying out the task. They possessed neither the trained staff nor the planning structures to implement this ambitious programme. Furthermore many of these small and medium-sized industries were badly designed and technologically ill-adapted to available infrastructures and manpower. Consequently at the end of 1979 over half the projects still remained at the design or study stage. A convincing argument can be made that the imported technology on which Algeria's development strategy has been based is incompatible with decentralisation of industry and the creation of small industrial units at the local level.

One of the most dramatic consequences of the massive state investment in the economy since 1967 has been the appearance of a dynamic private industrial sector alongside the public sector. By the late 1970s the private sector controlled 40 per cent of industrial value added, provided 23.3 per cent of all industrial employment (45 per cent in textiles, chemicals, plastics and building and public works), and contributed 33 per cent of production of capital and intermediate goods and 66 per cent of production of goods for final consumption. In certain branches of light industry, notably synthetic leathers (100 per cent), shoes (75 per cent) and textiles and clothing (75 per cent), the private sector was dominant. It was geographically concentrated in and around the three major cities, Algiers, Oran and Constantine, which accounted for 60 per cent of all privately-owned industrial enterprises. Spatial concentration was accompanied by a high level of capital concentration; eg., in 1974 84 enterprises in the textile branch (13 per cent of the total) employed 50 per cent of the workers and controlled 50 per cent of the turnover, while in building and public works a mere 3.5 per cent of all enterprises employed 52 per cent of the workers.

The increase in public investment and in public sector employment enlarged the basis of capital accumulation for the private sector, and resulted in the rapid expansion of the market for consumer goods and for construction; a market which the private sector has quickly penetrated. The state companies have been unable to carry out all the activities for which in theory they have a monopoly, providing numerous opportunities for private enterprise. The private sector has developed downstream of the public sector with the appearance of a division of labour whereby privately-owned factories concentrating on light manufacturing processes demanding relatively little capital have emerged on the periphery of the large, capital-intensive public enterprises. Inputs from the latter, raw materials and semi-finished goods – the product of costly investments, long lead times and difficult technologies, are purchased by the private sector at controlled prices which are often less than local cost price and even below the price on the world market. The state steel company, SNS, which sells 30 per cent of its products to the private sector, is one such example; another is SNMC which in recent years has lost at least 30 AD a ton on all cement produced or imported; 40 per cent of its sales (2.5 million tons a year) are to the private sector. These materials are transformed into finished goods using simple technologies, largely unskilled and cheap labour with little concern for conditions of work or the quality of the finished product. Profits in the private sector are therefore high. As Benanchenhou has observed, *'Il n'est pas alors exagéré de dire qu'une partie au moins de la rentabilité privée trouve son explication dans une partie au moins du déficit public'*(20). High profitability means that private industry is largely self-financed. It no longer needs to apply for assistance under the 1966 Investment Code which has ceased to act as an effective instrument of state control over the private sector.

THE AGRICULTURAL SECTOR

Although rapid industrialisation was given priority in the Algerian development model the success of this programme was closely linked to the development of the agricultural sector (21). Agriculture occupied a key position in the process of industrial integration and was crucial to achieving the introversion of the economy. It was required to produce foodstuffs to feed the growing population so that foreign exchange could be reserved for imports of industrial equipment; it could supply important raw materials for the industrial sector; and it provided a large potential market (47 per cent of the active population at the beginning of Algeria's development programme) for the products of Algeria's new industries – fertilisers, pesticides and farm equipment. Without the vast potential market of a modernised agriculture, Destanne de Bernis observed,*'l'industrialisation aurait dû se tourner vers la satisfaction de la demande de biens de consommation durables des classes sociales urbaines aisées, ce qui n'a jamais permis un véritable développement'*(22).

Nevertheless, in spite of government pronouncements in favour of the principle of a balanced development of agriculture and industry, *'marcher sur ses deux jambes'*, the proportion of planned investment allocated to the agricultural sector declined during the decade 1967-1977. Actual investment fell even more dramatically as the agricultural sector proved able to utilise only a part of the funds made available to it. Investment in the self-management sector achieved only 42 per cent of plan targets (12,000 million AD against 28,000 million AD) between 1966 and 1977 which represented about a third of what was needed to renew and maintain essential equipment. In effect, therefore, the self-management sector experienced the continuation of a period of disinvestment which had begun during the last years of colonialism. The reasons for this are complex. On the one hand within the *secteur autogéré* inappropriate management structures and procedures resulted in overconcentration of decision-making, long and complicated administrative circuits, weaknesses in the banking system and a serious shortage of trained personnel. On the other hand inputs from other sectors, notably from industry, were often insufficient or subject to long delays. Agricultural equipment was inadequate or underused because the state company possessing the monopoly over this branch of industry was unable to ensure the supply of new machines or repair existing machinery; consumption of fertilisers was low because of the difficulty in obtaining sufficient supplies from SONATRACH.

Only a small part of public investment in agriculture went to the private sector, and state aid in the form of credits and equipment practically disappeared after the agrarian reform in 1971. Credits which had been in the order of 120 million to 130 million AD a year fell to 45 million in 1971, 22 million in 1972 and 10 million to 12 million a year between 1973 and 1978. Furthermore they benefited essentially the medium and large landowners who utilised them to develop speculative livestock rearing and agricultural infrastructures; sometimes they were invested outside the agricultural sector.

Structural problems have been particularly serious for the agricultural sector. The dualistic structures inherited from French colonialism have not been eliminated and the *secteur autogéré* is essentially the *secteur colon* under a new form of management. These former European farms occupy 27 per cent of the cultivated area and 44 per cent of the irrigated lands (Table 5.6). They are located on the most fertile land, utilise modern farming methods and concentrate on the most intensive crops; average yields are higher than in the private sector. This sector is responsible for 45 per cent of total agricultural production; 32 per cent of cereals, 62 per cent of artificial fodder, 73 per cent of industrial crops, 35 per cent of vegetable crops and 83 per cent of wine and fruits. Since independence it has been assigned objectives at once ambitious and contradictory. It has been called upon to maintain and even increase the level of production for export and at the same time to satisfy local needs which involves the gradual replacement of export crops. Until 1971 exports were given priority and it was not until the Second Four Year Plan that the accent was placed on providing foodstuffs for the home market. Other problems have arisen from the vast size of the *domaines autogérés* (the individual farm units cover on average 1,158 ha) and their fragmentation, for which adequate management skills are not available; from the highly unsatisfactory performance of those state organisations providing necessary inputs and marketing outlets for the sector; and from the self-management system itself which has not functioned efficiently because of state intervention at all levels of activity. Many attempts have been made to reform the system but with little effect.

During the first ten years of independence the private sector was virtually ignored by the government whose attention was firmly focused on the self-management sector – in 1964 petroleum still represented only 50 per cent of exports, agricultural products 40 per cent. Neither the structure of ownership nor the relations of production underwent any substantial change. Programmes of agrarian

TABLE 5.6: CROP PRODUCTION AND CULTIVATED AREA BY SECTOR-SEASON 1977-1978

	Area h	Production quintals or hectolitres	Self-management sector		Agrarian reform sector		Private sector	
			Area %	Production %	Area %	Production %	Area %	Production %
Useful agricultural area	7,922,220		27		13		60	
Irrigated area	313,340		44		13		43	
Fallow	3,660,450		16		11		73	
Winter cereals	2,623,170	15,359,020	32	42	16	14	52	44
Artificial fodder	296,430		62		16		22	
Industrial crops	34,070	1,493,960	73	67	9	15	18	18
Vegetable crops	141,030	10,339,860	35	32	10	8	55	60
Vines for wine making	190,260	1,840,000	83	88	4	4	13	8
Citrus fruits	49,850	4,475,060	83	86	7	5	10	9
Fruits	49,660		49		8		43	

Source: G. Mutin, 'Agriculture et Dépendance Alimentaire en Algérie', Maghreb Machrek, 90 (1980), p.53.

reform were as old as the Algerian nationalist movement itself and after independence many promises were made but no action was taken. It was not until 1971 when rising food imports were beginning to pose a threat to the industrialisation programme that the government announced its *Révolution agraire* amidst a blaze of publicity (23). The first stage of the reform which ended in 1973 applied to collective lands, those belonging to communes, wilayat, state and religious endowments. The second stage affected private landowners. The reform placed a limit on the size of private ownership and excess land was expropriated. By the end of 1979 some 870,000 ha had been redistributed from the first phase of the reform, 500,000 ha from the second. A range of evasions, loopholes and misapplications of the reform measures may account in part for the limited amount of land expropriated – 9 per cent of privately-owned land. But expectations were also exaggerated. Mutin (24), for example, has argued that the number of large landed properties was limited – in 1973 properties of more than 100 ha covered only 600,000 ha – 11 per cent of the total area. Much of this land was devoted to extensive cereal cultvation so that the threshold of limitation was 60-80 ha, greatly restricting the area that could be nationalised.

By 1980 the 94,230 beneficiaries of reform land had been regrouped into 5,966 production cooperatives (25). The bulk of the recipients belonged to 4,873 *Coopératives Agricoles de Production de la Révolution Agraire* (CAPRA), which group together land and the means of production of the members, who collectively carry out farming operations, purchases and sales. Income is divided according to the hours worked. By contrast land remains in individual ownership in the 614 *Coopératives Agricoles d'Exploitation en Commun* (CAEC). While working their own land from which they draw their income, individual farmers have to follow a cultivation plan decided by all members of the cooperative. In the 479 pre-cooperative groupings or *Groupements de Mise en Valeur* (GMV) the aim is to improve uncultivated or undercultivated land and once an adequate production level has been achieved the GMV is promoted to the status of a CAPRA or CAEC. The new cooperatives (26) are much smaller than the *domaines autogérés* – their average area is 200 ha with an average membership of 13. The *secteur de la Révolution agraire* comprises an estimated 13 per cent of the country's useful agricultural area with cereal cultivation the dominant form of land use. In 1977-78 it contributed 14 per cent of the production of winter cereals, 15 per cent of industrial crops, 8 per cent of vegetables, 4 per cent of wine and 5 per cent of Mediterranean fruits. Only a minority of production cooperatives appears to be profitable, and they have had little impact on production or productivity. When they were set up they lacked agricultural machinery, livestock, farm buildings and even irrigation equipment because only the land had been redistributed. They were therefore heavily dependent on state assistance.

Private landholding has not been abolished by the land reform but little is known about the structure of ownership in the private sector. Since the reform, which mainly affected landholdings of over 50 ha, it has been estimated that the average size of holdings in the private sector is 7 ha, but 54 per cent of cultivators possess under 4 ha. They occupy some of the least fertile land and practise extensive farming. In 1978 private farms possessed only one fifth of all agricultural machinery, mechanisation affected only 26 per cent and a mere 10 per cent purchased fertilisers; almost half did not even use a metal plough. Although the private sector covers 60 per cent of the useful agricultural area, it contains only 43 per cent of irrigated lands but 73 per cent of fallow land. It contributes 52 per cent of cereals, 55 per cent of vegetables, 13 per cent of wine and 10 per cent of citrus fruits, but is dominant in livestock production with 92 per cent of the country's cattle and 75 per cent of sheep.

Very little progress has therefore been made towards achieving a greater uniformity of agrarian structures. The creation of a service cooperative, *Coopérative Agricole Polyvalente Communale de Service* (CAPCS), in virtually all rural communes represents one of the few attempts to unify the agricultural sector. CAPCSs are open to all agriculturalists with membership being obligatory for land reform production cooperatives as well as for the autogestion estates. They provide services for working the land such as seeds and machinery, market farm output and purchase inputs. The network of CAPCSs is seen as a system of technical, agricultural, political and administrative support for rural Algeria. But as yet not all CAPCS provide the full range of services, skilled personnel are in short supply and they ensure the commercialisation of only a small part of agricultural production.

Although the redistribution of land was a necessary step, it could not resolve the basic problem affecting Algerian agriculture, that of the shortage of cultivable land. The usable agricultural area is no more than eight million ha, a mere 3 per cent of national territory, and there are no large reserves of fertile land which can be brought into cultivation. Indeed an estimated 30,000 ha of some of the best farmland have been lost to urban development and industry since 1965. At Skikda the 2,000 ha industrial zone absorbed most of the small irrigated plain formerly devoted to citrus fruits. Between 1969 and 1974 the self-management sector lost 1,840 ha of arable land as a result of the expansion of the city of Oran. In order to increase production the existing agricultural land must produce more, and this intensification must be achieved mainly through the use of irrigation. Unfortunately since the late 1960s the irrigated area has actually declined, from 335,000 ha in 1973 to 300,000 ha in 1979. Programmes to extend the irrigated area by 51,000 ha during the First Four Year Plan and by 110,000 ha during the Second Four Year Plan fell far short of their targets; only 13,500 ha were completed during the first plan, 18,000 ha during the second. Competition for scarce water resources from urban areas and from industry has resulted in the loss of valuable irrigated land and a sharp decline in water resources available for agricultural use. Of the 130,000 ha lost to urban and industrial use, 10,000-12,000 ha were irrigated. Finally over large areas irrigation equipment is old and in urgent need of repair, while the lack of proper drainage of irrigated lands has resulted in a dangerous increase in soil salinity.

Algeria. The Contradictions of Rapid Industrialisation

Until 1975 the government's pricing policy for agricultural commodities actively discouraged the intensification of agricultural production. Prices were held stable at a time when the cost of farm machinery, fertilizers and labour rose substantially; the cost of labour increased by 55 per cent between 1969 and 1973, farm machinery by 37 per cent. These distortions in the terms of exchange between agriculture and industry discouraged investment in the private sector and resulted in low incomes for peasant farmers. But their most serious effects were on the self-management sector where those units cultivating intensive crops were unable to make a profit because of the low prices fixed for their production. Paradoxically the pricing system meant that those units practising extensive cereal cultivation had a greater chance of success than those devoted to dairying, fruits, vegetables and industrial crops. Since 1975, a year marked by massive imports of foodstuffs at a time when world prices were rising rapidly, prices have been more favourable to the producer and they have risen more rapidly than agricultural inputs. Between 1974 and 1978 cereal prices increased by 122 per cent; the price of milk, fruits, vegetables and industrial crops doubled during the same period. On the other hand the price of fertilisers and pesticides was maintained at the 1973 level throughout the Second Four Year Plan. Production in the self-management sector has been slow to respond to the new price structures, but in the private sector production of vegetables, tree crops and livestock has increased. However, these measures affect only a part of the private cultivators many of whom market little of their produce and in many cases are purchasers of agricultural products rather than vendors.

These complex problems have contributed to a general stagnation in agricultural production since independence with a distinct decline in some crops, notably vines, tobacco and cotton (Table 5.7). Agriculture's share in GDP fell sharply from 17.5 per cent in 1963 to a mere 7.7 per cent in 1978. At the same time with a population growth of 3.2 per cent a year demand within the country has grown constantly. Rapid urbanisation, changing patterns of consumption and higher living standards (per capita GNP=1200 US$ in 1980 compared to only $200 in 1962) have only aggravated the problem. Thus, per capita agricultural production has declined from an index of 100 in 1969-71 to 83 in 1977. Whereas 70 per cent of national food requirements were covered by production in 1969, the proportion had declined to 30 per cent by 1980. Similarly the proportion of agricultural imports covered by agricultural exports, largely wine, which was 98 per cent in 1967-68 had fallen to 11 per cent by 1978. Algeria's imports of cereals, meat and dairy products as well as tea, coffee and sugar have begun to weigh heavily in financial terms. Imports of milk and cheese quadrupled between 1964 and 1979 while imports of cereals have increased dramatically from 200,000 tons in 1963-66 to over 2 million tons since 1977 and could reach 4-4 and a half million tons by the year 2000. The cost of agricultural imports rose from 700-800 million AD in 1963-65 to 5,000 million AD in 1978. Since 1974 the value of net food imports has amounted to about a quarter of revenues from oil exports. The heavy dependence on imported foodstuffs also has a

TABLE 5.7: EVOLUTION OF AGRICULTURAL PRODUCTION 1970-77 (1967-1970 = 100)

	1970	1971	1972	1973	1974	1975	1976	1977
Crop production	100	102	110	92	98	133	115	81
Livestock production	105	110	103	114	125	127	134	143
Total production	101	104	110	100	108	132	121	106

Source: G. Mutin 'Agriculture et Dépendance Alimentaire en Algérie', Maghreb Machrek, 90, (1980), p.45.

TABLE 5.8: PLANNED INVESTMENT 1980-84 (IN 000 MILLION AD)

Sectors	Brought forward		New programmes		Investment 1980-84	
	Volume	%	Volume	%	Volume	%
Industry	79.5	40.3	132.2	36.2	154.5	38.5
Agriculture	17.8	9	41.6	11.4	47.1	11.7
Transport	2.4	1.2	13.4	3.6	13	3.3
Economic infrastructure	19.9	10	36.2	9.9	37.9	9.5
Housing	34.5	17.5	58	15.9	60	15
Education & training	30.3	15.4	35.4	9.8	42.2	10.6
Social infrastructure	6.7	3.4	15.3	4.2	16.3	4.0
Equipment for collectives	2.4	1.2	10.9	3.0	9.6	2.4
Productive enterprises	3.4	1.7	21.6	6.0	20	5
Total	196.9	100	364.6	100	400.6	100

Source: A. Benachenhou, Planification et Développement en Algérie 1962-1980, Presses de l' E.N. Imprimerie Commerciale, Algiers, 1980, p.249.

TABLE 5.9: STRUCTURE OF PLANNED INVESTMENTS 1967-1984

	1967-1969	1970-1973	1974-1977	1980-1984
Agriculture	16.9	14.9	13.2	11.7
Industry	48.7	44.7	43.6	38.5
Social	13.7	26.7	25.9	32.0

Source: A. Benachenhou, Planification et Développement en Algérie, 1962-1980, Presses de l' E.N. Imprimerie Commerciale, Algiers, 1980, p.250.

political dimension; over two-thirds of cereal imports are furnished by the USA and Canada (27). Without doubt, agriculture has become the 'Achilles' heel' of Algeria's development strategy.

EMPLOYMENT

A wide range of data sources are available on employment but they are often incomplete, sometimes contradictory and present considerable difficulties for any analysis and interpretation of the Algerian labour market since independence (28). Nevertheless through what often appears to be an impenetrable statistical maze, some of the main trends are clearly visible, although it is not always possible to quantify them in detail or with precision.

In a country characterised by a very high birth rate and an increasingly youthful population (47.5 per cent under 15 years of age), Algeria's active population represents a relatively small proportion of the total population; 23.2 per cent or 4 million people in 1978 according to Bernard (29). Thus, over three-quarters of the population are supported by the productivity of less than one quarter, giving a high dependency ratio.

Perhaps the most striking development since independence has been the massive exodus from rural areas (30) and from agricultural employment; the most visible manifestation of the profound crisis affecting the agricultural sector. The *Ministère de l'Agriculture et de la Réforme Agraire* estimate that some 100,000 persons a year left the countryside during the Second Four Year Plan, 132,000 in 1978 according to the *Secrétariat d'Etat au Plan* and even more according to other sources. The results of the 1977 census of population reveal a dramatic decline in the number of workers permanently employed in agriculture; a decline from 918,000 in 1966 (when they represented 54 per cent of the employed population) to 692,000 in 1977 (29 per cent of the employed population). If the proportion of the agricultural population in permanent employment had remained at the same level as in 1966 then the figure for 1977 would have been 1,200,000, indicating the scale of departures. As one writer has put it, *'L'image d'une Algérie où les fellahs sont majoritaires est une image du passé'* (31). Agriculture retains an aging population; the average age of the agricultural workforce is 39 years compared to 34 years for the active population as a whole; 12 per cent of the agricultural workforce are over 60 years of age, compared to only 6.5 per cent of the country's total workforce.

According to Mutin (32), the number of permanent workers in the self-management sector, for which the most detailed statistics are available, fell from 120,000 to 100,000 between 1967 and 1976 –a particularly disturbing trend as these farms occupy the country's most fertile lands. The problem was particularly serious in the coastal plains where the major new industrial complexes have been constructed in recent years. Many agricultural workers, notably the young and the skilled, have left the self-management sector, attracted by the higher wages offered by industry. As a result the *domaines autogérés* suffer from a high annual turnover of employees (as high as 20 per cent in some cases), an increase in the average age of the workers and a sharp decline in their level of qualifications.

Very little new employment has been created by the *Révolution agraire*. Some 100,000 beneficiaries received land under the reform measures but in most cases this did not represent new jobs. There are several examples of land transferred to cooperatives employing fewer workers than before the reform. Some beneficiaries have abandoned their lands and other lands have yet to be redistributed because of the lack of candidates. Sharp disparities between rural and urban incomes remain. Agricultural work is no longer attractive, and many peasant farmers see urbanisation as the only path towards improving their standard of living. Paradoxically, parts of the fertile coastal plains now suffer from a shortage of agricultural labour, even though in the country as a whole unemployment and under-employment remain a problem.

Underemployment rather than unemployment affects the vast majority of the agricultural population. In 1977 the *Secrétariat d'Etat au Plan* estimated that there were over a million agricultural workers 'in part-time employment' – two-thirds of the agricultural workforce. Many cultivate plots of land that are too small to support a family and their meagre earnings from agricultural work must be supplemented where possible from other activities or other sources. Until 1973 when the Algerian government suspended all new emigration, worker migration to France provided a vitally important safety valve for the rural underemployed: remittances from Algerians working in Europe supported an estimated 3 million rural inhabitants, some 600,000 families.

Non-agricultural employment, in sharp contrast, experienced a dramatic increase between 1966 and 1977, and the majority of the active population in regular employment is now concentrated in urban areas. Figures published by the *Secrétariat d'Etat au Plan* reveal that the number of workers in non-agricultural employment grew from 730,000 in 1966 to 1,730,000 in 1977. The creation of new jobs was particularly impressive during the Second Four Year Plan (1974-77) which identified an increase in employment opportunities as a major priority aim, a marked change in emphasis from the previous planning period. Between 1966 and 1973, the period covered by the Three Year Plan and the First Four Year Plan, the number of non-agricultural jobs rose by 480,000; 330,000 of these new jobs being created during the 1970-73 Plan. During the Second Four Year Plan, 523,000 non-agricultural jobs were created surpassing the plan target by 43,000.

Outside administration and transport employment in the tertiary sector was characterised by a slow rate of growth. Throughout this period the most notable increases in employment were recorded in the secondary sector: between 1973 and 1977 44 per cent of all new non-agricultural jobs were created in industry and building and public works. Within the industrial sector employment in light industries – textiles, food processing, leather and shoes – experienced a slow rate of growth, and the most rapid growth in employment was in the new branches of heavy industry – hydrocarbons, chemicals and iron and steel. In 1976 almost half the industrial workforce was employed in hydrocarbons, chemicals, iron and steel and metal production.

The creation of some half a million new jobs in the secondary sector during the development decade 1966 to 1977 is certainly impressive, but it is important to see this in perspective. Nearly half the workforce in the secondary sector are employed in building and public works where the new jobs created are highly unstable. The increase in employment in manufacturing industries, though impressive in absolute terms, is less so when set against the high level of investment in this sector. For example, investment in industry in 1974-75 totalled 19,650 million AD and 44,000 new jobs were created in this sector – an average investment of 446,590 AD per job. The cost has been very much higher in some projects – 2,600,000 AD per job in the gas liquefaction plants, 1,500,000 AD in cement works, 1,100,585 AD in the hot rolling mill at the El Hadjah steelworks and 672,727 AD in the phosphate fertiliser plant at Annaba. Several observers have pointed out that many more jobs could have been created if the industrial technologies adopted in at least some branches had been less capital-intensive. The adoption of the most modern and sophisticated industrial processes, even in light manufacturing, such as textiles and food processing, and at the same time official encouragement for all branches to employ as many workers as possible has resulted in serious overmanning in Algeria's new industries; a phenomenon sometimes refered to as 'disguised unemployment'. Bernard (33) argues that in some cases attempts have been made to resolve deficiencies in the internal organisation of industrial units by employing more workers. In others, enterprises have had to take responsibility themselves for activities such as transport and marketing thereby increasing the proportion of employees not directly involved in production – estimated at 25 to 30 per cent. In addition most state companies under pressure to employ more people have recruited staff for their offices rather than their workshops with negative effects on productivity and the risk of what Bernard terms 'industrial bureaucracy' (34).

Benachenhou (35) argues that the increase in employment opportunities during the decade 1966-77 has been accompanied by a decline in the productivity of the workforce in the industrial sector, building and public works and in administration. He suggests that a study of value added per worker in manufacturing industries and building and public works reveals a decline of 50 per cent in productivity for the two sectors. Benachenhou also points to the high level of mobility among the non-agricultural labour force, estimated at 18 per cent in the industrial sector. Recent studies of the state company SONACOME indicate that the rate of turn-over among labourers is 20 per cent, skilled workers 17 per cent, technicians and foremen 16 per cent and management 26 per cent; a situation which favours neither the training of the workforce, the efficient functioning of the enterprise nor increases in productivity.

The new jobs created in Algeria's emerging industrial economy are essentially for skilled workers. Some 70 per cent of the workforce possess some qualifications, and the level of qualifications of workers in the non-agricultural sector as a whole has increased since 1973. Skill levels are much higher in the new branches of heavy industry than in the more traditional branches of light industry. Whereas only 13 per cent of workers in the iron and steel industry were unqualified, 38 per cent in food processing industries were unskilled.

A considerable effort has been made since independence to expand the educational system and increase technical and industrial training, but there are still shortages of skilled workers. The majority of newly trained engineers are recruited by the hydrocarbon sector, followed by the metallurgical industry and the mines, leaving a shortfall in the mechanical and electrical industries. With the exception of hydrocarbons, all sectors are short of technicians and skilled workers are also needed in all branches. In many cases the quality of the training provided is unsatisfactory and poorly adapted to Algeria's needs. In 1979 the General Secretary at the Ministry of Planning and Regional Development admitted that during the Second Four Year Plan the training programme had not achieved its objectives.

> In some cases we found that firms were running well below their capacity, partly as a result of a lack of industrial discipline and skills. We consider that this is a price we have to pay and we use these factories as training schools, even if they are running at low capacity. We are making a revolution in the consciousness of the people. The first generation did not have an industrial consciousness, the second generation will (36).

Consequently Algeria continues to recruit foreign workers, particularly in highly skilled occupations. In 1976 71 per cent of foreign salaried workers in the non-agricultural sector were classified as managers and senior technicians; all foreign employees in the hydrocarbon sector and 89 per cent in the iron and steel industry belonged to this professional group. A general indication of the lack of technical expertise among Algerian personnel is given by the fact that some 5,000 contracts for technical asssistance were signed by state corporations between 1973 and 1978, about 80 per cent of these being with West European countries and a further 9 per cent with US concerns.

While Algeria continues to buy-in foreign labour, unemployment remains a problem. The magnitude of the unemployment problem is difficult to determine and estimates vary considerably. According to the 1977 Census of Population there were some 171,540 unemployed workers in urban areas between the ages of 18 and 59 years - 13.4 per cent of the active population; an improvement on the situation in 1966 when 28 per cent of the active population in urban areas was classified as unemployed. Benachenhou (37) using the 1977 census data but including male workers between 15 and 18 years and 59 and 65 years arrives at much higher estimates of urban unemployment - 291,692 or 20.9 per cent of the active population. He argues that the highest rates of unemployment are found among young workers and calculates that nearly half (47.6 per cent) of all the unemployed are under 25 years of age. Statistics published by the *Secrétariat d'Etat au Plan* on the other hand indicate that in 1977 the unemployment rate among the non-agricultural population was only 9 per cent, a figure challenged by the *Office National Algérien de Main d'Oeuvre* who insist that the level of unemployment is very much higher.

In spite of these differences most observers agree that the rate of unemployment among the non-agricultural population declined during the decade 1966-1977. A million new jobs were created in the non-agricultural sector during this period, 164,000 in 1977 alone. Though impressive, it must be remembered that population projections predict a rapid expansion in the number of persons in the 15-24 year cohort creating the need for continual growth in job opportunities within the Algerian labour market. Estimates suggest that a million new workers will enter the active population during the period 1980 to 1984. It remains to be seen whether Algeria's new industrial economy will be able to absorb the unemployed and create enough jobs for the 250,000 to 300,000 young Algerians who will be entering the labour market every year by the late 1980 s. This figure assumes that only a limited number of women continue to enter employment - in 1976 only 5.3 per cent of salaried workers in non-agricultural employment were women. On the whole the new entrants to this labour market will have achieved a higher level of education and have greater aspirations than their predecessors.

CONCLUSION - TOWARDS A BETTER LIFE?

The public debate on the National Charter in 1976, which preceded the announcement of a new constitution, provoked widespread criticism of many government policies. The new development plan which should have commenced in 1978 was delayed for two years partly in order to allow a thorough analysis of the adverse consequences of the 1974-77 plan and partly by the death of President Boumediène at the end of 1978. Debates in the Central Committee of the FLN and in the National Assembly on the future direction of development policy have been very comprehensive covering all major subjects in detail. Discussions have been frank and open with on occasion violent confrontation between opponents. As one observer put it 'Algeria interrogates itself'. Criticisms of the results of the development decade 1966-77 have focussed on the collapse of agriculture, low industrial productivity, the dangerous dependence on energy exports (in 1980 petroleum represented 98 per cent of total exports and 67.6 per cent of total government revenues) and the acute shortage of housing and social services. The 1977 Census of Population revealed an average of nine people to each home (38). With an annual population growth rate of 3.2 per cent (39) - one of the world's highest - the problem is rapidly worsening. Health provision has also not kept pace with population growth. In 1966 there was one hospital bed for every 300 inhabitants, in 1977 one bed for 390 inhabitants. Furthermore in spite of the progress made in expanding the education system in 1977 some 58 per cent of the population nine years and over were illiterate, 71 per cent of the population in rural areas.

The National Charter which embodies the major principles guiding the future shape of Algerian society underlines the need to maintain development coherence.

> The governing criterion of Algeria's development policy is that development is conceived as indivisible, that is, as a body of actions which will affect all aspects of political, economic social and cultural life, and which are interconnected, forming integral parts of a single process marked by unity of means and purpose. Development policy therefore rests on the establishment of close bonds designed to link industrial projects and the programmes undertaken in the various branches of education with operations for the restructuring of agriculture, the reorganisation of trade and the development of infrastructure, housing, and the organisation of communes and wilayate (40).

This concern to establish a better intersectoral balance and thus ensure balanced economic and social development was reflected in the new Five Year Development Plan (1980-84) finally adopted in 1980 (41). Projected investment under the plan totals 400,000 million AD, almost four times more than that proposed for the 1974-77 Plan (Table 5.8). Almost half total expenditure is being allocated to the completion of projects begun under the previous plan, notably in industry, housing, education and training. Under the new investment programme industry, with 38.5 per cent of planned investment, remains the basis of the government's long term strategy and the overall structure of planned investments in the new plan is not radically different from that of previous planning periods (Table 5.9). Nevertheless allocations to agriculture, housing, health and education, sectors which experienced serious delays under the last plan, have increased substantially in absolute terms. It remains to be seen whether these sectors will be able to utilise the increased funds made available to them more effectively than in previous years. For Benachenhou, *'La question centrale est, comme nous l'avons dit souvent, si l'allocation des ressources humaines et matérielles va suivre cette relative restructuration des dépenses'* (42).

The heavy industrialisation programme based on massive capital-intensive projects using sophisticated imported technologies has undergone a dramatic reappraisal under the new government of President Chadli. A number of major projects such as the third LNG complex at Arzew and the Bejaia refinery have been abandoned and others scaled down (43). The industrial options of the Boumediène era have been subject to fierce attacks in the Central Committee of the FLN. They have been held responsible for Algeria's huge foreign debt and a debt service ratio of 25 per cent in 1979 (44), for disastrous overdependence on imported high technology and for massive financial losses incurred by the construction of large-scale projects without sufficiently careful feasibility studies. In December 1981 M. Belaid Abdessalem, Minister of Industry & Energy under President Boumediène, and Sid Ahmed Ghozali, the Head of SONATRACH from 1966 to 1977, were suspended from the FLN'S Central Committee and there were indications that they might eventually be brought to trial for 'economic crimes'. Their eclipse marks a sharp break with the economic policies of the previous regime.

There has been a noticeable shift in policy away from investment in heavy industry towards greater emphasis on light industry. During the 1970s only 8 per cent of investment went to these industries and average production growth at 10 per cent per annum was insufficient to meet domestic demand. As a result there have been serious shortages of building materials, textiles and manufactured foodstuffs. While some of these projects will continue to rely on turnkey and product in hand contracts, smaller schemes will depend largely on simple labour-intensive techniques which draw increasingly on local resources for both studies and construction. In the annual development budget for the financial year 1980, the allocation for heavy industry was cut back to 7,800 million AD (as against 8,200 million AD in 1979) while in contrast light industry was given an increased allocation of 8,000 million AD as against 6,800 million AD in 1979.

As part of government efforts to improve productivity and promote more equitable regional development, a number of state companies in heavy and light industry have been split up into smaller units and management decentralised away from Algiers (45). Opposition to the reorganisation of public sector corporations reaches down into middle management, fearful of losing jobs and prestige and reluctant to leave the capital. According to the semi-official daily *El Moudjahid*, two years since it was announced, the reorganisation of the state oil company SONATRACH, a veritable state within a state with a turnover of 42,500 million AD in 1979, has still to be translated from paper to action. The restructuring of the public sector will not prove easy to implement.

The plight of the agricultural sector has become a major concern for the new regime. The accent has been placed on self-sufficiency in foodstuffs as 'the fundamental objective of the Revolution', a theme intended to mobilise public opinion rather than an economic objective to be achieved. A major operation to reorganise the heavily subsidised self-management estates (in 1981 the government devoted 1,500 million AD to cover deficits incurred by the autogestion and cooperative sectors during the 1978-79 session) is in progress and 1,500 agricultural engineers and 3,000 accountants are being trained with the help of the EEC. The government has decided to assist small and medium-sized landowners, and local authorities have been instructed to ensure that the private sector benefits more from state aid, notably by means of a *Banque Agricole pour le Développement de la Campagne* with its headquarters at Blida. The peasants are exempt from taxes, receive preferential rates of interest on all loans and benefit from other concessions. Some 23,000 million AD has been devoted to develop the country's water resources during the Five Year Plan; 16 dams are under construction and 25 more are planned to extend the irrigated area. A programme of reafforestation is underway and new housing is to be constructed to improve the living standards of the peasantry. To combat bureaucracy and encourage personal initiative, the President has declared that no measures will be introduced against the wishes of the peasantry.

Without doubt one of the most controversial actions of President Chadli's regime has been the new measures introduced to stimulate the private sector. Under the Boumediène Government and notably after 1971 and the *'tournant socialiste algérien'* the private sector was regarded with deep suspicion and various obstacles were placed on its development. Nevertheless even under adverse conditions the private sector grew to enjoy a not unimportant role in the national economy. It controls 60 per cent of the useful agricultural area (produces two-thirds of the country's cereal production, 90 per cent of meat and 85 per cent of milk production) and 40 per cent of industrial value added. Some 300,000 retailers and artisans enjoy a major role in distribution and services. It employs over a third of the active population, and in agriculture, commerce and services the private sector is the major employer.

Denounced as parasitic by the previous regime, the private sector is now being rehabilitated, and its existence and development are to be taken into account by the nation's planners. Following a recommendation by the Central Committee of the FLN a new investment code was drawn up and adopted by the government in March 1982. It gives private enterprises new guarantees and incentives. Private firms will be entitled to financial and fiscal incentives as well as assistance in preparing investment applications, accounting and management. Bank loans, state investment grants and tax benefits will be provided if projects are in line with the government's development objectives. Labour intensive projects in the backward interior will be encouraged. Previously ignored in economic planning, the private sector is now considered potentially important in creating jobs and improving the supply and quality of scarce goods and services.

In its resolution on the place of the private sector in the national economy, the FLN's Central Committee reaffirmed the role of the state as the basic economic driving force and emphasised that the private sector was not a substitute for a strong public sector. Nevertheless some observers interpret these measures and the other economic policies of President Chadli, as an attempt, under the guise of pragmatism, to abandon the socialist aims of the Revolution and dismantle the achievements of the Boumediène era. The eclipse of M. Abdessalem, a vigorous defender of the public sector built during the Boumediène presidency, and his suspension from the Central Committee, has only served to accentuate the worst fears of the vigilant supporters of socialist orthodoxy. They vigorously defend the public sector as perfectly viable, and blame any malfunctioning of the state system on sabotage by the enemies of socialism, some of whom, they maintain, occupy positions in the upper echelons of the state apparat. In reply the defenders of the present reforms reject the accusations of economic liberalisation *'à la Sadate'* and proclaim their allegiance to the socialist aims of the 1976 National Charter. This debate is not new; it is a fundamental one and will no doubt continue. For the Algerian masses forced to endure long years of austerity, and now promised a better life, this debate is far from academic.

NOTES AND REFERENCES

1. Useful references on the colonial economy include: S. Amin, The Maghreb in the Modern World : Algeria, Tunisia, Morocco, (Penguin Books, Harmondsworth, England, 1970); A. Benachenhou, Formation du Sous-développement en Algérie. Essai sur les Limites du Développement du Capitalisme en Algérie 1830-1962, (Algiers, 1978); W. Knapp, Northwest Africa : a Political and Economic Survey, (Oxford, 1977); Y.A. Sayigh, The Economies of the Arab World: Development since 1945, (Croom Helm, London, 1978), pp.521-578; T. Smith, The French Stake in Algeria, 1945-1962, (Ithaca, Cornell University Press, London, New York, 1978); A comprehensive bibliography on the colonial period and the economic policies of the independent Algerian government may be found in R.I. Lawless, Algeria - World Bibliographical Series, (Clio Press, Oxford, England and Santa Barbara, California, 1981).

2. A good analysis of the Plan de Constantine can be found in M. Raffinot and P. Jacquemot, Le Capitalisme d'Etat Algérien, (François Maspero, Paris, 1977), pp.33-38.

3. M. Cornaton, Les Regroupements de la Décolonisation en Algérie, (Les Editions Ouvrières, Paris, 1967).

4. P. Bourdieu and A. Sayad, Le Déracinement. La Crise de L'Agriculture Traditionnel en Algérie, (Paris, 1964); On the question of population regrouping see K. Sutton and R.I. Lawless, 'Population Regrouping in Algeria : Traumatic Change and the Rural Settlement Pattern'. Transactions of the Institute of British Geographers New Series, vol.3, no.3 (1970), pp.331-350.

5. Amin, Maghreb in the Modern World, p.243.

6. On the economic policies of Ben Bella's government see Raffinot and Jacquemot, Capitalisme d'Etat Algérien, pp.48-73; and G. Challand and J. Minces, L'Algérie Indépendante : Bilan d'une Révolution Nationale, (Francois Maspero, Paris, 1972).

7. On worker self-management in Algerie see F. d'Arcy, A. Krieger and A. Marill, Essais sur l'Economie de l'Algérie Nouvelle, (Presses Universitaires de France, Paris, 1965); T.L. Blair, The Land to those who work it' Algeria's Experiment in Workers' Management,, (Doubleday, Garden City, New York, 1969); I. Clegg, Workers' Self-management in Algeria, (Allen Lane, Penguin Books, London, 1971); G. Duprat, Révolution et Autogestion Rurale en Algérie, (Armand Colin, Paris, 1973); D. Helie, 'Industrial Self-management in Algeria' in I.W. Zartman. (ed). Man State and Society in the Contemporary Maghrib, (Pall Mall Press, London, 1973), pp.465-474; I. Koulytchiztky, L'Autogestion l'Homme et l'Etat : l'Experience Algérienne, (Mouton, Paris, Le Hague, 1974).

8. On the economic policies of the Boumediène era see K. Ammour, C. Leucate, J.J. Moulin, La Voie Algérienne : les Contradictions d'un Développement National, (François Maspero, Paris, 1974); A. Benachenhou, Planification et Développement en Algérie 1962-1980, (Presses de l'E.N. Imprimerie Commerciale, Algiers, 1980);

M.E. Benissad, L'Economie Algérienne Contemporaine, (Presses Universitaires de France, Paris, 1980); Challand and Minces, L'Algérie Indépendante; K. Farsoun, State Capitalism in Algeria, (Middle East Research & Information Project, Washington D.C. 1975); R.I. Lawless, Country Case Study – Algeria, (International Migration Project, University of Durham, Durham, England, 1978); Raffinot and Jacquemot, Capitalisme d'Etat Algérien; G. Viratelle, L'Algérie Algérienne, (Les Editions Ouvrières, Paris, 1973); also 'Chronique Economique Algérie', Annuaire de l'Afrique du Nord, (Editions du CNRS, Paris, 1962-).

9. J-P. Séréni, 'La Politique Algérienne des Hydrocarbures', Maghreb, no.45 (1971), pp.31-49.

10. Raffinot and Jacquemot, Capitalisme d'Etat Algérien, p.243.

11. Ibid., p.151.

12. The subject of emigration is discussed in detail in Lawless, Country Case Study – Algeria; R.I. Lawless, A.M. Findlay and A. Findlay, Return Migration to the Maghreb: People and Policies, Arab Papers no.10, (Arab Research Centre, London, 1982); S. Adler, International Migration and Dependence, (Saxon House, Westmead, Farnborough, England, 1977).

13. Benachenhou, Planification et Développement, p.78.

14. A useful series of articles on Algerian industrialisation can be found in C. Palloix et al., 'Algérie 1980' Revue Tiers-Monde, vol.21, no.83 (1980), pp.475-603; See also T. Said-Amer,L'Industrialisation en Algérie. L'Entreprise Algérienne dans le Développement, (Anthropos, Paris, 1978); A. Tehami, Le Programme Algérien des "Industries Locales", (Société Nationale d'Edition et de Diffusion, Algiers, 1979).

15. Raffinot and Jacquemot, Capitalisme d'Etat Algérien, p.186.

16. Ibid., p.187.

17. A. Benachenhou, Les Firmes Etrangères et le Transfert des Techniques vers l'Economie Algérienne, (Centre de Recherches en Economie Appliquée, Algiers, 1977).

18. These problems are discussed in Pôle de Développementet Arrière-Pays : le Cas de Annaba-El-Hadjar, (Association Algérienne pour la Recherche Démographique, Economique et Sociale, Algiers, 1979 and 1980) (4 vols); M. Mekideche, 'A Propos de Quelques Conséquences Negatives d'un Développement Par Pôle : Le Cas de la Zone Industrielle d'Arzew in Association Maghrébine pour l'Etude de la Population et Organisation Arabe du Travail, 4 Colloque de Démographie Maghrébine sur l'Emploi, (Hammamet, 9-13 June 1980), pp.103-113.

19. Raffinot and Jacquemot, Capitalisme d'Etat Algérien, p.203.

20. Benachenhou, Planification et Développement, p.111.

21. Basic references on agricultural development include Algeria's Agrarian Revolution, (MERIP Reports No.67, Middle East Research & Information Project, Washington D.C. 1978); C. Chaulet, La Mitidja Autogérée: Enquête sur les Exploitations Autogérées Agricoles d'une Région d'Algérie, (Société Nationale d'Edition et de Diffusion, Algiers, 1971); B. Etienne, et al., Problèmes Agraires au Maghreb,

(Editions du Centre National de la Recherche Scientifique, Paris, 1977); A. Hersi, Les Mutations des Structures Agraires en Algérie depuis 1962, (Office des Publications Universitaires, Algiers, 1979); J.C. Karsenty, 'La Politique Agricole Algérienne', Maghreb Machrek, no.77 (1977), pp.31-39; P. Knauss, 'Algeria's Agrarian Revolution : Peasant Control or Control of Peasants?, African Studies Review, vol.20, no.3 (1977), pp.65-78; G. Mutin, La Mitidja; Décolonisation et Espace Géographique, (Centre de Recherche et d'Etudes sur les Sociétés Méditerrannéennes, Paris, 1977); D. Sari, La Dépossession des Fellahs (1830-1962), (Société Nationale d'Edition et de Diffusion, Algiers, 1978); T. Smith, 'The Political and Economic Ambitions of Algerian Land Reform, 1962-1974' Middle East Journal, vol.29, no.3 (1975), pp.259-78.

22. Raffinot and Jacquemot, Capitalisme d'Etat Algérien, p.359.

23. Four articles on the réforme agraire are included in Palloix, 'Algérie 1980', pp.605-682.

24. G. Mutin, 'Agriculture et Dépendance Alimentaire en Algérie' Maghreb Machrek, no.90 (1980), p.52.

25. Some variation in total beneficiaries arises from a significant level of resignations from the production cooperatives and abandonment of land by beneficiaries dissatisfied with the quantity of land and the cooperative manner of working it. Benachenhou found 3958 examples of land abandonment (désistement) in the wilayat of Saida, Tihert, Sidi Bel-Abbes and Oum el-Bouaglis by late 1975, contributing to the problem of rural exodus.

26. The cooperatives of the agrarian reform are discussed in K. Sutton 'Agricultural Cooperatives in Algeria' in Yearbook of Agricultural Cooperation 1981, (The Plunkett Foundation, Oxford, 1982), pp.169-90.

27. H. Delorme, 'L'Algérie : Importations de Céréales. Blocage de la Production et Développpement de l'Etat', Maghreb Machrek, no.91 (1981), pp.7-23.

28. None of the official sources include employment in the so-called 'informal' sector or lower circuit of the urban economy (street traders, small shopkeepers, craftworkers) - jobs which provide the only source of livelihood for some Algerians and for others an essential supplement to their regular earnings. The numbers involved in informal sector employment are almost impossible to determine, but are far from negligible. For a thorough survey of the employment problem in Algeria during the 1970's see Lawless, Country Case Study - Algeria, pp.43-71.

29. Ch. Bernard, 'Occupation Massive et Sous-Activité. La Situation Algérienne de l'Emploi au Terme du 2e Plan Quadriennal (1973-77)' in Annuaire de l'Afrique du Nord 1978, (Editions du CNRS, Paris, 1979), p.297.

30. On this subject see A. Benachenhou, L'Exode Rurale en Algérie, (ENAP, Algiers, 1979); M. Nancy, 'Chronique Economique Algérie' in Annuaire de l'Afrique du Nord 1979, (Editions CNRS, Paris, 1980), pp.597-607.

31. Mutin, 'Agriculture et Dépendance', p.59.

32. Ibid., p.60.
33. Bernard, 'Occupation Massive et Sous-Activité', p.302.
34. Ibid., p.60.
35. Benachenhou, Planification et Développement, pp.222-224.
36. 'Interview with the general secretary at the Planning and Regional Development Ministry', Middle East Economic Digest, vol.23, no.49 (7 December 1979), p.9.
37. Benachenhou, Planification et Développement, p.221.
38. On this subject see D. Benamrane, Crise de l'Habitat: Perspectives de Développement Socialiste en Algérie, (Centre de Recherches en Economique Appliquée, Algiers, 1980).
39. After years of outspoken opposition to any official family planning programme, in 1980 there appeared to be a slight shift in policy with official sources including the press referring to the need for 'l'espacement des naissances'. This policy is to be encouraged through several hundred centres de protection maternelle et infantile (PMI). Details of this programme are given in D. Junqua, 'Algérie Entre les Principes Religieux et les Impératifs Démographiques', Le Monde, (20 August 1980), p.9.
40. National Charter, Ministry of Culture & Information, Algiers, 1981, pp.109-110.
41. Rapport Général du Plan Quinquennal 1980-84, (Ministère de Planification et de l'Aménagement du Territoire, Algiers, 1980); A summary may be found in The 1980-84 Algerian Five Year Plan, (Committee for Middle East Trade, London, 1981).
42. Benachenhou, Planification et Développement, p.250.
43. The gas liquefaction (LNG) plants have proved to be very expensive and subject to considerable operating problems. The lengthy reappraisal of export strategy has resulted in the decision to halt work on any further new LNG plants at least for the time being. This means that a growing proportion of the available gas will in future have to be exported by pipeline. A Trans-Mediterranean pipeline to Italy was completed in 1982 and is capable of carrying gas at an annual rate of 12 bn cu m. The Segamo project under study envisages the construction of a pipeline across the western Mediterranean linking Algeria and Spain. Under the new Energy Minister, Belkacem Nabi, government policy has been to achieve parity between oil and gas prices. Algeria made some progress towards this aim when France agreed in December 1981 to pay $5.20-$5.30mn Btu for its imports of Algerian gas compared to $2.45 rising to $3.20 agreed in early 1980. Algeria had originally demanded $6.11mn Btu but had to reduce its demands because of competition from the USSR.
44. Benachenhou puts it at a very much higher level of 39 per cent; Benachenhou, Planification et Développement, p.90.
45. A note on the new decentralisation policies is included in The 1980-84 Algerian Five Year Plan, p.38.

Chapter 6.

THE MOROCCAN ECONOMY IN THE 1970S

Anne M. Findlay

INTRODUCTION

Morocco, which in Arabic means 'the land of the farthest west', is politically and economically as well as geographically on the fringe of the Arab world. Although Morocco experienced colonial rule for a much shorter period than either Tunisia or Algeria, both its economy and spatial organisation underwent radical transformation. A reorientation of economic activities from the traditional centres of the interior to the coastal littoral took place, reflecting the pattern of penetration of colonial dominance. Rabat was nominated as the administrative capital while Casablanca rapidly emerged as the economic hub of the country. Of Morocco's 19.5 million population (1979) 10 per cent live in the Casablanca conurbation and large-scale rural to urban migration flows focus on the industrial zone of Casablanca-Mohammedia.

A considerable diversity of landscapes characterises Morocco. The plains of the Atlantic seaboard contrast with the rugged hilly landscapes of the Rif, the high mountains of the Atlas range and the pre-Saharan desert areas. Considerable agricultural potential exists in the climatically and physically favourable parts of the country. Morocco, although not an oil producing state, has rich deposits of phosphates. Phosphate exports are a principal source of foreign earnings, but sadly Morocco remains at the mercy of world market prices (1).

Although this chapter will consider the various sectors of the economy in turn it is emphasised that economic development must be more than the sum of sectoral growth. The distribution of resource exploitation is as critical to the economic development of the country as the type of resource utilisation. Santos (2) developing his concept of 'shared space', underlines the importance of the organisation of space in economic development, placing spatial integration of activities on a par with the choice of economic structures. The application of Santos' paradigm of economic development is of particular relevance to Morocco, as Moroccan choices concerning the spatial articulation of activities are as much responsible for the economic problems which face the country as the specific economic strategies which have been adopted during the 1970s (3). Morocco has achieved a considerable economic growth and the substantial transformation of its economy since independence. But it would appear that the course followed by Morocco has increased social inequalities as well as aggravated the extent of spatial non-articulation of activities in the national 'shared space'.

NATIONAL PLANNING, 1960-1978

Amin (4) described Morocco at the time of independence as an exemplary model of a well-developed colonial country. Basic industries had been established and welfare provision initiated. Following independence, the withdrawal of foreign capital and of consumers able to afford industrial goods resulted in a decline in private investment in the secondary sector. No comprehensive scheme was drawn up to develop Morocco's considerable physical resources in harmony with the needs of its still relatively poorly skilled and largely illiterate population.

During the 1960s a series of national plans were drawn up. These plans indicate the main aims of official policy-making. The central tenet of the first of these plans (1960-1964) was to assert Morocco's political liberation by encouraging greater economic independence. Political, social and economic structures were to be reformed by a programme of democratisation, Moroccanisation and modernisation. The plan claimed to seek the reduction of social and spatial inequalities as a high priority through the implementation of agrarian reforms and state intervention in industry. The *distribution* of economic growth was ostensibly considered as important as the *rate* of economic growth. Unfortunately this plan was never implemented due to considerable political opposition which it encountered from the powerful interest groups it sought to undermine. A second plan, known as the black version, was quickly drawn up following the replacement of the cabinet by a much more conservative one. The black plan reversed the priorities of the first plan but ironically it too was abandoned following the death of King Mohammed V in 1961.

A new attempt to formulate an economic plan was undertaken for the period 1965-1967 when *Le Plan Triennal* affirmed the intention to pursue the maximisation of economic growth at the expense of other goals. The 1968-1972 Plan continued this policy by encouraging large capital-dependent projects epitomised by the *'politique des barrages'*. It was claimed that the high dams project would favour the rapid growth of agricultural production, and this approach has dominated the government's agricultural investment policy during the 1970s. Under this policy it was hoped that 20 new dams would be constructed to irrigate one million hectares of land by the year 2000. In addition to increased production in the commercial agricultural sector, emphasis was placed on export-oriented crops which it was argued would assist the ailing balance of payments. The policy was enacted by the *Code d'Investissement Agricole* of 1969 which stipulated defined regions in which agricultural investment would be concentrated.

During the 1968-1972 Plan, economic growth exceeded the forecasted rate of growth. The annual growth rate of 5.6 per cent in

GDP was significantly higher than the expected growth rate of 4.8 per cent. Growth in both the agricultural and industrial sectors exceeded the Plan's estimations. A bumper harvest in 1968 was largely responsible for the 6 per cent per annum growth rate in the agricultural sector.

The unpredicted level of expansion in production was accompanied by an equally unplanned level of growth in consumption per capita. This increased by an average of 2 per cent per annum between 1968 and 1972, a rate almost double that envisaged by the planners. Despite this apparent national improvement in standard of living, disparities in wealth within society widened rather than decreased. The introduction to the 1973-1977 National Plan poignantly describes the problem: 'The overall improvement in living standards far from diminishing differentials in standards of living has to a certain extent accentuated the differentials'(5). This growth in economic inequalities can be clearly demonstrated from official statistics. In 1960 the value of consumption per capita was 1.7 times as great in urban as in rural areas, while in 1971 annual expenditure per household in rural areas was found to be 4,003 Moroccan dirhams (MD) compared with 8,057 MD in urban areas (or over twice as high) (6). In 1960 the richest and poorest 10 per cent of the Moroccan population consumed 25 per cent and 3.3 per cent of the total consumption respectively. By 1971 the situation had deteriorated, the richest 10 per cent of the population consuming 37 per cent of total consumption and the poorest 10 per cent only 1.2 per cent (7). Between 1973 and 1977 food prices rose by an average of 11.1 per cent per annum (a rate well above the level of wage increases), further exacerbating the economic hardship facing the poorest members of society (8). The gap between farmers involved in the upper and lower circuits of the economy also widened and despite limited agrarian reform in some areas the number of landless peasants increased. In addition to the social consequences, the widening of the gap between so-called upper and lower circuit workers had a spatial consequence. Beguin's analysis of the spatial development of the Moroccan economy during the 1960s concluded that the distribution of production had favoured the core area at the expense of the periphery.

The 1973-77 Five Year National Plan was the major policy document for investment in the 1970s. The Plan had a dual goal, firstly to assure maximum economic growth and secondly to achieve a better social and economic distribution of growth. Investment in the agricultural sector continued to be a priority although industry received a larger share than in previous plans but was still heavily reliant on private sector investment. In 1974 the world phosphates prices rose rapidly and the rise in revenue from phosphate sales encouraged economic optimism. In response to this optimism the plan allocations were revised. Agricultural investment was boosted by 80 per cent and a further new dam was planned but agriculture's share of the total budget declined relative to those of industry and infrastructure (Table 6.1). Administration and defence spending doubled proportional to other sectors in response to the Western Saharan troubles.

A comparison of growth in GDP by sector is given in Table 6.2 for

TABLE 6.1. THE SECTORAL ALLOCATION OF INVESTMENT OF THE MOROCCAN NATIONAL PLANS (% OF TOTAL INVESTMENT)

	1973–1977	1973–1977	1978–1980	1981–1985
		Revised Estimate		
Agriculture	24.8	19.4	16.2	17.7
Industry	14.2	11.0	34.8	39.7
Infrastructure	14.5	15.4	3.6	4.2
Education	14.0	8.3	6.2	6.4
Social Sectors	12.9	6.8	18.2	20.7
Administration/Security	9.9	22.3	19.3	6.0
Regional Development	9.4	16.5	1.7	5.3

Source: Author's compilation

for the 1960s and 1970s. Between 1970 and 1979 GDP grew at a faster rate per annum than in the 1960s. Growth in the industrial and manufacturing sectors was more rapid than in the 1960s and was accompanied by very rapid growth in the tertiary sector. By contrast agriculture stagnated during the 1970s despite the high levels of government investment in agriculture during the 1968-1972 plan. A marked shift in the structure of GDP occurred during the 20 year period, the mining sector expanding its share of GDP and the agricultural sector contracting. The share of manufacturing industry remained constant. It is significant that the tertiary sector expanded at a rate faster than the overall growth rate creating an imbalance between the tertiary and secondary sectors. Sectoral growth in GDP does not reflect sectoral investment by the government. Conversely despite government investment the agricultural sector has not expanded. The reasons for this are outlined in the following section. The world commodity markets appear to have been more significant than government planning in influencing the growth of GDP.

AGRICULTURE

In no sector of the economy can government policy so clearly be seen to have contributed to the bi-polarisation of the two circuits of the economy. Official statistics suggest that in 1979 53 per cent of the national labour force were employed in agriculture, but regional disaggregation of this statistic indicates that in the majority of regions a very much higher proportion of the population is employed in agriculture, whether it be in the commercial or subsistence sectors. As has been shown, large-scale agricultural projects have received a major share of national investment during the 1970s. This has not however been sufficient to reduce the gap between agricultural production and the consumption of agricultural produce. Food production declined from a base of 100 in 1971 to 83 in 1979 (10) reflecting an increasing dependence on imports and a failure to keep pace with demand. Programmes for investment in agriculture have favoured the already most commercialised zones and have virtually ignored peasant production systems.

Agricultural production has been characterised by extreme variability, largely resulting from the prevailing weather conditions. The bumper harvest of 1968 has not been matched during the 1970s, when by contrast a series of poor harvests were experienced leading to hardship throughout the country but particularly amongst the poorer small-scale subsistence farmers. The miserable harvest of 1978/1979 was caused by low rainfall early in the year which ironically was followed by floods in the Gharb plain at the same time as drought was parching the land in the south and east of the country. Table 6.3 highlights the problems of variability in crop production which have been encountered during the 1970s. Even industrial crops which are confined to the areas of irrigated agriculture such as sugar beet, whose growing conditions are closely monitored by the state agricultural boards, have been adversely affected by varying climatic conditions.

TABLE 6.2 GROWTH AND STRUCTURE GDP

Growth of Production (average annual growth rate)

	1960-1969 %	1970-1979 %
Agriculture	4.7	- 0.3
Industry	4.0	7.3
Manufacturing	3.8	6.3
Services	4.0	7.4
Total GDP	4.2	6.1

Source: World Development Report 1981, World Bank Washington D.C., 1981, p.136.

TABLE 6.3. AGRICULTURAL PRODUCTION

	Hard Wheat		Sugar Beet	
	(a)	(b)	(a)	(b)
1970-1971	1517	10.8	48	368.3
1971-1972	1503	10.8	60	277.6
1972-1973	1477	8.0	45	287.3
1973-1974	1388	9.9	57	336.8
1974-1975	1238	9.7	62	288.5
1975-1976	1454	11.4	67	352.5
1976-1977	1392	7.4	48	368.3
1977-1978	1297	11.1	59	409.0
1978-1979	1167	11.2	62	347.9
1979-1980	1269	10.5	63	347.5

(a) Area under cultivation (1000 ha)
(b) Yield (quintaux/ha)

Source: Statistiques Agricoles, Service des Statistiques et de la Documentation, Ministère de l'Agriculture et de la Réforme Agraire, Rabat, various dates.

The Moroccan Economy in the 1970s

The crisis in Moroccan agriculture is highlighted by the fact that before the Second World War Morocco was a net exporter of wheat. By contrast during the 1970s, with population growth averaging 2.9 per cent per annum, domestic production was incapable of meeting demand, the shortfall being made up by large quantities of imported wheat (Fig. 6.1). Between 40 and 50 per cent of wheat requirements were imported by the late 1970s. By 1978 almost four times as much wheat was being imported as in 1970 and wheat imports accounted for 8.9 per cent of the import bill compared with 3.7 per cent at the beginning of the decade.

Why should such a trend have emerged when the Moroccan Government has given priority to investment in the agricultural sector? The answer would seem to lie in the government's preoccupation with the extension of irrigation while almost ignoring the need for investment in the existing rainfed agricultural areas. Thus, the area under wheat cultivation, for example, which has traditionally been grown in rainfed areas, has actually declined during the last 20 years. It would seem that Morocco is now facing the unnecessary costs of neglecting the rainfed cereal-growing areas.

Not even the formal commercial agricultural systems of Morocco appear to have benefited from the policies for agricultural development. Other sectors of agriculture have also declined during the 1970s. Citrus fruit production, for example, has experienced decline. Citrus fruits are grown principally for export to the European Economic Community. In 1976/1977 184.4 million metric tons of citrus fruit were exported but in 1979/1980 this figure dropped to only 138.1 million metric tons. Moroccan fruit growers have failed to adapt to the stringent standards set by the European market. Improved quality of fruit could be achieved by means of increased greenhouse cultivation and the replanting of citrus orchards but these measures would again reflect a move towards an increasingly capital intensive form of production favouring upper circuit workers. The replanting programme is expected to yield a 22 per cent increase in the export potential of citrus fruit by 1985. Investment in agricultural sectors oriented towards export is vulnerable because of the tendency towards increasing trade restrictions by EEC nations with the imposition of product quotas.

Given the difficulties of providing sufficient food for the Moroccan population and the hazardous nature of investment in export-oriented agricultural systems, why have national plans continued to favour investment in expensive irrigation projects? One important aim of the irrigation programme would appear to be the idea of import substitution. For example, high levels of sugar imports in the 1950s and 1960s prompted efforts to increase domestic production. Sugar was first grown commercially in Morocco in the early 1960s. By 1973 Morocco was able to meet half the domestic requirement for sugar production from home production and by the late 1970s sugar beet had become Morocco's principal industrial crop. A 25 per cent increase in the area under sugar-beet cultivation between 1970 and 1978 was accompanied by higher yields per ha to give a significant increase in the level of production. Imported sugar fell from 4 per cent of the

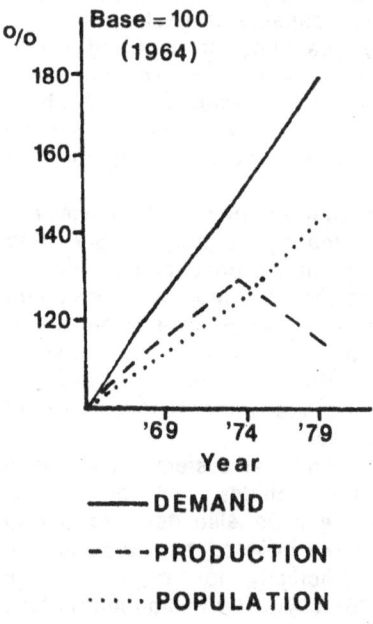
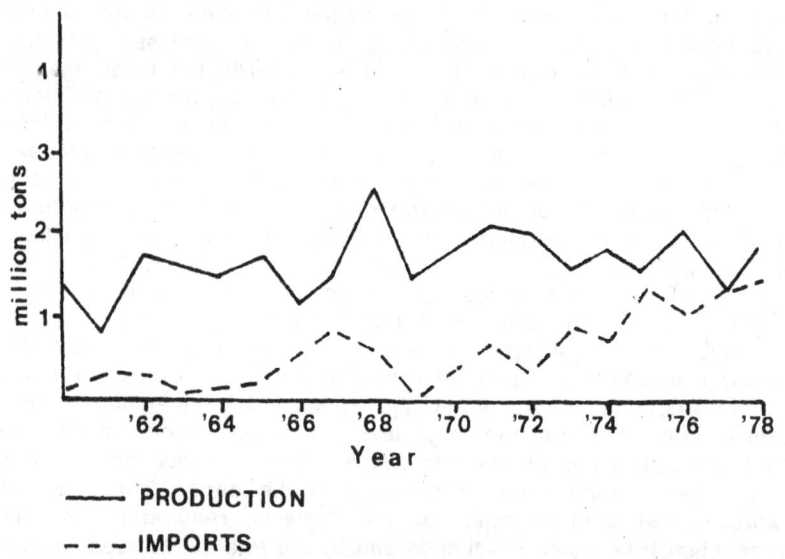

FIGURE 6.1   MOROCCO: TRENDS IN WHEAT PRODUCTION & DEMAND

import bill in 1970 to only 2.5 per cent in 1978.

Relationships between producer and market are strictly controlled, farmers selling their crops to specified processing plants. High profit margins for sugar beet have been more than sufficient to attract farmers of the upper circuit in the Gharb Plain and Tadla region into this profitable sector of the agricultural system. While progress in the cultivation of sugar beet has been impressive this must be set against the related increase in the bill for the import of other basic foodstuffs such as wheat, particularly in view of the immensely expensive irrigation projects involved.

Concentration of investment in the large dam schemes, and the related irrigation projects, might seem more justifiable if the programme itself had been more efficiently organised. Irrigation projects have been continually frustrated by the improper phasing of the installation of infrastructure and water distribution networks to the farms following the completion of the dams. Delays between the completion of the dams and distribution networks have retarded the rates of return on capital investment and have slowed up the long awaited increases in agricultural productivity. Examination of Table 6.4 indicates both the considerable unrealised potential for irrigation from the capacity of the existing dams and the very limited areas of Morocco which have benefited from irrigated agriculture. Despite the planners' assertions in 1973 to give priority to the completion of existing projects, the 1978-1980 Plan reiterated the need to complete the irrigation projects which have not as yet been operationalised.

While progress on Morocco's irrigation projects is slow, the implementation of a comprehensive land reform has yet to be undertaken (11). In 1977 23.4 per cent of farmers owned no land and 56.5 per cent owned units of less than 5 ha while only 0.5 per cent owned units of 50-100 ha. This same 0.5 per cent owned 17 per cent of the agricultural land.

Following independence the process of gradually repossessing land formerly owned by the French settlers was commenced. By 1966 some of this land had been redistributed to Moroccan farmers who were to work the land as members of agricultural cooperatives. According to the *Code d'Investissement de l' Agriculture* of 1969 land could be expropriated where necessary for new agricultural schemes. Allotments were subsequently resold in units of not less than 5 ha. Prices were generous and landowners experienced all the advantages of technical assistance and modern irrigation in addition to larger unfragmented units. As recently as 1973 the Moroccan Government negotiated compensation terms with foreign landowners as the final stage in the recovery of foreign-owned land. None of the above measures has contributed substantially towards remedying the problems of rural congestion, the fragmentation of holdings and the uneconomic size of most agricultural units found throughout the majority of the country where either colonial agriculture was less important or where, no irrigation schemes have been implemented.

The only major government scheme attempting to improve conditions in the rainfed farming zones was the DERRO project *Développement*

TABLE 6.4. IRRIGATION SCHEMES IN MOROCCO

a. The extension of irrigated land (ha), 1972-1978

Region	1972	Planned 1973-1977	Actual	1978
Moulouya	38,330	13,590	10,005	48,335
Gharb	36,200	49,100	28,590	64,790
Doukkala	22,400	11,100	8,860	31,260
Haouz	8,500	18,500	19,500	28,000
Tadla	85,000	15,400	19,868	102,368
Souss	-	25,800	20,317	20,317
Loukkos	-	12,200	1,500	1,500

b. Major Moroccan irrigation projects

Name of Dam	Area	Date of Completion	Irrigated Area(1978) (ha)	Potential Irrigated (ha)	Cost (million (MD)
Mohammed V	Moulouya	1967	45,000	61,000	
Bou Areg	Moulouya	1969		700	
Moulay Youssef	Haouz	1970	23,000	31,000	
Hassan Addakhil	Tafilalet	-	8,000	12,000	
Mansour Ed Dhabi	Ouarzazate	1972	19,500	25,000	
Idriss I	Gharb	1973	90,000	125,000	216
Youssef Ben Tachfine	Agadir	1973	-	20,000	193
Tleta	Tangier	(under construction 1978)	-	1,900	
El Massira	Doukkala	(under construction 1978)	-	95,000	340

Source: 'Maroc: bilan du plan quinquennial 1973-1977', Maghreb Développement no.8-9 (1978), p.5; 20 Ans d' Indépendance: Eau et Energie Electrique, Ministère des Travaux Publics et des Communications, Rabat, n.d.; Annuaire Statistique du Maroc, Direction de la Statistique, Secrétariat d'Etat au Plan et au Développement Régional, Rabat (various dates).

Economique et Rural du Rif Occidental). This project, concerning the western part of the Rif, comprised pasture improvement schemes, control of soil erosion, afforestation, replanting of orchards and rural infrastructure development. The 1973-77 National Plan wisely increased expenditure on the project. De Mas, in his study of the Rif (12), has underlined the pressing need for structural change in the rainfed agricultural areas if they are to support economically viable agricultural systems and make a substantial contribution to meeting the shortfall in domestic food production.

To summarise, the official Moroccan policy of encouraging irrigation projects and favouring export-oriented crops in a small number of areas has had detrimental consequences for the country's agricultural system. Limited land redistribution in the irrigated areas has created an upper circuit of agricultural activities which has links with the international market and which has operated in isolation not only from those parts of the rural population excluded from employment in this highly commercialised sector, but also relative to the domestic demand for basic foodstuffs. These agricultural policies have accentuated the differences between the lower and upper circuit of the rural areas as well as enforcing a distinct pattern of spatial inequality in agricultural investment.

MINING AND ENERGY

The crucial role of the mining industry in the Moroccan economy has already been emphasised. Phosphate exports contribute about 5 per cent of GNP and represent 35-40 per cent of all exports. Phosphate production is controlled by the *Office Chérifien des Phosphates*, a state company entrusted with the very critical task of managing the commercial exploitation of phosphates. About two thirds of the world's known phosphate rock reserves are located at Khouribga (Fig 6.2) where current production levels are 16 million tons per year. The government has attempted to increase production by bringing new mines into production both at Khouribga where two new mines are scheduled to open in the 1980s and at other sites such as Ben Guerir, Sidi Hajjaj (to open in 1985) and Meskala (to open in 1987), thus increasing production by over 13 million tons per year (13). This expansion is planned on the basis of Morocco penetrating new markets such as the USSR. Although the USSR is currently self-sufficient in phosphates, by the late 1980s it may be unable to meet its commitments to COMECON countries from Soviet reserves. Morocco also controls the 1,700 million reserves at Bou Craa in the former Spanish Sahara. Domestic demand within Morocco for phosphates is extremely limited and consequently the country is dependent on the vicissitudes of world market demand. This is well demonstrated by the painful experiences of the early 1970s. Increased world demand for fertilisers resulted in 1972 in a sharp rise in the price of phosphates. The tripling of the price of phosphates prompted an immediate revision of Morocco's 1973-1977 Development Plan with investment allocations being raised on the basis of the expected rise in export earnings. Subsequently world

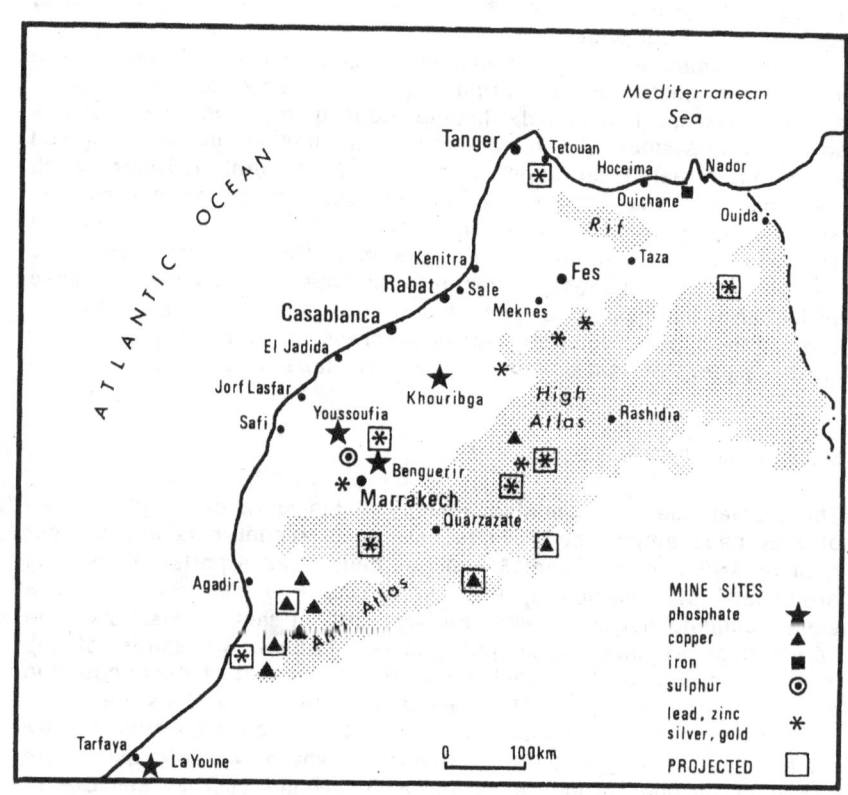

FIGURE 6.2   DISTRIBUTION OF MINERAL RESOURCES IN MOROCCO

The Moroccan Economy in the 1970s

demand slumped as rapidly as it had expanded and in 1975-1976 the price plummeted (Table 6.5).

Morocco has been concerned to increase domestic processing of phosphates in order to increase total revenues from phosphate sales. Consequently in recent years several new phosphate processing plants have been established. In addition to the three plants already in operation in Safi a fourth one is planned for 1982. The existing plants produce fertilisers, phosphoric acid and mono-amonium phosphate. A new port, specifically for the export of phosphates, is being constructed at Jorf Lasfar and future processing plants are likely to be located there. Although world demand for phosphate rock declined during the late 1970s, demand for phosphoric acid continued to increase, particularly in Europe. Strong opposition, on environmental grounds, to the siting of these processing plants in Europe has favoured the location of further 'nuisance' industrial units such as phosphoric acid plants in Morocco (14).

In addition to its phosphate rock reserves Morocco has smaller mineral deposits of iron, lead, zinc, pyrrhotine and copper. Despite extensive petroleum exploration no major oil reserves have been found in Morocco. Only one small oilfield at Sidi Ghalem is in commercial production. Oil exploration is still being carried out but efforts to extract oil from oil shale deposits offer a more promising, albeit uncertain, future. In 1979 82 per cent of Moroccan bulk energy needs were met from imports, domestic coal and hydro-electricity supplying only 11 per cent and 8 per cent of energy requirements respectively (15). In an attempt to reduce the cost of energy imports Morocco has expanded its oil refining capacity. In 1960 only 11.7 per cent of the tonnage of oil imports were crude oil but by 1973 91 per cent of imports were crude rather than refined oil, reflecting the success in increasing refining capacity. A new oil refinery is planned as part of the Jorf Lasfar port and industrial complex.

This review of the extractive sector of the economy has underlined Morocco's dangerous dependence on world prices, firstly for oil imports, and secondly for phosphate exports critical to the Moroccan balance of payments.

MANUFACTURING INDUSTRY

The industrial sector remains relatively underdeveloped as reflected in its low contribution to GDP. Industrial production consists of approximately 60 per cent consumer goods, 25 per cent intermediate goods and 13 per cent capital goods (16). The pattern of industrialisation remains highly concentrated on the Atlantic littoral, 52 per cent of modern industrial establishments being located in the Casablanca-Mohammedia agglomeration in 1972 and a further 7 per cent on other parts of the Atlantic coast. Furthermore the majority of enterprises are small. In 1966 only 220 industrial enterprises had more than 100 employees (17). This small nucleus of industries at the time contributed 75 per cent of the value added from the industrial sector. Official statistics from the 1970s reinforce

TABLE 6.5. PHOSPHATE EXPORTS, 1970-1980

Year	Production	Exports (1000 metric tons)	Income from phosphate exports (million MD)
1970	10,711	11,537	571
1971	12,493	11,868	588
1972	16,520	13,559	673
1973	18,389	16,109	788
1974	19,749	18,700	4,075
1975	14,119	13,110	2,836
1976	15,656	14,651	2,191
1977	17,572	15,791	2,111
1978	19,272	17,264	2,034
1979	20,031	17,867	2,214
1980	18,824	16,527	3,012

Source: 'Le secteur minier au Maroc', Revue Bimensuelle d'Information (Banque Marocaine du Commerce Extérieur), no.52 (1980), pp.2-18; Le Maroc en Chiffres, Direction de la Statistique, Secrétariat d'Etat au Plan et au Développement Régional, Rabat, various dates.

TABLE 6.6. GROWTH IN MANUFACTURING PRODUCTION 1970-1980
(Volume Index 1969=100)

	1970	1972	1974	1976	1978	1980
Foodstuffs	106	127	145	157	174	192
Textiles	95	106	105	121	121	106
Leather Goods	91	109	114	104	102	131
Wood Industries	107	124	112	87	116	139
Paper Industries	99	85	128	121	136	160
Processed Mining Products	119	128	166	185	199	220
Metal Fabrication	102	86	123	170	131	140
Metal Products	107	114	149	147	130	144
Transport Equipment	111	92	107	137	106	80
Electrical Industries	105	106	121	175	151	210
Chemicals	104	133	139	152	196	218
Rubber & Plastic	105	104	109	102	126	111
TOTAL	105	116	132	149	170	187

Source: 'Industrial production in 1979' Monthly Information Review, no.31 (1980), p.17; Le Maroc en Chiffres en 1980, Direction de la Statistique, Secrétariat d'Etat au Plan et au Développement Régional, Rabat, 1981, p.49.

the belief that even the capital-intensive upper circuit of the economy continued to be represented by only a very small number of large companies and many very small firms. The bias towards small-scale activities in the secondary sector is even greater when it is remembered that most lower circuit employment is excluded from the industrial surveys and that it consists predominantly of one- and two-man enterprises.

The major trends in industrial growth by sector during the 1970s are summarised in Table 6.6. Over the ten year period 1970-1979 it can be seen that some modest expansion in the industrial sector did occur, the most important contribution being made by the mineral processing industries. This capital-intensive, externally-oriented industry has provided little expansion of employment opportunities and has promoted little integrated industrial development.

The importance of import substitution in the Moroccan strategy for agricultural development has led to the encouragement of food processing industries. For example, in accordance with the 'Sugar Plan's' extension of the area of sugar beet cultivation, refining capacity has been increased with two new refineries coming into production in the mid 70s. The index of industrial growth (Table 6.6) indicates an above average rate of increase in the food processing industries but with some fluctuations attributable to the impact of poor harvests on the productivity of certain types of food processing such as fruit and vegetable canning. The fruit and vegetable canning industry is aimed at export rather than import substitution and with 80-90 per cent of products going to the export market it makes a significant contribution to the nation's exports as well as being an important source of employment. The industry creates up to 16,000 seasonal jobs per year but the capacity of the fruit and vegetable canning factories is underutilised due to the inadequacies of the industry's distribution and collection networks.

In line with the policies of import substitution adopted in other sectors the cement industry has been promoted. The demand for building materials accelerated during the 1970s due to the development of rapid urbanisation and projects for the improvement of transport and infrastructure. Between 1970 and 1975 a 30 per cent increase in consumption took place and by 1980 consumption was two and a half times as great as in 1970, totalling 3.7 million metric tons per year. This increase in consumption resulted in a change in the balance of supply and demand. In 1970 Morocco could satisfy 97.5 per cent of demand from domestic production but by 1977, despite increased domestic production, only 72.4 per cent of demand could be satisfied locally. By 1980 the opening of two new plants, the Oriental and Temara works, returned domestic supply to 98.9 per cent of demand. Proposals for two further cement works would raise production by 100,000 metric tons per annum giving Morocco a surplus of cement which it could perhaps export to the many other Arab countries currently importing large quantities of cement. The expansion in the construction sector has stimulated growth in related industries such as brickmaking where production capacity doubled between 1973 and 1977 and the construction of prefabricated buildings where seven new units were opened. The case of the cement industry appears to be one instance in which development plans have been successfully matched with trends in demand.

Moroccan industry is particularly weak in respect of the production of metallurgical, mechanical and electrical industries with only 30 per cent of national requirements being met from domestic production in these sectors. Private investment in this sector has been low and yet state involvement has remained minimal.

The government's stated policy of Moroccanisation of industrial ownership rather than state nationalisation has tended to ignore the shortage and unwillingness of Moroccan private capital to invest in many sectors of industry. The decree of 1973 requires that Moroccan citizens or Moroccan companies hold at least 50 per cent of the share capital and constitute a majority on the board of directors of industrial enterprises. While the decree is admirable in its intentions, it is inadequate in itself to ensure the development of a stable industrial base in Morocco. Table 6.7 indicates the number of enterprises which were Moroccanised between 1973 and 1977. With the exception of tourism and shipping the legislation has apparently affected the tertiary sector to a greater extent than the secondary one, and evidence suggests that the effects have not been entirely beneficial. A number of firms have either closed down or changed activity to avoid Moroccanisation. Most of the firms involved in the process of Moroccanisation have been very small, with less than ten employees.

Recognising the need for expansion of the industrial sector the investment codes of 1960 were finally revised in 1973 and extended to industry, mining, tourism and artisanal industries (19). The purpose of these investment incentives was to attract foreign capital, a policy which seems to be in contradiction to the Moroccanisation strategy. Incentives included tax and customs duty concessions and special conditions to facilitate the transfer of company profits and capital. The investment scheme has tended to encourage capital-intensive rather than labour-intensive industries as the incentives are geared towards high capital investment rather than to the level of job creation or the labour absorptive capacity of new industries. Furthermore the incentives make no provision for the promotion of particular types of industries and therefore do not contribute to rectifying the country's industrial imbalance. Although Morocco has established a system of industrial development areas in an effort to disperse industry, the 1978-1980 National Plan itself admits that past investment incentives have failed to endorse the policy of decentralisation. The investment incentives are designed to attract new industries rather than to meet specific industrial development objectives.

In the industrial sector, the promotion of capital-intensive high technology plants for processing phosphates, the proposed, although often postponed, Nador steelworks and the expansion of the sugar and cement industries have contributed little to bridging the gap between the once very profitable artisanal industries and upper sector activities. Moroccan industrial policies have achieved neither

TABLE 6.7. MOROCCANISATION OF ENTERPRISES 1973-1977

Sector	Number of Enterprises Moroccanised
Manufacturing Industry	252
Commerce	686
Insurance and Finance	227
Car repair	96
Transport	104
Other	127

Source: 'Maroc: bilan du plan quinquennial 1973-1977', Maghreb Développement, no.8-9, (1978), p.15.

TABLE 6.8. LABOURFORCE BY OCCUPATIONAL CATEGORY (%)

Category	Total employed	Unemployed	First time unemployed	Total labour force
A1 Professional and sub-professional occupations	0.9	1.2	16.0	1.0
A2 Professional occupations - Arts based	1.4	0.9	1.0	1.4
B Sub-professional and technical, 1-3 years post secondary school	2.9	2.7	1.9	2.9
C1 Skilled and semi-skilled, clerical	9.4	8.2	12.2	9.5
C2 Skilled and semi-skilled, manual	24.2	47.2	50.1	25.1
D Unskilled occupations	60.9	39.5	18.4	60.0

Source: A.M.Findlay, 'Geographical Patterns of Moroccan Emigration', unpublished MA thesis, University of Durham, 1978, p.60.

spatial nor economic integration in the secondary sector.

FOREIGN TRADE

France has traditionally been Morocco's major trading partner. In 1975 France accounted for over 35 per cent of exports and 31 per cent of imports. By 1980 although trade links with France remained strong they accounted for a lower percentage of exports (25.2 per cent). Other EEC countries such as Italy, Germany and the UK have become increasingly important trading partners with Morocco while trade with both the USA and the USSR has also grown in significance. Ironically Morocco has a very low level of trade with fellow Arab states. This is remarkable in view of the political dependence which has inevitably accompanied Morocco's continued concentration of trade links with EEC nations. No trading advantage appears to have resulted. EEC imports from the Maghreb countries have always remained below the level of EEC exports to the Maghreb, resulting in a continual economic dependence of the Maghreb nations on Europe (20). This has been evidenced by the worsening balance of payments problems experienced by Morocco in the 1970s.

In 1970 the balance of payments deficit was equal to 101 million US dollars but by 1979 had increased to 1,110 million US dollars. Debt service rose from 1.5 per cent to 5.2 per cent of GNP during the same period and from 7.7 per cent to 21.8 per cent of export earnings. Contributory factors to the relatively poor performance of the Moroccan economy have been the contraction in the phosphate market and the high increase in defence spending incurred as a result of the prolonged battle for the Western Sahara. Between 1972 and 1977 defence rose from 12.3 per cent to 16.3 per cent of government expenditure and defence spending per capita tripled. The cost of the Saharan war has become an excessive burden on the Moroccan economy. Dependence on the West for military equipment and technological back-up is however one of the many dependency strands which continue to link Morocco to the West and preclude trade and integration with other Arab states.

In 1972, in an effort to achieve greater integration between the EEC and its Mediterranean neighbours, a 'Global Mediterranean' policy was formulated expanding EEC trade links with countries in the region. This strategy was formalised in 1976 when negotiations by Morocco succeeded in gaining what was termed 'preferential access' to EEC markets for the country's agricultural produce. The 1976 Agreement was an extension of earlier trade agreements between Morocco and the EEC and gave Morocco an 80 per cent concession on customs duty on citrus fruit, wine, olive oil, sardines and exemption on customs duty for all industrial products. This policy, however, still carefully protected EEC producers from direct competition from Moroccan imports by a system of Community preference prices for fruit and vegetables. Other EEC protectionist measures include quotas, import calendars and specific safeguards against competition. For example, Moroccan tomato exports are eligible for a 60 per cent tariff concession only between

November and April when European producers have little marketable produce.

In contrast with the trade agreements of the 1960s recent links have been concerned not only with trade but also with financial, social and technical cooperation. Morocco received loans from the EEC worth 130 million European units of account (EUA) for the period 1978 to 1981 which included a large loan towards the construction of the Jorf Lasfar port.

About 90 per cent of Moroccan textile exports are destined for the European market and 11 per cent of fruit and vegetables. Morocco, like its Maghreb neighbours, has recently become concerned at the accession of southern European countries to the EEC. At an EEC-Moroccan cooperation council in 1980 Moroccan Ministers seeking improved tariff concessions and product classification expressed concern over the enlargement of the Community.

Spain exports 20 per cent of citrus fruit traded on the world market, while Morocco exports 13 per cent. During the 1970s Spain lagged behind other countries in obtaining privileged access to EEC markets, having only a 40 per cent tariff concession compared with the Maghreb's 80 per cent concession. By contrast Spain's entry to the EEC is likely to give her a monopoly of EEC markets for citrus fruit to the considerable detriment of the Maghreb states. Morocco is also vulnerable as the biggest exporter of tomatoes to the EEC particularly as countries such as Greece are currently increasing out-of-season cultivation (23). Furthermore free movement of labour within the EEC could deal the final death blow to the precarious Moroccan migrant community, as Spanish and Greek workers will receive preferential status. In short, the increasing self-sufficiency of the EEC, resulting from the accession of new southern European states, will severely disfavour Morocco and the rest of the Maghreb.

MANPOWER

From an analysis of the labour market it appears that Morocco faces problems both of labour surplus and structural imbalance in the labour market (24). Between 1960 and 1971 the labour force increased at a rate of 1.8 per cent per annum compared with 2.5 per cent for the population as a whole. The former statistic represents a formidable rate of growth in demand for employment in a period when expansion of secondary and tertiary activities in the upper circuit were dominated by capital- rather than labour-intensive activities. The latter statistic (overall population growth rate) reflects the even greater problems faced by manpower services in the 1970s and 1980s as they seek to accelerate the rate of job creation in line with the rising number of new entrants from the bulging cohorts of Morocco's youthful population. The participation of women in the labour force increased from 10.6 per cent to 15.2 per cent in the 1960s. This represented a further pressure on both the upper and lower circuits as women have increasingly sought to obtain wage employment.

A number of changes have taken place in the distribution of

employment by sector. In both 1960 and 1971 agriculture remained the dominant economic activity involving more than 50 per cent of the labour force, but an increasing proportion of the labour force has found employment in the secondary sector with employment in the construction industry rising rapidly.

Table 6.8, compiled from the 1971 census data, attempts to classify the labour force on the basis of their skill levels. Some 94.5 per cent of the labour force are categorised in the three least skilled categories C1, C2 and D. A shortage of category B personnel exists and compared with, for example, Tunisia, the labour market is characterised by structural imbalance. Of those entrants to the labour market in the 15-24 age cohort, 89.1 per cent were classified in categories C2 and D. It is ironic that although large labour surpluses exist at the base of the labour market shortages of more skilled personnel may increasingly become an obstacle to the development of industry and agriculture, particularly in the projects involving technological expertise favoured by the Moroccan government.

While official estimates of unemployment are clearly inadequate they do indicate some of the general problems of the labour market. In 1971, 35 per cent of the population were recorded by the census as unemployed or underemployed. Great differentials in both unemployment and underemployment rates occurred. For example in the province of Al Hoceima 65 per cent of the workforce were registered as unemployed or underemployed. The highest labour surpluses existed in the peripheral and rural areas of the country, areas in which present development strategies have had a limited impact.

Approximately half those recorded as unemployed were aged less than 24 years and 60.2 per cent had no education. Even amongst first time jobseekers 44 per cent had no educational qualifications. The possibility of these low-skilled and unskilled persons finding a place in modern sector activities seems negligible. Little or no attempt has been made to foster intermediate technology which might permit a more labour-intensive pattern of development to emerge or to consider alternative futures for the very large number of Moroccans who have no chance of ever benefitting from the Western-oriented sector of the economy.

An important ingredient of the employment matrix has been the role of international migration. During the early 1970s large numbers of migrants left Morocco, mainly for France in the hope of gaining permanent wage employment in foreign labour markets. Many succeeded in gaining temporary access to employment in Europe as agricultural workers, builders and service workers. The earnings of migrants soon constituted an important source of revenue for the Moroccan economy (Table 6.9). The Moroccan Government responded by investing in a programme to promote emigration, incorporating emigration as an element of national planning with moderate success during the initial planning period. By 1973 there were 192,000 Moroccans working in Europe, with the largest single group in France (25). Following the downturn in the European economies in 1973 there has however been a halt to further worker migration. Indeed there has been the possibility of large numbers of return migrants. As the author has

TABLE 6.9. INCOME FROM REMITTANCES (MILLIONS MD)

Year	Income
1970	316
1971	480
1972	640
1973	1,021
1974	1,557
1975	2,159
1976	2,417
1977	2,652
1978	3,176
1979	3,696

Source: L'Economie Marocaine en 1979, Banque Nationale de Développement Economique, Rabat, n.d., A.M. Findlay 'Geographical Patterns of Moroccan Emigration', unpublished MA thesis, University of Durham, 1979, p.42.

TABLE 6.10. INVESTMENT PROJECTS AGREED 1979 BY MAJOR CENTRES

	% Industry	%Tourism
Casablanca)		
Mohammedia)	43.5	54.0
Marrakech	1.6	26.8
Tanger	11.0	-
Fes	6.2	3.4
Rabat	5.2	4.2
Salé	-	-
Agadir	2.4	5.6
Meknes	1.0	5.9
Oujda	0.7	-
Other Areas	28.4	-
TOTAL	100.0	100.0

Source: L'Economie Marocaine en 1979, Banque Nationale de Développement Economique, Rabat, n.d., p.21.

previously shown the impact of migration levels on the overall balance of the labour market has been critical in keeping labour surpluses from rising to astronomical levels. The cessation of migration and the possibility of large scale return of migrants has more serious consequences at the regional level in exacerbating already chronically congested local labour markets such as in the northern provinces of Tetouan and Al Hoceima where remittances play a critical role in household subsistence.

It is creditable that the 1973-1977 National Plan projections for employment expansion were largely fulfilled in the upper circuit of the economy. However for lower circuit workers and for those seeking permanent wage employment but with low skill levels, the 1970s were a period when the Moroccan labour market offered few new opportunities.

The government's main scheme (known as *Promotion Nationale*), which aimed at providing work for the massive labour surpluses of young unskilled workers, failed to meet its targets. Projects undertaken by Promotion Nationale have been mainly concerned with the provision of rural infrastructure (26). Promotion Nationale has failed to constitute a valid employment policy. The projects undertaken have had a very limited impact on the surrounding region and have not resulted in substantial employment opportunities but have offered only short-term employment.

With regard to job creation it seems unlikely that the optimistic projections of the 1978-1980 Plan will be fulfilled, particularly due to the reliance of the plan on private investment. Actual levels of investment have been lower than expected, and consequently it is not surprising that only 13,800 new jobs were created in 1978 compared with an expected 71,400 (27).

The shortcomings of Morocco's economic and manpower strategies appear to be forcing the country into taking more severe economic measures to conserve the country's fragile stability. In 1978 the 10 per cent inflation rate, coupled with a massive jump in the trade deficit and increases in the debt-servicing ratio, resulted in the announcement of a spectrum of austerity measures. These measures included a 20 per cent curb on imports and the alignment of the Moroccan dirham and the French franc in an attempt to encourage workers to repatriate their savings. Severe import restrictions were introduced, prohibiting the import of luxury products and requiring a licence for others, while firms had to make a pre-shipment deposit to the value of 25 per cent of the goods to be imported.

Originally a Five Year Plan had been scheduled for 1978-1983 to continue along the same lines of expansion as the 1973-1978 Plan pursuing the policy of extreme austerity announced in June 1978. The capital-intensive development ethic of the 1973-1978 Plan was fundamentally revised in order to correct the disequilibria created by the over-ambitious Five Year Plan. No major new projects were proposed in the Plan but the need to complete projects which had been initiated was underlined. An overall growth rate of only 4.6 per cent in GDP per annum was set. In the agricultural sector it was hoped that the full potential created by the dams for irrigation could be realised by completion of the distribution networks. As previously more than half the agricultural budget was directed to the irrigated sector. Import substitution remained a key objective in the secondary sector. New projects proposed by the plan were small-scale, low capital investment projects and the plan relied heavily on private rather than public investment. Cuts in public spending coupled with a good harvest in 1978 suggested that the policy was at least partially successful in restoring balance to the critical monetary situation.

REGIONAL PLANNING

The 1973-1977 National Plan had two goals - the first to maximise economic growth and the second to ensure a more equitable social and geographical distribution of economic growth. It has already been shown that although aggregate economic indicators suggest moderate rates of growth have been achieved, this has been at the expense of forfeiting some of this country's economic and political independence. It has also incurred the emergence of considerable sectoral imbalances. The spatial distribution of growth is a critical ingredient in achieving economic development. It is pertinent now to examine the plan's second objective and to consider to what extent the second goal has been achieved. De Mas (28) attempted to answer this question by relating the proportion of investment allocated to each region by the 1973-1977 Plan, to the proportion of the national population in each area. He concluded that investment allocation under the 1973-1977 Plan continued to favour those areas which were already the most prosperous. Although Fez, Marrakech, Meknes, Oujda and Agadir were designated as growth poles, only Agadir and Oujda actually received an adequate level of investment. The rural areas of the periphery received a lower level of investment than was appropriate given the magnitude and composition of their populations, and the provinces of Al Hoceima and Nador were particularly disfavoured (29). Investigation of investment by sector showed that irrigated agricultural areas were favoured over rainfed areas, the industrial littoral was favoured over the centre and that the Casablanca-Mohammedia zone and the Atlantic littoral also received a disproportionate share of social investments. De Mas (30) concluded that the government had made productive investments only where the chances of maximum growth were highest. This explains why regional inequalities have increased and the second goal of the plan has been neglected in practice with little productive investment in the peripheral areas.

The 1978-1980 Plan's emphasis on small-scale rather than large-scale development projects is appropriate but rather than being interpreted as a positive change in strategy this redirection must be regarded as merely the government's response to financial constraints imposed from without (31). The renewed emphasis on private investment is likely to favour the already growing sectors of the economy and prosperous regions even more strongly than did previous plans where public investment in projects was greater.

The 1978-80 Three Year Plan like its predecessor stressed the need to reduce social and spatial inequalities stating that:

> this situation (of overconcentration of activities on the Atlantic littoral) requires attention from all departments and a limitation on the size of some conurbations must become a priority. Publicly financed projects should be located, as far as is possible, outwith the Kenitra-Casablanca area (32).

In order to implement this policy the plan recommended that investment incentives should be drawn up and regional development boards created. But like previous plans, no effective planning machinery was available to enforce the spatial policy objectives which were identified. Table 6.10 lists the projects which had been agreed for investment by region for two sectors - industry and tourism. The Casablanca-Mohammedia region with 12.2 per cent of the Moroccan population clearly again received a disproportionate share of investment. A foretaste of the 1981-1985 Development Plan indicated that similar aims have been reiterated (33).

Sayigh (34) concluding his analysis of the Moroccan economy stated that a satisfactory growth rate was not a substitute for comprehensive and integrated development which has the support of the mass of the population and which is oriented towards their requirements. Moroccan planners are not blind to the need for regional development and deconcentration of resources, growth and investment. It is to Morocco's credit that planners have freely stated the need for greater social and spatial equality, but the absence of the necessary legislative frameworks to permit structural and spatial changes has frustrated the execution of the plans. The designers of Morocco's national plans have little influence on the national policy-makers who direct the course which the country follows. The very regrettable gaps which exist between policy formulation and policy implementation and between technical planning and structural reform have been, and continue to be, the major blockages in the progress of Moroccan economic development.

Investment in capital-intensive projects in both the agricultural and industrial sectors has done little to bridge the gap between rich and poor, and centre and periphery as such investments have accentuated the spatial non-articulation of economic activities rather than stimulating integrated economic development. In Morocco development policies, influenced by the exigencies of the domestic economic situation and the vicissitudes of world markets, have served to fossilise existing social and spatial structures. King Hassan II has himself asserted the need for the reduction of both spatial and social disparities, and the 1981-1985 National Development Plan has put forward a series of measures for this purpose including fiscal reforms, regional planning and investment policies and priorities for employment promotion (35). If these intentions can be successfully implemented Morocco's economic future would be more optimistic and the total result of its economic development would amount to more than the sum of the sectoral growth.

NOTES AND REFERENCES

1. Data for the analysis of the Moroccan economy has been drawn from a wide range of official publications. The following publications have been used extensively: Annuaire Statistique du Maroc, (Direction de la Statistique, Secrétariat d' Etat au Plan et au Développement Régional, Rabat); La Situation Economique au Maroc (annual publication) (Direction de la Statistique, Secrétariat d' Etat au Plan et au Développement Régional, Rabat); Le Maroc en Chiffres (annual publication) (Direction de la Statistique, Ministère au Plan et au Développement Régional, Rabat); Statistiques Agricoles (annual publication), (Service des Statistiques et de la Documentation, Ministère de l' Agriculture et de la Réforme Agraire, Rabat); Revue Bimensuelle d' Informations, (Banque Marocaine du Commerce Extérieur, Casablanca); Monthly Information Review, (Banque Marocaine du Commerce Extérieur, Casablanca).

2. M. Santos, The Shared Space : the Two Circuits of the Urban Economy in Underdeveloped Countries, (Methuen, London, 1979).

3. Santos distinguishes between so-called formal modern sector activities characterised by vertical linkages (upper circuit) and informally structured activities characterised by horizontal economic linkages (lower circuit).

4. S. Amin, The Maghreb in the Modern World : Algeria, Tunisia, Morocco, (Penguin Books, Harmondsworth, England, 1970), Chapter 6.

5. Plan de Développement Economique et Social 1973-1977, (Direction de la Statistique, Secrétariat d' Etat au Plan au Développement Régional et à la Formation des Cadres, Rabat, 1973), vol.I, p.14.

6. La Consommation et les Dépenses des Menages au Maroc, (Direction de la Statistique, Secrétariat d'Etat au Plan, au Développement Régional et à la Formation des Cadres, Rabat, 1972), vol.1, p.19.

7. P. de Mas, 'The Place of Peripheral Regions in Moroccan Planning' Tijdschrift voor Economische en Sociale Geografie, vol.69, no. 1-2 (1978), p.90.

8. 'Maroc : Bilan du Plan Quinquennial 1973-1977', Maghreb-Développement no.8-9 (1978), p.5.

9. H. Beguin, L'Organisation de l' Espace au Maroc, (Académie Royale des Sciences d' Outre-Mer, Brussels, 1974).

10. World Development Report 1981, World Bank, Washington D.C., 1981, p.134.

11. K. Griffin, Land Concentration and Rural Poverty, (Macmillan, London, 1976), Chapter 2.

12. de Mas, 'The Place of Peripheral Regions', p.90.

13. 'The Mining Sector' Monthly Information Review (Banque Marocaine du Commerce Extérieur), no.28 (April-May 1980), p.22.

14. 'EEC-Morocco' Telex Mediterranean, no.85 (Dossier supplément) (1979), p.6.

15. L' Economie Marocaine en 1979, (Banque Nationale pour le Développement Economique, Rabat), n..d., p.86.

16. R. Aliboni (ed.), Arab Industrialisation and Economic Integration, (Croom Helm, London, 1979), p.46.
17. Beguin, L'Organisation de l'Espace; J. Bouquerel, 'Aspects Géographiques de l'Industrialisation du Maroc', unpublished thesis, Université de Lille III, 1974, 3 vols.
18. Répertoire des Etablissements - Industrie, Commerce, Services, (Direction de la Statistique, Secrétariat d'Etat au Plan et au Développement Régional, Rabat, 1976).
19. 'Maroc : Bilan du Plan Quinquennal', p.16; 'The Moroccan Investment Codes', Monthly Information Review (Banque Marocaine du Commerce Extérieur), no.6(1977), pp.16-26.
20. A. Robert 'The EEC and the Maghreb and Mashreq countries' in D. Seers and C. Vaitsos eds. Integration and Unequal Development, the Experience of the EEC (Macmillan, London, 1980), pp.264-265.
21. World Development Report, p.180.
22. Ibid., p.180-181.
23. A. Tovias, EEC Enlargement - the Southern Neighbours, (Sussex European Research Centre, Brighton, 1979), Sussex European Papers, no.5.
24. A.M. Findlay, 'Geographical Patterns of Moroccan Emigration' unpublished MA thesis, University of Durham, 1978.
25. Ibid., p.24.
26. R. Andriamanjara, 'Labour Mobilisation : the Moroccan Experience', in W. Rijckeghem ed., Employment Problems and Policies in Developing Countries,, (Rotterdam University Press, Rotterdam, 1976), pp.134-211.
27. L'Economie Marocaine en 1979, pp.21-22; Plan de Développement Economique et Social 1978-1980, (Direction de la Statistique, Secrétariat d'Etat au Plan et au Développement Régional, Rabat), n.d.; p.173; L. Jaidi, 'Chronique Economique Maroc',Annuaire de l'Afrique du Nord, 1978 pp.483-524.
28. de Mas, 'The Place of Peripheral Regions'.
29. Ibid., p.92.
30. Ibid., p.93.
31. Jaidi, 'Chronique Economique Maroc', p.523.
32. Plan de Développement Economique et Social 1978-1980, p.209.
33. 'The 1981-1985 Plan : a Summary', Monthly Information Review (Banque Marocaine du Commerce Extérieur) no.39 (January-February 1982), pp.3-47.
34. Y. Sayigh, The Determinants of Arab Economic Development, (Croom Helm, London, 1978), p.171.
35. Plan de Développement Economique et Social 1981-1985, (Ministère du Plan et du Développement Régional, Rabat), 1980, vol.1, p.155.

Chapter 7

TUNISIA: THE VICISSITUDES OF ECONOMIC DEVELOPMENT

Allan Findlay

External forces were dominant in moulding Tunisia's economic development in the 1970s. Extroversion of economic affairs is not new to Tunisia which served once as commercial base for the Phoenicians, later as granary to the Roman empire and more recently as a raw material export economy under French colonial administration. The nature of external intervention in the 1970s was, however, new and had a profound effect on the country's economic structure.

The full implication of foreign investment and of the influence of international political forces on Tunisia is not adequately expressed by aggregate economic indicators such as the Gross National Product (GNP), but require more detailed analysis. Per caput growth of GNP at 5.7 per cent per annum in the period 1970-78 is nevertheless a noteworthy achievement, and requires explanation in view of the much weaker economic performances of Morocco and Algeria during the same period. They recorded 3.1 per cent and 2.1 per cent growth rates respectively. This chapter hopes to demonstrate on the one hand that Tunisia's apparently more successful economic record was not directly attributable to its government's liberal economic policies. On the other hand it hopes to indicate that criticism of these policies, which in many respects can be shown to have had detrimental effects, should be tempered by the realisation that only a very limited number of options have been open to Tunisian leaders in directing the course of the country's economic development. To a very great extent the future prosperity or pauperisation of the economy continues to rest on the vicissitudes of international political and economic trends which lie beyond the control of the Tunisian government.

THE RESOURCE BASE OF THE COLONIAL ECONOMY

Prior to assessing economic trends in the 1970s it is appropriate to examine Tunisia's resource base as developed during the colonial era, and to review briefly the country's recent economic history.

Tunisia's location on the southern shores of the central Mediterranean has strategic significance, lying as it does between the Arab East (Machrek) and Arab West (Maghreb). Variation in environmental conditions occurs however on a north-south axis, with

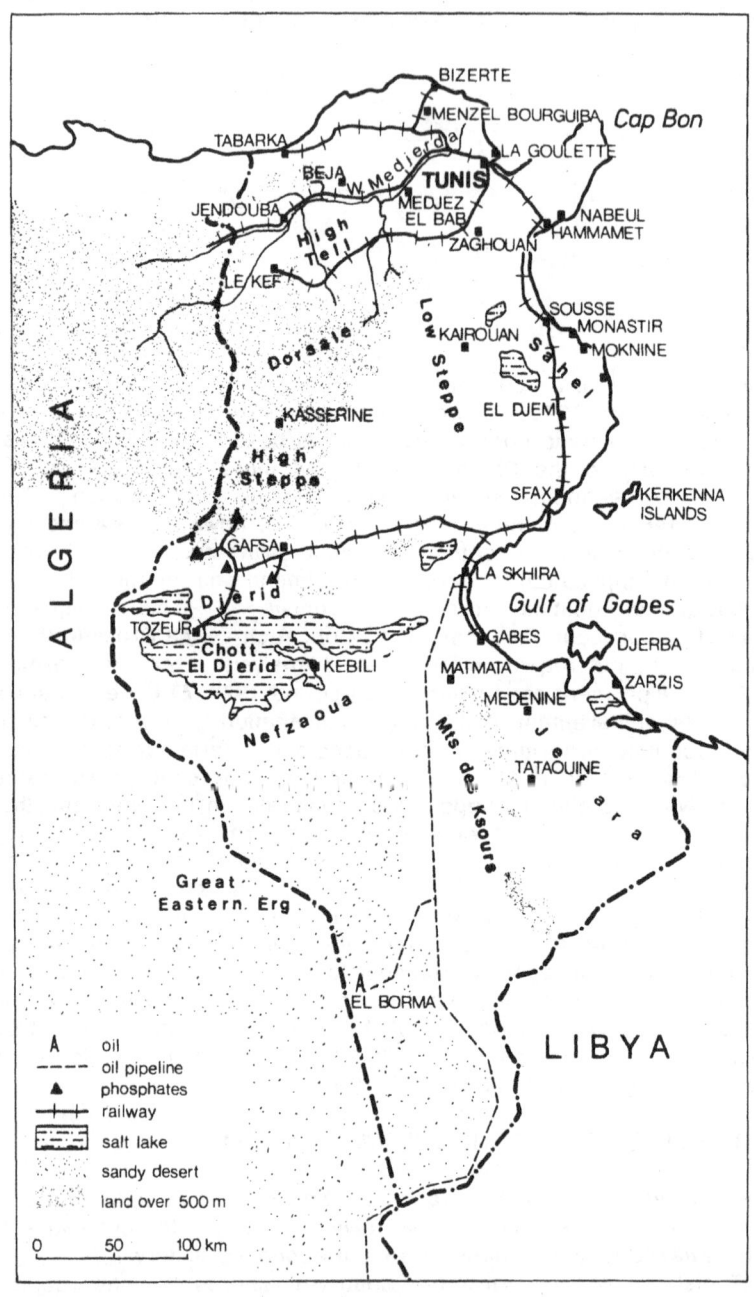

FIGURE 7.1   LOCATION MAP OF TUNISIA

aridity increasing with distance from the country's northern coast. The potential for settled agricultural cultivation is greatest on the discontinuous coastal plains or *sahel*. High rural population densities of over 100 persons per square kilometre are found in the lowlands around Bizerte, in the lower Medjerda valley, the Cap Bon peninsula and the *sahels* of Sousse and Sfax, as well as island fishing communities such as on Djerba and the Kerkennahs (1). In the more mountainous north-west, sometimes called the Tell, in the semi-arid interior and in the deserts of the south, pastoralism is practised at varying intensities dependent on the availability and sustainability of pastureland.

Historically nomadism and semi-nomadism proved an ecologically harmonious response to the scarcity of pasturelands in the arid areas of Tunisia. For many centuries following the original Islamic invasions of the seventh century and later the arrival of the Beni Hilal and Sulaim tribes in the eleventh century nomadism persisted as a major force right into the nineteenth century with as many as 600,000 nomads estimated to be living in Tunisia in 1860. This exceded the size of the settled population (500,000) (2).

The advent of European colonialism, and specifically the establishment of the French Protectorate in Tunisia in 1881 reversed the balance of power between nomadism and the settled population. This reversal led to the virtual demise of nomadism by the middle of the twentieth century. The French perceived Tunisia's agricultural potential as lying with the Mediterranean crops of the type familiar to them from Languedoc, Corsica and the Rhone lowlands. Citrus fruit, olives and cereal culture were encouraged in the moister coastal areas, while the agricultural resources of arid areas were almost ignored. This perception of Tunisia's environmental resources and agricultural potential persisted throughout the colonial era, and remains to the present day.

Prior to French colonisation Tunisia's mineral resources were almost unexploited. This is not surprising since little or no modern industrial activity existed, the towns being centres only of artisanal activities such as the production of *chechias* (religious caps) in Tunis and carpets in Kairouan. The French discovered and exploited the large phosphate reserves located in central Tunisia to the west of Gafsa. Railways had to be constructed to facilitate movement of these phosphates to the coast for export to Europe, and it is to this that the dendritic railway network of central Tunisia owes its origin. The year of maximum phosphate production during the colonial era was 1930 when 3.3 million tons of phosphate rock were quarried, making Tunisia at the time the world's second largest producer (3). Tunisia's phosphates proved less rich than those of deposits found later in other parts of the world, and as a result production declined in the late 1930s and 1940s. Phosphates remain, however, one of Tunisia's major exports, and in the 1970s, when world demand for phosphates soared, production levels once again passed the 3 million ton mark in Tunisia, rising yet further in the late 1970s to a peak level of 4.5 million tons in 1980 (Table 7.1).

Other minerals found in commercially exploitable quantities

TABLE 7.1: TUNISIAN PHOSPHATE AND OIL PRODUCTION
(millions of tons)

	Phosphate Rock	Crude Petroleum
1966	3.22	0.77
1970	3.02	4.15
1974	3.83	4.14
1978	3.71	4.94
1980	4.50	5.63

Source: Banque Centrale de Tunisie, 1981, Statistiques Financières, 60, p. 61.

TABLE 7.2: TUNISIAN POPULATION GROWTH AND OTHER DEMOGRAPHIC CHARACTERISTICS, 1936-1980

	Population excluding foreigners (thousands)	Crude Death Rate (per thousand)	Life Expectancy at birth
1936	2,325	n.d.	n.d.
1946	2,904	26.0	37
1956	3,602	20.0	43
1966	4,463	17.0	55
1975	5,626	13.0	59
1980	6,323	14.0 (1978)	60

Source: République Tunisienne, 1980, L'économie de la Tunisie en Chiffres, 1979, 18. Institut National de la Statistique: Tunis, and Bulletin Mensuel de Statistique, 1967, La Mortalité et le Coût de la Santé Publique en Tunisie, Université de Tunis: Tunis.

during the colonial era were iron ore, lead and zinc. The deposits were generally rather small or low grade and have not proved to be a stimulus to industrial activity. The production levels of both iron ore and lead have dwindled rapidly since independence. The only other major natural resource to be found in Tunisia is oil, but this was not discovered and exploited until 1966, by which time Tunisia's relative paucity of other natural resources had already operated as a severe constraint on the course of the country's economic development.

At the same time as the French were expanding Tunisia's natural resource base through the discovery of phosphates and other minerals, they also, perhaps unwittingly, were influencing the development of the country's human resources. The transference of European medical knowledge (4) had the effect of reducing the Tunisian death rate without eliciting any parallel drop in the birth rate. Population statistics suggest an overall growth in the number of people from 1.5 million in 1870 to 2.3 million in 1936 and 3.6 million in 1956 (Table 7.2).

Provision of educational services and training facilities for the growing population does not appear, however, to have been a high priority during the colonial era. On the eve of independence 75 per cent of the population remained illiterate, reflecting the relatively low quality of the human resources with which independent Tunisia was expected to achieve economic development.

Even more serious, the colonial experience of Tunisia left the country's natural and human resources almost totally unintegrated, and dependent on foreign management. Natural resources had been exploited mainly to serve the needs of the French economy as reflected by the fact that most colonists were merchants or administrators rather than industrialists or entrepreneurs interested in establishing productive units in Tunisia. In 1901 62 per cent of French colonists were employed in commercial or service activities. Even after the Second World War industrial production in Tunisia remained minimal, there being as few as 48,000 employees in industry in the entire country in 1952 (5). Independent Tunisia therefore inherited a highly imbalanced economy, with few activities in the secondary sector of the economy to absorb the ever growing number of persons unable to find employment in agriculture.

POLITICAL ECONOMY, 1956-1969

The early political and economic history of independent Tunisia has been reported in detail elsewhere (6), and only the most important developments need to be repeated here. Political independence from France did not precipitate immediate economic reform. Habib Bourguiba, who had led the struggle for independence became head of state and promoted conservative strategies to permit a gradual adjustment to the loss of colonial skills and finance. The policy was moderately successful and decolonisation proceeded slowly with the departure of the majority of the large French and Italian populations over several years rather than months as occurred in Algeria.

While no major attempt was made to reorganise the use of the country's natural resources or redirect the nation's economic orientation, major policies concerning the country's human resource base were introduced which had long-term consequences for the country's economy and particularly for the labour market in the 1970s and 1980s. A Code of Personal Status was approved in 1956 which amongst other rights established a minimum legal age for marriage. Attempts were made to improve the status of women and an official family planning programme was launched. These changes combined with efforts to improve the distribution and quality of health and medical services resulted in a reduction in the rate of infant mortality, a lowering of the death rate and an increase in life expectancies (Table 7.2).

The newly established government also chose to allocate a large proportion of national resources (19 per cent of government spending in 1955-6) (7) to the improvement of education services, hoping that this would lead in the long run to a more skilled and adaptable labour force. The impact of this decision was indeed substantial with enrolment in primary schools doubling and numbers in secondary schools quadrupling within a decade of independence. While the benefits of increasing national literacy and importing other skills was undoubtedly very substantial the policy also stimulated problems for the future by raising the aspirations of the population and by creating a new demand for jobs in semi-skilled and skilled professions which the nation would find hard to provide. Nevertheless, the overall result of these social and demographic policies must be accepted as beneficial to the Tunisian economy in leading to a vast improvement in the quality of the country's human resource base.

A major attempt to reorganise the structure of production in the Tunisian economy did not commence until 1962, some six years after independence. In this year a ten year development plan designed by the Secretary of State for Planning and Finance, Ahmed ben Salah, was published. This plan was to mould the course of economic development for the remainder of the decade. The vastly over-ambitious targets of the plan included the establishment of a minimum monthly income level of 50 dinars per caput, a reduction in dependence on foreign aid and by 1971 an increase in the level of national savings to some 26 per cent of the GNP (8). The plan identified agrarian reform as the first priority in the creation of a socialist state, but also outlined a course for industrial growth starting from the basis of a few basic industries such as oil refining and steel production.

In agriculture Tunisification of the land was achieved through the expropriation in 1964 of remaining colonial properties. These lands together with ground held by the government since the abolition of the *habous* lands were used to establish state co-operative farms. The full co-operative experiment only ran for a few years (1965-1969) before it encountered insuperable difficulties. In the north the co-operatives were intended for cereal cultivation and were laid out in units of between 500 and 1000 ha to facilitate rapid mechanisation. In the centre and south even larger units were established for arboriculture and the extensive grazing of large herds of livestock.

The chief opposition to the co-operatives came from the large land owners, but they raised the support of many small holders and landless peasants who found that constraints on small-scale private cultivation within the co-operative system were too great. Clumsy over-centralised decision making was also responsible for many inefficiencies on the co-operatives, and often involved unwise and expensive investments yielding no short-term benefits. Bad management, poor weather conditions and the problems arising from widespread opposition to the co-operatives resulted in agricultural production levels actually falling during the 1960s (9), with some farm labourers receiving lower rewards than even in the colonial era.

The industrial sector fared better with the state investing in new phosphate treatment and processing plants at Gabès and Sfax, an oil refinery at Bizerte and expansion of the nation's cement and steel production capacity. These industries reduced Tunisia's dependence on imported basic products, but they failed to create much new employment in the secondary sector. With agriculture ailing under the co-operative experiment and with ever increasing cohorts of potential employees entering the labour market every year, Tunisia faced a growing demand for jobs in manufacturing production rather than in capital intensive industries. The inability of agriculture to absorb further manpower is illustrated by the declining percentage of the labour force in the primary sector, which declined from 67 per cent in 1956 to only 43 per cent in 1966. The transfer of labour out of agriculture during this period was only possible because of the swelling of commercial and service employment opportunities in the towns and cities of Tunisia following decolonisation, but in-migration to urban areas far exceeded rates of employment expansion and by the late 1960s the larger cities were centres of high unemployment and under-employment (10). By 1969 the financial losses of the co-operative experiment, combined with the major problems of other aspects of the economy became unsustainable and Tunisia's era of socialist economic planning came to a catastrophic conclusion. In the late summer and autumn, floods inundated the Tunisian landscape damaging and destroying much of the infrastructural investment of the 1960s. At the same time President Bourguiba chose to replace ben Salah with a new team of politicians sympathetic to a liberal economic approach. The result was a reorientation of the Tunisian economy towards so-called 'free' market forces. The economic performance of Tunisia in the 1970s was to show that these forces were not entirely unkind to Tunisia, but that the most potent forces were dominantly external to the Tunisian economy, and consequently favoured further extroversion of Tunisian economic activities towards the economies of more developed nations rather than towards integrated internal development of Tunisia's natural and human resources.

EXTERNAL ECONOMIC FORCES AND THEIR INFLUENCE ON TUNISIA IN THE 1970s

Tunisia's geographic and historical links with the nations of Western Europe has meant that it has always been strongly influenced (in both positive and negative respects) by the developments in their economies. The rapid growth of the Western economies in post-war years proved to generate an insatiable demand for one particular raw material in which Europe had only the most negligible reserves in the 1960s: oil. Concentration of production in the Arab states of the Gulf and Iran was a threat to Western economic stability and so international oil companies began a world-wide search for new sources of oil to supply energy to the hungry West. Very fortuitously for Tunisia, small but nevertheless valuable oil reserves were discovered in the south of the country which permitted oil production to commence from the El Borma field in 1966. As Table 7.3 shows, production did not reach a significant level until the 1970s, but the knowledge of the existence of the reserves provided promise for future revenue, from which a Tunisian goverment could choose to finance at least some development policies which would be independent of Western intervention.

By 1980 the El Borma and Ashtart oil fields together with a number of smaller oilfields were producing 5.6 million tons of crude petroleum making Tunisia the twelfth largest Arab oil producer. At this production level reserves should last 30 years. Proven natural gas reserves found in association with the petroleum exploration equal 33 million tons of oil equivalent (1977) but production was still only 0.4 million tons in 1980, although projected to rise to 2 million tons in 1986 (11).

The rising value of Tunisia's limited oil and gas reserves is due entirely to international economic forces. The use of the 'oil weapon' by Arab oil producers after the Yom Kippur war of 1973 resulted in the price of oil rising very rapidly to the benefit of the world's oil exporters. Subsequent moves by the organisation of Arab Petroleum Exporting Countries (OAPEC), of which Tunisia was not a member in the 1970s, ensured that oil prices continued to rise ahead of the level of inflation. For Tunisia, the result has been continually increasing revenues from its oil exports. Between 1972 and 1974, for example, the value of oil exports more than trebled, while the volume of exports remained almost constant (Table 7.3).

A second external force strongly influencing Tunisia in the 1970s has been the evolution of international labour migration. The aforementioned expansion of the West European economies in the post-war period led to labour shortages in certain sectors of the industrial economies by the mid 1960s. In order to sustain economic growth, labour immigration from neighbouring labour surplus countries was encouraged. Many Tunisians, unable to find secondary and tertiary employment in the country's domestic labour market, quickly accepted the opportunity of foreign employment. The most important host nation was France, where the size of the resident Tunisian population rose from 52,000 in 1965 to almost double this level in 1970. For the Tunisian government international migration provided an apparent panacea to the nation's overburdened urban labour markets, and labour transfers to France and Germany were encouraged through the creation of a special agency (Office de la Formation Professionelle à l'Etranger) to link up jobseekers with foreign employment opportunities. The departure of migrant workers reached a peak in

TABLE 7.3: VOLUME AND VALUE OF TUNISIAN PETROLEUM AND PETROLEUM PRODUCT EXPORTS

	Volume (1000 tons)	Value (1000 Dinars)	Exchange Rate (Dinars per US$)
1970	3,407	26,081	0.523
1972	3,856	40,751	0.477
1974	3,863	142,802	0.410
1976	3,792	143,271	0.429
1978	4,846	180,294	0.408
1980	4,829	474,825	0.418

Source: Banque Centrale de Tunisie, 1981 Statistiques Financières, 60, p. 70.

TABLE 7.4: PROJECTS AND JOBS CREATED AS A RESULT OF LAWS 72-38 AND 74-74 FROM CONTRACTS SIGNED 1973-1978 (21)

Region	Projects	Jobs
Tunis and North East	2,302	45,896
North West	,146	3,027
Sahel of Sousse	,759	21,708
Centre	,151	2,793
Sfax	,645	8,722
South	,212	4,322
Total	4,215	86,468

Source: Agence Promotion des Investissements: Tunis

Tunisia: The Vicissitudes of Economic Development

1973 when no less than 20,900 left on official contracts to work in France, bringing the total Tunisian population there (counting workers and their families) to almost 150,000. For the Tunisian government international migration to Europe in the early 1970s, can be seen as an opportunity to tackle the problems of the domestic labour market, while temporarily benefitting from the absence of a large number of workers who might otherwise have been unemployed. Recession in Europe in late 1973 and in the years that followed led to a termination of further immigration, but for Tunisia the opportunity to export surplus labour continued as the neighbouring oil-rich state of Libya began to seek foreign labour. The oil price rises of 1973 led to a staggering upward revision of the Libyan development plan with investments being increased by 68 per cent over the previous plan. As a result immigrant labour from Tunisia and Egypt was suddenly required in order to achieve the ambitious new agricultural and infrastructural projects which the plan had identified. By 1975 there were 38,000 Tunisians in Libya and many more migrated in 1977 and 1978, when, after an unfortunate lapse in Libyan-Tunisian relations the border between the two countries was reopened.

In the late 1970s hostility against the many Tunisian and other North African workers remaining in France rose, the migrant community being unfairly blamed for the high levels of unemployment amongst French nationals (12). In 1977 France launched a scheme to encourage return migration offering a 'million centimes' to foreign workers willing to leave. The threat of the large Tunisian community being forced to return home further to burden the Tunisian labour market remained a very real one throughout the remainder of the 1970s with several further measures being taken by the French to try and stimulate a return flow. Few migrants wished to return home voluntarily, however, since salary and job opportunities remained much poorer in Tunisia than France. On the contrary the migrant community in France continued to grow through natural increase and through family (as opposed to worker) migration. In 1979 the Tunisian presence had reached 203,000 persons.

It has been shown that external economic forces, in a different way from natural and human resources, present both opportunities and problems for Tunisian economic development. One of the most potent forces creating problems for Tunisia's imbalanced and underdeveloped economic structure, has been the growth of the European Economic Community. The Tunisian economy, oriented as it was during the colonial era towards raw material export to the industrialised nations, has proved particularly sensitive to the trade barriers and tariffs established by the EEC against non-member countries. For example, Tunisia found during the 1970s that the export of its Mediterranean crops was severely hindered, and that increasingly the agricultural base which it had inherited from the French was a wasting asset. Mediterranean competitors such as Italy who found themselves within the EEC were given preferential access to the European market, reducing the demand for Tunisian produce and therefore forcing down its price. As recently as 1972 olive oil was, for example, Tunisia's single most valuable export earning 46 million dinars, yet because of the declining demand for Tunisian olive oil the value of exports in the period 1976-1980 was only 86 per cent of that in the previous five years 1971-1975, and this was despite price inflation throughout the decade. Other examples of the influence of EEC growth and protectionism will become apparent when individual sectors of the economy are examined in a later section.

A final external force having a considerable impact on Tunisia in the 1970s was the growing tendency for capital from the industrialised nations to seek investment opportunities in the Third World. This trend, and its compatibility with the liberal economic views of the Tunisian government in the 1970s, led Tunisian politicians to choose a development strategy which positively encouraged foreign investment in Tunisia. This policy will now be studied in greater detail along with other aspects of Tunisian industrialisation.

TUNISIAN INDUSTRIALISATION LEGISLATION AND ITS CONSEQUENCES

There were only a limited number of economic courses which Tunisian politicians could follow in the 1970s. The recent failure of the co-operative experiment closed the door to further major upheavals in the agricultural sector. Large labour surpluses made the creation of some labour intensive activities highly desirable, and the economy which had been virtually bankrupted by the co-operative experiment was, momentarily at least, forced to find private capital and foreign loans to finance new projects and these sources of capital demanded short term profits from any investments rather than lower returns over the long term. Given these constraints it was not perhaps surprising that the new emphasis to emerge in Tunisian economic planning was on labour intensive manufacturing industry financed dominantly by private investors.

The new political regime under the leadership of Hedi Nouira, a former director of the Bank of Tunisia, devised a disengagement of state finance in the industrial sector, opening the sector instead to private finance through a new range of legislation. It took till 1972 before the first new law emerged offering incentives to foreign investors interested in establishing production units in Tunisia. This law (72-38) guaranteed approved industrial projects a wide range of tax concessions (13) and the duty-free import of capital equipment, raw materials and semi-processed goods. The new industries were to produce dominantly for export, hence reducing even less the linkages with the Tunisian economic base and giving rise to the term 'offshore industries' since the only major contribution which Tunisia was to make to these industries was a tax haven proximate to cheap labour supplies. Foreign investors were exempted under law 72-38 from corporate income tax during the first ten years of operation and amongst other benefits were permitted to repatriate profits free of tax. The only visible advantage of offshore industrialisation for the Tunisian economy was therefore the absorption of some of the country's labour surpluses in productive employment with consequent wage multiplier effects for the areas in which the new jobs were created. Offshore industrialisation was promoted under decree 73-19 by which the Tunisian government established and financed an agency to publicise the new investment opportunities (*Agence de Promotion des Investissements:* API), and to streamline the investment procedure by introducing potential investors to the legislative mechanisms and by establishing in advance industrial sites with the appropriate infrastructure for development (14). The economic climate was right for these moves, with many foreign investors and multi-national companies eager to profit from the generous investment laws. Between 1973 and 1978 no less than 523 foreign firms established factories under law 72-38 investing some 57 million dinars in industrial projects (15).

A second industrial investment law was introduced in 1974 (law 74-74) which sought to relate incentives more closely to employment creation. Under law 72-38 incentives had been linked to the volume of investment but under law 74-74 industrial licences were costed inversely to the number of jobs created by a project. Law 74-74 was also intended to encourage Tunisian private investment, which had previously been less favoured than foreign involvement. Once again law 74-74 encouraged the extraversion of industrial production with manufacturers receiving major tax concessions during their first five years of operation if more than ten per cent of their produce was oriented towards export markets. By 1978 some 614 million dinars had been invested under this scheme in light manufacturing industry, reflecting its immense popularity with private investors. Only seven per cent of the projects operating under this scheme directly involved foreign capital, but it was abused by some international companies who found that the law permitted the establishment of assembly plants under Tunisian management which used components produced entirely abroad giving them subsequent preferential access to the Tunisian domestic market for their manufactures.

The most positive consequence of laws 72-38 and 74-74 was the rapid growth of manufacturing employment. Between 1973 and 1978, 86,500 new jobs were created in light manufacturing industry according to the records of the API. By any accounts this represents a remarkable achievement given the almost complete absence of employment growth in this sector in the previous decade. API claim to have sustained this rate of employment expansion during the course of Tunisia's Fifth National Plan (1977-1981) (16). Surveys of the new industries of the '70s show that the achievement has not, however, been as beneficial to Tunisia as might at first be thought. For example in the textile sector no less than 90 per cent of the new jobs created under the investment laws were filled by women (17). While growth of employment opportunities for the female population can in some respects be viewed as progress, it cannot be entertained as a major contribution to reducing the critical labour surpluses of the Tunisian economy which continue to consist dominantly of unemployed male jobseekers.

Three major problem areas may be identified associated with Tunisia's industrial investment legislation. Firstly, the structure of industrialisation resulting from private capital investment has been highly imbalanced, and no mechanism has been established within the legislation to correct for over-concentration of investment in some activities to the detriment of others. By the end of 1977 54 per cent of new investment and 87 per cent of employment created under law 72-38 was in the textile, clothing or leather goods industries, while less than four per cent of new jobs went to the mechanical or engineering industries or to the production of building materials or glass. Agricultural and food processing industries received a meagre one per cent of investment under this particular law. It should be noted that textiles and clothing, the sector to attract most private investment, promised the most rapid returns on capital and involved the least labour skills.

A second problem resulting from the policy was the growth of dependence on European markets for the sale of Tunisia's industrial produce. Tunisia's industrialisation strategy resulted in an increased extroversion of the agricultural and food processing industries and of the textiles industry. In the latter case the trend was startling, exports rising from only four per cent of total production value in 1969 to 44 per cent by 1975 (18). Even more worrying was the concentration of exports to the EEC countries. In 1976 the EEC was the destination for 74 per cent of all Tunisian export manufactures, and considering textiles alone the figure was as high as 95 per cent (19). The dangers of this situation were amply demonstrated when in 1977 the EEC imposed new tariff barriers on textile imports. In the following year 19 of Tunisia's new textile factories closed down involving the immediate loss of 2,000 jobs. Recession in other factories led to a further 3,000 persons being temporarily made redundant (20). The uncertainties associated with export dependence seem likely to increase rather than decline with time, as unemployment levels continue to rise in Western Europe and as more countries join the EEC and seek protection for their own producers.

A third difficulty associated with laws 72-38 and 74-74 has been the virtually uncontrolled location of new plants in only a few regions of Tunisia. This has strengthened existing regional inequalities and through accentuating spatial variations in employment opportunities has contributed towards encouraging further population migration towards the already congested north-eastern region of Tunisia. Some 55 per cent of the 4200 new industrial units agreeing between 1973 and 1975 to enter production in Tunisia chose a location either within the Tunis agglomeration or in its immediate hinterland of north-eastern Tunisia (Table 7.4). By contrast many of the interior districts of the country such as Sidi Bou Zid, Kairouan, Gafsa and Kasserine which previously had almost formed an industrial void together received only 3.6 per cent of the new factories. Only in the late 1970s did the Tunisian government apparently become concerned about this imbalance and tried to introduce regional incentives to persuade some industries to locate in the less developed parts of the country.

INDUSTRIAL PERFORMANCE IN THE 1970s

Indices of industrial production for the 1970s indicate that although liberalisation of the economy may have attracted private capital to the industrial sector during this period, this in itself did not guarantee an increase in output. Table 7.5 shows that highly variable rates of expansion were experienced by different sectors of manufacturing industry. Textiles and leather received 82 per cent of their investment from the private sector between 1970 and 1976 yet in textiles industrial output actually fell slightly over this period while the leather industries experienced only a modest expansion. Much more successful were the electrical and metallurgical industries whose output more than doubled during the same period. The chemical industries, which because of the large sums of capital required for development continued to be financed largely by the state, also grew rapidly. Analysis of tables 7.5 and 7.6 would suggest that most of the industrial sectors which were left to private investment for their development in the early 1970s, experienced slow or only moderate rates of growth, while in those sectors where state investment was maintained higher levels of production were also achieved. One exception was the food processing industry which under dominantly private ownership performed well throughout the decade. In other sectors, however, it seems that lack of basic state investment in infrastructural extension and improvement was a blockage to growth and may even have deterred sustained private investment.

The emergence of these blockages led to a re-emphasis in Tunisia's Fifth Plan (1977-81) on public investment, but only as a support to private sector developments. Projects to establish an industrial base, which had been shelved at the end of the socialist era were reintroduced such as the development of a second petrol refinery in order that by the mid-1980s the nation's refining capacity will at least match the volume of oil production. New cement plants were initiated and projects to extend Tunisia's iron and steel producing capacity were begun. Table 7.6 shows that higher levels of public investment in several sectors of industry were in fact achieved during the first three years of the plan. Ironically Tunisia had difficulty in financing its Fifth Plan and had to seek funds to undertake belatedly these projects from foreign banks and through aid agencies. In the first two years of the plan 36 per cent of funding came from abroad compared with 29 per cent as originally intended (22).

State involvement in industrialisation has also been necessary to rebalance development. The bias towards investment in some sectors of manufacturing has already been mentioned, but within sectors certain vital production activities failed to attract any private investment and required state assistance. For example, in the food processing industries law 74-74 led to privately financed units for the production of soft drinks and lemonade and the processing of jam while basic food production such as sugar refining and creameries were ignored because of the lower profit margins and the longer term nature of investment. As a result the Tunisian dairy industry failed to keep

TABLE 7.5: INDICES OF TUNISIAN INDUSTRIAL PRODUCTION
(100 = base year : 1970)

	1970	1973	1976	1978
Energy:	100	113	132	170
Other Mineral Extraction:	100	109	93	101
Manufacturers:				
Building Materials	100	120	140	174
Electrical Engineering and Metals	100	143	220	258
Textiles	100	119	98	97
Leather	100	113	108	102
Food	100	135	139	168
Chemicals	100	118	134	169
Paper	100	132	127	148
Others	100	140	161	180

Source: République Tunisienne, 1980,
Annuaire Statistique de la Tunisie, Années 1978-79, 24.
Institut National de la Statistique: Tunis

TABLE 7.6: PERCENTAGE DISTRIBUTION OF PUBLIC AND PRIVATE INVESTMENT BY MANUFACTURING SECTOR

	1962-69		1970-76		1977-79	
	Public	Private	Public	Private	Public	Private
Building Materials	93	7	69	31	80	20
Electrical, Engineering and Metals	92	8	54	46	47	53
Textiles and Leather	83	17	18	82	13	87
Food	72	28	30	70	37	63
Chemical	62	38	70	30	94	6
Others	79	21	23	77	18	82
Total	84	16	47	53	64	36

Source: Signoles, P. and Ben Romdane, M., 1981, see footnote 16.

up with domestic demand for its produce and milk products had to be imported in ever increasing quantities. In 1970 dairy product imports cost Tunisia three million dinars: by 1980 the import bill was 17 million dinars. In the building sector a similar imbalance illustrates the same problem. Private investors dominated the production of bricks and tiles, yet important building projects were delayed because of the continual scarcity of cement in the country and the inability of the private sector to invest the 100 million dinars necessary to establish a new cement works (23).

AGRICULTURAL PERFORMANCE IN THE 1970s

The co-operative system was rapidly dismantled and replaced by private ownership. Tunisian farmers were allowed to repossess their land, while former colonial farms were placed under the control of a government agency *(Office des Terres Domainales:* OTD). The OTD sold some 270,000 ha to the private sector and rented many more hectares to large landowners. Of the remainder of the OTD land some was organized as *Agro-Combinats* or *Unités Co-opératives de Production* while the rest was used to establish pilot farm projects. Many of the small peasant farmers who received land found either that they had insufficient capital to develop, or that their plots were too small to be viable. Consequently they sold up to the large landowners, who were particularly eager to buy ground in the most fertile irrigated areas.

Between 1972 and 1976 Tunisia experienced favourable weather conditions which helped to provide large and profitable harvests of all the main cereal, citrus and vegetable crops (Table 7.7). Cereal production which had been as high as 575,000 tons in 1960 had fallen under the 400,000 ton level in 1969, but recovered dramatically in the early 1970s reaching 1,236,000 tons in 1975.

The total value of agricultural production rose by no less than 70 per cent between 1970 and 1975, encouraging further investment by large private financiers and by foreign aid organizations, who were eager to extend mechanisation and technical innovation in agriculture. Progress was rapid in the richest agricultural areas, but elsewhere the government was slow to give state support to improve rural conditions. Only in 1974 were schemes established to provide village electrification and piped water to all village communities irrespective of their agricultural potential.

Between 1977 and 1979 poorer weather conditions meant that cereal harvests were poorer than earlier in the decade and production of other important crops such as olives also declined. An even greater threat than the uncertainty of weather conditions was, however, the erosion of Tunisia's place in the Western European market. In 1976 87 per cent of Tunisia's olive oil was exported to the EEC, and the country was the chief supplier to Western Europe. This position was however threatened by the application of Tunisia's nearest rival in the olive oil trade, Spain, to join the EEC and therefore to have preferential access. Likewise the addition of Greece to the EEC had a detrimental effect on Tunisia's export opportunities.

TABLE 7.7: PRODUCTION OF SELECTED CROPS (1000 tons)

	1969	1972	1975	1978
Cereals	396	1210	1236	906
Olives	275	900	468	625
Tomatoes	153	173	260	280
Citrus	108	120	131	220
Melons	75	162	210	230

Source: République Tunisienne, 1980, Annuaire de la Statistique: Années 1978-79, Institut National de la Statistique: Tunis, p.105

TABLE 7.8: PERCENTAGE DISTRIBUTION OF TUNISIAN EXPORTS BY SECTOR

	1964	1968	1972	1976	1980
Primary Produce:					
Food	59.0	30.3	41.2	19.3	4.4
Minerals	21.8	19.0	10.4	8.9	3.1
Oil, gas	0.0	19.8	27.1	42.3	53.0
Semi-processed goods:	16.6	27.2	16.7	15.0	18.6
Finished Products:					
Machinery & capital goods	0.5	0.7	0.5	1.2	2.0
Consumer goods	2.1	3.0	4.1	13.2	18.9
Total	100	100	100	100	100
Total value of merchandise exports (million Tunisian Dinars)	57.3	82.8	150.3	338.3	891.4

Source: Banque Centrale de Tunisie, 1981, Statistiques Financières, 60, p.66

While agriculture has proved moderately prosperous during the 1970s, a further worrying trend should be noted: the inability of the agricultural sector to keep pace with the range and quantity of foodstuffs demanded within the domestic market. This is apparent not only from the vastly increased volume of cereal, sugar and dairy imports which Tunisia had to buy after 1977, but also from the deteriorating balance of trade in foodstuffs. Between 1971 and 1974 the value of food exports from Tunisia consistently exceeded the value of the imports. Thereafter the situation has been reversed with food imports costing almost twice the value of exports in 1979 (24).

ECONOMIC STRUCTURE AND TRADE

It has been shown that the government's industrialisation policy had a number of drawbacks, but one gain which might have been expected was an improvement in the balance of payments as a result of a boost in exports. By comparison with the 1960s the structure of Tunisian trade certainly shifted, with exports relying much less heavily on unprocessed raw materials and other primary produce such as foodstuffs (Tables 7.8 and 7.9). In 1964 the value of these exports amounted to 80.8 per cent of the total while by 1980 they were only worth 7.5 per cent of all export value. By contrast consumer goods exports did rise rapidly during the 1970s and earned some foreign revenue for Tunisia. The most important change was, however, the emergence of oil and gas as a major export. In the mid 1960s oil and petroleum products made only a trivial contribution, while by 1980 they earned 475 million dinars for Tunisia or 53 per cent of all export earnings.

Regrettably liberalisation of the economy has permitted the influx of many foreign manufacturers and at a value exceeding that of Tunisia's exports. The government's desire to over-rapidly achieve industrial growth in the manufacturing sector in order to create employment and a facade of modernity also led to the import of many expensive items of capital equipment in order to provide machinery and furnishings for the new factories. A slower rate of manufacturing expansion might have permitted some of these goods to be produced in Tunisia, rather than adding unnecessarily to the country's import bill. The net effect of these trends has been that imports have consistently exceeded the value of exports. On average between 1970 and 1979 exports only covered 61.2 per cent of the cost of imports and had it not been for oil the imbalance would have been much greater, and might have forced the country to follow quite a different development course involving greater integration of the different sectors of the economy. Tables 7.8 and 7.9 clearly show that it was oil exports rather than the growth of light manufacturing industry which was the major source of foreign revenue in the 1970s, giving the Tunisian government credibility amongst foreign financiers and permitting it to follow an economic policy which contributed more to the management of the urban labour market than to stimulating long-term economic growth.

Helping to close the gap between the value of merchandise imports and exports has been the growing revenue earned from the sale of

TABLE 7.9: PERCENTAGE DISTRIBUTION OF TUNISIAN IMPORTS BY SECTOR

	1964	1968	1972	1976	1980
Primary Produce:					
Food	15.4	19.6	18.9	12.3	12.0
Minerals	0.7	3.9	1.5	2.2	3.8
Oil, gas	5.2	1.6	6.8	11.1	20.0
Semi-processed goods:	31.3	33.0	28.4	26.6	25.9
Finished products:					
Machinery & capital goods	27.0	26.6	29.6	31.9	22.9
Consumer goods	20.3	15.4	14.8	15.8	15.3
Total	100	100	100	100	100
Total value of merchandise imports (million Tunisian Dinars)	110.8	114.5	222.2	656.7	1391.7

Source: Banque Centrale de Tunisie, 1981, Statistiques Financières, 1981, 60, p.66.

TABLE 7.10: TUNISIAN INVESTMENT FOR THE SIXTH PLAN
(Units: Million Tunisian Dinars)

	Fifth Plan		Sixth Plan	
	Amount	%	Amount	%
Agriculture	575	13.8	950	13.6
Manufacturing	787	18.9	1,400	20.0
Non-manufacturing industry	880	21.1	1,700	24.3
Services including tourism	1,509	36.2	2,350	33.5
(Tourism)	(62)	(1.5)	(250)	(3.6)
Public services	417	10.0	600	8.6
Total	4,168	100.0	6,250	100.0

Source: République Tunisienne, Ministère du Plan

Tunisian 'services'. The most important of these has been tourism which earned for Tunisia some 219 million dinars in 1979 and 259 million in 1980. The number of visitors has expanded throughout the 1970s from less than 400,000 in 1970 to over 1,500,000 in 1980 (25), but as a source of income tourism has proven no more reliable than the other sectors of the Tunisian economy which depend on a foreign market. The fragility of the tourist sector was demonstrated in 1973-74 when numbers dropped dramatically as a result of the world economic crisis and the temporary decline in demand for Mediterranean holidays amongst workers from the industrial regions of Western Europe. The policy to encourage the very rapid growth in tourism has also suffered many of the same problems as the government's industrialisation policies, with the materials and furnishings for the major hotel complexes at Sousse and Djerba having to be imported rather than manufactured in Tunisia. Tourism remains a highly lucrative source of foreign revenue for the Tunisian economy, but its future lies largely in the hands of a small number of large foreign operators who seem little concerned with the wasteful use of Tunisia's resources which tourism has so far involved. The average length of stay of tourists in 1980 was less than eight days, bed occupancy rates were only 60 per cent and employment was highly seasonal often distracting young Tunisians away from productive agricultural work to the more lucrative temporary employment of the tourist trade. Despite its many problems Tunisia depended on tourism for 20 per cent of its trade receipts in 1978.

Less important but even more vulnerable are Tunisia's service earnings from migrant remittances. These have continued to rise throughout the 1970s despite the halt on further migration to Europe. They accounted for 11.5 per cent of balance of payment receipts by 1978, but in addition to the 92 million dinars received through official channels it should be remembered that many more remittances and consumer goods were transferred to Tunisia by migrants returning home on holiday.

ECONOMIC PROBLEMS, POLITICS AND FUTURE PROSPECTS

Despite the many problems of Tunisian economic development in the 1970s, its economic performance remained substantially superior to that of either Algeria or Morocco. This in large part has been due to the moderately favourable way in which international economic forces have influenced Tunisia relative to other Third World countries, but as has been indicated this has often been entirely fortuitous rather than intended.

The government's decision to encourage the extroversion of the Tunisian economy has in many respects forfeited Tunisia's ability to determine its own economic future and many potential pitfalls seem to lie ahead. Within this context, however, certain positive features of the country's economic development must be credited to the country's leaders. Stability of political leadership under Bourguiba during the three decades since independence has reduced economic uncertainty and has given valuable continuity to the country's development course.

Tunisia: The Vicissitudes of Economic Development

Although this stability has not been achieved without some level of repression of alternative political viewpoints, the Tunisian political system has permitted internal debate over its economic and social policies, and some would view the growing public expression of opposition within Tunisia as a backhanded complement to the openness of the existing regime. The absence of major internal and external military conflicts has avoided wasteful absorption of both human and physical resources in the defence sector, and unlike so many developing nations, Tunisia has not had to pay the very substantial opportunity costs of tying up its scarce financial resources in buying a large stock of arms and weapons rather than in channelling these funds towards more profitable investment.

Stability has resulted in positive economic gains for Tunisia which has received tertiary functions from other Arab nations and has come to be recognised as a centre of international organisations within the Arab world. The civil war in Lebanon, for example, stimulated the flight of capital from Beirut, as the former centre of the Arab banking community, and many of the large financial organisations relocated their headquarters subsequently in Tunis. Similarly the political ostracism of Egypt by other Arab nations, following the Israeli-Egyptian peace treaty and the signing of the Camp David Agreements in 1978, led to the movement of the headquarters of the Arab League from Cairo to Tunis. The positive benefits accruing from being a leading centre within the Arab world have been cultivated by Tunisia which has recently aligned itself with other Arab oil producers, culminating in its membership of the Organization of Arab Petroleum Exporting Countries (OAPEC) in 1982. Likewise, the government's former policy of encouraging Westernisation through the erosion of certain Islamic traditions has been halted and reversed, with overt approval now given to the observance of Islamic festivals such as the month of Ramadan.

More problematic has been the Tunisian government's decision to encourage the growth of international tertiary functions controlled by multi-national companies and western capital. Under a new 1981 Law (81-56) investment incentives were extended to foreign companies interested in investing in service sector activities (as opposed to the manufacturing activities favoured by laws 72-38 and 74-74). The new law hopes to encourage the location of warehousing and distribution services for multi-national companies in Tunisia which will serve the entire Arab world (26). Offshore banking has also been welcomed by Tunisia, with foreign banks being allowed to receive deposits from, and lend to, non-resident companies and societies. The influx of foreign capital, free from exchange controls, may make Tunisia a regional banking centre for North Africa and ensure easier access for the country to international money markets; but whether the long-term effect for Tunisia's fragile economy will be beneficial remains to be proven.

Many severe problems face the future economic development of Tunisia. The country cannot continue to rely on oil revenues and earnings from service activities to sustain its economy. Projections for petroleum demand within the domestic economy, based on the tripling of demand which occurred in the 1970s, indicate that by 1986 Tunisia may consume over 4 million tons per annum. The net benefits from oil production can therefore be expected to decline throughout the 1980s as internal demands rise to match supply.

Tunisia's Sixth Plan identifies the main problem for the years 1982-86 as the continued pressure on the national labour market. The number of new job seekers leaving schools and colleges will continue to rise rapidly and yet most of the obvious opportunities for job creation have already been taken up by the labour intensive industrial projects of the 1970s. Some 320,000 jobs need to be created during the five year period of the plan in order to keep pace with the expansion of the labour force, and the optimistic targets for the Sixth Plan project a growth in jobs for no more than 75 per cent of this demand. Even this target can only be achieved through a plan which calls for a 50 per cent increase in investment over that attained in the previous five years, and through the further extroversion of the economy and dependence on large scale private investment (27). The sectoral allocations for the Sixth Plan, shown in Table 7.10, indicate that despite the many problems of the 1970s, the government intends to pursue similar economic policies in the 1980s with industry and tourism being favoured rather than agriculture, and with over 20 per cent of investment in the plan coming from foreign sources. Tunisia, with its large labour surpluses and limited natural resource base, appears to have chosen to pursue an economic course dependent on the vagaries of international markets and foreign capital, rather than based on integrated internal economic development of the human and physical resources which lie within its own control.

NOTES AND REFERENCES

1. J.I. Clarke, 'Population Patterns, Pressures and Policies' in J.I. Clarke and W.B. Fisher (eds.), Populations of the Middle East and North Africa, (University of London Press, London, 1972) pp. 362-3.
2. J. Ganiage, 'La Population de la Tunisie vers 1860', Population, vol.21, (1966) pp. 857-886.
3. S. Amin, The Maghreb in the Modern World, (Penguin, Harmondsworth, 1970) p. 40.
4. M. Rouissi, Population et Société au Maghreb, (Ceres, Tunis, 1977) pp. 56-59.
5. F. Leduc, 'L'industrialisation de la Tunisie', Industrialisation l'Afrique du Nord, (Bibliothèque l'E.P.H.E., Colin, Paris, 1952) pp. 276-290.
6. See Chapter 3; and W. Knapp, North West Africa: A Political and Economic Survey, (Oxford University Press, Oxford, 1977) pp. 341-402.
7. M. Bchir, 'L'enseignement' in M. Fakhfakh, Atlas de Tunisie, (Jeune Afrique, Paris, 1979) p. 58.
8. République Tunisienne, Ministère du Plan et de Finances, Perspectives Décennales de Développement 1962-71, (Tunis, n.d.).

9. Holding prices constant at 1966 levels, the primary sector of the economy is recorded as contributing 81.7 million dinars in 1955, 103.8 million in 1965 and only 101.9 million in 1970.
10. A. Findlay, 'Labour Mobility and Manpower Planning in Tunisia' in J.I. Clarke and H. Bowen-Jones (eds.), Change and Development in the Middle East, (Methuen, London, 1981) pp. 242-251.
11. 'The Energy Situation in the Arab World: Tunisia', OAPEC Bulletin, vol.8, no.6 (1982), pp. 11-15.
12. R.I. Lawless, A. Findlay and A. Findlay, Return Migration to the Maghreb: People and Policies, (Arab Research Centre, London, 1982).
13. Agence Promotion des Investissements, Direction des Etudes et du Suivi: Rapport, (A.P.I., Tunis, 1976).
14. This was achieved in association with the Agence Foncière Industrielle.
15. Agence Promotion des Investissements, Rapport Suivi: Etat des Réalisations des Projets Agréés durant les Années 73- 78, (A.P.I., Tunis, 1979).
16. P. Signoles and M. Ben Romdane, 'Les Formes Récentes de l'Industrialisation Tunisienne' in proceedings of GRESMO colloquium on L'Industrialisation du Bassin Méditerranéen, (Gresmo, Grenoble, 1981).
17. P. Signoles, 'Les Effets Géographiques des Investissements Industriels Etrangers en Tunisie', Etudes Méditerranéenes, Vol. 1, (1978) pp.3-60.
18. Signoles and Ben Romdane, 'L'Industrialisation Tunisienne, p. 27.
19. C. Secchi, 'The Mediterranean Policy of the E.E.C. and the N.I.E.O. with particular reference to North African Countries' in proceedings of GRESMO colloquium in L'Industrialisation du Bassin Méditerranéen, (Gresmo, Grenoble, 1979).
20. P. Blum, 'Tunisia aspires to be Regional Banking Centre', Middle East Economic Digest, (4.5.1979) pp. 10-15.
21. The regional definitions used in Table 7.4 are as follows:
Tunis and North East: Governorates of Tunis, Zaghouan, Bizerte, Nabeul
North West: Beja, Jendouba, Siliana, Kef
Sahel of Sousse: Sousse, Monastir, Mahdia
Centre: Kasserine, Gafsa, Kairouan, Sidi Bou Zid
Sfax: Sfax
South: Gabes, Medenine
22. Blum, 'Regional Banking Centre', p. 10.
23. Signoles and Ben Romdane, 'L'Industrialisation Tunisienne', p. 17.
24. In 1979 food imports cost 149.8 million dinars compared with 89.4 million for food exports.
25. Banque de Développement Economique de Tunisie, Exercice 1980, (B.D.E.T., Tunis, 1981).
26. M. Frost and P. Blackburn, 'Tunisia Widens Investment Window', Middle East Economic Digest, (9.1.1981) pp. 4-5.

27. P. Blackburn, 'Tunisia Faces the Challenge of its unemployed', Middle East Economic Digest, (27.3.1981) p.43.

Chapter 8.

LIBYA: PROBLEMS OF A *RENTIER* STATE

Stace Birks and Clive Sinclair[*]

INTRODUCTION

Libya sits oddly amongst her North African neighbours. They are, in the main, poor countries with limited mineral or oil endowment. For most of these states, economic development – or even, from certain perspectives, merely economic survival – is their main pre-occupation. Algeria is an exception to this observation, but even she is poor in comparison with Libya.

Table 8.1 shows the population and GNP of selected North African countries. Libya has the smallest population – a tiny 2.7 million in comparison with the 40 millions of Egypt and the 19 millions of Morocco. Concurrently, Libya has the highest level of income per capita: US$ 6910 (1978). This figure compares with US$ 140 in the case of Chad, the poorest country in the group.

Chad's problems – her harsh climate, absence of coastline, and limited endowment of resources – inflict an austere life upon her citizens. Without oil, economic conditions in Libya would not be so very different to those found in Chad, though Libya does have the advantage of a Mediterranean coastline.

Libya's fickleness in international relations may be caused partly at least, by fears deriving from the disparity between herself and her neighbours' populations and per capita incomes. It must have occurred to the Libyan leadership that living conditions in neighbouring states might become so harsh that their annexation of oil-rich and under-populated Libya seems the only alternative to economic disaster (1).

A more natural group with which to compare Libya is the other oil endowed states of the Arab Middle East (Tables 8.2 & 8.3). Libya occupies a middle position in a league table of GNP per capita comprising countries from this group. In terms of oil production, revenues and reserves, Libya is comparable with Iraq. At 1978 oil production levels she will enjoy a further 36 years of oil life. This

[*]The views contained in this paper are those of the authors. Opinions expressed here should not be attributed to any international agency with which the authors are, or have been associated.

TABLE 8.1. POPULATION AND GNP PER CAPITA OF NORTH AFRICA, 1978

	Population (million)	GNP/Capita (US dollars)
Egypt	39.9	390
Morocco	18.9	670
Algeria	17.6	1,260
Sudan	17.4	320
Tunisia	6.0	950
Niger	5.0	220
Chad	4.3	140
Libya	2.7	1,760

Source: World Development Report, 1980 World Bank, Washington, 1980, p.110.

TABLE 8.2. GROSS NATIONAL PRODUCT PER CAPITA, (US DOLLARS) 1978

State	Gross National Product per capita (US dollars)
Kuwait	14,890
United Arab Emirates	14,280
Qatar	12,740
Saudi Arabia	8,040
Libya	6,910
Bahrain	4,100
Oman	2,570
Iraq	1,860
Algeria	1,260

Source: World Bank, World Bank Atlas, 1979, World Bank, Washington, 1980.

TABLE 8.3. OIL PRODUCTION RESERVES, REVENUES AND DURATION OF OIL RESERVES IN 1978 FOR SELECTED ARAB STATES

State	Production (1978) million b/d	Reserves (1.1.79) million barrels	Revenues (1978) US dollars million	Anticipated Duration of Oil at 1978 Prdn levels
Saudi Arabia	8.2	169,500	34,600	57
Iraq	2.6	33,500	10,700	35
Kuwait	2.0	73,800	9,300	101
Libya	1.9	25,000	9,000	36
U.A.E.	1.8	32,400	3,500	49
Algeria	1.2	8,000	6,500	18

Source: Naft-Al-Arab, Kuwait, (February and March, 1980), OAPEC News Bulletin, vol. 5, no.12.

TABLE 8.4. LIBYA : PLAN ALLOCATIONS, 1973-1975, 1976-1980, MILLION LD

Sector	Revised Intermediate Plan, 1973-75	%	Transformation Plan 1976-1980	%
Agriculture	159	6.2	1,476	16.0
Industry	262	10.2	1,205	13.0
Public Works	295	11.5	1,131	12.2
Communications	199	7.7	930	10.0
Education	186	7.2	522	5.6
Health	70	2.7	276	3.0
Total	2,571	100.0	9,250	100.0

Source: Economic & Social Transformation Plan, 1976-1980, Ministry of Planning, Tripoli, 1976.

is not the same as the oil life of Kuwait, nor does Libya have the income of Saudi Arabia, but nonetheless, it does provide a real opportunity to create an at least partly self-sufficient economy.

In the current development plan, the Second Five Year Plan, 1980-85, a lower level of oil production is envisaged of about 1.5 million b/d (2). If that option were followed it would lengthen the life of the oil reserves by about 13 years.

Libya's present oil-derived wealth contrasts starkly with her poverty in the early 1950's. At that time Libya qualified for favourable loans and grants from development agencies, because the country, ravaged by war, was visibly and acutely poverty-stricken (3). Even in 1961, GDP was only US$194 per capita (4).

Inevitably, Libya's oil production transformed her economic prospects. Production began in 1961 when some 18,000 barrels of oil were produced per day. By 1971 this had risen to 1 million b/d. Today Libya faces the same predicament as the oil-rich states of the Arabian peninsula: how best to secure an income independent from oil before the oil revenue terminates. Libya also shares with these states the handicap of a small under-educated population and she too relies, fairly extensively, on migrant labour.

Libya's avowed socialism, which under close scrutiny seems to have a rather cosmetic quality, is unusual amongst the more wealthy capital-rich states. Muammar al-Qadhafi, the Libyan leader, has made explicit a proposed style of development for the Jamahiriya (the 'state of the masses') which is contained in the 'Green Book' (5). It is a state run on Islamic and socialist lines, which comprises a 'third style' of development, existing conceptually somewhere between imperialism and communism.

The practical impact on the economy of this vision has been indeterminate. In an international context, Libya continues to participate in world markets, particularly the market for oil. Countries which have free enterprise economies such as the Federal Republic of Germany are major partners in Libya's development. Domestic development planning proceeds on predictable conventional lines; industrial development is a major component of Libya's development, and ventures are established with the justification that they will be profitable.

Libya's socialism is more visible in rather specific measures as, for example, in the official termination of the private sector. The private sector is being dismantled progressively and inexorably. Progress has presently (1981) reached the point where private bakeries and butcheries have been taken over. They have been replaced by large supermarkets, state-owned and state-run, in which prices are subsidised. More broadly however, it has been impossible to direct Libyan development on a course close to the outline given by the Green Book. This is partly because the Green Book is a confused document and also because the injunctions it contains are at times quite impracticable. As a result, despite the pedigree of the authorship, the Green Book has had less effect on actual economic development in Libya than one might imagine from the publicity it has been given (6).

The authors of the Second Five Year Plan, faced with the

practical and immediate task of developing the country, have taken a more conventional view of 'development'. For them, the expansion of the non-oil sector, the development of human and physical resources and self-sufficiency in food are the principal economic objectives. These are both familiar and appropriate to a developing country with a small productive base to the economy. However, in many respects they sit uncomfortably alongside the injunctions of Muammar al-Qadhafi which, at the very least, do not appear to support a conventional style of development, and on occasion are in direct opposition to the views of the planners (for example on the question of women's participation in the economy) (7).

Libya's oil wealth permits her leadership to engage in political and social experiments without apparent cost. More realistically, the rather poor quality of data combined with the favourable interpretations often placed on extant facts by commentators make it difficult to see exactly what these costs are (8). Indeed, measuring foregone development is a near impossible task. However, we shall argue in this chapter that the latent cost of these experiments and the conflicts of objectives between the strategy behind the Green Book and that of the more pragmatic planners are high, particularly if a long-term perspective is taken. Two such major costs can be identified, amongst others as – the permanent loss of Libya's water resources and the atrophy of her human resources.

ECONOMIC DEVELOPMENT

Development Planning
The government has taken a major part in development planning during the 1970s. Muammar al-Qadhafi's socialist perspective and the increasingly large sums paid in oil revenues to the government have been contributory factors to the enhanced role of central government in development. Three development plans have been announced: The Intermediate Plan, 1973-1975; the Transformation Plan, 1976-1980, and the Second Five Year Transformation Plan, 1981-1985 (9). Each of these has been progressively more ambitious in scope and financially more costly.

The Intermediate Plan initially had a budget of 1.1 billion Libyan dinars (LD), though this was revised to 2.6 billion LD; the Transformation Plan's budget was originally 7.8 billion LD, subsequently raised to 9.2 billion LD, and the authors of the current plan envisage expenditure in the region of 18.5 billion LD.

The growth in development expenditure reflects the increase in income that Libya has received from oil during the 1970s. From 1973 to 1974, oil income almost increased threefold. From 1974 onwards it increased to 1979 at a rate of 17 per cent annually.

Despite the innovative sounding titles of these plans and the fanfare of publicity they enjoyed at their inception, each one has been conventional in substantive content and, broadly speaking, typical of the development plans of other more 'conservative' capital-surplus economies in the Middle East.

The 1973-1975 Plan's economic aims were to improve the country's infrastructure, to develop industry (at that stage, foodstuffs, building materials and petrochemicals) orientated towards import substitution and to improve the agricultural sector so that Libya should be self-sufficient in food within a decade. The intermediate Plan (Table 8.4) was also typical in setting a highly ambitious annual growth target of 10.5 per cent in real terms for non-oil GDP. This rate was actually exceeded by some margin, but the base was small, and the efficiency of investment may not have been high.

The existing infrastructure in Libya was not able to cope with the sudden explosion in demand; ports and roads were congested, manpower was scarce, and many projects had to be delayed or postponed because of an inadequate administrative capacity.

The Transformation Plan was equally ambitious in its objectives: and annual real growth in GDP of 10.7 per cent was targetted for the economy as a whole and 14.1 per cent for the non-oil sectors. Moreover, this was a plan with more sophisticated objectives than those of the Intermediate Plan. Economic diversification away from oil had become extant as a, if not the, primary objective. This was to be accomplished by further developing industry and agriculture. Self-sufficiency in food and in manufactured goods were specific objectives though, in the event neither was to be even partly achieved. Many intended industrial ventures were not complete at the end of the Plan, agricultural output fluctuated indifferently, and non-oil GDP rose by only 10 per cent per annum, a little less than the intended 14 per cent. Manpower shortages persisted and were exacerbated by Libya's poor relations with her neighbours, notably Egypt.

The current Plan's aims are yet more sophisticated than those of the Transformation Plan. Economic diversification away from oil is to continue, and oil production is to be reduced to levels required to finance development and to ensure a balanced overseas payments account. There is again considerable emphasis on the agricultural sector (which has not lived up to past expectations) and on industry. Libya is about to begin an excursion into heavy industry with an iron and steel mill at Misurata (Fig. 8.1), further investment in petrochemicals, and an aluminium smelter. A greatly stressed innovation is the heightened emphasis on the productivity of manpower, in evaluating the extent to which their targets are met. Libyan planners are now arguing that the measures of success in achieving development objectives should no longer be the capacity to invest; rather it should be the rate of project completion and the efficiency of operation.

Rather than examine an intermediate list of plan targets and actual performances, we proceed to look at some of the key elements of the Libyan economy over the entire period of modern Libyan planning. We start with an overview of the whole economy.

Economic Growth

In an assessment of an oil-based economy it is important to distinguish between those elements of GDP and economic growth which derive from oil and those which do not. The Libyan economy is sustained by oil, and the wealth it has brought to Libya has influenced development profoundly. Oil will continue to be crucial to the economy for the foreseeable future, but the criterion by which the economy should now be measured is essentially the extent of growth of non-oil GDP. Naturally, much of Libya's industrial development is linked to oil and natural gas, for example her petrochemical industries, but in the long run it will be the capacity of the economy to earn a living from activities other than oil sales and directly related income which will decide whether or not Libyans will continue to enjoy their present standard of living.

National Income
Despite the efforts at diversification, Libya's national income remains heavily dominated by oil revenues and since these were first paid, national income has risen accordingly (Table 8.5). Since about 1968 national income has tended to be about two and one half times as great as oil revenue. A major pre-occupation amongst Libyan planners has been to break this link, and to create a high volume of non-oil GDP.

Table 8.6 shows the structure of Libya's national income, measured by the expenditure method. Government expenditure, investment, and private consumption all contribute roughly equal proportions to national income. In 1980 the largest proportion of expenditure was accounted for by the government, and this proportion is growing a great deal more rapidly than is Gross Fixed Capital Formation.

In the Second Five Year Plan (1981-1985), national income may well fall, as oil output is constrained to a level sufficient to meet government domestic expenditure and investment. The level at which this balance should occur is around 1.5 million barrels per day, a significantly lower level of output than that prevailing in 1980.

In 1970, the petroleum, mining and quarrying sector accounted for about 61 per cent of GDP (Table 8.7). The other large contributor to GDP was the public services sector, which includes government administration, education, health and other budgets such as military expenditures. The agriculture and manufacturing sectors made particularly small contributions of 2.5 per cent and 1.7 per cent respectively at that time.

This distribution of economic activity is typical of the other oil states of the Arab region at an early stage of their development. By 1978 however, the dominance of oil had tempered slightly as infrastructural development began in earnest.

Domestic Investment
The emphasis early in the 1970s on infrastructure and agriculture is borne out by the pattern of investment, which Table 8.8 shows. Social services and infrastructure absorbed large proportions of the total investment in 1975. This is not surprising however, since there was an acute absence of infrastructure which became particularly obvious when domestic expenditure rose in line with oil income. The limited provision of social services in the early 1970s also occasioned

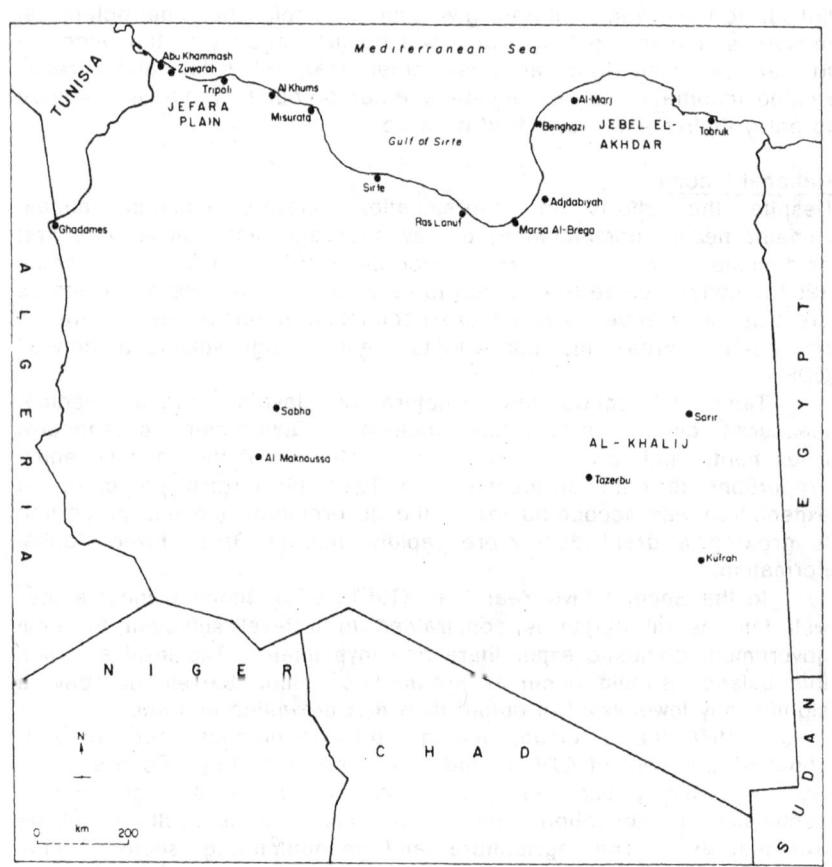

FIGURE 8.1   LOCATION MAP OF LIBYA

TABLE 8.5. LIBYA: OIL PRODUCTION, REVENUE, TAKE PER BARREL AND GROSS NATIONAL PRODUCT, 1962-1981

	Oil Production (thousand b/d)	Oil Revenue (LD million)	Average take per barrel LD	GNP million LD
1962	182.3	14.2	0.4	164
1963	441.8	38.5	0.5	241
1964	862.4	75.2	0.5	307
1965	1,218.8	125.4	0.6	436
1966	1,501.1	186.7	0.8	559
1967	1,740.5	223.3	0.8	649
1968	2,602.1	357.8	0.9	883
1969	3,109.1	419.7	0.8	1,144
1970	3,318.0	482.6	0.9	1,210
1971	2,760.8	593.7	1.4	1,416
1972	2,239.4	514.0	1.4	1,519
1973	2,174.9	663.6	1.9	1,928
1974	1,521.3	1,776.0	7.4	3,534
1975	1,479.8	1,510.3	6.4	3,380
1976	1,932.6	2,220.4	7.2	4,389
1977	2,063.4	2,620.0	8.0	5,182
1978	1,982.5	2,486.8	7.9	5,407
1979	2,090.1	3,848.7	11.7	n.a
1980	1,700.0	n.a	n.a	n.a
1981	1,600.0	n.a	n.a	n.a

Source: Compiled from figures provided by Petroleum Economist, Secretariat of Planning and H.M.Yahya, 'Oil and Economic Development in the Socialist Peoples Libyan Arab Jamahiriya : A Great Challenge'. OPEC Review, vol.5. (1981), pp.33-52.

TABLE 8.6. LIBYA NATIONAL EXPENDITURE (INCOME) ACCOUNTS 1975-1980

	1975		1976		1977		1978		1979		1980	
	LD million	%	LD million	%	LD million	%	LD million	%	LD million	%	LD million	%
Government Consumption	1,044	27.6	1,185	23.7	1,378	24.0	1,590	26.9	n.a.	n.a.	2,210	27.4
Gross Fixed Capital Formation	1,055	27.9	1,226	24.5	1,360	23.7	1,450	24.5	n.a.	n.a.	1,830	22.7
Private Consumption	1,194	31.6	1,337	26.7	1,490	25.9	1,657	28.0	n.a.	n.a.	2,070	25.6
Increase in Stocks	100	2.6	-50	1.0	40	0.7	-	-	n.a.	n.a.	100	1.2
Exports minus Imports	387	10.3	1,210	23.1	1,482	25.7	1,215	20.6	n.a.	n.a.	1,864	23.1
Gross Domestic Product	3,780	100.0	4,907	100.0	5,750	100.0	5,912	100.0	n.a.	n.a.	8,074	100.0
Less Factor Payments Abroad	-400		-518		-548		-505		n.a.	n.a.	n.a.	n.a.
Gross National Expenditure	3,380		4,389		5,182		5,407		n.a.	n.a.	n.a.	n.a.

Source: International Financial Statistics, (International Monetary Fund, Washington), vol.34, no.5, 1981.

TABLE 8.7. LIBYA: DISTRIBUTION OF GROSS DOMESTIC PRODUCT BY ECONOMIC SECTOR, 1970 AND 1978 (AT CURRENT PRICES)

	1970	1978
Agriculture & Fishing	2.5	2.0
Petroleum, Mining & Quarrying	61.2	54.4
Manufacturing Industries	1.7	2.6
Construction	6.6	10.9
Electricity & Gas	0.5	0.6
Trade, restaurants & hotels	3.5	5.5
Transport, storage & communications	3.2	4.0
Public Services	20.8	20.0
Total	100.0	100.0

Source: *Annual Report*, Central Bank of Libya, Tripoli.

TABLE 8.8. LIBYA: GROSS FIXED CAPITAL FORMATION IN 1975 AND 1980 (CONSTANT 1975 PRICES) AND CUMULATIVE GROSS FIXED CAPITAL FORMATION 1981-1985 (1979 PRICES)

Economic Sector	1975* LD million	%	1980** LD million	%	1980-85 LD million	%
Agriculture	149.9	14.2	205	14.1	1,400	12.5
Manufacturing	121.5	11.5	218	15.0	2,000	17.9
Electricity & Water	135.1	12.8	223	15.4	1,600	14.3
Transport & Communication	157.8	15.0	241	16.6	1,800	16.1
Housing	235.5	22.3	158	10.9	1,500	13.4
Public Services	91.4	8.7	150	10.3	1,000	8.9
Education & Health	99.3	9.4	135	9.3	1,000	8.9
Other (Oil,Trade etc)	64.2	6.1	121	8.4	0,900	8.0
Total	1,054.7	100.0	1,451	100.0	11.2	100.0

* Constant 1975 prices
** Constant 1979 prices
Source: *Second Five Year Plan*, Secretariat of Planning, Tripoli.

substantial investment in government services. In such areas as education and health, Libya's standards in these fields are improving dramatically (10).

Agriculture received a substantial share of investment expenditure both in 1975 and 1980 (Table 8.8). In 1980 the share accounted for by industrial investment is anticipated as increasing to the point where it almost absorbs the highest share of investment. This trend towards an increasing emphasis on industry is echoed in the current 1981-1985 Plan, to the point where it absorbs 18 per cent of all investment in the period 1981 to 1985. Taken together however, 'electricity and water' and 'transport and communications' comprise 30 per cent of total investment. Infrastructure will therefore continue to be a major component of Libyan planning and domestic expenditure. Table 8.9 shows the evolution of Libya's non-oil income, and the growing significance of manufacturing industries is clear.

Balance of Payments
Despite some short-term concerns Libya's balance of payments has been in surplus since 1965, as exports have exceeded imports by a considerable margin. Libya's only export of any significance is oil, and the real price of oil has risen steeply during the 1970s on two occasions: first in 1973 and again in 1979. On each occasion Libya's current account balance rose sharply, from US$1.5 billion in 1973 to US$4.0 billion in 1974 and from US$9.7 billion in 1979 to about US$12 billion in 1980 (Table 8.10).

Libya's oil output has been more or less stable during the 1970s, falling slightly in recent years, while export earnings have soared. Libya's imports have been increasing rapidly in recent years also. Libya's internal development relies very heavily on imported products, technology and manpower. At this stage in her development, the demand for foreign services is massive. Naturally, government planners hope that as internal development moves beyond the infrastructural and initial investment stage that the demand for imports will decline.

Although import prices have moved quite sharply upwards over the decade, the spectacular improvements in the price of oil has served to achieve favourable terms of trade for Libya. Table 8.11 shows that in 1980 Libya's terms of trade index stood at 172 (1974=100). However, since 1980 these will have begun to deteriorate, rather as they did after 1974.

Libya's exports of oil are sold mainly to OECD countries, and in particular the United States of America, Italy and the Federal Republic of Germany. Libya's imports come mainly from Italy and the Federal Republic of Germany.

AGRICULTURE

Libya is a comparatively large country of some 1.8 million square kilometres. Most of the country comprises arid desert, and only a small area is suitable for intensive cultivation (11). Present land use is shown on Table 8.12.

Libya's rainfall tends to be low, except for some coastal areas

TABLE 8.9. LIBYA: DISTRIBUTION OF NON-OIL GROSS DOMESTIC PRODUCT BY ECONOMIC SECTOR, 1975, 1980 & 1985 (1979 prices)

Economic Sector	1975	1980	1985*
Agriculture & Fishing	5.3	4.4	4.9
Other Mining & Quarrying	1.3	1.2	1.1
Manufacturing Industries	3.6	6.7	11.5
Construction	35.0	27.8	6.0
Electricity & Gas	0.9	1.4	2.2
Trade, restaurants & hotels	13.1	11.9	11.0
Transport, storage & communication	10.1	8.8	8.5
Finance	5.9	6.3	6.8
Public Services	23.2	29.9	26.6
Other Services	1.6	1.6	1.4
Total	100.0	100.0	100.0

* estimate
Source: Second Five Year Plan, Secretariat of Planning, Tripoli.

TABLE 8.10. LIBYA: BALANCE OF PAYMENTS 1970-1980
(US DOLLARS MILLION)

	1970	1971	1972	1973	1974	1975	1976	1977	1978	1979	1980
Merchandise Exports (fob)	2,379	2,714	2,470	3,528	7,803	6,418	8,748	10,405	9,900	15,915	22,579
Oil Sector	2,389	2,709	2,458	3,509	7,796	6,410	8,737	10,393	9,888	15,904	22,561
Other Sectors	8	5	12	19	7	8	11	12	12	11	18
Merchandise Imports (fob)	-674	-930	-1,290	-2,011	-3,746	-4,424	-4,277	-4,929	-5,764	-6,160	-8,851
Trade Balance	1,723	1,784	1,180	1,517	4,057	1,994	4,471	5,476	4,136	9,755	n.a.
Exports of Services	139	172	225	216	434	375	349	379	468	559	n.a.
Imports of Services	-1,059	-1,034	-758	-1,237	-1,372	-1,553	-1,574	-1,574	-1,607	-2,192	n.a.
Balance of Goods & Services	803	922	647	496	3,119	816	3,246	4,248	2,789	8,212	n.a.
Transfers (private)	-45	-48	-306	-273	-350	-260	-257	-857	-577	-669	n.a.
Transfers (official)	-113	-90	-102	-156	-69	-164	-144	-98	-91	-178	n.a.
Current Account Balance	645	784	239	-67	2,700	392	2,845	3,293	2,121	7,365	n.a.

Source: Compiled from International Financial Statistics, various years, (International Monetary Fund, Washington).

TABLE 8.11. LIBYA: TERMS OF TRADE, 1974-1980

	1974	1975	1976	1977	1978	1979	1980
Export Prices	100	84	92	103	92	161	276
Import Prices	100	112	116	124	136	146	160
Terms of Trade	100	75	79	83	67	110	172

Source: Compiled from: *International Financial Statistics*, vol.34, no.5,(May 1981).

TABLE 8.12 LIBYA: LAND USE IN 1979

Land Use Type	Area km2	% total area
Urban	500	0.03
Agriculture - arable and orchard	18,000	1.10
Agriculture - pasture and grassland	70,000	4.00
Forest and scrub-land	5,000	0.30
Wastelands	1,666,000	94.57
Total	1,760,000	100.00

Source: *National Physical Perspective Plan 1981-2000*, UNDP, Tripoli, March 1979, p.36.

to the west and to a lesser extent, coastal zones to the east (12). The climate tends to make modern cultivation in much of the country extremely difficult and expensive in terms of capital and water.

In terms of agricultural activities and resources, the country can be roughly divided into three parts. There are two coastal strips where the bulk of Libya's intensive cultivation takes place, notably the Jefara area and Jebel Al Akhdar coastal strip. These two coastal strips enjoy about 200 mm of rainfall annually, and the Jefara has significant, if now reduced, water supplies from underground aquifers which have been the basis for intensive irrigation of land. The Jebel Al Akhdar region tends to be used for growing citrus fruits and dairy farming. From the perimeters of these areas and in between them, south to a distance of about 50 kilometers, runs a strip of marginal land, suitable only for extensive grazing.

The remainder of the country consists of barren desert, interupted only by very occasional natural oases, such as exist in the south west, around Sabha, and still less frequently by a man-made oasis, such as those in the south east at Kufrah. Abundant underground water reserves exist in the desert in particular parts of the Al Khalij region, notably at Sarir and Kufrah (13).

Agriculture and Oil

The development of Libyan agriculture since 1950 has been erratic. Initially, the agricultural sector was a principal means of livelihood for the majority of the populace (14). With oil came the opportunity of an easier life in towns and adjacent areas. The internal migrations which occurred when oil revenues were first received had a debilitating effect on the agricultural sector.

Table 8.13 shows that agricultural production dropped quite significantly from 1950 to 1982, exports of food dwindled while food imports soared. The significance of the agricultural sector as a source of GDP and as an employer has been decimated by the advent of oil in Libya.

This is hardly a surprising development. Indeed it is entirely predictable and, from the perspective of Libyan economic development, in some respects a welcome one. The agricultural sector was characterised by low levels of productivity and income, and demanded an exacting life-style from those living off the land.

Libya's discovery and exploitation of oil dramatically changed her economic situation. Her scarce resource suddenly became manpower and water, not finance. The appropriate economic response would have been to adopt policies which enhanced the productivity of labour through the use of capital-intensive techniques and to select a product blend which maximised the return to water. With the exceptions of the wheat schemes in the south (which we deal with later) the government chose to do neither of these. Large farms have been broken up into smaller ones, with the effect that labour intensity had increased, and, in general, returns to water have probably declined as water usage has increased with the advent of diesel powered pumps which are often used inefficiently.

The aim of government policy in the agricultural sector can be

TABLE 8.13. LIBYA: SELECTED AGRICULTURAL INDICES, 1958, 1962 1967 AND VARIOUS RECENT YEARS (LD MILLION).

	1958	1962	1967	Various	
Total value of agricultural production (1964 prices)	20.0	17.3	21.0	42.6	(1977)
Value of agriculture output as per cent of GDP	26.1	9.4	3.4	2.0	(1978)
Value of food exports (current prices)	2.7	1.8	0.6	0.0	(1977)
Value of food imports (current prices)	5.1	8.4	19.2	19.0	(1977)
Food deficit (value)	2.4	6.6	18.6	19.0	(1977)
Agricultural labour (per cent of total labour force)	70	50	33.9	20	(1975)
Value of petroleum exports	0	49.0	417.3	2617	(1978)
Value of petroleum production as per cent of GDP	6.9	28.5	54.7	54.4	(1978)

Source: 1958, 1962, 1967 E.E. Penrose, J.A. Allan & K.S. McLachlan (eds) Libyan University - London University, Joint Research Project on Libya, vol.I, Agriculture & Economic Development of Libya, 1969, p.16.

summarised as an attempt to maximise output and to support the incomes of individual farmers. The oft repeated objective of 'self-sufficiency' in food had dominated government thinking. As a result, the agricultural sector has absorbed, or at least received, between 1963 and 1980, 14 per cent of all development expenditure. In 1980, gross fixed capital formation in agriculture was 1,402 LD per agricultural worker, and some 205 million LD in all.

Yet, despite the large sums devoted to agriculture, output growth has been indifferent. Table 8.14 shows the fluctuations which have characterised agricultural output during the 1970s.

In some cases, the levels of production and cultivation were lower in 1977 than in 1970, for example in the cases of wheat and olives. In most cases, though production tended to rise through the 1970s, large fluctuations occurred.

The impact of oil wealth has been shown in broad terms on Table 8.13, but from Table 8.14 its detailed impact can be observed on output over the period 1973 to 1974. Output in 1974 was lower in practically every item recorded on Table 8.14 than it was in 1973.

The economic changes experienced at that time were essentially a repetition of the period 1958 to 1960, when attitudes and aspirations changed suddenly, urban opportunities increased, and farmers left rural areas for towns.

More recent data is available for 1976 to 1980, and is shown on Table 8.15. Overall value added grew at 6.2 per cent per annum in the agricultural sector. This is not unimpressive by itself, but in the context of Libyan investment in agriculture, it is poor. Wheat and barley production grew rather modestly, given the extent of investment in irrigated land.

Current Development in Agriculture

The government is currently engaged in a range of schemes to promote the sector to greater levels of efficiency and production. Not insignificant amongst these is the government's policy of supporting farm units through the provision of loans and grants to farmers. The official vehicle for this task is the National Agriculture Bank which offers Libyan farmers credit for farm expenditures which fall into particular categories.

The average 'long term loan' in 1977 (of which some 1,150 were made) was US$9,500. One suspects that the accessibility of such loans may be a reason for the retention of so many Libyans in the agricultural sector. Moreover, the injection of such large sums into quite small farming units has probably not been entirely beneficial.

Water. The extensive mechanisation of the sector and, in particular, the increasing use of tractors and water pumps on the coastal belt may be contributory factors to an eventual and inevitable demise of the sector, brought about by the exhaustion of Libya's now most precious resource: water.

In the coastal belt, water depletion has reached a crisis point, and managing the water resources of the country is the major challenge to Libyan planners in the agricultural sector. Hydrologists believe

TABLE 8.14. LIBYA: INDEX OF OUTPUT OF SELECTED AGRICULTURAL ITEMS, 1970 to 1977

	Area Harvested		Quantity Produced												
	Barley	Wheat	Barley	Wheat	Potatoes	Onions	Groundnuts	Tomatoes	Apples	Figs	Olives	Poultry	Cattle	Goats	Sheep
1970	100	100	100	100	100	100	100	100	100	100	100	100	100	100	100
1971	31	34	6	23	230	75	104	91	162	122	7	84	95	92	106
1972	76	70	220	41	495	118	128	119	123	130	136	95	98	90	105
1973	133	95	387	86	791	166	104	122	177	161	212	366	113	81	143
1974	155	85	274	49	657	117	85	72	77	183	33	273	142	93	132
1975	171	92	363	58	898	199	118	134	123	13	215	360	178	137	193
1976	181	107	348	81	806	239	120	150	154	204	220	390	184	150	208
1977	66	65	110	35	999	252	122	122	200	270	60	362	169	123	177

Source: Statistical Abstract (various years), Ministry of Planning and Scientific Research, Tripoli.

TABLE 8.15. LIBYA: GROWTH OF SELECTED AGRICULTURAL INDICES, 1976-1980

Item	Annual Growth Rate, 1976-1980 %
Value Added	6.2
Wheat	9.9
Barley	2.7
Fruits	9.2
Vegetables	0.9
Fodder	7.3
Milk	0.8
Meat	7.3
Eggs	12.5

Source: Second Five Year Plan, Secretariat of Planning, Tripoli.

TABLE 8.16. LIBYA: EXPANSION OF ENROLMENT IN PRIMARY SCHOOLS 1950/51 TO 1976/77

	Number of Pupils		
Year	Boys	Girls	Total
1950/51	28,470	3,650	32,120
1960/61	97,560	25,870	123,430
1969/70	203,800	107,050	310,850
1976/777	299,480	262,120	561,600

Source: various Educational Yearbooks, Tripoli.

TABLE 8.17. LIBYA: ENROLMENT OF LIBYANS IN SCHOOLS, COLLEGES, UNIVERSITIES, 1976/77

	Number of Pupils		
Level	Boys	Girls	Total
Primary	299,480	262,120	561.600
Preparatory	96,530	50,450	146,980
Secondary	14,700	4,480	19,180
Vocational	4,450	440	4,890
University	9,650	1,840	11,490

Source: Annual Report, 1976/77, Secretariat of Education, Tripoli.

that the cultivable parts of the Jefara plain, presently irrigated from underground aquifers, will become uncultivable in the forseeable future, unless irrigation water reserves are conserved. The rate of extraction around Benghazi is believed to be three to six times the rate of natural recharge. As a result, the saline content of the aquifers is rising, and the land proximate to the coast becoming sterile (15).

It is now planned to pipe large quantities of water from Sarir to Sirte and Ajdabiya. The needs of Libya's industry and townships for water are increasing, but the consumption of water by small-scale farms vastly exceeds either of these other uses.

Piping water from Sarir to the coast will alleviate the problem of supplying water to industry and for domestic consumption. It is not relevant to the question of Libya's use of water for agriculture from aquifers on the Jefara plain. It is the cumulative effect of the drawing off of water by innumerable individual farmers that contributes most substantially to that problem.

It is in the use of water that Libya must make explicit her economic priorities. Libya desires self-sufficiency in agricultural produce, in manufactured goods, and a large non-oil element to GDP.

The country cannot have all three, if it is to preserve its water resources. Indeed, an unwise or over-rapid depletion of water resources will result in the loss of part of Libya's cultivable land, namely those parts of the Jefara adjacent to the sea. There is in fact a partial solution, albeit a temporary one, namely to produce desalinated water from the sea. To do this would defeat the purpose of Libya's aims of self-sufficiency in food, since if to produce agricultural produce and manufactured goods Libya is obliged to invest in desalination plants, her products will not be competitive in world markets. However, as long as Libya enjoys substantial oil revenues, planners can ignore this detail. Nevertheless, it would mean that in reality Libya was not achieving a self-sustaining economy independent of food imports and oil revenues, capable of existing in the post-oil era. Indeed, the day Libya's oil income ended, so would these uneconomic and subsidised agricultural and industrial ventures.

It would, at that time, be patently obvious that tomatoes can be bought in Tunisia for less than it costs to grow them in Libya, that wheat can be bought abroad at a fraction of the true cost to Libya of producing her own wheat, and so on.

The desire to persist with domestic production of these goods may continue, but in the post-oil era, the finance to do so will not. More importantly, Libya's natural water resources may have been so squandered that domestic production is by then impossible in any case. It would be appropriate at this stage for Libyan planners to reassess their entire agricultural strategy and simultaneously to look again at national development objectives. If water and manpower are scarce, then intensive land use via irrigation is a nonsense. One authority on Libyan agriculture has even argued that all irrigated farming should cease on the Jefara plain (16). The point is that, sooner or later, Libya will have to abandon the dreams of making the desert bloom, and being self-sufficient in food. She will have to face up to the realities and responsibilities of being a partner in a complex and inter-dependent world.

In this world, trade is a pre-requisite, and will remain so, especially for Libya. Libya cannot close herself off from the rest of the world, however appealing that alternative might appear to Libya's leaders. There is a strong case for abandoning the capital-intensive wheat schemes, government support to Libyan farmers and forbidding the irrigation of land from underground sources in the Jefara. One suspects that however radical these suggestions now appear, in 15 years time they will seem commonplace.

The Wheat Schemes. Libya's most ambitious farming venture has been the cultivation of wheat and fodder crops in the desert at Al Maknoussa, Sarir and Kufrah, using water from underground water reservoirs. Crops are cultivated on land irrigated by mechanically-powered rotating sprinklers.

From an economic perspective, these ventures have little justification. The climate in the south is adverse, being extremely hot and dry, occasionally experiencing a burning wind. The initial investments in these projects were enormous. Yields are low, being 2-3 tons per ha at Kufrah and Sarir, and between 5-6 tons per ha at Al Maknoussa. All three places are distant from Tripoli and Benghazi. Labour is scarce or non-existent, currently consisting of mainly foreign workers from Egypt, Tunisia and the Indian sub-continent.

The technology required to irrigate large land areas correctly is very advanced, and in the case of Al Maknoussa, is based on a computer in America. By the time a ton of wheat arrives at the markets of Tripoli and Benghazi, it is said to have cost US$1,350. One suspects that this price, inevitably an estimate, is based on current costs, and does not take depreciation into account. It compares with a world and Libyan market price of US$241 (17).

The only rational justification for these ventures is a variance between the market price and a governmental shadow price for domestically produced wheat, which the government notionally values very highly. It does so for, one might say, ideological reasons, namely the same oft-repeated desire to be independent of food imports. While these schemes have been marginally successful in proving an almost inconceivable feat possible, they have not been a panacea to Libya's food production requirements nor have they proved, according to economic criteria, to be anything approaching a success.

A great amount of political (not to mention financial) capital is tied up in these desert ventures, and the signs are that although government now perceives the scale of the problem, they will be at least maintained, and in the case of Al Maknoussa, receive yet further investment in social infrastructure.

OIL AND INDUSTRY

Libya took the first steps towards producing oil in the mid fifties, when she created the legal framework under which exploration concessions could be granted. Libya's oil exploitation was unusual amongst the oil producers in that it involved a large number of companies all of whom were operating separately, though most were American-based. This was significant for two reasons. First, the discussions over ownership, production and pricing agreements, which every oil producer was involved in from the late 1960s onwards, were made easier for Libya by the number of companies competing with each other for further concessions. Thus Libya tended to be negotiating in a sellers' market, which naturally worked in her favour. Secondly, and less importantly, Libya's oil installations tended to proliferate as each company created installations, and in particular pipelines, catering for their particular concession (18).

Discoveries were made in the late fifties, and production began in 1961. It quickly rose, and by 1968 Libya was producing 2.6 million b/d.

The revenue from oil has risen with increases in the price paid for oil. Table 8.15 shows how steeply these rose in 1974 and again in 1979. Libyan oil has always enjoyed a slight premium over Arabian Gulf oil, for two reasons: its proximity to the European markets and its quality.

At present Libyan reserves are quoted by OPEC as being about 25 million barrels. A production level of about 2 million b/d implies, as noted, an oil life of around 34 years. However, the view taken by Libyan planners is that oil resources will largely be exhausted by the end of this century, some 20 years hence.

The comparatively limited life of Libyan reserves has encouraged Libyan planners to seek urgently for a non-oil base to the economy and to set policies to limit oil production to the level required by internal development. The equilibrium level where domestic requirements are met from oil revenues is, presently, around 1.5 million b/d.

In addition to her oil, Libya has sizeable natural gas reserves; in 1979 these were estimated at some 4 billion barrels oil equivalent, though there are probably untapped reserves besides those proven ones. In 1979, Libya produced some 828,000 million cubic feet of natural gas, of which she flared only 21 per cent. This figure would be higher if oil production rose, but gas utilisation plans are well advanced (19).

As a first step to creating a non-oil revenue based economy, Libya has made large investments in petrochemicals, which have the general objectives of producing fuels for Libya's domestic development, using more of her natural gas, and transforming crude oil into a more valuable end product, thus enhancing Libya's revenues.

Petrochemical and non-oil industrial developments are all located on the coast, but particularly at three sites: Marsa Al Brega, Misurata and Ras Lanuf.

Marsa Al Brega is the centre for petrochemical development, already having ammonia, urea, methanol, LNG and NGL plants and expansion is envisaged for each product. A little way to the west, at Ras Lanuf, another petrochemical complex is planned, including a large oil refinery and an ethylene plant. Another oil refinery will open at Tobruk in 1981, but Libya's conflict with Egypt persuaded the government to use Ras Lanuf as the major site for petrochemical development instead of Tobruk.

Over the country as a whole, Libya currently refines 51 million barrels of oil. However, assuming contractors meet their deadlines, total refining capacity will be 122 million barrels by 1985. A growing amount of refined products are consumed domestically. In 1980 some 6.5 million barrels of gasoline were consumed within the country. The steel mill at Misurata and the aluminium plant at Zuwarah represent a new facet of Libyan industrial development, namely the move into explicitly non-oil-related heavy industries, though both these assume a cheap energy source such as natural gas.

Misurata is the site for a massive steel mill, and there are equally large complementary projects related to the production of steel. It is hoped that output will reach 1.2 million tons per year by 1985. Initially, ore will be imported, but later the deposits of iron ore at Sabha may be used. Equally ambitious is the proposed development of an aluminium smelter at Zuwarah, west of Tripoli.

The ancillary infrastructural investment required by these various industrial projects is massive. All require port facilities, roads, power supplies, and last but not least, a sizeable workforce which in turn will require housing, social services and water. Initially a township capable of accommodating 180,000 persons was to be built at Misurata, but more recently a figure of 40,000 has been mentioned (19).

Apart from these investments in heavy industries, other industries are planned, including a car assembly plant, further development of food processing and electrical goods manufacture.

The production figures available for Libya's industrial sector up to 1976 show rather odd fluctuations from one year to the next. Some manufacturing establishments appear to have closed altogether, in others, such as 'canning and preserving of fruit', production fell in 1976 to 3 per cent of 1975 levels. Under-utilisation of capacity is a widely accepted and acknowledged problem in Libyan industry, as is the unwillingness of Libyan labour to work in industrial environments, and their lack of motivation and skills. To an outsider, a disinclination amongst erstwhile farmers or traders to participate in industry is hardly surprising. The importation of many foreigners has become, and will remain, essential.

Apart from simple labour problems, industry has to cope with the political climate. Since 1978 all businesses have been nationalised and are run, nominally, by People's Committees. In the consequent muddle which pervades the Libyan modern sector, only the oil sector remains unscathed. Many commercial enterprises have seemingly lost their *raison d'être*, as ownership has passed to the 'people'. Economic efficiency is no longer an accepted criterion of survival, since the government subsidises establishments run by People's Committees which make a loss.

This process of democratisation has not reached the really large industrial plants yet. Many of these are still under construction, hence the presence of foreign contracting companies. The oil industry, and possibly its off-spring, the petrochemical industry, may well continue to remain under the control of foreign oil companies, and hence be run conventionally. The same may apply to the steel mill and the aluminium plant. The result of lengthy deliberation by People's Committees on the day-to-day running of these large enterprises would lead, in conventional terms to bankruptcy or, conceivably, to disaster.

In the short term, Libya can afford to pay the price of her present experiment in socialism, namely economic inefficiency, but there may also be less obvious but very costly elements, such as the atrophying of the economic motivation of her indigenous workforce. In many respects, Libya's human resources are more crucial to her long-term development than a large and artificially created non-oil element in GDP. We now turn to the question of Libya's manpower.

MANPOWER

Libya's population of some 2.7 million persons is small in relation to her land and oil endowment. At the end of the Second World War Libya enjoyed only limited economic development and physical infrastructure. The state of her human capital was equally unfavourable. With oil revenues came the capacity to rectify this situation, by providing the funding for educational facilities. Table 8.16 shows the rapid pace at which primary school enrolment expanded.

However, even with this impressive increase in enrolment, in 1973 some 61 per cent of the total population remained illiterate. The educational pyramid in Libya is fairly broad, though there is an obvious bias towards male education particularly at levels above the primary. Libya's two universities enrolled, in 1976, some 11,490 Libyan students, (Table 8.17) two thirds of whom were studying non-scientific subjects. Thus the bias in tertiary education, so common in other Arab countries, is found again here.

Labour Force

Since oil revenues have been received, the crude participation rate (the share of the population which is economically active, expressed as a percentage) has fallen, and today is about 20 per cent. This decline has been the result of increased urbanisation, which has reduced the frequency of female participation. Generally higher income levels have probably also contributed to this trend, as the economic necessity for women to work on farms has been reduced.

About a quarter of all Libyan manpower that is economically active is employed in agriculture, and this proportion has changed very little since 1973 (Table 8.18). It is a remarkable facet of Libyan development, that in a time when GNP per capita rose from US$3,116 (1977) to US$9,590 (1980), the proportion of the country's labour force working in agriculture should remain constant. This statistic illustrates clearly how little in fundamental terms the economy of Libya changed over the period, despite the surge in oil revenue.

Nonetheless, a growing proportion of Libya's indigenous manpower is working in the productive sectors, here defined as manufacturing,

TABLE 8.18. LIBYA: DISTRIBUTION OF NATIONALS' EMPLOYMENT BY ECONOMIC SECTOR, 1973, 1975 and 1980.

Economic Sector	1973 No.	1973 %	1975 No.	1975 %	1980 No.	1980 %	Annual Growth Rate 1975-1980 %
Agriculture	110.4	25.5	115.5	25.4	130,300	24.5	2.4
Petroleum & Gas	) 8.2	2.0	8.0	1.8	8,600	1.6	1.4
Mining & Quarrying	)		4.1	0.9	5,300	1.0	5.3
Manufacturing	13.3	3.1	19.1	4.2	32,700	6.1	11.3
Electricity Gas & Water	8.6	2.0	9.4	2.1	14,100	2.6	8.4
Construction	30.6	7.1	34.6	7.6	42,800	8.0	4.3
Trade, Restaurants & Hotels	34.2	7.9	40.8	9.0	40,000	7.5	-0.4
Transport, Storage & Communication	42.1	9.6	47.2	10.4	60,000	11.3	4.9
Finance, Insurance & Real Estate	5.2	1.2	6.1	1.3	7,100	1.3	3.1
Social & Personal Services	180.1	41.6	169.6	37.3	191.9	36.1	2.5
Total:	432.7	100.0	454.4	100.0	532.8	100.0	3.2

Source: Based on information contained in J.S.Birks and C.A.Sinclair, The Kingdom of Saudi Arabia and the Libyan Arab Jamahiriya: The Key Countries of Employment, World Employment Programme Research Working Paper, International Labour Office, Geneva, 1979 and J.S.Birks & C.A.Sinclair, Arab Manpower: The Crisis of Development, Croom Helm, London, 1980.

electricity, gas and water, and construction. In 1973 the proportion working in these sectors was 12 per cent; by 1980 this had risen to 17 per cent. In this respect Libya is comparatively unique amongst the oil-rich states of the Middle East. Few of these states have managed to persuade their nationals to work in these sectors. Moreover, equally unique is the declining proportion of total Libyan employment accounted for by 'services'. This, however, is due more to the demise of the private commercial sector in Libya than to a deliberately restrained growth of government employment.

Migrant Workers
Libya's small population and workforce have required the importation of quite large numbers of migrant workers. Table 8.19 shows their rapid growth through the 1970s up to 1976. In 1975 they represented about 33 per cent of the entire workforce.

There is a sharp discrepancy in Libya between official figures of the number of migrant workers after 1975 and the calculations of the authors. The number of migrant workers in Libya given by official government sources is a great deal less than that estimated by the authors. The difference is illustrated by Table 8.19.

One simple reason for a discrepancy between government estimates (and that, indeed, is all that the government figures are) and the number of migrant workers postulated here could be the extent of illegal and undocumented immigration. Libyan officials are either unwilling or unable to take account of its full extent in official planning documents. The discrepancy is not academic, since it is of major significance for analysis of investment efficiency and productivity in such sectors as agriculture and construction. It also raises the very important question of productivity levels of nationals. From this point forward we discuss the distribution of migrant workers between economic sectors using official figures, but deal with the topic of migrant workers using personal estimates. Until a new census of manpower survey is held in Libya, this rather important aspect of Libyan development will remain obscure. In the absence of such a survey we argue that the government estimates of the number of migrant workers (and similarly of migrant populations) err seriously on the low side.

Libya's migrant workforce are of all skill levels and are widely dispersed throughout the economy. The construction sector is the principal provider of non-national employment, followed by educational services, agriculture and manufacturing. In future years, the contribution of non-Libyans to the manufacturing sector will grow, while their employment in construction declines. At least, it will decline if Libya's demand for housing and her infrastructural and development spending ever ends.

In reality, the labour-intensive construction phase of development is likely to draw to a close some time after 1985, when the number of migrant workers in this sector will decline.

Table 8.20 shows that a small but significant number of migrants work in the agricultural sector, and this illustrates another remarkable facet of Libya's development, namely the agricultural

TABLE 8.19. LIBYA: GROWTH OF MIGRANT WORKERS IN LIBYA, OFFICIAL AND ESTIMATED FIGURES

Year	Official Data	Authors' Estimates
1970	50,000	
1971	64,000	
1972	81,000	
1973	118,350	
1974	169,770	
1975	223,000	323,000
1976	262,600	n.a
1977	n.a	n.a
1978	252,300	n.a
1979	n.a	n.a
1980	280,000	518,500

Source: <u>Official Data;</u> various official publications of the Secretariat of Labour and the Secretariat of Planning. <u>Authors' estimates;</u> 1975 figure is based on J.S.Birks and C.A.Sinclair, <u>International Migration and Development in the Arab Region,</u> ILO, Geneva, 1980, Tables 10 & 13. The 1980 figure is based on three sources of information (a) macro-economic projections of Libya's economy and labour market (by economic sector); (b) data on labour emigration from neighbouring countries, particularly Egypt; (c) data from the Secretariat of Labour on work permits issued for 1980.

TABLE 8.20. LIBYA: DISTRIBUTION OF MIGRANT WORKERS BY ECONOMIC SECTORS, 1975 and 1980

Economic Sector	1975		1980	
	No.	%	No.	%
Agriculture	17.6	7.9	23.1	8.2
Petroleum & Gas	2.7	1.2	2.9	1.0
Mining & Quarrying	2.8	1.3	3.7	1.3
Manufacturing	13.8	6.2	23.2	8.3
Electricity, Gas & Water	3.6	1.6	5.4	1.9
Construction	118.0	53.0	129.5	46.2
Trade, Restaurants & Hotels	7.7	3.5	4.5	1.6
Transport Storage & Communications	6.2	2.8	11.7	4.2
Finance Insurance & Real Estate	1.6	0.7	2.5	0.9
Public Administration	5.2	2.3	6.0	2.1
Education	14.1	6.0	30.6	10.9
Health	9.8	4.3	18.2	6.6
Other	19.6	8.8	18.7	6.8
TOTAL	222.7	100.0	280.0	100.0

Source: 1975; J.S.Birks and C.A.Sinclair, <u>International Migration and Development in the Arab Region,</u> ILO, Geneva, 1980.
1980; Official Estimates.

sector's dependence on expatriate labour. Almost certainly these immigrants work in those parts of the agricultural sector which are 'modern', in the sense of being capital-intensive, using modern technology, and where labour productivity is relatively high. There may, however, be to a limited extent, a certain number of immigrants on traditional farms where they will earn very low wages, and exhibit low production.

Libya's experience with expatriate labour has not been a happy one. Since 1975 Libya has suffered a shortage of manpower. The 1975-1980 Development Plan was compromised greatly by a lack of skilled manpower; businessmen and commentators regularly agree about labour shortages.

From an objective viewpoint, there is no reason at all why Libya should experience labour shortages, provided of course she is prepared to admit migrant workers. She has the financial capacity to pay migrant workers and is surrounded by potential labour suppliers, including Tunisia, Egypt and Sudan, not to mention Morocco, Syria, Jordan and Turkey only slightly further afield. This is notwithstanding some critical skill shortages which are pervasive throughout the Arab region.

Libya's manpower shortages are aggravated partly by political and partly by social reasons. On the political front, Libya's relations with Egypt deteriorated in the mid 1970s to the point where in 1977 Libya and Egypt broke off diplomatic relations. The practical upshot of this essentially border dispute was that Libya dropped Tobruk as an industrial centre and is said to have expelled 100,000 Egyptian workers. Many Egyptian workers left, either voluntarily or involuntarily, and Libya certainly lost a sizeable proportion of her migrant workforce, albeit temporarily. Many Egyptians returned to Libya, inconspicuously, a short time later. It remains to be seen whether Sadat's assassination has any ramifications for the Egyptian community in Libya.

Libya's political relations with Tunisia and Sudan have blown hot and cold, though without quite the extremes to which her policies towards Egypt led. Nevertheless, Tunisians now, and the Sudanese for some time, have not felt particularly welcome in Libya, and as a result they have opted, where ever possible, to work in the Arabian Peninsula rather than Libya. The tightening regional labour market for skilled labour has facilitated this option.

The second point is related. Given a choice, migrant workers from within the Middle East prefer to work in Western Europe, the Gulf and Arabian Peninsula states are a second choice, and Libya their last choice. The conditions under which migrant workers are required to live in Libya are harsh. Islamic social mores and customs are applied rigorously, and this tends to reduce the already few pastimes open to migrant workers.

The nationality blend of Libya's migrant workers has altered significantly since 1975, since when the relative importance of Arab migrants was reduced by 17 percentage points (Table 8.21). The Asian community increased quickly as have Europeans (East and West), and Turks. Libya's immigrants come from an unusually diverse number of

TABLE 8.21. LIBYA: MIGRANT WORKERS IN 1975 and 1980

Sending Country	1975 No.	%	1980 No.	%
Egypt	229,500	69.1	225,000	43.4
Jordan & Palestine	14,150	4.3	30,000	5.8
Syria	13,000	3.9	30,000	5.8
Lebanon	5,700	1.7	5,700	1.1
Sudan	7,000	2.1	21,000	4.1
Maghreb	41,000	12.3	65,600	12.7
Somalia	-	-	5,000	1.0
(All Arab)	(310,350)	(91.4)	(382,300)	(73.9)
Pakistan	4,500	1.4	25,000	4.8
India	500	0.2	17,000	3.3
Other Asian	500	0.2	10,000	1.9
(All Asian)	(5,500)	(1.8)	(52,000)	(10.0)
OECD & Europe	7,000	2.0	30,000	5.8
African & Other	500	0.2	2,200	0.4
Turkey	9,000	2.6	52,000	9.9
Total	332,350	100.0	518,500	100.0

Source: 1975; J.S.Birks and C.A.Sinclair, International Migration and Development in the Arab Region, ILO, Geneva, 1980.
1980; Authors' estimates.

countries, compared to most other major labour importing states.

The number of Egyptians working in Libya has remained more or less static since 1975. Although the 1980 figure is a little lower than that of 1975, the number of Egyptians should increase appreciably by 1985 following Muammar al-Qadhafi's remarks welcoming Egyptian migrant workers back to Libya. The cool response from Sadat will not deter many would-be migrants, many of whom pay scant regard to the vicissitudes of inter-Arab relations, even those of their own country. Indeed, so far as the issue of labour migration goes, economics generally tends to take preference over politics, though, rather surprisingly, this is not always the case as the Libyan example shows.

Libya's ties with Turkey are growing; in 1981 some 30 Turkish companies were working in Libya with a commensurately large workforce. There are a large number of nationals from Eastern European countries in Libya, notably Bulgarians, Czechs, Yugoslavs and Rumanians. Libya's economic relations with these countries have been strengthening since 1975.

A Dual Labour Market
Libya shares with Saudi Arabia a duality of labour market. Practically all oil-endowed states in the region have a split in their labour markets between nationals and non-nationals, in the sense that rates of pay, employment conditions and even economic sectors of work are different for the two groups. That division exists in Libya, but not especially strongly. We are here concerned with a slightly different duality, namely that which occurs within the national labour market. This duality is most obvious in the continual presence of so large a proportion of Libyan manpower in the traditional, rather unproductive, agricultural sector while concurrently most non-Libyan manpower in the Jamahiriya participates actively in the modern sector. Libya's economic policy of sustaining the agricultural sector, and in particular of providing financial support to Libyan farmers, has encouraged illiterate Libyans to remain on their farms, at least on a part-time basis. Many part-time farmers also have second jobs in cities, such as taxi driving or guarding. However, the demise of the private sector has reduced the opportunities for this part-time participation in the modern sector, so ensuring that uneducated Libyans remain on farms.

By importing migrant workers into the modern sector of the economy, opportunities for Libyan entry are reduced. A vicious circle therefore develops. Because Libyans have limited or non-existent modern sector skills, migrant workers are imported. Contemporaneously, Libyans develop no wish to work in occupations held presently by migrants, nor does the opportunity to do so then arise. In the absence of able and willing Libyans, further immigration occurs, and a self-reinforcing process becomes established. The entrenchment of Libyans in agriculture is ensured by government policies towards agriculture, in particular, that of supporting the income of Libyan farmers, and by growing dependence on migrant workers to run the modern sector.

CONCLUSION

The pattern of Libya's oil-stimulated development, and the problems posed by it remain surprisingly similar to those found in, for example Iraq and Saudi Arabia. Libyan development might best be characterised as conventional (to oil-rich states) but rather more confused. However a significant element of confusion exists in all the capital-surplus states because of their conflicting social and economic aims.

Libya's problems might well be considered more acute, however, because the economy is, in many respects founded on a resource base of smaller dimensions. Oil reserves are much more limited than other Arab oil-exporting states, and the projected life at realistic rates of extraction is low. Yet, paradoxically, Libya is now having increasing difficulty in selling as much oil as it would like. Water supplies, much more limited than past reports have implied, are being mined at a rate well beyond their level of natural replenishment. The Libyan population is even smaller than that of Saudi Arabia and, in the short term, large proportions of it are showing a similar disinclination to enter the modern sector on an economically realistic basis. Thus, although not normally described as such, Libya might well be considered a marginal oil producer, rather than a truly capital-rich state.

This whole syndrome is exacerbated by the large share of Libyan GNP directed towards military expenditure, and the similarly large proportion of the national workforce drawn into the armed forces.

From the authors' perspective, then the economic development of Libya is on a short fuse. Libya has less potential than many other oil-rich states to 'buy herself out of her mistakes'. This means that it is time for a detailed and careful but radical and all-encompassing re-evaluation of Libyan economic and social development. This is not to assert that Libya should move towards the more overt capitalism of Saudi Arabia, nor to the Islamic socialism of Iraq. Perhaps Muammar al-Qadhafi is absolutely right in shunning both these models as ill-fitted to Libyan development. But he must also come to terms with the fact that Libya cannot be economically independent from the rest of the world market, before or after oil. It is a sobering thought that, at present assessment, Libya is more likely to collapse economically after the cessation of oil reserves than any other oil-endowed state in the Arab world. This is less comment upon the ideology of development in Libya, than upon the reality of the marginal nature of the oil and water resource bases. Hence the urgency for a reassessment of development strategy in Libya.

Yet, it is almost impossible for a central planning authority to change development labour market trends which result from the individual decisions of thousands of employers, individuals, and an entrenched pattern of government expenditure. These are, in many respects, a natural consequence of the country's economic conditions. However, a factor working towards the possibility of an economic reassessment and an ending of the labour market duality which so prejudices long-term Libyan prospects, is the increasing and more widespread provision of education. The experience of education by the mass of the population serves both as a stimulus to enter the modern sector, and could also provide a basis for the acceptance of the government's necessary reassessment of the domestic agricultural policies which are widely criticised outside Libya. If the present arrangements for generous long-term loans to Libyan farmers were curtailed, that alone would have an impact. But only education of farmers can make this a realistic possibility, no matter how pressing an issue this might be in terms of depletion of natural resources.

If Libyan economic development is not redirected, and the country's resource base is squandered in a manner that does not engender a self-sustaining economy in the post oil era – a very proximate period in the Libyan case – then the fears of Libyan expansion might become increasingly well-grounded.

NOTES AND REFERENCES

1. McLachlan makes special reference to the impact of population distribution in the Maghreb on Libya's regional planning. See K.S. McLachlan, 'Strategies for Agricultural Development after 1951' paper presented at a Conference on Economic and Social Development of Libya held at the School of Oriental & African Studies, University of London, July 1981.

2. Preliminary Conceptual and Quantitative Framework of the Second Five Year Transformation Plan, 1981-1985, (Secretariat of Planning, Tripoli, 1980), p.72.

3. See International Bank for Reconstruction and Development, The Economic Development of Libya, (Johns Hopkins, Baltimore, 1960); General Economic Appraisal of Libya, (United Nations, New York, 1952).

4. Authors' calculations based on Y.A. Sayigh, The Economies of the Arab World, (Croom Helm, London, 1978).

5. The Green Book, Part 1, The Solution of the Problem of Democracy, Part 2, The Solution of the Economic Problem, (Public Establishment for Publishing, Advertising & Distribution, Tripoli, 1977).

6. See J.A. Allan, Libya : the Experience of Oil, (Croom Helm, London 1981), pp.252-308. Allan analyses the Green Book in depth and details the inconsistencies and inadequacies of the book, describing it as 'ill thought out and ill thought through', 'based on ill-founded assumptions and ill-thought argument'. He concludes 'the Green Book has had a very limited impact...' See also O.I. Fathaly and F.S. Abusedra, 'The Impact of Socio-Political Change on Economic Development in Libya', Middle Eastern Studies, vol.16, no.3 (1980), pp.225-235.

7. Volume 111 of the Green Book deals with the nature of womenhood and argues that women should confine themselves to their homes and to rearing children. Libya's planners see the swelling ranks of educated Libyan women as one of the few possibilities of augmenting the national workforce.

8. See Allan, Libya : the Experience of Oil, p.211 on

this point.

9. The Plan of Economic & Social Transformation, 1976-1980 A.D., (Ministry of Planning and Scientific Research, Tripoli, 1976); Second Five Year Transformation Plan.

10. See Allan, Libya : the Experience of Oil, Chapter 8 Spending and Distributing Oil Wealth Since 1969, pp.232-252.

11. Readers interested in Libyan agriculture should consult J.A. Allan, K.S. McLachlan and E.T. Penrose, Libya : Agriculture and Economic Development, (Frank Cass, London, 1973). More recent works include, K.S.McLachlan, 'Strategies for Agricultural Development'; J.A.Allan, 'Capital has not Substituted for Water in Agriculture', paper presented at a Conference on Economic and Social Development of Libya, held at the School of Oriental & African Studies, University of London, July 1981; J.A. Allan, 'The Kufrah Agricultural Schemes', Geographical Journal, vol.142 (1976), pp.48-56; J. Howell, 'Libya's Free Farm Policy', World Crops, vol.30, no.6 (1978), pp.264-267; K. Moran, 'The Sarir Story', World Crops, vol.32, no.4 (1980), pp.96-100; S.E. Moomem and C.W. Barney, 'A Modern Technique to Halt Desertification in the Libyan Jamahiriya', Agricultural Meteorology, vol.23, no.2 (1981), pp.131-136; W.M. Edmonds & E.P. Wright, 'Groundwater and Recharge and Palaeoclimate in the Sinte and Kufrah Basins', Journal of Hydrology, vol.40, no.3/4 (1977), pp.215-242; O. El Fathaly and M. Palmer, 'Opposition to Change in Rural Libya', International Journal of Middle East Studies, vol.11, no.2 (1980), pp.247-261.

12. Allan, Mclachlan, Penrose, Agriculture & Economic Development.

13. See Allan, 'Capital has not Substituted for Water'.

14. See S. Ghanem, 'The Subsistence Economy : Libya without Oil', paper presented at a Conference on Economic and Social Development of Libya, held at the School of Oriental and African Studies, July 1981.

15. See Allan, 'Capital has not Substituted for Water' for detailed analysis of this point.

16. Ibid.

17. Middle East Economic Digest, 20.6.80.

18. For a comprehensive account of the development of oil in Libya, see F.C. Waddams, The Libyan Oil Industry, (Croom Helm, London, 1980).

19. OAPEC Bulletin, August/September 1980, p.39.

20. Middle East Economic Digest, 16.1.81.

INDEX

Abbas, Ferhat 8-9, 42
Abdallah-Khodja, Kamel 26
Abdelghani, Col. Mohamed B. 19, 21-2, 35-6, 40
Abdessalem, Belaid 25-6, 32-3, 35, 184, 186
'Abduh, Muhammad 59
Abu-Nasr, Jamil 59
Achour, Habib 105, 108-9, 111, 113
Addi ou Bihi 70
agriculture: Algeria 11-17, 29, 155-8, 166, 172-80, 185; Libya 127-8, 131, 243, 246-7, 251-3, 257-62, 265-7; Morocco 68, 77, 84-7, 192-201, 210-11; Tunisia 106-7, 219, 222-3, 226-7, 229, 232-5; see also cooperatives; investment; irrigation; land; production; reform
Aherdane, Mahjoubi 71
Ait Ahmed, Hocine 9-10
al-Aynayu, Ma' 55
al-'Aziz, 'Abd 53, 55, 57
al-Basri, Muhammad 72-3, 75, 77-8
al-Fassi see 'Allal
al-Glawi, Madani 54, 64-5
al-Hafidh, 'Abd 54-6
al-Hiba 55-6
al-Kattani, Ibrahim 61
al-Khaliq, Torres 'Abd 64
al-Krim, 'Abd 63
al-Majid, 'Abd 53
al-Malik al-Mtougi, 'Abd 54
al-Qadhafi, Muammar 120, 126, 134, 138-9, 144-5, 150, 244-5, 272-3
al-Qadir, 'Abd 51

al-Rahman, Muhammad ibn 'Abd 51
al-Sadiq, Muhammad 52
al-Susi, Mukhtar 61
al-Wahhab, Muhammad ibn 55, 58
al-Wazzani, Muhammad 61
al-Yazzidi, Muhammad 61-2
Algeria: economy 153-90, 242; agriculture 11-17, 29, 155-8, 166, 172-80, 185; colonial inheritance 153-6; currency exchange rate xiii; employment 156, 168, 179-83; industrialisation, rapid, contradiction of 153-90; industry 11, 16, 155-63, 167-72, 180-5, 243; maps xv, 154; oil and gas 6, 156, 159-160, 163, 167-8, 243; state capitalism era 160-7; worker self-management, contradiction of 156-60
Algeria, socialism 5-49; Boumediène and end of Oujda clan 17-23; Chadli's new course (1979-81) 31-40; change, political (1975-7) 23-6; demobilisation and construction of state (1962-71) 8-11; factionalism and empirical mode of development 5-8; remobilisation, political and agrarian revolution

277

11-17; rise of FLN
 (1977-9) 26-31
'Allal al-Fassi 59, 61,
 63-4, 66-7, 74, 79-80
Allan, J.A. 257
Amin, Samir 68, 137, 147, 149, 157
 187, 192
Amir, Mohamed, 25, 32
Arab Socialist Union, Libya 144
Arabisation policy, Algeria 33-4, 41
'Arafa, Moulay 65-7, 71
Arbaoni, Abdallah 26
armed forces: Algeria 10, 14-15,
 21-2, 25, 36-7; Libya 132-4, 273;
 Morocco 77; Tunisia 114
Ayache, G. 51, 91

Ba Ahmad 53
Baccouche, Taieb 111
Ballafrej, Ahmad 61-2, 71
Balta, P. 16, 45
Belhouchet, Col. Abdallah 21-2,
 35-7, 40
Belloucif, Col. Mustapha 37
ben Ammar, Wassila 106
Ben Barka, Ahmed 8-10, 17, 21, 33,
 36, 40, 72, 74, 90, 157-60
Ben Romdane, M. 231, 239
ben Salah, Ahmed 104-8, 112, 222-3
ben Siddiq, Mahjoub 72
Ben Tobbal, Lakhdar 10, 43
ben Youssef, Salah 103-5
Benachenhou, Abdellatif 30, 47,
 165-6, 169, 178, 181-2, 184,
 188-90
Bencherif, Col. Ahmed 22, 25, 32,
 35, 40
Benhamouda, Boualem 32, 35-6
Benissad, M.E. 158
Benyahia, Mohhamed Seddik 14, 32,
 35, 40
Berbers 9, 38-9, 57-8, 60; see also
 Mouvement Populaire
Bererhi, Abdelhak 30, 47
Bernard, Ch. 179, 189-90
Berque, J. 50, 90
Berrada, Hamid 75
Birks, S. 241, 266, 268-9, 271, 276
Bitat, Rabah 24, 35
Blum, L. 61
Bouabid, Abdurrahman 72, 78, 81, 90

Bouarfa, Mustapha 40
Boubenider, Salah 11, 43
Boucetta, Muhammad 80-1
Boudjellab, Omar 25
Bouhara, Abderrazak 30, 33, 47
Boumediène, Houari 9, 11-41,
 160, 167, 183-4, 186
Bourdieu, P. 7, 41, 156, 187
bourgeoisie 101-2, 107-8,
 131-2
Bourguiba, Habib 102-6, 109-
 23 passim, 236
Bouteflika, Abdelaziz 9-10,
 17-20, 23, 31-7, 40-1
Britain 51-2, 54, 129-30, 139
Brown, K. 60, 94
Bu Himara 54

capital formation, Libya 251
capitalism: international
 121-6; state, Algeria 160-7
Catroux, General 66
Chaabani, Col. Mohamed 10, 14,
 43
Chadli Benjedid, Col. 21-2,
 27, 31-8, 40-1, 83, 184,
 186
Cherif Belkacem 10, 17, 23,
 25, 30
Clifford, B. 5, 41
climate and agriculture 195,
 252, 256, 262
colonialism: Algeria 153-6;
 Libya 128-30; Morocco 50-
 80 passim; Tunisia 101
 -3, 109, 116, 217-21, 224,
 226
Communist Party: Algeria 14,
 31, 38; Morocco 63, 65;
 Tunisia 113
cooperatives, agricultural:
 Algeria 12-13, 15, 175-6;
 Tunisia 106-7, 222-3, 232;
 see also agriculture
Cornaton, M. 156, 187
currency exchange rates xiii

De Gaulle, C. 62, 155
De Mas, P. 213, 215-16
debts 52, 83, 101

Democratic Socialists, Tunisia 111-12, 115
Destanne de Bernis, G. 161, 172
Destour Party, Tunisia 102
development *see* plans
Dlimi, Col. 76
Draia, Ahmed 25, 32-3, 35
Drummond-Hay, Sir J. 52
dual labour market 272
Dunn, J. 16, 45
Duprat, G. 27, 47

economies of Northwest Africa 150-2; Algeria 153-90; Libya 241-75; Morocco 67-9, 76-7, 191-216; Tunisia 217-40
education: Algeria 11, 182-4; Libya 133, 260, 274; Morocco 58-9, 210; Tunisia 102-3, 221-2
Eikenberg, C. 87, 98
emigration: Morocco 86, 210-12; Tunisia 224, 226, 236
Emmanuel, A. 136-7
employment: Algeria 179-83; Libya 128, 133, 138-9, 145, 265-72; Morocco 204-6, 209-13; overseas 86, 210-12, 224, 226, 236; Tunisia 224-8, 238
energy *see* oil and gas
Etienne, B. 20, 45-6
European Economic Community 208-9, 224, 226, 229, 232
exchange rates xiii
exports: Algeria 163; Libya 252-6; Morocco; Tunisia 107, 223-9, 232-4, 236; *see also* trade

Fadel, Abdallah 25-6, 46
Farhat, Abdullah 109
Farouk-Sluglett, M. 50, 276
Fathaly, O.M. 126, 147
Ferroux, F. 161
Findlay, Allan 150, 217, 276
Findlay, Anne 191, 194, 207, 216, 276
First, R. 120-1, 146-7
FLN *see* Front de Libération
foreign enterprises, nationalised 160
foreign investment: Morocco 83, 87; Tunisia 102-8, 227-8, 237

foreign workers: in Algeria 156, 168, 182; in Libya 138, 145, 267-72
France: Algeria and 153-6; Libya and 129; Morocco and 50-68, 79, 208, 210; Tunisia and 101-3, 109, 116, 219, 221, 224, 226
Front de Libération, Algeria 6-8, 103, 113; under Boumediène 17-31; under Chadli 31-40

General People's Congress, Libya 139
Germany: Morocco and 55, 62; Tunisia and 103, 107, 116, 224
Ghazi, Muhammad 61
Ghozali, Sid Ahmed 25, 32, 184
Glavanis, P. 120, 276
Goudjil, Salah 30, 33, 47
'Green March' 80
gross domestic and national products: Algeria 158, 164-5, 242; Libya 241-2, 247, 251, 253, 273; Middle East 241-4; Morocco 193, 196, 241-2; Tunisia 217, 242; USA 124
see also production
Guédira, Ahmed Rida 73-4
Guennez, Col. Mahmoud 24, 36, 40
Guillaume, A. 65-6

Hached, Farhat 65
Hadjerès, Lt. Col. El Hachemi 22, 36
Hamdani, Smail 25
Harbi, Mohamed 8
Hassan I of Morocco 52-3
Hassan II of Morocco 70, 73-5, 77-83, 89-90, 214
health care 15, 183, 222
Hirschmann, A.D. 161
Hoffman, Slimane 30, 47
Hone, A. 136, 149

Ibrahim, Abdullah 72, 78, 90
immigrants *see* foreign labour

imports: Libya 133, 246, 252, 254–6; Morocco 203, 205; Tunisia 234–5; see also trade
income see wages
income, national, Libya 247, 250
independence and movement towards 124; Algeria 157; Libya 126, 130; Morocco 51, 54, 60–71; Tunisia 103–4
industry: Algeria 11, 16, 155–63, 167–72, 180–5, 243; Libya 128, 131, 134–8, 247, 249, 251–3; Morocco 68, 77, 86–9, 194–5, 199, 203–8, 211, 214; Tunisia 106, 218–38 passim; see also investment, oil, phosphates, production, reform; inflation 78, 131, 133, 212 see also prices
international capitalism 121–6
international trade see trade
investment: Algeria 166–73, 178, 181, 184–5; foreign 83, 87, 107–8, 227–8, 237; Libya 128, 247, 252, 258; Morocco 83, 86–7, 193–9, 206, 210–11, 214; Tunisia 107–8, 227–32, 235, 237–8
irrigation: Algeria 176; Libya 261–2; Morocco 68, 86, 192, 197, 199–201; see also agriculture; water supply
Islam: Algeria 38–9; Morocco 50–1, 56–9; Tunisia 113–14
Isma'il, Khedive 52
Istiqlal Party, Morocco 62–5, 69–73, 76–7, 81–2
Italy 128–9

Jacquemot, P. 161, 170, 188
Juin, A. 63–5
Julien, C.-A. 51, 55, 91, 93

Kabyle Berberists 9, 38–9
Kafi, Ali 10, 43
Kaid Ahmed 10, 17–19, 21, 23, 30
Kharroubi, Mohamed Cherif 32, 36
Khatib, Ahmed 71
Khider, Mohamed 9, 18, 42
Knapp, W. 85, 99

Labonne, E. 63
labour force see employment
labour migration see emigration foreign labour
Lacheraf, Mustapha 15, 19, 25–6, 32–3
land: ownership 60, 68; reform and redistribution 77, 84–5, 106–7, 122, 157, 175–6, 199; use, Libya 255; see also agriculture
Laraki 81
Laroui, A. 57, 91
Latreche, Lt. Col. Abdelhamid 36–7
Lawless, R.I. 153, 276
Leca, J. 7, 28, 41, 43, 47
legislation: Libya 143, 145; Tunisia 227–9
Liassine, Mohamed 25–6
liberalisation, Tunisia 105, 107–8, 110–11
Libya, economy, problems of rentier state 241–75; agriculture 127–8, 131, 243, 246–7, 251–3, 257–62, 265–7; currency exchange rate xiii; development 245–52; employment 133, 138–9, 145, 265–72; industry 128, 131, 134–8, 247, 249, 251–3; maps xv, 248; oil and gas 121, 126–46 passim, 241–9, 252–8 passim, 262–5, 273
Libya, state and labour 120–49; revolution (1969) 126, 130, 132–4, 142; state and international division of labour 121–6; state in revolutionary Libya 134–46; state, socio-historical formation 126–32; Tunisia and 113, 270
Lyautey, General 50, 54–60, 69
Lyazidi, Muhammad 61–2

McLachlan, K.S. 257
Maghrabi, Suleiman 140–3

280

Mahmud II of Morocco 53
Mahroug, Smail 26
Mammeri, Mouloud 34
manpower see employment
maps: Algeria xv, 154; Libya xv, 248; Morocco xv, 198, 202; Tunisia xv, 218
Marxist Left, Algeria 8-9, 14, 31, 38
Masmudi, Muhammad 112-13
Materi, M. 102
Mauriac, F. 65
Mazouzi, Mohand Said 32, 35
Medeghri, Ahmed 10, 17-23
medicine see health care
Mehri, Albdelhamid 32, 39
Mendès-France, P. 103
Merbah, Lt. Col. Kasdi 36-7
Messaadia, Mohamed Charif 27, 37, 40, 47
Messaoudène, Said Ait 25
Mestiri, Ahmed 110-12, 115
Michel, H. 12, 44
Middle East 241-4
migration see emigration; rural depopulation
mineral resources and mining: Morocco 201-3; Tunisia 102, 218-21, 224-5, 234, 237-8; see also oil and gas
Mohand ou el Hadj 11, 43
Montagne, R. 58, 66
Morocco, economy 67-9, 83-9, 191-216; agriculture 68, 77, 84-7, 192-201, 210-11; currency exchange rate xiii; industry 68, 86-9, 194-5, 199-208, 211, 214; maps xv, 98, 202; phosphates 67-9, 79, 81, 86-8, 191, 193-208; planning, regional and national 192-5, 213-14; trade 208-9
Morocco, politics: conquest and resistance 59-67; 'constitutional experiment' 1961-3), 73-5; independence: direct rule from throne (1965-74) 75-8, early years (1956-60) 69-73, economy in 83-9, struggle for 51, 54, 60-71;
in 1912 51-6; politics and society (since 1975) 80-3; as protectorate 56-9; Sahara, Western 78-82
Moroccanisation 192, 206-7
Moulay, Col. Abdelkadir 36
Mouvement Populaire, Morocco 71, 73, 75-6, 81
Mouvement d'Unité Populaire, Tunisia 107, 112, 115
Muhammad V of Morocco 51, 60-70, 73, 89, 192
multinationals, Tunisia 237
Muslims see Islam
Mutin, G. 174-5, 178-9, 189
Mzali, Muhammed 110

Nabi, Belkacem 32
Nasser, G. 131, 140
nationalisation 106, 122, 157, 159-62
nationalism see independence
Neihum, Rajab 140
Neo-Destour Party, Tunisia 102-6 (later Socialist Destour Party)
Noguès, General 61
nomadism 219
Nouira, Hedi 108-10, 113-14

OAPEC see Organization of Arab Petroleum etc
oil and gas: Algeria 6, 156, 159-60, 163, 167-8, 243; Libya 121, 126-46 passim, 241-9, 252-8; passim, 262-5, 273; Morocco 203; prices 136-7, 252; Tunisia 218, 220, 224-5, 234, 237-8
Organisation of African Unity 83
Organisation of Arab Petroleum Exporting Countries 224, 237, 242-4
Oufkir, General 75-7
Oujda clan, Algeria 9-10, 17-23, 26, 160
Ould Dadda 79
Ould Khalifa, M. Larbi 36
Oumeziane, Mouloud 9, 11, 24, 44

Ouseddik, Omar 11, 43

Palmer, M. 126, 147
Penrose, E.T. 257
phosphates: Morocco 67-9, 79, 81, 86-8, 191, 193-206; Tunisia 218-21
Pinay, A. 67
plans, development: Algeria 35, 155-7, 164, 166, 170, 180, 184; Libya 243-7, 270; Morocco 71, 84, 192-3, 201, 212-14; Tunisia 106-7, 222, 228, 230, 238-9
politics of Northwest Africa 1-4; Algeria 5-49; Libya 120-49; Morocco 50-100; Tunisia 101-19
Poncet, J. 108
population 220 see also rural; urban
poverty see wages
prices: Libya 129, 131, 133; Morocco 78, 82, 87, 193, 196, 212; oil 136-7, 252
private property 13, 15, 157
private sector: Algeria 171, 173, 175-6, 186; Libya 244; Tunisia 106-7, 232
production, agricultural: Algeria 158, 173-4, 177-8; Libya 131, 247, 251, 253, 257-60; Morocco 195-8; Tunisia 233; see also agricultural
production, industrial: Algeria 158, 160-9, 181; Libya 131, 247, 249, 251, 253; Morocco 204-6; Tunisia 231; see also industry
protectorate: Morocco as 56-9, 69; Tunisia 101-3, 219
Puaux, G. 62

Qadhafi see al-Qadhafi

Raffinot, M. 161, 170, 188
Reagan, R. 83
rebellions see independence
reform agricultural: Algeria 11-17, 155-7, 175, 180; Morocco 77, 84-6, 192-3; Tunisia 106; 222-3; see also agriculture

reform, industrial 11, 16, 77, 155-6 see also industry
reform land 72, 84-5, 106-7, 122, 157, 175-6, 199
revolution: Algeria 6; Libya (1969) 126, 130, 132-4, 142
Revolutionary Command Council, Libya 134, 138-9
Roberts, H. 5, 276
Roosevelt, F.D. 62
Ruf, W. I, 4, 101, 116-18, 276
rural depopulation: Algeria 156, 179; Libya 133; Morocco 86, 191, 193; Tunisia 107-8, 229
rural population: Morocco 69-71, 86; Tunisia 229; see also agriculture

Sadat, A. 270, 272
Sahara, Western 78-82, 88, 201
Said, Mohammedi 11, 43
Santos, M. 191, 215
Sayad, A. 156, 187
Sayigh, Y. 214, 216
Sayyah, Muhammad 109, 112
Sharqawi, Ahmad 61
Shiteh, Salem 139-40
Signoles, P. 231, 239
Sinclair, C. 241, 268-0, 271, 276
Sluglett, P. 50, 276
socialism 244; see also Algeria
Socialist Destour Party, Tunisia 106-11 (earlier Neo-Destour Party)
Spain: Morocco and 51-2, 54-6, 63-4, 79-80, 209; Tunisia and 232
stability, Tunisia 236-7
state: Algeria 160-73, 178; Libya 121-32, 134-46, 244, 258; Morocco 87-8; Tunisia 106, 230-1
strikes: Algeria 33-4, 38-9; Libya 141; Morocco 75; Tunisia 108-9; see also trade unions
students: Algeria 14, 18, 33-4, 39; Morocco 75; Tunisia 102, 112

Taleb Ibrahimi, Ahmed 25
taxation 53, 84
Tayebi, Mohamed 17, 23, 32-3, 35, 40
Temmam, Abdelmalek 25
Tilli, Ahmed 105
Tobal, Nrahim 104
tourism 211, 214, 236, 238
trade: Algeria 163; Libya 133, 246, 252-6, 262; Morocco 88, 192, 196-7, 201, 203, 205, 208-9; Tunisia 107, 223-9, 232-6
trade unions: Algeria 9, 18, 29, 31, 33-4, 38-9; Libya 138-45; Morocco 65, 71-3, 75, 81-2; Tunisia 102-12, 115
traditional structures, preserved 56-8
Tunisia, economy 217-40, 242; agriculture 106-7, 219, 222-3, 226-7, 229, 232-5; colonial resource base 217-21; currency exchange rate xiii; employment 224-8, 238; external forces (1970s) 223-7; future 236-8; industry 106, 218-38 passim; Libya and 113, 270; oil and gas 218, 220, 224-5, 234, 237-8; phosphates 218-21; political economy (1956-69) 221-3; trade 234-6
Tunisia, politics 101-19; independence, struggle for 103-4; independent party and state 104-11; in 1980s 111-16; protectorate 101-3

unemployment 133, 182-3, 207
Union Nationale des Forces Populaires, Morocco 65, 72-8, 80-2, 84, 89-90
United States 62, 107, 116, 124
urban population 69, 131-2, 191, 193

wages and poverty: Algeria 15; Libya 128-9, 131, 138, 143, 241; Morocco 76, 78, 82, 193, 196; Tunisia 108
water supply, Libya 245, 258, 261-2; see also irrigation
Waterbury, J. 67, 72, 95
women 222
worker participation: Algeria 16, 156-60; Libya 264; see also industry
World Bank 107-8

Yahiaoui, Mohamed Salah 22, 30-1, 33-5, 37-8, 40
Yahya, H.M. 249
Yaker, Layachi 24, 26
Yala, M'hamed Hadj 25-6
Yata, 'Ali 80
Youssefists, Tunisia 110, 113
Yusuf, Sultan 55
Yusufi, Abderrahman 72

Zaibek, Abdelkadar 24, 26
Zbiri, Col. Tahar 11, 14, 33, 36, 40, 44
Zerguini, Col. El Hadj Mohamed 25